SIGN, SENTENCE, DISCOURSE

SIGN, SENTENCE, DISCOURSE

Language in Medieval Thought and Literature

Edited by

JULIAN N. WASSERMAN

and

LOIS RONEY

Syracuse University Press

First published 1989
98 97 96 95 94 93 92 91 90 89 88   6 5 4 3 2 1

The paper used in this publication meets the minimum requirements of American National Standard for Information Sciences—Permanence of Paper for Printed Library Materials, ANSI Z39.48–1984. ∞™

Library of Congress Cataloging-in-Publication Data

Sign, sentence, discourse.

Includes index.
1. Languages—Philosophy—History. 2. Philosophy, Medieval. 3. Literature, Medieval—History and criticism. I. Wasserman, Julian N. II. Roney, Lois Y.
P106.S5427 1988   409'.4   88-20177
ISBN 0-8156-2445-X
ISBN 0-8156-2451-4 (pbk.)

Manufactured in the United States of America

For Susan, who has her own joyful way with words
and
For Deirdre, whose *sentence* enlightens

CONTENTS

CONTRIBUTORS

Peter L. Allen, Assistant Professor of French and Comparative Literature at Pomona College, is currently a Mellon Fellow at the University of Southern California. He has published articles on Ovid's *Metamorphoses* and Chaucer's *Legend of Good Women*, and is working on a book entitled *Love Poetry and the Art of Love: Love Poetry and Literary Theory from Ovid to* Le Roman de la Rose.

Glenn C. Arbery, Assistant Professor of English at the Thomas More Institute for the Liberal Arts, has published essays on Dante and Dostoevsky. His current research interests include a study of Shakespeare and political theory.

Ross G. Arthur, a Canada Research Fellow in the Humanities at York University, is the author of *Medieval Sign Theory and* Sir Gawain and the Green Knight (1987). His published work also includes essays on *Sir Gawain and the Wife of Bath's Tale* as well as on Provençal poetry.

Kathleen M. Ashley, Associate Professor of English at the University of Southern Maine at Gorham, has published widely on medieval drama and its relation to late medieval thought and philosophy. Her research interests also include both French and Spanish literature, including the *Cantigas de Amigo*.

Edith Joyce Benkov, Associate Professor of French at San Diego State University, teaches Medieval and Renaissance literature with an emphasis on Women's Studies. Among her publications are articles on Chrétien de Troyes, the farce *Le Cuvier*, and Louise Labe. Her current projects include a monograph on Labe as well as a book-length study of Protestant women in southern France during the Reformation.

Judith Ferster, Associate Professor of English at North Carolina State University, has written *Chaucer on Interpretation* (1985) and articles on Chaucer and Alain de Lille. She contributed an article on hermeneutics and the *Franklin's Tale* to *Medieval Literature: Criticism, Ideology, & History* (1986).

Joan Tasker Grimbert, Assistant Professor of French at the Catholic University of America, has published several articles on Chrétien de Troyes, as well as a monograph, *Yvain dans le miroir: Une Poétique de la reflexion dans le Chevalier au lion de Chrétien de Troyes* (1988). Her current work involves a comparative study of Robert de Baron's *Joseph d'Arimathie* and an early prose rendering.

David W. Hiscoe has taught in the English departments at North Carolina State University, Duke University, the University of North Carolina at Greensboro, and Loyola University of Chicago, as well as at Rice University where he was a post-doctoral Mellon Fellow. He has published work on Chaucer's *Troilus and Criseyde* and Gower's *Confessio Amantis*. At present, he writes marketing literature for the telecommunications industry.

Peggy A. Knapp, Associate Professor of English at Carnegie Mellon University, edits *Assays: Critical Approaches to Medieval and Renaissance Texts*. Her work has appeared in such journals as *PMLA, ELH, Speculum, Philological Quarterly, Criticism, College English,* and *Modern Language Notes*. She is currecently writing a book on the *Canterbury Tales*.

Phillip Pulsiano, Associate Professor of English at Villanova University, has co-edited and translated *Baroar saga Smaefellsass* (1984) and compiled *An Annotated Bibliography of North American Doctoral Dissertations on Old English Language and Literature* (1988). He is general editor of *Medieval Scandinavia* (Vol. 1 of the Garland Medieval Encyclopedias).

Liam O. Purdon, Associate Professor of English at Doane College, has published articles on Spenser's *Faerie Queene* and short verse English romances, as well as the works of the *Pearl*-Poet. He is currently engaged in a longer study of chivalric ideals and the concept of youth in Middle English literature.

Edmund Reiss has published extensively on medieval literature. His books include *Sir Thomas Malory, Elements of Literary Analysis, The Art of the Middle English Lyric, William Dunbar, Boethius,* and *Arthurian Legend and Literature*. He has also published some sixty essays and articles, and is a founder and early editor of both the *Chaucer Review* (1965) and the *Journal of Medieval and Renaissance Studies* (1970).

Lois Roney, Assistant Professor of English at St. Cloud State University, has published articles on the *Wakefield Shepherds' Plays* and the *Canterbury Tales*. She has just completed a book entitled *Chaucer's "Knight's Tale" and Universal Psychology: Theories of Faculty Structure, Thinking Processes, and Language Use at the Beginning of the* Canterbury Tales.

R. A. Shoaf, Professor of English at the University of Florida at Gainesville, is the author or editor of four books on medieval and Renaissance literature and literary theory and is founding editor of *Exemplaria: A Journal of Theory in Medieval and Renaissance Studies*.

Julian N. Wasserman, Professor of English at Loyola University of New Orleans, is editor of collections of essays on Chaucer and Edward Albee, as well as co-author of book-length studies on Gottfried von Strassburg and Thomas Hardy. He has published widely on the *Pearl*-Poet.

ACKNOWLEDGMENTS

"The thanks so great, the page so short," as Geoffrey might have observed. Nevertheless, we wish to attempt to acknowledge some of the many people who have helped us produce this volume. We would begin by thanking the scholars who have entrusted their work to us, especially for their patience during the unforeseen delays that inevitably accompany any such project. We would especially like to thank our home institutions—in particular, our departmental colleagues for their many "unremembered acts of kindness," the sort of encouragement and support that allow any project to see its own completion. Nor could we possibly have completed this project without the kind support of the community of our fellow medievalists who are fortunately friends as well as colleagues: Jane Chance, Lorraine Stock, Mimi Miller, Steve Russell, Robert J. Blanch. Thanks are also due Martin B. Shichtman for his thoughtful suggestions in reviewing the manuscript. In addition, we would like to thank Loyola University for underwriting many of the expenses incurred by this project through a faculty research grant. We would also express our gratitude to the Criterion Group and Continental Airlines, sponsors of "The Glory of the Page" exhibition at the Houston Museum of Fine Arts, for their generous travel grant.

Other members of the Loyola community who added immeasurably are Bobbie Porter, John Campbell, Cassandra Mabe, Gary Talarchek, Nye King and Anne Marie Juul. Special thanks are also due to Dean William W. Edison for his support as well as his tolerance of the frequent disruption of his office staff, and especially to Charlene Floyd whose good humor and patience in "yielding the computer" at a moment's notice was and is greatly appreciated. In regard to computers, we received invaluable assistance from James O'Meara and Daniel Goldstein. Our gratitude also extends to Bernie Meisner of the University of St. Thomas in Houston, Texas, as well as to his colleagues at the Doherty Library—Peter Kupersmith, Lillian Chen, Becky Goldman, Pat Gerson, and Kerri Jara—whose wise stewardship of the OCLC terminal and help in obtaining materials were greatly appreciated, as were the unceasing efforts of Vicky Bullock of the library at the University of Texas at Dallas.

Finally, we offer our sincere thanks to Laurie Winship for meticulous copyediting. Our most sincere thanks go to Walda Metcalf, not only for her encouragement of the publication of medieval studies at Syracuse University Press but also for the humane values that she has brought to the business of publishing.

INTRODUCTION

$\mathcal{T}$he heart of the artist, as Lollius reminds us in his *Legend of Troy*, is to be found in the broad strokes of plot and theme; his mind, if it is to be glimpsed at all, is in the details. For example, the careful attention paid to details by Chaucer's Man of Law reveals a great deal about this lawyer whose attention to language is so meticulous that no man might "pynch" at his writing. So it is especially important to note that, having firmly anchored his tale in the world of miracles, Chaucer's Lawyer suddenly interrupts his narrative of a woman cast adrift without food for seven years in order to treat that most practical of details, her language. How does Custance, washed ashore on a strange and possibly hostile land, make herself understood? "A maner Latyn corrupt was hir speche, / But algates therby was she understonde." While the laws of physics and of human sustenance may be suspended, the laws of language remain fast. Why, we ask, this drop into realism; why, when so many other details are passed over in the willing suspension of disbelief that inevitably accompanies a genre rooted in the miraculous, why this attention to language?

The answer lies in the fact that, in the fictive world evoked by the Man of Law, language is not a detail, not something pushed to the periphery by other more important elements. Rather, words are the very substance of which the tale is made, the paste that holds the work together. Thus, the first cause of Custance's adventures is rumor. Syrian merchants, "fadres of tydynges," hear tales of her virtue. The motive power of their language is so strong that the young Sultan whom the merchants serve falls in love with Custance merely by listening to their reports of her beauty. And as the Sultan is falling in love with that verbal image of Custance, the narrator apostrophizes concerning "thilke large book / Which that men clipe the hevene [in which] ywriten was" the birth and death of the Sultan as well as of all mankind. Moreover, within the tale, the two hostile camps are each defined by their allegiance to a text. There are those loyal to the "Alkaron" of Islam, and there are those who keep faith with the book of the "Evaungiles." And later, in Northumbria, there is the fixed language of the formally sworn oaths as well as the mutable signs of the altered letters sent to and from King Alla. And throughout the tale there is the constant discourse of prayer. Everywhere one looks within the tale there is evidence of the import of language as a theme.

Of course, at first glance it is tempting to ascribe this preoccupation with words written and spoken to the character of the Man of Law, himself a professional talker and skilled and successful writer and speaker. Yet Chaucer's other pilgrims are equally concerned with language. Their tales consistently take up such issues as how to speak, when to speak, why we speak. For them as well as for the Man of Law, language is substance rather than accident. *Homo loquens,* as Chaucer presents him, is above all self-conscious of his linguistic identity.

Indeed, if we pull back to consider the pilgrims as a whole, we find the same theme of language throughout the descriptive tapestry of the *General Prologue.* In fact, it is difficult not to notice the attention and space given over to describing the spoken and written language of the various Canterbury pilgrims. For example, we know the physical qualities of their speech. The Prioress speaks through her nose. The Friar lisps from wantonness. The Pardoner has a voice like a goat. We know their vocal mannerisms. The Host is "boold of his speeche," whereas the Clerk "Noght o word spak . . . moore than was neede / And that was seyd in forme and reverence / And short and quyk." We know the content of their speech. The Knight never yet "no vileynye ne sayde," whereas the Miller is a "janglere and a goliardeys." We know the relative value of their speech. The Man of Law's "wordes weren so wise" that no man could them "pynch," whereas the Sommoner's "fewe termes" in "Latyn" are devalued since "a jay / Kan clepen 'Watte' as wel as kan the pope." We know how they feel about reading. The Monk hates to read, while his counterpart the Clerk takes "moost cure and moost heede" of "studie." The Physician has read a great deal but in the wrong book. We know what they write. Besides Geoffrey, the prolific author whose gregarious nature and proclivity for speech first serves to bind together the diverse company at the Tabard Inn, two other pilgrims, the Squire and the Friar, compose poetry. In all, the portraits of two-thirds of the pilgrims contain explicit information concerning how they write, speak, or read.

And, of course, this theme of language, so prominent in Chaucer, is by no means something that sets him off from his times. Students new to *Beowulf* routinely find their expectations confounded by the fact that there is considerably more talking than fighting in that poem. In Bede's account of Caedmon, the ability to compose is the stuff of miracles. Beyond the realm of English poetry, we see versions of the Tristan legend—Anglo-Norman, French, and German—in which linguistic and semiotic themes abound. The onomastic intricacies of the legend begin with the naming of its protagonist and the seeming connection between name and fate of the person to whom it is applied. Such themes continue with Tristan's change of character under his new name, "Tantris." And there is not one, but three, Isoldes. So real is the power of a name that Tristan loves Isolde of the White Hands simply because she bears the same name as Isolde the Fair. Further, there is within the same legend the polysemous phrase *"le mer,"* and there is the infamous linguistic contortion of the oath taken at Isolde's ordeal. Similarly, in the romances of Chrétien we find the silences of Enide and Perceval, the rash oaths of the King and the rude remarks of Sir Kay, and the identity changes which take place as knights change speech habits, armors, and ensigns, the signs which identify them to the rest of the world. Indeed, as we read Chrétien, we are constantly reminded that a world given over to heraldry is one which wears its semiotic self-consciousness on its sleeve. In fact, in romance in general, it is clear that knowing both how and when to speak is as important as knowing how and when to bear arms, a fact attested to in the nonfictive world by the wealth of manuals designed to teach would-be knights the art of proper discourse, most notably that of the good Andreas.

The theme of language is not, however, limited to the elevated realm of the chevalier. It is equally present in the scatological world of the fabliau. With its double entendres and semantic slapstick, the verbal tricksters who populate the fabliaux have much in common with their more noble kinsmen. In fact, the goliard, in his endless fascination with abused language and the power of a name, has not a little in common with the preacher of the popular sermon and even with the Latin Fathers with their elaborate explorations of the creative nature of the Word. One recalls Augustine beginning his *Confessions* with an account of his own linguistic development and ending that same work with a consideration of the ontological and phenomenal dimensions of the creative speech act in Genesis. As for the philosophers, theirs was the debate between Realism and Nominalism, over the reality or the arbitrariness of names. The short poem, the epic, the romance, the fabliau, the popular sermon, the commentary, the *summa,* the treatise on logic, the books of virtues and vices, the moral treatise—all share this great preoccupation with language. In short, despite the self-congratulatory tone that pervades much of our modern writing about language, many issues at the heart of our own critical/theoretical debates can be found already foreshadowed in the works of the Middle Ages, a period that may well outstrip our own in both popular and academic interest in and awareness of language. As Lollius reminds us, sometimes we stand on the shoulders of giants, not to look through the window, but to study the stains of the glass.

The following essays consider such issues as the relationship between language and identity—individual and social; the indeterminacy of text and the radical instability of signs; the conventionality and arbitrariness of language; the attempt to control reality by controlling signs; the relation of language to thought; language as a behavior, both sexual and social, as well as the larger issue of language and gender; the differences between public and private language, and human and divine; and even the internal dialogue by which a society is reshaped by its language. In fact, like signs themselves, the subjects (and meanings) of these essays are too rich for simple schematizing. Of necessity, an order has been imposed on them, but others were equally possible. For example, while there is no category of language and gender, several essays dwell upon the subject, and the contents might have been ordered to accommodate that category at the expense of another. The same might have been done for the theme of manipulating reality through the manipulation of names. Or essays might have been grouped differently; for example, Grimbert with Allen in regard to silence. However the essays are grouped, what emerges is the richness of diversity. To that end, the collection is as diverse in subject matter as in critical approach, containing essays on literature written in French, Italian, and Spanish as well as English. Moreover, the literary works that are the subjects of these essays range widely in topic and genre, from knightly adventure to moral allegory, fabliau to popular sermon, philosophical treatise to comic tale, short verse romance to religious epic. The scholar who comes looking for an essay on Chaucer will discover parallel concerns in works in other vernaculars, perhaps even other disciplines as well. Although readers often come to collections such as this in search of a particular essay on a particular author or work, the essays are ordered to build on each other, so that the effect on the reader looking for an overview of medieval concerns about language is cumulative. To that end, each chapter begins with a brief headnote which not only introduces the essays that follow but also attempts to draw connections between those essays and others in the collection.

SIGN, SENTENCE, DISCOURSE

PART I

OF FIGS AND *FIGURA*

The Search for Origin
through the Breaking Up of the Word

EDITORS' INTRODUCTION

The Vedas tell of a conversation between a young man, Shvetaketu, and his father concerning what the son had learned in his education. Pointing to a fig tree, the father asked, "From whence cometh the tree?"—to which the son replied, "from the fig." "From whence did the fig come?"—to which the son replied, "the fig seed." "And from whence the fig seed?" the father continued. "From whatever is inside the seed," the son replied and, pausing, was told to break open the fig seed and describe what was there. "Nothing" exclaimed the boy in surprise, to which the father replied, "That thou art, Shvetaketu."

In his essay "Medieval Studies after Derrida after Heidegger," R. A. Shoaf sets forth what are some common themes (and methodologies) in this collection—the suspicion of ("anxiety over") language that results from recognizing its instability and arbitrariness; and the respect for language as a transcendental medium standing between phenomena and ideas, and therefore a possible avenue back to purer ontological states. In short, we break open the word seeking origin much as Shvetaketu dissects the fig.

And the result of this parsing is much like that in the Vedic parable. There are those who find nothing in the seed and those who find its emptiness substantive. As Shoaf asks,

> Does such breaking up give evidence of the fullness or the emptiness of the text or the word? . . . The question asks whether a text or word is an archival deposit of an original and originary proper, in which case a dictionary would be the last word on words; or whether a text or a word is a node in a skein of relations constantly changing its contours as it, the text or word, assimilates to other texts or words, in which case a dictionary would be out of date practically the day it was published.

In regard to the essays that follow, we could in the same terms contrast Joan Grimbert's "meaningful silence" as sign and Peter Allen's observation that the name "Silence" in *Le Roman de Silence* is merely a "placeholder." Into the first of these camps we might, at least to some degree, place the essays of Liam Purdon and Phillip Pulsiano with their emphasis on language redeemed; into the latter, those of Judith Ferster and Julian Wasserman with their emphasis on the privatization entailed in the act of reading. Or we might take Peggy Knapp's discussion of Chaucer's Knight and Miller as providing models, or at least congruencies, of the same dichotomy.

In the first essay, R. A. Shoaf, as his title indicates, claims Heidegger and Derrida as his models. In the former's "verbal mysticism," Shoaf finds a somewhat positivist celebration of "the pure delight of becoming stillness," not far removed from the essence or fullness which Shvetaketu's father found in the "emptiness" of the fig seed. To discover that *essence*, the father began with the tree and worked backward. In Heidegger we find a corollary belief that the part (the emanation) is the microcosm of the whole, even if the whole is beyond comprehension. Like an unseen planet whose effects of mass and orbit can nevertheless be felt and measured, the "relation of all relations" has Platonic substance and Reality.

In Derrida the emptiness is also a fullness. To break up a word or text, or for that matter a fig, is to fill it. Both Shvetaketu and his father see the "Nothing" as something, although radically different somethings that are projections of themselves. Due to the incomplete nature of any text and sign, to read a text is to rewrite it, as several of the succeeding essays remind us. Using Dante's famous letter to Can Grande, Shoaf notes that it is the reader who provides the missing levels of allegory. In the end, Derridian interplay between present and absent behaves like two poles of a simple electric motor, the alternating movement and pull from one to the other generating its own energy, creative excitement, danger, and even comic possibilities.

In the second essay in this chapter, Glenn Arbery's "Adam's First Word and the Failure of Language in *Paradiso* XXXIII," we encounter in Dante's effort at "breaking up" Adam's speech the poet's dismay at finding there both fullness and emptiness; hence, confirmation of Shoaf's assertion that, in regard to the word as both "archival deposit" and "node" in a changing skein, the Middle Ages can answer affirmatively to both possibilities. The foundation of Arbery's second essay is its conclusion: that language is supplemental, that the word is neither the phenomenon nor the idea of the rose—that Adam's first word "El" is outside both God and the concept of God. Nevertheless, the sign has substance as a medium, and what is unnecessary in Eden is necessary in a fallen world. Being supplemental, language resides outside the human world, but being beyond that world is transcendental. For Dante, as for many medieval thinkers, language is privileged: prayer is the link, perhaps the only avenue, to our original state. Thus, although "supplemental" in Paradise at the first moment of consciousness, language becomes increasingly necessary in the fallen world as the world becomes increasingly distanced from the moment of creation.

On "breaking apart" Adam's words, Arbery finds both fullness and emptiness. Adam's first word, although "supplemental," is clearly a success. Its fullness comes from its proximity to its origin which is Real in the Platonic sense. Arbery notes that since Adam did not devise his first word—and he could not, since it came with his first breath and moment of consciousness—then it must have been inscribed in his mind by God. Hence, the language that proceeds from Adam is the product of "Derridian good writing"—in this case divine writing that precedes speech. The emptiness that one finds in Adam's words is the "Paradisal failure of language," the result of an apparently Derridian tension between absence and presence, between the good writing of the Trinity and the bad writing of the figure of man in Dante's final vision. There the sign is the signifier of that which cannot be conceived—Shvetaketu's "Nothing" and, as we shall see, Allen's placeholding "Silence." While both emptiness and fullness are found in the signs, the final vision in canto XXXIII of "one of the most logocentric of western writers" is, as Arbery presents it, a positivist vision. The tension creates infinite possibilities, the *coincidentia oppositorum* of the Augustinian Creation, a product of God's speech whose unfolding meaning is both fluid and fixed, empty and full.

1

MEDIEVAL STUDIES
AFTER DERRIDA AFTER HEIDEGGER

R. A. SHOAF

[D]enn die Worte und die Sprache sind keine Hülsen, worin die Dinge nur für den redenden und schreibenden Verkehr verpackt werden. Im Wort, in der Sprache werden und sind erst die Dinge.

(Words and language are not wrappings in which things are packed for the commerce of those who write or speak. It is in words and language that things first come into being and are.)

> Martin Heidegger, *An Introduction to*
> *Metaphysics* (translated by Ralph Manheim)

Die Sprache ist . . . das Verhältnis aller Verhältnisse. . . . Dieses Zerbrechen des Wortes ist der eigentliche Schritt zuruck auf dem Weg des Denkens.

(Language is . . . the relation of all relations. . . . This breaking up of the word is the true step back on the way of thinking.)

> Martin Heidegger, *The Nature of Language*
> (translated by Peter D. Hertz)

Si les mots et les concepts ne prennent sens que dans des enchaînements de différences, on ne peut justifier son langage, et le choix des termes, qu'à l'intérieur d'une topique et d'une stratégie historique. La justification ne peut donc jamais être absolue et définitive. Elle répond à un état des forces et traduit un calcul historique.

(If words and concepts receive meaning only in sequences of differences, one can justify one's language, and one's choice of terms, only within a topic [an orientation in space] and an historical strategy. The justification can therefore never be absolute and definitive. It corresponds to a condition of forces and translates an historical calculation.)

> Jacques Derrida, *Of Grammatology*
> (translated by Gayatri C. Spivak)

O ne of the frequent attacks on Heidegger, especially the late Heidegger, argues that he practices something like a verbal mysticism.[1] Those who hold this position can point, with justice, to the German language, and, with perhaps even more justice, to Heidegger's way with the German language—a way we might describe as excavation, leaving no syllable unturned, of a ground ever receding from human grasp.[2] The readiest example of this way is Heidegger's turning and mining, and occasional overturning and undermining, of the many words deriving from the prolific verb *stellen*—such as *bestellen, vorstellen, sicherstellen, nachstellen, verstellen, herstellen, darstellen,* and perhaps most important, *Gestell*—words he is continually breaking up to get at the senses of *pose, place, order, arrange, supply, set.*[3]

I do not number myself among Heidegger's attackers (though neither am I a disciple). Still, I sympathize with the complaint: the constant "breaking up" of words looks dangerously like the kind of childishly destructive game any clever person can play. However, this is not so, I believe, in Heidegger's case—nor, for that matter, in Derrida's either (although clearly Derrida more openly invites such criticisms).[4] In Heidegger, the "breaking up of the word" serves a quest for the *how* of relations, for the *way* in which Being summons man to answer for the human—to declare himself for the fate of the human. And I, as a medievalist studying literatures in which everything relates to everything, through an agency named Providence, find Heidegger's quest and, in particular, his instruments, especially useful just because they seek the "relation of all relations," or language.[5]

The Relation of Relations: The Breaking Up of the Word

Heidegger's quest is successful, as I believe he himself would have also admitted, only fleetingly. He surprises "the relation of all relations" once, I think, in *A Dialogue on Language:* language there he likens to "Blütenblätter, die aus der lichtenden Botschaft der hervorbringenden Huld gedeihen" ("flower petals that flourish out of the lightening message of the graciousness that brings forth") where "graciousness" has "der Sinne des reinen Entzückens der rufenden Stille" ("the sense of the pure delight of the beckoning stillness").[6]

I would like, provisionally, to propose an analogy between language, as Heidegger describes it here, and the Gothic cathedral—Notre Dame de Paris, for example—which, like language, also is "the petals that stem from . . . the happening of the lightening message of the graciousness [the pure delight of the beckoning stillness] that brings forth."[7] The analogy I am suggesting is a fruitful one, I believe. The Gothic cathedral is "gracious" in "the sense of the pure delight of the beckoning stillness." The Gothic cathedral would thus be a figure for language understood as "the relation of all relations." And "the breaking up of the word" that "is the true step back on the way of thinking" would then be the concentration on the petal—be it the flying buttress or the caryatid or the arch or the vault or the stained glass window—which re-duces or leads back to the thought of the whole, hitherto impossible, at just that moment when it became possible through the articulation of the petals.

The thought of the Gothic cathedral without breaking it up into its many articulations is unthinkable. One can look at it without such breaking up. But one cannot think it, be beckoned by it, without taking this "true step back on the way of thinking"—the thought of the Gothic cathedral must think the articulation of relations.[8]

Heidegger was, early in his career, a medievalist.[9] He submitted his *Habilitationsschrift* in the summer of 1915, on a speculative or, strictly speaking, *modistic,* grammar, then ascribed to Duns Scotus, now known to have been the work of Thomas of Erfurt.[10] Heidegger was also one of the last of the major German Romantic medievalists. He came at the end and is arguably one culmination of a centuries-old *Forschung* into the ontology of language that began with Enlightenment and Romantic recovery of German and classical Antiquity.

And his anxiety over language emerges from a Romantic conviction which is also demonstrable in medieval contexts. This is the conviction that because words are, as Aristotle says, "symbols of that which suffers in the soul," they somehow relate to man's relation, through the world, to the earth, and to his body, which is a product of the earth.[11] If words are "symbols of consciousness" ("that which suffers in the soul"), then somehow they are related to the agents of that suffering, or the "things" (objects, events, etc.) of the world; words are somehow the mark or the scar or the trace left in the soul by the world during the sojourn of the human being on the earth. And if only one could somehow follow the trace back to its origin, then one could grasp the world, and, through the world, the earth. One could perhaps name the relation of language to relation itself.

For a medievalist, the quest for this name is necessary and important. All medieval writing posits relations among this or that discrete, individual entity, person, or thing, and other entities, within structures of ever-increasing articulation and hierarchical interconnectedness.[12] Thus, for example, if just before the Parson begins his *Tale* at the end of the *Canterbury Tales,* Chaucer refers to the astrological sign Libra, he is telling us in effect that the Scales or the Balance is related to this moment in the pilgrimage; and this because the issue of justice, and of the Last Judgment, is also related to this particular moment; and this relation further relates to the most important scales or balance in medieval Christianity, or the scales of the Cross on which, in the person of the Crucified, the good and the evil of a person's life are weighed for final judgment.[13] The relations, I hasten to admit, are more complex and obviously more involved than my brief description indicates; I am oversimplifying to have a ready, introductory example. But even oversimplified, the example does suggest how relation, the phenomenon of relatedness, enjoys such extraordinary importance in medieval writing.

Moreover, the example shows how "breaking up" (which is the literal sense of the word *analysis*) is necessary to think the relations: we must break the text up into ever finer parts to discover and to think its total articulacy. Sometimes, as for example with a line of Dante, this process can go on for scores of pages, for some medieval writers, and especially Dante, can articulate an entire world in one line or one figure—"luce intelletüale, piena d'amore" ("intellectual light, full of love"), for example.[14] But such breaking up, be it brief or extended, of a text or a word, can still be submitted to a very serious, searching question.

Does such breaking up give evidence of the fullness or the emptiness of the text or the word?[15] One immediate response to this question would be to "deconstruct" it in order to expose how it rests on a differencing (fullness/emptiness) in service of an illusion of logical or logocentric reasoning; so deconstructed, this differencing would appear as the trace of a nostalgia for idealism within the self-presence of the logos. I am not unsympathetic to this gesture; and I will return to it and some of its implications shortly. But for now, I would like to try a different response to the question, in order to test what the logical presence is that it would present.

The question asks whether a text or a word is an archival deposit of an original and originary proper, in which case a dictionary would be the last word on words; or whether a text or a word is a node in a skein of relations constantly changing its contours as it, the text or word, assimilates to other texts or words, in which case a dictionary would be out of date practically the day it was published.[16] Ordinary, educated opinion assumes, I suspect, that the Middle Ages automatically answers in the affirmative to the first alternative, and ordinary, educated opinion is to a certain extent correct. But the Middle Ages also answers affirmatively to the second alternative, although this fact is only beginning to inform ordinary opinion.[17] And it is the dual answer, sometimes given apropos of the same text or word, that makes at least some medieval writing accessible to the Heideggerean understanding of language as "the relation of all relations."

Dante's "Epistle to Can Grande" will provide a useful illustration. In this epistolary preface to the *Commedia* and to the *Paradiso* in particular, Dante offers what we know, in light of the work of Judson Allen and Bruno Sandkühler, is a typical medieval *accessus ad auctores,* or "introduction to the author and his work."[18] In the course of this preface or introduction, Dante enters an extraordinary description of the sense of the poem:

It should be understood that there is not just a single sense in this work; it might rather be called *polysemous,* that is, having several senses. For the first sense is that which is contained in the letter, while there is another which is contained in what is signified by the letter. The first is called literal, while the second is called allegorical, or moral or anagogical. And in order to make this manner of treatment clear, it can be applied to the following verses: 'When Israel went out of Egypt, the house of Jacob from a barbarous people, Judea was made his sanctuary, Israel his dominion' [Psalm 113:1–2]. Now if we look at the letter alone, what is signified to us is the departure of the sons of Israel from Egypt during the time of Moses; if at the allegory, what is signified to us is our redemption through Christ; if at the moral sense, what is signified to us is the conversion of the soul from the sorrow and misery of sin to the state of grace; if at the anagogical, what is signified to us is the departure of the sanctified soul from bondage to the corruption of this world into the freedom of eternal glory. And although these mystical senses are called by various names, they may all be called allegorical, since they are all different from the literal or historical. For allegory is derived from the Greek *alleon,* which means in Latin *alienus* ["belonging to another"] or *diversus* ["different"].

This being established, it is clear that the subject about which these two senses play must also be twofold. And thus it should first be noted what the subject of the work is when taken according to the letter, and then what its subject is when understood allegorically. The subject of the whole work, then, taken literally, is the state of souls after death, understood in a simple sense; for the movement of the whole work turns upon this and about this. If on the other hand the work is taken allegorically, the subject is man, in the exercise of his free will, earning or becoming liable to the rewards or punishments of justice.[19]

My only concern in this dense and often difficult passage is narrowly with the illustration of the fourfold method of Scriptural exegesis.[20] Here would appear to be the perfect, brief example of the fullness of God's text: he has written the Book of Scripture and the Book of the World in such a way as to fill them with his inexhaustible meaning.[21] One psalm verse relates in three extra-literal ways to the most basic conditions of the soul in this life.[22] And yet, if we attend carefully to what Dante has written, we can see, I think, how this fullness of Scripture "is" emptiness (Derrida would write this "is" *sous rature* ["under erasure"]): the extra-literal meanings clearly are to be occupied, filled, by each reader, with himself; and to be so occupied, they must, just as clearly, in some sense, be empty—to be so applicable to a given individual's discrete, historical situation, these meanings must be full only in such a way as to be empty.[23] So also with the extra-literal meaning of Dante's poem itself: it is empty as full insofar as each of us can insert himself into the articulations of rewards and punishments—find himself or herself in a type that is also an individual. In both cases, in short, and to make the crucial point, to read the text is to write it, is to write oneself into it and ultimately after it. Every reading of these texts, every medieval reading, is a supplementary writing of the texts.[24] And what fullness there is does not obtain without its answering emptiness.[25]

Examples of such reading as writing can be found in numerous sources.[26] Even as late as the seventeenth century, in John Milton, for instance, in many ways a profoundly medieval poet, it is the will to be a poem oneself: "He who would not be frustrate of his hope to write well hereafter in laudable things, ought him selfe to bee a true Poem, that is, a composition, and patterne of the best and honorablest things."[27] With Chaucer's Troilus, it is the recognition, perhaps too late, that one's life has become a story,[28] in accordance with the poetry one has been reading and writing. In *Hamlet*, with typical Skakespearean poignancy, it is the realization that though Ophelia's speech is nothing, yet we do and must make of it something:

> *Gentleman:* Her speech is nothing,
> Yet the unshapèd use of it doth move

The hearers to collection—they yawn at it,
And botch the words up fit to their own thoughts;
Which, as her winks and nods and gestures yield them,
Indeed would make one think there might be thought,
Though nothing sure, yet much unhappily.[29]

Here, indeed, is a description of—some might say a prescription for—reading as writing. And if it be objected—But she is mad! Surely, this is no paradigm of human signification—then one can only reply, after reading-*and*-writing her subsequent lyrics, offered in response to Gertrude and Claudius: if this be madness, make the most of it.

But whatever illustration we choose, it remains the case that the fullness of the word in at least some medieval writing is emptiness— probably ultimately on the pattern of Christ's self-emptying, or *kenosis* (Phil. 2:6)[30]—and the way to thinking this phenomenon often does lie through the breaking up of texts or words. (Think of the way the text of the Bible is broken up into small bits on the folium of a manuscript or of a Renaissance printed edition and then surrounded by gloss which reads it, but also writes and re-writes it and then writes it again, on that very folium).[31]

To break up a text or a word, we can go on to observe now, is to fill it with, empty it of relations hinted at or suspected but otherwise silent in the everydayness or the historical opacity of writing. It is to disseminate anew possibilities of perceived relations in texts or words whose usage has hardened their fictionality or metaphoricity into a pseudo-proper, a meaningless meaningfulness. Take a difficult example, a proper name—in this case, the name of Constance in Chaucer's *Man of Law's Tale*. It is useful, following Heidegger, to break this word up into its abstract noun relative, or "constancy," and then to argue that this tale of a merchant, as the Man of Law calls it (*CT* II, 131–33), is concerned—a merchant's tale would be—with the constancy and inconstancy of media, such as money or female sexuality or indeed words, as these media travel from one border to another, from one rate of exchange to another. Then, having said this, in Heidegger's way, we can argue further that this concern with the constancy of media, as inconstant as they usually are, also helps to explain Chaucer's long list, in the Man of Law's *Prologue*, of the women he writes about in *The Legend of Good Women*: that is to say, a poet of Chaucer's sophistication would be anxious to establish the *constant* value of one of his works, made up of media or words as it is, by an accurate and authentic list of its (so to speak) "Table of Contents." At this point, the crucial observation that the list in the *Prologue* is inconstant with the work as it comes down to us leads directly to Chaucer's irony: the Man of Law, so good a lawyer that "ther koude no wight pynche at his writyng" (*CT* i, 326), nonetheless makes a mistake, commits an error, in his list of Chaucer's works— and suddenly we can pinch at his writing anyway.[32] And we find later in the *Tale* that if we do not pinch at it, it and the Man of Law will pinch at us: the Man of Law uses every rhetorical means at his disposal to persuade us to a view of women and the world that is definitely self-serving.[33]

Another example of Heidegger's way can be drawn from the *Franklin's Tale*.[34] If we break up Middle English *astoned* ("to be astonished") in the following passage, we can argue that it also says *a-stoned* or "turned to stone." Aurelius has just shown Dorigen the coast of Brittany, with the rocks (apparently) away:

> He taketh his leve, and she *astoned* stood;
> In al hir face nas a drope of blood.
> She wende nevere han come in swich a trappe.
> 'Allas,' quod she, 'that evere this sholde happe!
> For wende I nevere by possibilitee
> That swich a *monstre* or merveille myghte be!
> It is agayns the proces of nature.'
> (*CT* v, 1339–45 [emphasis added])

The key here is the word *monstre*. It occurs only three times in the *Canterbury Tales*, only eleven in all of Chaucer's works.[35] It tells us that what Dorigen sees is a Medusa, the monster that turns to stone.[36]

But in what sense exactly is Dorigen turned to stone? In Dante, Medusa is a figure of literalism, of the letter that kills (2 Cor. 3:6), and correspondingly, of that kind of reading which insists on the letter and resists figuration, that reading which refuses to lift the veil or, indeed, if need be, to rend the veil, to see underneath.[37] Just so, Dorigen cannot see beneath the waves magically wrought by the Clerk of Orleans to cover the rocks on the Coast of Brittany; just so, Dorigen is blinded by the illusion, by the surface of the ocean—and by extension, by the surface of the letter of *fin'amors*—to the truths of Aurelius's expediency and her own shallowness. Shallow herself, without depths to penetrate, neither can she penetrate the depths of others or of the Other—her reading, as we would say, is superficial only, and thus like all victims of the Medusa of literalism, she is turned to stone.

Similarly, we, as readers of the *Franklin's Tale,* must break up its illusion of "gentilesse." We must penetrate its sleight of hand, prestidigitatory evocation of moral profundity, we must see through the Franklin's status-anxious mimicking of the Knight with his *demande d'amour* or *questione d'amore* (cf. *CT* I, 1347–48), or we too will be turned to stone. We will be turned to stone by his literalism, his manipulation of the letter of *fin'amors* conventions and of us such that we never penetrate the illusory gentility of wondering "which was the most fre?" (*CT* V, 1622) to see that we are asking this question, playing this silly game, about four of the most self-serving moral adolescents that Chaucer ever invented.

But we must not be turned to stone, if we would be the sort of readers Chaucer wanted. We must penetrate the text, break it up; we must not let it be what Aurelius's wound is said to be, a *sursanure* (*CT* V, 1113), or a wound healed over on the surface (*sur-sanure*) but still festering beneath.[38] We must probe to find the foreign body, the alien sense (recall Dante's *alienum*), and lift it out: in short, we must find and open the holes in the text if we would see it whole.

And when we have done just this, we will see that the Franklin is full of holes.[39] Each of us, to be sure, is full of holes; we depend on holes for life itself. Stop up our holes, impede the flow of life into us and out of us, and very soon we die. The flow of life (life is flow) necessitates the always perilous, sometimes joyous rhythm of opening and closing in which we move every day and have our being.[40] But the Franklin is afraid of his and everyman's (w)hole(i)ness; his son, after all, flowing out from him has disappointed him; his anxieties escaping his elaborate coverings of self-defense betray him. And so, afraid of holes and just possibly wholes, also, the Franklin would cover them all, especially our, his readers' or auditors', eyes and ears. For if our holes are covered, then, of course, his will be, too.

A final example from Chaucer will be useful. Throughout *Troilus and Criseyde*, Chaucer elaborates a figure of the *mewe*, or "place where hawks are put to molt" (*Middle English Dictionary* M:405).[41] The ground of the figure is the echolalia between *mewe* and the first syllable of "mutability" (see *T&C* III, 822). By means of the figure, Chaucer is able to suggest that Troilus and Criseyde are both falcons, noblest of raptors, who are also, and at the same time, victims of mutability. This irony becomes especially moving in Book iv when the dark syllable *mewe* returns, inside the word *transmewe*.

The figure of the *mewe* describes both, and often at the same time, the grandeur and the misery of the two principals, Troilus and Criseyde. They are falcons, birds of nobility, who soar high and possess if not always great courage then certainly great beauty. At the same time, however, the one, Criseyde, is actually more the hunted than a hunter and a bird who leaves the *mewe*, molting place and place of restriction both, only to return to it, inevitably, " 'trans*mewed*'," as she herself says, " 'in cruel wo' " (*T&C* iv, 830; emphasis added). And the other, Troilus, though indeed a prince of a bird, is neither so free nor so powerful in flight as, sadly self-deceived, he thinks he is: he too must molt and the feathers of philosophy with which he is plumed anew do not liberate him from the weight of earth and its mortality and mutability. For that he would have, cruel irony, as he himself says, to become unfeeling earth itself: " 'Thow moost mee first trans-*mewen* in a ston' " (*T&C* iv, 467; emphasis added). Both birds, in fact, however noble, all the same succumb to the lot of those who look to the world for what the world cannot give, satisfaction of the appetite for felicity. Both birds, though they toil in the hunt of *fin'amors* with a good deal more dignity and a good deal less sordidness than most, cannot finally escape the gravity of our condition, that this flesh is not spirit and cannot endure.

This mutability, inescapable as well as so often cruel, Chaucer also inscribes, we can observe now, in the word *transmewen*. His willingness to imagine *transmewen* as, in Heidegger's sense, "broken up" so that he can repeat the dark root *mewe* in a different but related context is evidence of his understanding that such repetition in language itself attests to mutability, to the uncanny phenomenon of doubling, to the radical instability of signs. Thinking through the word broken up, Chaucer discovers anew the contingency of discourse on time and the arbitrary. And thus the word is what it says, and this repetition, in its turn, only further underwrites Chaucer's design—language never rests from mutability. Whatever it shows, it shows distortingly, from within the turns and re-turns, the tropes, of its relentless historicity.

One last example, perhaps, will be useful, this one from Dante's *Inferno*, the opening lines of canto 24, first of the cantos of the thieves:

In quella parte del giovanetto anno
che 'l sole i crin sotto l'Aquario tempra

> e già le notti al mezzo dì sen vanno,
>   quando la brina in su la terra as-*sempr*-a
> l'imagine di sua sorella bianca,
> ma poco dura a la sua penna tempra,
>   lo villanello a cui la roba manca
> si leva, e guarda, e vede la campagna
> biancheggiar tutta, ond'ei si batte l'anca
>   ritorna in casa, e qua e là si lagna,
> come 'l tapin che non sa che si faccia,
> poi riede, e la speranza ringavagna,
>   veggendo 'l mondo aver cangiata faccia
> in poco d'ora, e prende suo vincastro
> e fuor le pecorelle a pascer caccia.
>   (*Inferno* XXIV, 1–15 [emphasis added])

(In that part of the youthful year when the sun tempers his locks beneath Aquarius, and the nights already wane towards half the day, when the hoarfrost copies on the ground the image of his white sister, but the temper of his pen lasts but short while—the peasant, whose fodder fails, rises and looks out and sees the fields all white; at which he smites his thigh, returns indoors and grumbles to and fro, like the poor wretch who knows not what to do; then he comes out again and recovers hope when he sees how in but little time the world has changed its face, and taking his crook, drives forth his sheep to pasture.)[42]

Clearly what we have here is a convincing description of a rural scene Dante probably witnessed more than once during his lifetime, especially perhaps during his exile. But just as clearly what we have here is also an extended trope of writing itself, its instability and evanescence.

The frost makes an image of the snow, and does so with its pen. The crucial verb here, *assempra*,[43] not only insists on representation but also on the inevitable temporality of representation since, if, following Heidegger, we *break* this verb *up*, within it we also hear, ironically, *sempr*[e] (*always*)—ironically because the next line will subvert the *sempr*[e] with its radical insistence on mutability and evanescence—"ma poco dura a la sua penna tempra." The pretensions of writing to permanence are thus dismissed and primarily because writing is constantly subject to misinterpretation by the reader—or, in this case, the *vilanello*, who misinterprets the *brina*: he is the figure of all readers, who jump to conclusions and miss the point, not waiting for the text, like the world, "to have changed face"—not waiting, in short, to break the text up, to analyze its face, its appearance, so as to see and understand what it implies.

De Meun and Derrida: Identity and Difference

All these arguments need much greater elaboration and defense than I have given them here. But still they will serve, I think, to illustrate just briefly how a medievalist can practice his trade after Heidegger.

And how he can practice it after Derrida can be illustrated by returning to and taking up the deconstructionist response to the question of fullness or emptiness. This response can, in fact, be predicted from a common position of medieval thought, set forth most clearly perhaps in Jean de Meun's conclusion to his continuation of *Le Roman de la Rose:*

> Ainsinc va des contreres choses,
> les unes sunt des autres gloses,
> et qui l'une an veust definir,
> de l'autre li doit souvenir,
> ou ja, par nule antancion,
> n'i metra diffinicion,
> car qui des .II. n'a connoissance,
> ja n'i connoistra differeance,
> san quoi ne peut venir en place
> diffinicion que l'an face.

(Thus things go by contraries; one is the gloss of the other. If one wants to define one of the pair, he must remember the other, or he will never, by any intention, assign a definition to it; for he who has no understanding of the two will never understand the difference between them, and without this difference no definition that one may make can come to anything.)[44]

If I argue that the position that Jean de Meun articulates here is the same as a very famous one assumed by Derrida, it is only because Derrida has helped us to see that the same is the same because it is different (that is, not identical, where identity is understood to cancel difference).[45] Both men, Jean de Meun and Jacques Derrida, are concerned with what the latter encounters in "différance comme temporalisation . . . la non-présence de l'autre inscrite dans le sens du présent . . . la rapport à la mort comme structure concrète du présent vivant" ("difference as temporalization . . . the nonpresence of the other inscribed within the sense of the present . . . the relationship with death as the concrete structure of the living present").[46]

Jean de Meun is concerned with "the relationship with death as the concrete structure of the living present" primarily because of the anxiety of the proper which he and his contemporaries had begun to experience. If a word is defined by its opposite—by opposition—then its proper (sense) is always the property of another: no word is secure from an archaeology of mind because no word is innocent of structure and its contingency. It was this discovery, this realization, that so troubled and moved Alan of Lille—one of Jean's principal precursors—who, in the famous opening metrum of the *De planctu Naturae,* recognizes the collapse of linguistic property in the decay of sexual propriety:

> Veneris monstro naufraga turba perit.
> . . . .
> Activi generis sexus, se turpiter horret
> Sic in passivum degenerare genus.
> Femina vir factus, sexus denigrat honorem,
> Ars magicae Veneris hermaphroditat eum.
> Praedicat et subjicit, fit duplex terminus idem,
> Grammaticae leges ampliat ille nimis.
> . . . .
> Ars illi non placet, imo, tropus.
> Non tamen ista tropus poterit translatio dici,
> In vitium melius ista figura cadit.

([L]arge numbers are shipwrecked and lost because of a Venus turned monster. . . . The active sex shudders in disgrace as it sees itself degenerate into the passive sex. A man turned woman blackens the fair name of his sex. The witchcraft of Venus turns him into a hermaphrodite. He is subject and predicate: one and the same term is given a double application. Man here extends too far the laws of grammar. . . . Grammar does not find favor with him but rather a trope. This transposition, however, cannot be called a trope. The figure here more correctly falls into the category of defects.)[47]

Promiscuous coupling, especially when it is homoerotic, defines linguistic and sexual perversion alike.[48] But promiscuous coupling, whether homo- or heteroerotic, as the twelfth and thirteenth centuries were beginning to see, is the irrational and uncontrollable corollary of the very rationality of history.[49] Language like sex will not be confined by laws precisely because it is governed by laws.[50] And either's transgression of the law is its "encounter with death as the concrete structure of the living present."

Given that this is so, Jean de Meun as well as Jacques Derrida would recognize in the opposition fullness/emptiness an ever unstable ground, an energy of signification, an entropy of structuration, such that election of one "meaning" over the other would be only a logocentric illusion masquerading as a law (people, of course, we should observe, manage most of the time quite well on illusions, which, regrettably, most of the time have precisely all the force of laws). Jean de Meun as well as Jacques Derrida would accept that fullness is ("under erasure") emptiness—if it is also agreed that "one is the gloss of the other" or that "le signifié [est] originairement et essentiellement . . . toujours déjà en position de *signifiant*" ("the signified is originarily and essentially . . . always already in the position of the *signifier*").[51] Both thinkers, separated though they are by a chasm that cannot be crossed (only for the moment crossed out), still recognize, each on his own horizon, the endless finitude of thought. Both accept "death as the concrete structure of the living present."

If I practice medieval studies after Derrida after Heidegger, it is because, like Heidegger, I also read St. Augustine, whose concern with signification I hardly need emphasize here.[52] In particular, I study Book 12 of the *Confessions,* especially certain affirmations in chapters 18 and 31 which exemplify language as "the relation of all relations":

> Dum ergo quisque conatur id sentire in scripturis sanctis, quod in eis sensit ille qui scripsit, quid mali est, si hoc sentiat, quod tu, lux omnium veridicarum mentium, ostendis verum esse, etiamsi non hoc sensit ille, quem legit, cum et ille verum nec tamen hoc senserit?

> (Provided, therefore, that each of us tries as best he can to understand in the Holy Scriptures what the writer meant by them, what harm is there if a reader believes what you, the Light of all truthful minds, show him to be the true meaning? It may not even be the meaning which the writer had in mind, and yet he too saw in them a true meaning, different though it may have been from this.)

Ego certe, quod intrepidus de meo corde pronuntio, si ad culmen auctoritatis aliquid scriberem, sic mallem scribere, ut quod veri quisque de his rebus capere posset, mea verba resonarent, quam ut unam veram sententiam ad hoc apertius ponerem, ut excluderem ceteras, quarum falsitas me non posset offendere.

(For my part I declare resolutely and with all my heart that if I were called upon to write a book which was to be vested with the highest authority, I should prefer to write it in such a way that a reader could find re-echoed in my words whatever truths he was able to apprehend. I would rather write in this way than impose a single true meaning so explicitly that it would exclude all others, even though they contained no falsehood that could give me offense.)[53]

To these moments in the *Confessions,* I should add at least one from the *Enarrationes in Psalmos,* from the comment on Psalm 126:

Sed est alia sententia quam praetermittere non debemus. Ideo enim forte obscurius positum est, ut multos intellectus generet, et ditiores discedant homines, quia clausum inuenerunt quod multis modis aperiretur, quam si uno modo apertum inuenirent.

(But there is another opinion also which we ought not to pass over. For perhaps the words are rather obscurely expressed for this reason, that they may call forth many understandings, and that men may go away the richer, because they have found that closed which might be opened in many ways, than if they could open and discover it by one interpretation.)[54]

Perhaps it is perversely Abelardian of me to *sic et non* Augustine on Derrida. And yet, perhaps not. I juxtapose Augustine and Derrida because I am a juxtologist—pursuing a poetics of duality through the method of juxtology.[55] Juxtology emerges from the ancient epistemology of knowledge by contraries and pursues, by comparisons— be they of thinkers and their ideas or of the minutest items of a text, syllables and even individual letters—the aleatory juxtapositions of minds or of sounds that produce the phenomena of meanings.[56] So doing, juxtology recognizes the ontology of error and its necessity: we humans come to the truth only by wandering. For Derrida such wandering consists in detours.[57] For Augustine, it is pilgrimaging, to the Truth who is no one's private property.[58] Hence the ground of my juxtaposition, my Abelardian comparison (and also, obviously, contrast) of the two thinkers.

For Heidegger, finally, such wandering is the way (not without "irren" [error][59]) to the relation of all relations. In this way he learned and teaches that "das Sich-verdanken ist als Danken auf die Freude gestimmt" ("owing oneself as thanking is attuned to joy")[60] and also that—this is even more important—"das Fragen ist die Frömmigkeit des Denkens" ("questioning is the piety of thought").[61]

Notes

I would like to take this opportunity to acknowledge with gratitude the National Endowment for the Humanities for a Fellowship for Independent Study in the academic year 1982–83 which enabled me to pursue the research for this and other studies.

1. For a helpful explanation of Heidegger's practice, see Ronald Bruzina, "Heidegger on the Metaphor and Philosophy," in Michael Murray, ed., *Heidegger and Modern Philosophy: Critical Essays* (New Haven: Yale University Press, 1978), pp. 184–200; consult also Murray's introduction, pp. vii–xxiii. See also Frederick A. Olafson, *Heidegger and the Philosophy of Mind* (New Haven: Yale University Press, 1987), pp. 185–93, esp. p. 192; the essays in Joseph J. Kockelmans, ed., *On Heidegger and Language* (Evanston: Northwestern University Press, 1972); and Samuel B. Southwell, *Kenneth Burke and Martin Heidegger, With a Note Against Deconstruction*, Humanities Monograph 60 (Gainesville: University of Florida Press, 1987), pp. 7–8. An extremely enlightening introduction to Heidegger, his methods, and his meaning is found in Ernesto Grassi, *Heidegger and the Question of Renaissance Humanism: Four Studies* (Binghamton, N.Y.: Medieval and Renaissance Texts and Studies, 1983).

2. The collection of Heidegger's papers on language most important to the present essay is *Unterwegs zur Sprache* (Pfullingen: Neske, 1971). Most of these essays have been conveniently translated by Peter D. Hertz, *On the Way to Language* (New York: Harper and Row, 1971). Another collection of essays in convenient translation, not all on language, is *Poetry, Language, Thought,* trans. Albert Hofstadter (New York: Harper and Row, 1971).

3. See the helpful note on this verb by William Lovitt, trans., *The Question Concerning Technology* (New York: Harper and Row, 1977), p. 15.

4. Southwell's attack is particularly vehement—see pp. 87–105.

5. It is interesting and instructive to compare Heidegger with Luther in this regard: "Luther held that God was to be encountered not in his substance, which was unknowable and terrifying, but 'in the category of relation' (L[uther] W[erke])"— Georgia B. Christopher, *Milton and the Science of the Saints* (Princeton: Princeton University Press, 1982), p. 21.

6. Martin Heidegger, "Aus Einem Gespräch von der Sprache," in *Unterwegs zur*

Sprache, pp. 153, 141.

7. I should observe, if only tangentially at this point, that a Derridean critique of this definition of language would begin with distress over how graphic a translation it is of just two Japanese words, *Kota ba,* and perhaps then go on to stress the idealism urgent in the differencing of the numerous abstractions against the organic and sensuous *petals.* As interesting as I find this Derridean detour to the definition, it is not at this moment our principal way, which lies rather in a different direction. For related comment, see, below, pp. 20–22.

8. See Otto von Simson, *The Gothic Cathedral: Origins of Gothic Architecture and the Medieval Concept of Order,* Bollingen Series 48 (Princeton: Princeton University Press, 1956), pp. 4–20, esp. p. 6. See also Erwin Panofsky, *Gothic Architecture and Scholasticism* (New York: New American Library, 1976), pp. 31–35, and Robert M. Jordan, *Chaucer and the Shape of Creation* (Cambridge, Mass.: Harvard University Press, 1967), p. 42.

9. For this and other biographical details, see Thomas Sheehan, "Heidegger's Early Years: Fragments for a Philosophical Biography," in *Heidegger, the Man and the Thinker,* ed. Thomas Sheehan (Chicago: Precedent Publishing, Inc., 1981), pp. 3–19.

10. See *Die Kategorien- und Bedeutungslehre des Duns Scotus* (Tübingen, 1916); and consult G. L. Bursill-Hall, *"Grammatica Speculativa" of Thomas of Erfurt* (London: Longman, 1972), p. vii, along with his *Speculative Grammars of the Middle Ages* (The Hague: Mouton, 1971).

11. For Aristotle's famous definition of words "των ἐν τῃ ψυχῃ Παθημάτων συμβολα," see the *Peri Hermenias* I, trans. Harold P. Cooke, Loeb Classical Library (Cambridge, Mass.: Harvard University Press, 1938), pp. 114–15.

12. The single most important example of this phenomenon is allegory, on which so much has now been written that even an introductory or preliminary bibliography is impossible in a mere footnote. Still, most bibliographies would probably include Judson B. Allen, *The Ethical Poetic of the Later Middle Ages: A Decorum of Convenient Distinction* (Toronto: University of Toronto Press, 1982); Hennig Brinkmann, *Mittelalterliche Hermenutik* (Tübingen: Niemeyer, 1980); Angus Fletcher, *Allegory: The Theory of a Symbolic Mode* (Ithaca: Cornell University Press, 1964); Maureen Quilligan, *The Language of Allegory: Defining the Genre* (Ithaca: Cornell University Press, 1979); Jon Whitman, *Allegory: The Dynamics of an Ancient and Medieval Technique* (Cambridge: Harvard University Press, 1987).

13. See Chauncey Wood, *Chaucer and the Country of the Stars* (Princeton: Princeton University Press, 1970), pp. 272–97.

14. *Paradiso* 30.40 in *La Commedia secondo l'Antica Vulgata,* 4 vols., ed. for the Società Dantesca Italiana by Giorgio Petrocchi, Edizione Nazionale (Milan: Mondadori, 1966–67); my translation.

15. Compare Roland Barthes on the text and the *vide,* in *Critique et Vérité* (Paris: Éditions du Seuil, 1966), pp. 56–57.

16. On the "proper" and the problematics of "property" in regard to the senses of words, see the now classic essay by Derrida, "White Mythology: Metaphor in the Text of Philosophy," *New Literary History* 6 (1974): 5–74. At issue is the question whether, if words have a "proper" sense, they also in some way then "own" that sense (as when, speaking loosely, we say, "this or that is the ap*prop*riate sense of the word"). Is there an obligatory, *essential* connection between a word and its sense? A connection of "ownership"? From one perspective, this is among the oldest problems in Western philosophy. Plato is concerned with it, for example, in the *Cratylus.* Heidegger

addresses it especially in the essays collected in *Early Greek Thinking: The Dawn of Western Philosophy*, trans. David Farrell Krell and Frank A. Capuzzi (San Francisco: Harper and Row, 1975), in particular, the essay "Logos" (Heraclitus, Fragment B 50)," pp. 59–78.

17. See, among others, R. Howard Bloch, *Etymologies and Genealogies: A Literary Anthropology of the French Middle Ages* (Chicago: University of Chicago Press, 1983), esp. pp. 75–87, 115–27, 131–58; Giuseppe Mazzotta, *Dante, Poet of the Desert* (Princeton: Princeton University Press, 1979), esp. p. 190; R. A. Shoaf, *Dante, Chaucer, and the Currency of the Word: Money, Images, and Reference in Late Medieval Poetry* (Norman, Oklahoma: Pilgrim Books, 1983), esp. pp. 7–16, 93–94; Shoaf, *The Poem as Green Girdle: "Commercium" in "Sir Gawain and the Green Knight,"* Humanities Monograph 55 (Gainesville, Fla.: University Presses of Florida, 1984), pp. 66–75; Brian Stock, *The Implications of Literacy* (Princeton: Princeton University Press, 1983); and Eugene Vance, *Mervelous Signals: Poetics and Sign Theory in the Middle Ages,* Regents Studies in Medieval Culture (Lincoln: University of Nebraska Press, 1986) plus his review of Stock's book in *Diacritics* 15 (1985): 55–64, esp. p. 55.

18. See Allen, pp. 71–73; and Bruno Sandkühler, *Die frühen Dante kommentare und ihr Verhältnis zur mittelalterlichen Kommentartradition* (Munich: M. Huber, 1967), pp. 13–46.

19. Ad evidentiam itaque dicendorum, sciendum est quod istius operis non est simplex sensus, immo dici potest *polysemum,* hoc est plurium sensuum, nam alius sensus est qui habetur per literam, alius est qui habetur per significata per literam. Et primus dicitur literalis, secundus vero allegoricus, sive mysticus. Qui modus tractandi, ut melius pateat, potest considerari in his versibus: 'In exitu Israel de Aegypto, domus Iacob de populo barbaro, facta est Iudaea sanctificatio eius, Israel potestas eius.' Nam si literam solam inspiciamus, significatur nobis exitus filiorum Israel de Aegypto, tempore Moysis; si allegorium, nobis significatur nostra redemptio facta per Christum, si moralem sensum, significatur nobis conversio annimae de luctu et miseria peccati ad straum gratiae; si anagogicum, significatur exitus animae sanctae ab huius corruptionis servitute ad aeternae gloriae libertatem. Et quamquam isti sensus mystici variis appellentur nominibus, generaliter omnes dici possunt allegorici, quum sint a literali sive historiali diversi. Nam allegoria dicitur ab *alleon* graece, quod in latinum dicitur alienum, sive diversum.

His visis, manifestum est quod duplex oportet esse subiectum, circa quod currant alterni sensus. Et ideo videndum est de subiecto huius operis, prout ad literam accipitur; deinde de subiecto, prout allegorice sententiatur. Est ergo subiectum totius operis, literaliter tantum accepti, 'status animarum post mortem simpliciter sumptus.' Nam de illo et circa illum totius operis versatur processus. Si vero accipiatur opus allegorice, subiectum est 'homo, prout merendo et demerendo per arbitrii libertatem Iustitiae praemianti aut punienti obnoxius est.'

Epistola x, ed. E. Moore, in *Tutte le Opere di Dante Alighieri,* 3rd ed. (Oxford: Oxford University Press, 1904), pp. 415–16; trans. Robert Haller, *Literary Criticism of Dante Alighieri* (Lincoln: University of Nebraska Press, 1973), p. 99.

20. The principal study remains that by Henri de Lubac, *Exégèse médiévale: les quatre sens de l'Écriture* (Paris: Aubier, 1959–64). Supplementing it now are the studies by G. R. Evans, *The Language and Logic of the Bible: The Earlier Middle Ages* (Cambridge: Cambridge University Press, 1984), esp. pp. 114–22, and *The Language and*

Logic of the Bible: The Road to Reformation (Cambridge: Cambridge University Press, 1985).

21. On God's two Books, see the discussion by Charles S. Singleton in *An Essay on the "Vita Nuova"* (1949; reprint, Baltimore: Johns Hopkins University Press, 1977), pp. 38–40.

22. See further the helpful remarks in Robert Hollander, *Allegory in Dante's "Commedia"* (Princeton: Princeton University Press, 1969), pp. 3–57, esp. pp. 40–47.

23. For a related but finally different approach to the same issue, see Judson B. Allen, "The *Grand chant courtois* and the Wholeness of the Poem: The medieval *assimilatio* of text, audience, and commentary," *L'Ésprit Créateur* 18 (1978): 5–17.

24. For an elaboration of this argument, see my study "Literary Theory, Medieval Studies, and the Crisis of Difference," forthcoming in *Reorientations: Literary Theory, Pedagogy, and Social Change,* ed. Bruce Henricksen and Thais Morgan (Urbana: University of Illinois Press, 1989).

25. Compare the stimulating remarks on "le blanc" in Dante's writing by Roger Dragonetti in Alexandre Leupin, "L'enjeu et l'événement: Entretien avec Roger Dragonetti, Alexandre Leupin et Charles Méla," *L'Ésprit Créateur* 23 (1983): 5–24, esp. p. 13. Compare also the provocative argument by Stephen Nichols that "as the trope for womb, Mary conveys the alternate condition of presence and absence associated with that term: the womb is either full or empty, although its potential as a generator of being remains at all times. We then see how "womb" and consequently Mary . . . becomes also a metonym for mind, or heart, those medieval seats of understanding in humans where Christ . . . could either be present or absent, although the potential for presence remained possible at all times"—*Romanesque Signs: Early Medieval Narrative and Iconography* (New Haven: Yale University Press, 1983), p. 119.

26. See Allen, *The Ethical Poetic of the Later Middle Ages,* pp. 32 and 61n48.

27. "An Apology against a Pamphlet," in *The Complete Prose Works of John Milton,* gen. ed. Don M. Wolfe (New Haven: Yale University Press, 1953–82), 1: 890. For commentary, see my *Milton, Poet of Duality: A Study of Semiosis in the Poetry and the Prose* (New Haven: Yale University Press, 1985), pp. 56–59.

28. See *Troilus and Criseyde* v, 582–85, ed. Stephen A. Barney, in *The Riverside Chaucer,* gen. ed. Larry D. Benson, based on *The Works of Geoffrey Chaucer,* ed. F. N. Robinson (Boston: Houghton Mifflin, 1987); all citations of Chaucer in this paper are from this edition. For further commentary, see Shoaf, *Currency of the Word,* p. 148.

29. *Hamlet* 4.5.7–13, ed. Frank Kermode in *The Riverside Shakespeare,* ed. G. Blakemore Evans (Boston: Houghton Mifflin, 1974), pp. 1135–97, p. 1172.

30. An excellent introduction to the concept of the *kenosis* is P. Henry, S.J., in *Dictionnaire de la Bible, Supplement,* ed. L. Pirot (1928–), 5 (1957): 7–161, s.v. "Kenose."

31. A good example of the sort of book I am thinking of is the *Biblia Sacra cum Glossis, Interlineari et Ordinaria, et Moralitatibus Nicolai Lyrani* (Lyons, 1525).

I would like to recognize here the estate of the late Judson Boyce Allen and to thank the family for permission to consult materials in his library of rare and modern books, where I have studied this edition of the Bible.

32. See Patricia J. Eberle's explanatory notes to the *Introduction* to *The Man of Law's Tale* in *The Riverside Chaucer,* p. 854b. For a recent helpful discussion of *The Man of Law's Tale,* see V. A. Kolve, *Chaucer and the Imagery of Narrative: The First Five Canterbury Tales* (Stanford: Stanford University Press, 1984), pp. 257–358.

33. Here I am drawing from " 'Unwemmed Custance': Circulation, Property, and

Incest in *The Man of Law's Tale,*" a chapter of my book in progress, tentatively entitled, *"The Substaunce is in Me": An Essay on Error in "The Canterbury Tales."* A version of this chapter was read at the Mellon Conference on Medieval Studies at Rice University in February 1986. I would like to take this opportunity to thank the organizers of the conference for inviting me to participate.

34. Here I draw on my study, "Chaucer and Medusa: *The Franklin's Tale,*" *Chaucer Review* 21 (1986): 274–90.

35. I rely for my statistics here on J. S. P. Tatlock and A. G. Kennedy, *A Concordance to the Complete Works of Geoffrey Chaucer* (1927; reprint, Gloucester, Mass.: Peter Smith, 1963), s.v.

36. For Medusa as *monster,* see Ovid's *Metamorphoses* 5. 216–17, ed. G. Lafaye, 3 vols. (1930; reprint, Paris: Société d'Édition "Les Belles Lettres", 1972).

37. See John Freccero, "Medusa: The Letter and the Spirit," *Yearbook of Italian Studies* (1972): 1–18. The essay is reprinted under the title "Dante's Medusa: Allegory and Autobiography," in D. L. Jeffrey, ed., *By Things Seen: Reference and Recognition in Medieval Thought* (Ottawa: University of Ottawa Press, 1979), pp. 33–46; it is also available now in *Dante: The Poetics of Conversion,* edited and with an introduction by Rachel Jacoff (Cambridge, Mass.: Harvard University Press, 1986), pp. 119–35. I have reviewed this and other recent books on Dante in "The 'Threshing Floor' of Recent Dante Studies," *Envoi: A Review Journal of Medieval Literature* 1 (1988): 58–68.

38. See, further, Shoaf, "Chaucer and Medusa," pp. 277 and 288n11.

39. See, further, my study "The Play of Puns in Late Middle English Poetry: Concerning Juxtology," in *On Puns: The Foundation of Letters,* ed. Jonathan Culler (London: Basil Blackwell, 1988), pp. 44–61.

40. Compare the stimulating remarks on equilibrium and flow in nature and in human life by Michel Serres in *Hermes: Literature, Science, Philosophy,* trans. Josué V. Harari and David F Bell (Baltimore: Johns Hopkins University Press, 1982), pp. 73–74 and 118.

41. See my study *"Troilus and Criseyde:* The Falcon in the Mew," forthcoming in the AMS/Georgia State University Literary Studies Series, vol. 7 (1990), ed. Hugh T. Keenan, "Typology and English Medieval Literature."

42. Trans. Charles S. Singleton, *The Divine Comedy, Inferno,* Bollingen Series LXXX (Princeton: Princeton University Press, 1970–1975).

43. According to Francesco Mazzoni, *assempra* "deriva da *exemplare* (così *assempro* da *exemplum)* e significa trascrivere, ritrarre, rendere imagine ecc"; see his edition of *La Divina Commedia: Inferno,* con i commenti di Tommaso Casini—Silvio Adrasto Barbi e di Attilio Momigliano (Firenze: Sansoni, 1972), p. 469.

44. Ed. Félix Lecoy, *Le Roman de la Rose,* 3 vols. (Paris: Aubier, 1966–70), 3:148, lines 21543–52; trans. Charles Dahlberg, *The Romance of the Rose* (Princeton: Princeton University Press, 1971), p. 351.

45. Jacques Derrida, "Différance," in *Marges de la philosophie* (Paris: Les Éditions de Minuit, 1972), pp. 3–29; trans. Alan Bass, *Margins of Philosophy* (Chicago: University of Chicago Press, 1982), pp. 1–27.

46. *De la Grammatologie* (Paris: Les Éditions de Minuit, 1967), p. 103; trans. Gayatri Chakravorty Spivak, *Of Grammatology* (Baltimore: Johns Hopkins University Press, 1976), p. 71.

47. *De planctu Naturae,* ed. Migne, *Patrologia Latina* 210: 431; trans. James J. Sheridan, *Plaint of Nature* (Toronto: Pontifical Institute of Medieval Studies, 1980), pp. 67–68.

48. See, further, Jan Ziolkowski, *Alan of Lille's Grammar of Sex: The Meaning of Grammar to a Twelfth-Century Intellectual*, Speculum Anniversary Monographs 10 (Cambridge: The Medieval Academy of America, 1985).
49. See Bloch, pp. 64–158.
50. Compare Boethius: "Quis legem det amantibus?" *Philosophiae Consolatio*, ed. L. Bieler, *Corpus Christianorum Series Latina* 94 (Turnhout: Brepols, 1957), Book 3, *metrum* 12, p. 64. Compare also St. Paul's psychological insight, "I had not known sin except by the law" (Romans 7:7).
51. Ibid., p. 108, Derrida's emphasis; Spivak, p. 73.
52. See Kenneth Burke, *The Rhetoric of Religion: Studies in Logology* (Berkeley: University of California Press, 1970); consult also Southwell's commentary, pp. 30–31.
53. *Confessionum Libri XIII*, ed. Pius Knöll, *Corpus Scriptorum Ecclesiasticorum Latinorum*, 33, section 1, part 1 (Vienna: Tempsky, 1896), pp. 328 and 343 respectively; trans. R. S. Pine-Coffin, *The Confessions* (Harmondsworth: Penguin Books, 1961), pp. 296 and 308.
54. *Enarrationes in Psalmos*, 126, ed. E. Dekkers, O.S.B. and J. Fraipont, *Corpus Christianorum Series Latina* 40 (Turnhout: Brepols, 1956) p. 1865; trans. by Members of the English Church, *Expositions on The Book of Psalms by St. Augustine* (Oxford: J. H. Parker, 1857), 6:28. Compare also *De doctrina Christiana* 2.6.7–8.
55. See *Milton, Poet of Duality*, esp. chapters 1 and 2; also "The Play of Puns in Late Middle English Poetry: Concerning Juxtology," esp. pp. 60–61.
56. At present I am preparing a position paper on juxtology—"For There Is Figures in All Things': A Theory of Duality in English Poetry from Chaucer to Milton," a version of which was read as one of the Plenary Addresses at the 6th Citadel Conference on Literature, "The Poetry, Prose, and Drama of the Renaissance and Middle Ages," Charleston, S.C., 10 March 1988. I would like to take this opportunity to thank the organizers of the conference, especially David G. Allen, for inviting me to participate.
57. See esp. "Des Tours de Babel," trans. Joseph F. Graham, in *Difference in Translation*, ed. J. F. Graham (Ithaca: Cornell University Press, 1985), pp. 165–207.
58. See *Confessions* 12.25:

Si autem ideo ament illud, quia verum est, iam et ipsorum est et meum est, quoniam in commune omnium est veritatis amatorum. . . . domine, tremenda sunt iudicia tua, quoniam veritas tua nec mea est nec illius aut illius, sed omnium nostrum, quos ad eius communionem publice vocas, terribiliter admonens nos, ut nolimus eam habere privatam, ne privemur ea. nam quisquis id, quod tu omnibus ad fruendum proponis, sibi proprie vindicat et suum vult esse quod omnium est, a communi propellitur ad sua, hoc est a veritate ad mendacium. qui enim loquitur mendacium, de suo loquitur.

(If, on the other hand, they love them because they are true, they are both theirs and mine, for they are the common property of all lovers of the truth. . . . We must dread your judgments, O Lord, because your truth is not mine alone nor does it belong to this man or that. It belongs to us all, because we all hear your call to share it and you give us dire warning not to think it ours alone, for fear that we may be deprived of it. If any man claims as his own what you give to all to enjoy and tries to keep for himself what belongs to all, he is driven to take refuge in his own resources instead of what is in common to all. For he who utters falsehood utters what is his alone—Pine-Coffin, p. 302).

59. See *Aus der Erfahrung des Denkens* (Pfullingen: Neske, 1965), esp. pp. 5, 17; trans. Hofstadter, pp. 3, 9.

60. "Das Wort," in *Unterwegs zur Sprache,* p. 234, trans. Hertz, p. 152.

61. "Die Frage nach der Teknik," in *Vorträge und Aufsätze,* 4th ed. (Pfullingen: Neske, 1978), p. 40; trans. Lovitt, p. 35.

2

ADAM'S FIRST WORD AND THE FAILURE OF LANGUAGE IN *PARADISO* XXXIII

GLENN C. ARBERY

"The first idea," writes Wallace Stevens in *Notes Toward a Supreme Fiction,* "was not our own. Adam / In Eden was father of Descartes."[1] Beginning a supreme fiction requires a relentless evaluation of previous ones, and Adam dominates all other fictions of beginning. Like Marvell's speaker in "The Garden," the poet desiring to achieve a "pure" originality must undertake a process of "Annihilating all that's made / To a green thought in a green shade."[2] But Stevens recognizes the impossibility of a purely undetermined state of consciousness. In saying that Adam was "father of Descartes," he suggests (among other things) that Descartes's *cogito* was not a genuine beginning because it was "fathered" by the influence on his thought of the garden myth—the fiction of a pristine thinker of the first idea. When Descartes drew in upon himself in order to annihilate "all that's made" and to pluck certainty from his own green thought, he did so because of the paradigm of solitude in Genesis; his "first idea," his *cogito,* was grounded in the myth of himself as Adam.

Dante also in his own great fiction and in the Latin work that justified his use of the vernacular, turned to the figure of Adam. Although Dante is hardly proposing a myth to supplant the Bible, as Stevens or Descartes may have been, he recognizes that Adam must be his starting point. The first man governs any image of an original, clean perception of what exists—any "first idea." For Dante, Adam was not so much a submerged, determining pattern as a binding archetype, like the sun in Stevens's poem. As Joseph Cremona has pointed out, "It is not easy for the modern mind to grasp the significance that the figure of Adam must have had for the medieval. . . . Created fully grown, [Adam] was the incarnation of God's idea of human nature, a perfect image."[3] In other words, Adam embodies man himself in his first idea. In the *Paradiso,* Dante confronts this "perfect image" just after his examination in the theological virtues and just before his ascent to the final regions of Paradise—a placement suggesting that Dante's approach to God is an approach to the source of his poetic enterprise, a discovery of himself in the figure of the perfect man, the new Adam.

One of the questions prominent in Dante's discussion with Adam is Adam's language, a topic on which Dante had written some years before in *De vulgari eloquentia*. In the earlier work, Adam's central importance lies in his speaking of the first word: "rationabiliter dicimus ipsum loquentem primum, mox, postquam afflatus est ab animante virtute, incunctanter fuisse locutum" ("We may reasonably say that this first speaker at once, after having been inspired by the vivifying power, spoke without hesitation" [I, v, 1]).[4] The first utterance constitutes a return to God, in the breath of his speech, of the power that gave him bodily life. In emphasizing the necessity of Adam's physical breath (his first) in making this sound, Dante appears to associate sinlessness and divine presence with an original spoken word. Such an emphasis upon speech, breath, and presence implies that writing is fallen and secondary. Derrida has argued that a more or less unconscious rejection of writing taints Western philosophy, and Dante apparently falls into the usual pattern. Derrida points out this pattern in "Plato's Pharmacy":

> While presenting writing as a false brother—traitor, infidel, and simulacrum—Socrates is for the first time led to envision the brother of this brother, the legitimate one, as *another sort of writing*: not merely as knowing, living, animate discourse, but as an *inscription* of truth in the soul. . . . According to a pattern that will dominate all of Western Philosophy, good writing (natural, living, knowledgeable, intelligible, internal, speaking) is opposed to bad writing (a moribund, ignorant, external, mute artifice for the senses). And the good one can be designated only through the metaphor of the bad one.[5]

Dante's subscription to this pattern could not be more prominently placed: in the beatific vision of *Paradiso* XXXIII, the human effigy appears to him as an image *painted* in the second circle:

> Quella circulazion che sì concetta
>   pareva in te come lume reflesso,
>   da li occhi miei alquanto circunspetta,
> dentro da sé, del suo colore stesso,

mi parve pinta de la nostra effige:
per che 'l mio viso in lei tutto era messo.

(That circle—which, begotten so, appeared
in You as light reflected—when my eyes
had watched it with attention for some time,
within itself and colored like itself,
to me seemed painted with our effigy,
so that my sight was set on it completely.)
(*Paradiso* XXXIII, 127–32)[6]

The corporeal form seems distastefully artificial—"ignorant, external, mute"—a graven image on the breathing perfection of the divinely spoken Word. At the journey's ultimate moment (which is the "first idea" of the poem) the "bad" excluded term re-emerges as the sign for what is included and defined as "good," as if God could be signified only by the inscription of man in His image.

The difficulty with bringing Derrida to bear upon Dante, of course, is that one can hardly assert that the poet is unconscious of the "bad" excluded term that provides his metaphor, since the bad writing here is man himself. In fact, this most "logocentric," most judgmental of poems deliberately makes the tension between the "good writing" of the Trinity's circle and the "bad writing" of the human effigy the poem's final—and first—mystery. This tension expresses itself not only in the *pilgrim's* bafflement but also in the *poet's* repeated claim to be unable to say what was inscribed on his heart during the vision. The inadequacy of language before such a mystery involves the failure of any sign to signify what the mind cannot wholly conceive: ultimately, it involves the problem of naming God. The poem falters upward past the limit of the atmosphere of language into the light where essence and existence coincide, the vacuum of the sign. The paradisal failure of language, which is analogous to Stevens's problem with naming the first idea, contrasts with Dante's account in *De vulgari eloquentia* of a success: Adam's first word.

The most striking thing in each case is the presence of what Derrida calls the "supplement" which is both "an addition" and "a substitute."[7] For Derrida, writing itself is such a supplement since it both adds to and substitutes for speech. But speech cannot be defined without recourse to the metaphor of writing, and the supplement is therefore essential to what attempts to reject it. In *De vulgari eloquentia,* Dante does not explicitly invoke the metaphor of writing, but he does claim that "a certain form of speech was created by God together with the first soul. And I say 'a form'," he continues, "both in respect of words and their construction and of the utterance of this construction. . . ." ("Dico autem formam, et quantum ad rerum vocabula, et quantum ad vocabulorum constructionem . . ." [I, vi, 4]). If Adam did not devise his own words, then the language had to be written (the metaphor seems inevitable) into Adam's soul. Adam did not need to ponder what he would say, for he spoke, Dante says, immediately after he had received his first animating breath, a breath that must have contained the entire Hebrew language.

What did he say? According to Dante, reason should tell us that Adam's first word was *El*, the earliest Hebrew word for God. Reason might also tell us, as Dante points out, that it was not necessary for Adam to speak aloud since God knew his thought:

> Now I have no doubt that it is obvious to a man of sound mind that the first thing the voice of the first speaker uttered was the equivalent of God, namely *El*. . . . It seems absurd and repugnant to reason that anything should have been named by man before God, since man had been made by him and for him! . . . but if anyone raises the objection that there was no need for him to speak, as he was, so far, the only human being, whilst God discerns all our secret thoughts without any words of ours, even before we do ourselves, we say with that reverence which we ought to use in judging anything respecting the eternal will, that though God knew, nay, even fore-knew (which is the same thing in respect of God) the thought of the first man who spoke, without any words being said, still he wished that the man should also speak, in order that, in the unfolding of so great a gift, he himself who had freely bestowed it might glory. (I, iv, 4; I, v, 2)[8]

Precisely at this point a major problem arises: the word *El* seems intrusive. Dante's explanation does not seem to help a great deal: he says only that God wanted Adam to use human speech so that "he himself who had freely bestowed it might glory." Very deliberately, Dante makes us see that the first use of language has nothing to do with communication or exchange. The spoken word—the echo of a prescribed and foreknown sign—is supplemental. It is an addition to the conception *(conceptum)* within Adam that God already sees, and it is an unnecessary substitute for that conception. Adam's demonstration of the characteristic human gift seems to introduce an unnecessary artifice into what could have been God's unmediated beholding of the word he had written into Adam's intellect. Oddly, the final puzzle of the *Paradiso* is also the puzzle of the supplement:

> verder voleva come si convenne
> l'imago al cerchio e come vi s'indova;
> ma non eran da ciò le proprie penne:
>
> (I searched that strange sight: I wished to see
> the way in which our human effigy
> suited the circle and found place in it—)
>   (*Paradiso* XXXIII, 137–39)

In his gaze at the begotten circle of the Godhead, when Dante finally sees "our effigy" *(nostra effige)* painted within it, he wonders at the addition which seems to be incommensurable with the conception for which it substitutes.

In moving between these two instances of the problematic supplement, let us turn to the key term in both cases: the "conception," the internally begotten realization of the truth. This is the traditional locus of what Derrida calls "the inscription of truth in the soul." In an earlier passage of *Paradiso* XXXIII, Dante exclaims:

> O quanto è corto il dire e come fioco
> al mio concetto! e questo, a quel ch 'i' vidi,
> è tanto, che non basta a dicer "poco."
>
> (How incomplete is speech, how weak, when set
> against my thought [*concetto*]! And this, to what I saw
> is such—to call it little is too much.)
>   (121–23)

He does not say that his speech is feeble next to what he saw, but that it is feeble next to his "conception" *(concetto)*, his inner formulation of what he saw. The conception always mediates between what is known by the intellect and what is said. In this case, the conception falls far short of his vision. Charles Singleton suggests that the poet's later memory fails, but it is certainly possible that, gazing into the Trinity, Dante simply sees more than he can conceive.[9] Despite its inadequacy, however, Dante implicitly compares his conception to the begotten circle, the *Logos* conceived within the Godhead. In making such a comparison, he draws on a long tradition, for in attempting to explain the procession of the Word within the Trinity, both Augustine and Thomas Aquinas use the analogy of an idea formed in the mind but not spoken. In his article on whether there is procession in God, Thomas writes that

> Whenever we understand, by the very fact of understanding there proceeds something within us, which is a conception of the thing understood, a conception issuing from our intellectual power and proceeding from our knowledge of that thing. This conception is signified by the spoken word, and it is called the word of the heart signified by the word of the voice. . . . Procession, therefore . . . is to be understood by way of an intelligible emanation, for example of the intelligible word which proceeds from the speaker, yet remains in him.[10]

A few lines after speaking of his own conception of what he saw, Dante writes of "that circling which, thus begotten *(si concetta),* appeared in Thee as reflected light . . ." His own conception is analogous to the conceived or begotten Divine Word, and language falls so far short of his conception that it seems supplemental by nature. To speak or write of his conception of God will necessarily be distractingly artificial compared to the simplicity of his experience; the words will be a misleading substitute for what he has already realized.

Yet the same problems were surely in force when Adam first addressed himself to God. Why, then, did God wish him to speak? If we bring Thomas's terms to bear, we see that God did not want Adam to rest with the "intelligible word which proceeds from the speaker, yet remains in him." Even in addressing God Himself, Adam had to use the "word of the voice." Dante says that God wanted to glory in "the unfolding of so great a gift," but it is not immediately clear why God sees it as great. I think that the answer lies in the implied analogy between the spoken word and the Incarnation. If the word that remains within the speaker is like the procession of the Word from the Father, it follows that the word that goes out from the speaker is like the Word that becomes flesh, the visible sign of the invisible conception. Dante does not imply that the body and soul of Jesus are an inadequate sign of God's begotten Word: rather, in the light of this sign, he points to a way beyond the supplemental nature of signs toward a recovery of their sacramental possibilities.

What, for instance, does the supplemental sign *El* accomplish? This word, "written" into Adam as the sign appropriate for his conception of God, is spoken to the being it signifies. The word is returned to God, addressed to him as an answer—a condition that Dante is careful to point out. Although Adam cannot see God, he can see the created order (including his own *cogito*), and he can either restate its implied question or answer it. If the word were put as a question (*El?*), it would imply the necessity of further revelation: Adam's intention in speaking the word would not be to signify what was beyond his own conception but to conceive what the word signifies, which he could never do. As a question, the word would be philosophic, the name of the philosopher's uncertainty before being. But as an answer, Adam's word represents an act of faith; it is the sensible sign of the ineffable *Logos,* referring not to Adam's conception, but to God's, with whom it becomes one. If it were addressed to any other being, the significance of the word would be limited by the conception of God in the hearer, but when God "hears" the word, he perfectly conceives it in the Son, the Word, his conception of his own nature. God wants Adam to speak because the very first thing Adam says will be an acceptance of the "word of the voice" to be "spoken" in the Incarnation, even though Adam himself has not yet fallen. Precisely because it is not spoken out of necessity, the supplement signifies the communion of the divine nature with man and reveals the action of unmerited grace.

In *Paradiso* XXVI, Dante returns to some of the central concerns of *De vulgari eloquentia* and revises them. Once again, Adam's language interests Dante most. When Adam himself appears to the pilgrim, he answers Dante's unspoken wish to know certain things about Eden. There is no need for speech, Adam says, since he can see Dante's conception reflected in God, reflected so well that he claims to discern it "better than / you can perceive the things you hold most certain" ("meglio / che tu qualunque cosa t'è più certa" [104–5]). Dante's wish (the word of the heart) is reflected in God, I suggest, because Christ has now entered time as the word of the voice addressed to the Father as an answer: although God still wants the exercise of his gift of the sensible sign, that gift is now the Incarnation of the Son, in whom Adam sees Dante's desire perfectly expressed. Several of Adam's other remarks, however, are not so easily reconciled to *De vulgari eloquentia:*

> La lingua ch'io parlai fu tutta spenta
> innanzi che a l'ovra inconsummabile

fosse la gente di Nembròt attenta:
ché nullo effetto mai razïonabile,
    per lo piacere uman che rinovella
    seguèndo il cielo, sempre fu durabile.
Opera naturale è ch'uom favella;
    ma così o così, natura lascia
    poi fare a voi secondo che v'abbella.
Pria ch'i' scendessi a l'infernale ambascia,
    I s'appellava in terra il sommo bene
    onde vien la letizia che mi fascia;
e *El* si chiamo pòi:

(The tongue I spoke was all extinct before
the men of Nimrod set their minds upon
the unaccomplishable task; for never
    has any thing produced by human reason
been everlasting—following the heavens,
men seek the new, they shift their predilections.
    That man should speak at all is nature's act,
but how you speak—in this tongue or in that—
she leaves to you and to your preference.
    Before I was sent down to Hell's torments,
on earth, the Highest Good—from which derives
the joy that now enfolds me—was called *I;*
    and then He was called *El.*)
                    (*Paradiso* XXVI, 124–36)

In *De vulgari eloquentia,* Dante had considered Hebrew the divinely ordained language written into Adam. Here he has Adam state that languages are arbitrary and that neither Hebrew nor Latin enjoys a special status. Since all languages are products of reason, no language is privileged. Moreover, the Bible does not record any of the primal language; the words ascribed to Adam, Eve, the serpent and God in Eden are already translations of lost and ultimately arbitrary original signs. Dante does make a point of correcting the one word that he had given Adam in *De vulgari eloquentia;* instead of *El,* the first word for God was *I,* a word that Dante probably invented for his own purposes in the poem. If the rest of Dante's appeal to reason in the earlier work remains intact, then *I* was the first word Adam said. Notably, this word was not "written" into Adam, as Dante had earlier thought. Rather, it is a product of human reason, the first supreme fiction. When Adam speaks it, he prefigures Dante's poetic act. It is fitting, then, that this word is superior to *El* in several ways. For instance, it is not a composite of two sounds; its simplicity more closely reflects the simplicity of the divine nature. Moreover, Singleton points out that *I* is both the first letter of the later names of God and the Roman numeral for one.[11] Most noteworthy, however, is the fact that the name becomes a number only when it is written. When Dante writes down the sound Adam speaks, the mute, external artifice reveals the numerical principle of unity. Speech enjoys no privilege over writing. Both proper name and number, *I* becomes the undetermined, humanly invented signifier of God to Himself. Adam's first word, then, is not only like the human image in the circle of the Word; in some senses, it is that image—the supplement as sacrament.

Let us turn once more to this final image of the *Divine Comedy*. One of the most troubling things about it, as we have seen, is the apparent coldness with which Dante gazes at the appearance of the Savior in the reflected circling of God. At the crucial moment, the Incarnation becomes a vexingly impossible geometrical problem. But even more distancing, I think, is the description of Christ that immediately precedes this simile. I mean, of course, Dante's admission that the circle "seemed to (him) painted with our image within itself" ("pinta de la nostra effige" [*Divine Comedy*, par. xxxiii, 131]). Even Charles Singleton backs down from the implications of *pinta,* translating it as "depicted," which avoids some of the connotations of "painted"; he argues that the word "does not suggest an addition of color, but simply affirms appearance, that which the wayfarer beheld."[12] But this explanation, I think, avoids the fact that Christ in the flesh appears artificial to the pilgrim. To say that the human image is painted in the circle need not mean an addition of color in order to imply that the Incarnation seems accidental and exterior to the divine nature—a distracting, if not disfiguring, addition to its simplicity. The word reflects the pilgrim's sense that the body of Christ seems essentially mimetic, a painting of the human exterior, at a remove both from man and from God. To put the matter even more explicitly, Jesus Christ appears to be the "supplement" both to God's divinity and to man's humanity—the addition, the substitute, the intrusive sign. Our painted effigy stands out in its character as the "bad writing" on the perfect mathematical form of God.

Dante's apparent coldness, I think, reflects the extent to which he had prepared himself for a purely spiritual vision, as if he were capable of becoming purely spiritual himself. The pilgrim looks at the figure of Jesus as incommensurable with the circle and the superrational reality it signifies:

> Qual è l' geomètra che tutto s'affige
>   per misurar lo cerchio, e non ritrova,
>   pensandro, quel principio ond' elli indige,
> tal era io a quella vista nova:
>
> (As the geometer intently seeks
> to square the circle, but he cannot reach,
> through thought on thought, the principle he needs,
>   so I reached that strange sight . . .)
>   (*Paradiso* xxxiii, 133–36)

The geometer trying to measure the circle is like Dante trying to make the human image conform to the Godhead. Dante sees the necessity of the circle, but he cannot understand why the human image needs to appear as the sign signifying it. Why measure perfection with the body that one must discipline and overcome even to begin the ascent toward such perfection? Before the human effigy appeared, he had seemed to enjoy a direct intellectual sight of the conception within God. But at this point, as with Adam's first word, the fleshly sign apprehensible even by the senses intrudes, disrupting the purely intellectual conception of the divine nature by interposing the human likeness. Thus, the poet subtly presents his last mistake as the pilgrim—a failure to recognize that even the circles themselves are only signs and that God's spiritual nature cannot be made visible to him without the supplement that at first repels him.

At first Dante looks at this likeness as though it were a sign directed to him, which in some ways it is. It distracts him, however, because it is *only* our image he sees. As long as he looks at it with puzzled distaste, it arouses in him a "wish" to understand the principle of conformity:

> verder voleva come si convenne
>   l'imago al cerchio e come vi s'indova;
>   ma non eran da ciò le proprie penne:
>
> (I wished to see
> the way in which our human effigy

suited the circle and found place in it—
and my own wings were far too weak for that.)
(*Paradiso* XXXIII, 136–39)

As he has been discovering throughout his ascent with Beatrice, Dante needs a supplement to his own intellect. He needs to understand something that exceeds his own powers of comprehension, and he therefore cannot retain either the conception or the power to conceive it:

se non che la mai mente fu percossa
da un fulgore in che sua voglia venne.
A l'alta fantasia qui mancò possa.

(But then my mind was struck by light that flashed
and, with this light, received what it had asked.
Here force failed my high fantasy.)
(140–141)

In the flash that gives him his wish, I suggest, the human image is revealed as a sign of love directed to Dante *and* to God, to the circle it signifies. That is, it cannot communicate the true significance of the circle to Dante if it is addressed only to him, just as the word *I* cannot truly signify God to Eve, if the meaning of the word is limited to her own conception. But if Christ's humanity is a sign wholly intended to signify God *and* wholly addressed to the Father, then this sign, like *I,* achieves a perfect commensurability with the divine Word in whom God knows himself. It *is* the Word. What happens in the "flash" is that Dante conceives Adam's first word. But this word is now the person of Christ. As Dante gazes at the human image, it suddenly becomes his own conception, and the divine Word proceeds *in* his own intellect with a perfection inconceivable *by* his intellect. Because he did not and cannot father the conception within him, there is a sudden reversal of perspective: the image of Christ conceived within him becomes *answer* that includes the whole being of the pilgrim. He is subsumed in the love of the Son for the Father, and the Father mercifully inscribes Dante in the person of his own begotten Word.

Dante's logocentric structure finally comes to reveal the human image, even in the Incarnation itself, as what Derrida would call bad writing—"a moribund, ignorant, external, mute artifice for the senses." But at the same time that it is bad writing, it is good, it is supremely good, because, as a sign, it makes no claim whatsoever to self-presence. On the contrary, it acknowledges at every moment that anything conveyed to human conception must be realized by means of some sign, even if the "word of the heart" is divinely inscribed, and the sign implies the absence of what it signifies—what Derrida calls *différance*. The way around this *différance* between man and the God beyond his conceiving is a rather simple strategy: prayer. As the poem moves toward the vision of the end of *Paradiso* XXXIII, the instances of invocation or prayer increase. For instance, when Dante begins to recount his vision of the Trinity, he prays in this manner:

> O somma luce che tanto ti levi
>   da' concetti mortali, a la mia mente
>   ripresta un poco di quel che parevi,
> e fa la lingua mia tanto possente,
>   ch'una favilla sol de la tua gloria;
>   possa lasciare a la futura gente;
> ché, per tornare alquanto a mia memoria
>   e per sonare un poco in questi versi,
>   più si conceperà di tua vittoria.

> (O Highest Light, You, raised so far above
> the minds of mortals, to my memory
> give back something of Your epiphany,
>   and make my tongue so powerful that I
> may leave to people of the future one
> spark of the glory that is Yours, for by
>   returning somewhat to my memory
> and echoing awhile within these lines,
> Your victory will be more understood [*concepera*].)
>   (*Paradiso* XXXIII, 67–75)

Language fails, but in its failure it addresses the Light in whom its failure is meaningless; by means of that address, the reader's mind necessarily turns toward the divine completion of its own language-borne conception.

At the end of the poem, the reconciliation of the truth and its imperfect likeness takes place in the "flash" that ends Dante's bafflement and moves his will in accordance with love. By excluding any explanation of the one moment of presence that generates and includes the whole text, Dante does not fix the significance of his poem. Rather, he sets the possibilities of significance into a ceaseless motion, like the circling of the stars moved by divine love. Both the text and the created world it imitates are fundamentally written, never self-present; their meanings always center on the God who is always conceptually beyond them, therefore always "present" only to the sign of the human answer. If the poet's prayer is effective, there is just enough power in the poem to generate "one spark" of the divine glory as its sign. Precisely at the point that language, the medium of the "lofty phantasy," fails altogether, the signifying spark, impelled by the intensifying force of 100 cantica, leaps across time, across the inevitable changes in the forms of language, through the silence onto which the sacred poem opens, to kindle conception and move the living to the communion of the word.

Notes

1. Wallace Stevens, *Notes Toward a Supreme Fiction* IV, vv. 1–2 in *The Collected Works of Wallace Stevens* (New York: Knopf, 1955).

2. Andrew Marvell, "The Garden," vv. 47–48 in *The Poems and Letters of Andrew Marvell, Vol I: The Poems*, ed. H. M. Margoliouth, 3rd ed. rev. Pierre Legouis and E. E. Duncan-Jones (Oxford: Clarendon Press, 1971).

3. Joseph Cremona, "*Paradiso* XXVI" in *Cambridge Readings in Dante's Comedy*, ed. Kenelm Foster and Patrick Boyde (Cambridge: Cambridge University Press, 1981), p. 184.

4. All citations of the Latin text of *De vulgari eloquentia* are taken from *Il Tratto De Vulgari eloquentia Di Dante Alighieri*, ed. Pio Rajna (Firenze: Successori Le Monnier, 1897). All translations are taken from *A Translation of the Works of Dante Alighieri* (London: J. M. Dent and Sons, Ltd., 1940), pp. 1-124.

5. Jacques Derrida, *Dissemination*, trans. Barbara Johnson (Chicago: The University of Chicago Press, 1981), p. 149, his italics.

6. All citations of the Italian text of the *Paradiso* are taken from Charles S. Singleton, *Paradiso, Vol. I: Italian Text and Translation*, Bollingen Series LXXX (Princeton: Princeton University Press, 1975). Translations are taken from *The Divine Comedy of Dante Alighieri: Paradiso*, trans. Allen Mandelbaum (Toronto: Bantam Books, 1986).

7. Barbara Johnson, "Translator's Introduction," to Jacques Derrida, *Dissemination* (Chicago: University of Chicago Press, 1981), p. xiii.

8. Quid autem prius vox primi loquentis sonaverit, viro sane mentis in promptu esse non titubo ipsum fuisse quod Deus est, scilicet *El*. . . . Absudum atque rationi videtur horrificum ante Deum ab homine quicquam nominatum fuisse, cum ab ipso et in ipsum factus fuisset homo! . . . Si quis vero fateur contra

obiciens, quod non oportebat illum loqui, cum solus adhuc homo existeret et Deus omnia sine verbis archana nostra discernat etiam ante quam nos, cum illa reverentia dicimus qua uti oportet cum de eterna voluntate aliquid iudicamus, quod licet Deus sciret, ymo presciret, quod idem est quantum ad Deum, absque locutione conceptum primi loquentis, voluit tamen et ipsum loqui, ut in explicatione tante dotis gloriaretur ipse qui gratis dotaverat.

9. Charles Singleton, *Paradiso, Vol* II: COMMENTARY, Bollingen Series LXXX Princeton: Princeton University Press, 1975), p. 582.

10. Quicumque autem intelligit, ex hoc ipso quod intelligit, procedit aliquid intra ipsum, quod est conceptio rei intellectae, ex ejus notitia procedens. Quam quidem conceptionem vox significat, et dicitur verbum cordis significatum verbo vocis. . . . sed . . . emanationem intelligiblem, ut pote verbi intellibilis a decente, quod manet in ipso.

The Latin text is taken from *Vol. I, Summa Theologica* (Paris, 1887). The translation is taken from *Thomas Aquinas I*, trans. Fathers of the English Dominican Province, Britannica Great Books 19 (Chicago: Encyclopedia Britannica, Inc., 1971).

11. Singleton, *Commentary*, p. 423.

12. *Ibid.*, p. 534.

PART II

THE NATURE OF SIGNS
The Varieties of Receiver Experience

EDITORS' INTRODUCTION

*A*s Edmund Reiss notes in a subsequent essay, Augustine argues that men should first learn to recognize signs as signs and then learn to understand their meanings. The two essays in this section address these two tasks. The first, by Joan Tasker Grimbert, presents a survey of the wealth of signs, both visual and verbal, found within the works of Chrétien and by implication in medieval fiction as a whole. The second essay, by Ross Arthur, presents a complimentary discussion of the ways in which such signs can be and are read by both the characters and the readers of the Middle English *Emaré*. Leaving aside for the moment the first third of the Jakobsonian Addresser-Message-Addressee model of the speech act—the "origin" that is so much the subject of the previous essays—Grimbert and Arthur respectively take up the two remaining elements wherein meaning may reside.

Professor Grimbert's essay on Chrétien begins where Glenn Arbery's on Dante leaves off, with the discrepency between "reality" and the signs used to represent it, noting that this theme is one of the most common in the works of the French poet. Indeed, Grimbert argues that Chrétien repeatedly shows his characters "exploiting the polyvalence of sign" in order to explore the "relationship between being and being said."

Beginning with non-verbal signs, Grimbert discusses Perceval's muddled attempt to make rational sense of sensory perceptions. Dazed by the brilliant armor of the passing knights, the young Perceval has much in common with Arbery's Dante, overwhelmed by the geometric sign and the painted effigy of man. If, as Grimbert demonstrates, Chrétien's visual signs consistently mislead and confuse, the same may be said of his verbal signs, which likewise are noted for their "opacity" and especially for their ability to evoke antithetical meanings. As a result, what Grimbert finds in Chrétien is a "fundamental distrust of language." That distrust—also Shoaf's "anxiety"—makes deeds, visual signs, necessary. Language most often fails because complementary, mutually validating visual and verbal signs are taken separately, so that the part is taken to signify the

47

whole. Such "failure" of interpretation, inevitably the result of selective speaking or observation, constitutes, as Grimbert notes, an important part of Chrétien's romances, with their emphasis on understanding (*entendre*) and thinking (*penser*) as well as their emphasis on the perceiver's subjectivity. But, at base, Grimbert reveals within Chrétien a strong positivist bias, for there is in his works a strongly felt assumption that signs do, in fact, possess authorized— that is "correct"—meanings, and that understandings which deviate from such "correct" meanings are simply wrong, are fictions without substance.

Professor Arthur's study of Emaré's gem cloak uses that particular object as a visual sign for the starting point of a discussion of the ways that signs, such as those outlined by Grimbert, may be read. As with Grimbert, there is a strong positivist assumption of a correct and absolute reading of any sign. Interestingly enough, in *Emaré* the belief in this Platonic connection between signifier and signified leads to attempts among the tale's characters to manipulate reality by manipulating the signs which represent it. In this discussion of *Emaré*, we encounter the first of many references to attempts to control reality by changing the names used to describe it, a theme equally prominent in the essays by Professors Allen, Benkov, and Ashley. In regard to this theme, the incident in which the king's mother changes the content of the letter announcing the birth of Segramour by describing the infant as a "monster" is interesting in that her charge is both true and false. Segramour is not literally a "monster," at least not to anyone other than the Queen Mother. But surely he is a type of Yeatsian "Rough Beast" that threatens the status quo. In a sense, then, misreadings are also authorized as possible understandings of the text. Like Grimbert, Arthur stresses that the meaning of a sign is determined by those who perceive it. However, Arthur goes on to imply that misreadings are not only built into the signs themselves but also into the consciousness of the reader, whose (mis)readings fall into certain definable categories according to his or her particular predisposition. As David Hiscoe notes in a subsequent essay on Genius in Gower's *Confessio Amantis*, "the process of assigning meaning mirrors the spiritual condition of the humans" who engage in such activity. Likewise following Augustine, Arthur notes that there are three types of responses to signs and finds in the world of Emaré's cloak ample evidence of those readings. In the end, Emaré's cloak acts as a discriminatory sign that reveals not only the differences among the tale's characters but among its critics as well. As in Allen's subsequent study of *Le Roman de Silence,* the extratextual reader's responses parallel those of the characters within the text, implying that such responses are universal modes of perception, habits of consciousness that transcend the particulars of time and culture—a structuralist proposition of which Augustine would approve.

3

MISREPRESENTATION AND MISCONCEPTION IN CHRÉTIEN DE TROYES

Nonverbal and Verbal Semiotics in Erec et Enide *and* Perceval

JOAN TASKER GRIMBERT

𝕿he discrepancy between reality and the signs used to represent it is one of the most pervasive themes in the romances of Chrétien de Troyes. Time and again it is brought to the fore as Chrétien's characters discover the difficulty of deciphering the verbal and nonverbal signs which make up their universe, itself but an obscure reflection of the reality beyond.[1] It becomes abundantly clear that the information presented to ears and eyes must be processed carefully, for sensory perceptions in their brute state are extremely deceptive.[2]

Chrétien puts great emphasis both on the possibility of exploiting the polyvalence of signs (for good and for ill) and on the consequent need for perspicacity in all social situations, from the most banal to the most extraordinary. His characters run the full gamut from the shrewd, perceptive confidant, Lunete, to the naive Welshman, Perceval. Those who evolve in the course of the romances usually grow in their ability to interpret their experiences, while those who are part of the regular cast—Gauvain, Keu, Arthur— are content to play out the same role. The latter act as static foils to the former, each of whom embarks on an *aventure* which, though composed of a number of physical encounters, turns out to be chiefly intellectual.

Chrétien illustrates in myriad ways the difficulty of interpreting nonverbal and verbal data; the notion informs his poems structurally as well as thematically. I have shown elsewhere how in *Le Chevalier au lion (Yvain)* he sets up a network of signs (words and deeds) which alternately confirm and contradict each other. Protagonist and reader experience repeated disappointment of their expectations and are led gradually to understand the importance of interpreting what is presented to their senses.[3] This process, by which the poet engages his audience in the kind of active reflection required ultimately of his characters, appears to be at work in all of his romances. But appearances can be deceiving. By extending my study to Chrétien's first and last of these poems, *Erec et Enide* and *Le Roman de Perceval ou le Conte du Graal*, I hope to demonstrate that the problem of representation and interpretation was a constant preoccupation of the poet.[4]

The eye is as easily deceived as the ear, and Chrétien relates numerous instances of misunderstanding arising from the polyvalence of both nonverbal and verbal signs, i.e., the opacity of nonlinguistic data, on the one hand, and that of language, on the other. In the following pages, I will be exploring each of these major categories successively in the context of examples taken from *Erec et Enide* and *Perceval*. These examples are so varied, and so many involve signs both nonverbal and verbal (sometimes set in opposition to each other), that it would be impossible to form rigid subgroups.

Nonverbal Signs

There is no better place to begin a discussion of semiotics in Chrétien than with that most naive of heroes, Perceval. Perceval's first exposure to knighthood is a veritable feast for ears and eyes, and his initial conclusions as to the meaning of these sounds and sights represent one of the earliest stages of a boy's attempt to make rational sense out of sensory perceptions. The five knights create such a terrible din as they come through the forest, with their armor clanking and their lances and shields striking against the branches of the trees, that Perceval thinks they must surely be devils, for his mother has told him that devils are the ugliest of creatures. When the knights finally come into sight, however, Perceval is dazzled by the play of the sun on their armor and the bright colors of their regalia. Endowed at this point with but a primitive system of values admitting of no nuances between good and evil, he has no alternative, if he is to revise his first judgment, than to arrive at the opposite conclusion: surely these must be angels, for his mother has told him that angels are the most beautiful of creatures.

Witnessing Perceval's unsuccessful attempts to decipher the various aspects of the new world that open to him at this point is amusing, but it is also instructive, because it reminds us of the tortuous process by which a child learns to interpret all that assails its senses. Perceval is not the fool he appears to be; he simply has not had a chance to realize that things are not always as they seem. When he discovers that the knights are not devils, he does not know what place to assign them on his simple scale of values except that hitherto reserved for angels. Upon returning home, Perceval accuses his mother of having lied to him when she told him angels were the most beautiful of creatures; he can imagine nothing that could surpass the beauty of the knights.

And he longs to know that beauty firsthand. When his mother learns that he intends to have King Arthur knight him, she fears greatly for his safety. Her husband and elder son died in combat, though they were wise in the ways of the world. She cannot imagine how the sheltered Perceval could possibly survive. What will he do when it comes to actually bearing arms? However will he manage to *do* what he has never *done* nor even *seen done*? She concludes that he will be most incompetent:

> "Qu'il n'est merveille, ce m'est vis,
> S'en ne *set* che c'on [n'] a apris;
> Mais merveille est quant on n'aprent
> Ce que on *ot* et *voit* sovent."
>
> (523–26)

("For it's no wonder, it seems to me, not to *know* what one's never learned; the wonder's when one fails to learn the things one often *hears* and *sees*.")

But more is involved in learning than simply seeing and hearing, as we are reminded when in a later scene Gornemant de Gorhaut asks Perceval if he knows anything of arms, and the boy answers that he knows how to put them on. From Perceval's point of view, it is a sensible answer, for he has come straight from his first combat as a knight, a victory obtained simply by heaving a javelin at his opponent, in sum, a feat that must have seemed no different from killing a wild animal. Squire Yvonet's ceremonious arming of him afterwards was the only new aspect of the experience. Despite this earlier misconception, Gornemant apparently feels that the use of signs (demonstration) is still the most effective method for teaching someone of Perceval's level, and this time the boy does manage to correctly translate what he sees into knowledge.[5]

The difficulty Perceval has in interpreting sense data stems in part from his sensuality. He is virtually blinded by his senses. He is so caught up with the various aspects of the knights' regalia that he barely hears their request for information about the group they are pursuing. He steadfastly refuses to acknowledge their queries until he has heard about every new article that fires his imagination. Similarly, his mother's grief over his discovery leaves him cold, and her lengthy account of family history falls on deaf ears:

> Li vallés *entent* molt petit
> A che que sa mere li dist.
> "A mengier, fait il, me donez;
> Ne *sai* de coi m'araisonnez."
> (489–92)

(The boy *hears* very little of what his mother says to him. "Give me something to eat," he says. "I don't *know* what you're talking about.")

The verb *entendre* is somewhat ambiguous: it usually means either to hear or to understand.[6] In many passages Chrétien uses it to signify the latter, and if here it seems to mean the former, the point is that if Perceval fails to *hear*, it is mainly because he cannot *understand* anything that does not appeal directly to his sensual nature. Since grief is a stranger to him, an abstraction, the widow's story can hold no interest for him.

Nor does he really understand the advice his mother gives him before he departs. Impatient and eager to be off, he retains only the most salient features. For example, concerning her advice to honor and aid women (and to accept only a kiss and ring if offered), he remembers only the tangible elements: Kiss! Ring![7]

Perceval's limited scale of values and his sensuality are also to blame for his unseemly treatment of the maiden he encounters shortly after leaving home. He enters the pavilion because it is so fair he thinks it must be a church, and his mother has told him to worship God in His house. The sight of the lovely maiden causes him to make other associations with the advice he has just heard and only partially retained, which is why he insists on kissing her and taking her ring despite her vehement protests. Blinded by his boyish sensuality and his limited knowledge, he conducts himself thoughtlessly.

Curiously, the girl's lover (aptly named *li Orgueilleus*, 'the Proud One') is scarcely more reflective. Confronted with the physical traces of Perceval's passage ("ces *ensaignes* que chi *voi*": "these *signs* that I *see* here" [788]) and the verbal explanation offered, he arrives at an interpretation that is dictated by both his intense jealousy and his adherence to the misogynous nature of conventional lore. Despite the girl's claim that she was kissed against her will, her lover is convinced she enjoyed the experience:

> "Ainçois vos sist, et si vos plot;
> Onques nul contredit n'i ot,"
> Fait cil cui jalosie angoisse,
> "*Cuidiez* que je ne vos *conoisse?*
> Si fas, certes, bien vos *conois;*
> Ne sui si borgnes ne si lois
> Que vostre falseté ne *voie.*"
> (813–19)

("No! It was as you wished, and pleased you well! He found no great resistance!" he cries, in jealous anguish. "Do you *imagine* I don't *know* you? I do indeed, I *know* you well! I'm not so blind or squint-eyed that I can't *see* your falseness!")

The striking rhyme *angoisse/conoisse* highlights the fact that the knight is misled by his anguished jealousy. The series *conois/lois/voie* emphasizes how dependent his knowledge is on his sight, which is indeed "squint-eyed," despite his claim to the contrary.

The second source of his error is brought out later when he recounts the incident to an apparent stranger (Perceval himself), using a string of sententious statements about the insatiable desire of women in general to buttress his belief concerning his own woman's conduct, as is evident from the conclusion: "Por che *quit* je qu'il jut a li": "That's why I *believe* he lay with her" (3877). This statement not only demonstrates the folly of relying on conventional truths to interpret a situation; it reveals the degree to which the knight's active imagination has, over time, further impaired his ability to understand what actually transpired, for now he is convinced they did not stop at a kiss.

We have seen how a dominant sensuality or strong emotion can influence one's interpretation of physical data, and we have some indication of the insidious authority of proverbial wisdom.[8] The problem posed by this latter notion becomes clearer as we consider the perspective of the average person. This perspective, the conventional sensibility, is brought out in crowd scenes. Chrétien often describes events such as tournaments as seen through the eyes of onlookers watching from an upper balcony or tower.[9] Since the poet's audience is usually better informed than the eyewitnesses through whose perception the events are filtered, the effect is one of dramatic irony. But, as in the case of Perceval, humor is not the only purpose of this device; it also serves admirably to highlight the process by which ordinary people arrive at (often erroneous) conclusions by bringing to bear on a situation the most conventional notions or standards, that is, common sense.

In this context, it is worth recalling Peter Haidu's observation regarding a famous scene in another of Chrétien's romances, the debate between Reason and Love which precedes Lancelot's decision to get into the cart driven by the dwarf who promises to lead him to the Queen. As Haidu notes, the arguments by which Reason attempts to dissuade the enamored knight from riding in the infamous cart represent little more than a vulgar appeal to one's fear of incurring dishonor by defying convention.[10] One does not always gain by conforming to custom, as is evident later on when Lancelot learns that despite all he has done to effect her rescue, the Queen begrudges him his momentary hesitation to obey Love's command to get into the cart.

Of all Chrétien's characters, it is no doubt Gauvain who is most concerned with appearances (as is borne out by his categorical refusal to ride in the cart).[11] Therefore, it is amusing to see him become, in the second half of *Perceval,* the object of a gross misconception on the part of casual onlookers. In the episode of the "Girl with the Narrow Sleeves," Gauvain, who has vowed to refrain from combat until he has cleared himself of a charge of treason, shows no interest in participating in the tournament of his host Tybaut. This arouses the curiosity of Tybaut's daughters and their entourage, and their attention is frequently diverted from the tournament to the mysterious knight sitting idly by. When he arrived with his two shields, seven squires, and as many horses, the ladies had been excited because they thought they would see two knights arming themselves for the tournament. But then they were, successively, chagrined to discover he was alone, curious as to why he might need two shields, and, finally, disappointed that he showed no sign of preparing for combat.

Physically, Gauvain appears every bit the handsome, skilled, and courteous knight that he is. But his bizarre conduct, which seems to offer contradictory evidence, sets the girls speculating. Perhaps he's a pacifist, says one. He's a merchant with horses to sell, suggests another; while still another claims he's a money-changer, transporting bags and boxes stuffed with money and silverware. The younger daughter, who is intent on proving there exists a knight handsomer and braver than her elder sister's love, reproaches her companions for their malicious talk and stands obstinately by the simple evidence of her eyes, setting off a spirited exchange with the others:

> "Chevaliers est il, bien le *samble*."
> Et les dames totes ensamble
> Li dïent: "Por che, bele amie,
> S'i[l] le *samble,* ne l'est il mie.
> Mais il le se fait *resambler*
> Por che que ensi quide embler
> Les costumes et les paages."
>
> (5079–85)

("He's a knight, for well does he *look* like one." But the ladies all reply together: "If he *looks* it, my dear, he's certainly not. Rather, he is trying to *look* it to evade duties and tolls.")

The ladies are right to caution the girl not to assume that things are as they seem, for that *samblance* could well be a façade deliberately constructed to mislead. Of course, in this instance things *are* precisely as they *seem,* and it looks as though the ladies' sophisticated attempts to be lucid actually lead them into error. However, they are probably teasing; having noted the girl's determination to defend Gauvain, they have perversely assumed the opposite stance.

Gauvain, who is pained by the ladies' jeers, knows that the only way he can prove he is indeed what he seems is by agreeing to join the tournament, which he finally does, ostensibly for the sake of the younger sister. His combat with the elder sister's favorite is extremely brief: within no time he shatters his opponent's lance and sends him crashing headfirst to the ground. Triumphantly, the younger sister points out that the man her sister prized so highly the day before now lies vanquished, adding:

> "Or i *pert* che que je *dis* hier,
> Or *voit* on bien, se Diex me saut,
> Que il i a tel qui miex vaut."
>
> (5536–38)

("Now it's *clear* what I *said* yesterday; now, by God, you can *see* there's one of greater worth than he.")

This speech highlights the most effective way of resolving semiotic ambiguity: time and again characters will resort to actual deeds to prove they are (or are not) as they seem or pretend to be. It is then possible to compare these two kinds of visual evidence: the simple appearance of, say, prowess, and the actual display.

Another, quite different, instance involving both visual ambiguity and the efforts of crowds to decipher their impressions occurs towards the beginning of *Erec et Enide* when Yder, whom Erec has defeated, approaches the court under the wondering gaze of a group stationed in the upper balconies. Chrétien devotes eighty-two verses to the knight's approach and the attempts of the onlookers to identify him and divine his mission. Keu spots him first, and concludes from the presence at his side of a maiden and a dwarf that it is the very knight who insulted the Queen's maid the day before. Gauvain is inclined to agree, given the evidence of the trio, but since the knight's ravaged shield prevents identification, he suggests calling the Queen to verify. The conversation with Guenièvre is recounted *in toto*. Keu tells her what he has *seen* and what the sight appears to signify if his eyes have not lied ("se mi oel ne m'ont manti" [1119]). The Queen, in turn, suggests they go *see* if it is so, because she assures him she will tell him the truth as soon as she *sees* him. Keu agrees to conduct her to the point where they *saw* the knight approaching.

Guenièvre's arrival marks the second stage of the deciphering process. She immediately confirms the knight's identity and declares that he has been in combat. Although she surmises that Erec attempted to avenge the insult, she cannot be sure whether he was successful or not. However, she does note that there is more red than white on the knight's blood-stained hauberk. Gauvain is reluctant to conclude anything from this evidence except that it is clear he has fought, and fought hard. He expresses confidence that they will soon *hear* testimony that will confirm one of two hypotheses: that the knight defeated Erec or was himself defeated. The Queen agrees; and the others, in unison like an epic chorus, express their comically neutral opinion that this could well be the case.[12]

It is, then, Yder's account of his defeat by Erec which will clear up the mystery, and indeed, verbal signs are often used to interpret a situation that is visually ambiguous. But if the congruence of visual and verbal information resolves the ambiguity, the evidence presented by the verbal testimony alone is often no more conclusive than nonverbal data. Let us now consider several instances in which language misleads or is misconstrued.

Verbal Signs

The term 'verbal signs' is used here to denote what is conveyed both by language and by what is perceived as meaningful silence, the kind of silence known in French, paradoxically, as *parlant,* 'eloquent'. There are numerous examples in Chrétien's romances of misconceptions caused by ambiguous speech or an ill-timed silence. In *Cligès,* *Yvain,* and *Lancelot,* the lovesick protagonists pour out their contradictory feelings in long, tortuous monologues which abound in wordplay calculated ultimately to lead them to the conclusions at which they want so desperately to arrive. In contrast to their eloquence when they are alone, they are often tongue-tied in the presence of their beloved.[13]

As in the case of nonverbal signs, the density of language in Chrétien's romances points to the importance of context for interpretation. Even in the love monologues, which seem so precious and superficial, ambiguity is dependent on twists and turns resulting from the lover's alternate espousal of two fundamentally different perspectives. For example, when Yvain falls in love with the widow of the knight he has just slain, he uses rhetoric to transform his apparently hopeless situation into a hopeful one. His conclusion that his mortal enemy is actually his friend depends entirely on his willful confusion of subject and object: although he knows Laudine is his enemy *(enemie)* because she hates him, he claims he can call her his friend *(amie)* because he loves her!

Erec et Enide and *Perceval* do not contain nearly as many examples of sophistic reasoning as Chrétien's other three romances.[14] The sources of verbal ambiguity are much less obvious, though they are in some ways a good deal more significant, because the opacity of a particular statement does not depend on verbal acrobatics or simple wordplay, but rather on a misconception that is often quite profound.

No doubt the purest example of verbal ambiguity occurs towards the end of *Perceval* when Gauvain is talking to a maiden (his sister) at the Roche de Canguin. Gauvain's mother and grandmother look on with delighted approval and speculate on what might come of this conversation, for they are unaware that the two are siblings. The grandmother hopes they might marry and love each other as much as Eneas and Lavinia. Her daughter, in turn, prays it please God that they should love each other like brother and sister and be of one flesh. The narrator breaks in to say that this wish will be granted, but not in the way she means. She thinks she is describing in only figurative terms the love that should exist between the two, but she will soon learn that those terms are literally true:

> En sa proiere *entent* la dame
> Qu'il l'aint et qu'il le praigne a fame.
> Cele ne reconnoist son fil:
> Come frere et suer seront il,
> Que d'autre amor point n'i avra
> Quant li uns de l'autre savra
> Qu'ele est sa suer et il ses frere,
> Et s'en ara joie la mere
> Autre que ele n'en atant.
>   (9065–73)

(The lady *means* by her prayer that Gauvain should love her and take her for his wife; she does not recognize her son. They will indeed be like brother and sister, for there will be no other kind of love between them once they know that she is his sister and he her brother; and their mother will rejoice for a reason other than she expects.)

It is curious that the verb *entendre,* which usually refers to the way a message is received (heard or interpreted) is used here to signify the way in which the speaker construes her own message. (The verb *penser,* 'to think', can be used similarly.) The ambiguity, then, is quite unintentional. In the following discussion, we will see the great extent to which language can imperfectly represent reality, and the misunderstandings that are created, many intentionally.

We have observed how difficult it is for Perceval to deal with nuances in his efforts to interpret what he sees and hears, and we have noted the unfortunate consequences of his failure to understand his mother's advice because he retains only the elements which strike his fancy. This advice would not seem ambiguous to anyone with a normal capacity for processing it, but Perceval's mind is like a grossly constructed filter through which slips anything that is not concrete; abstract concepts elude him, as does innuendo.

Perceval demonstrates his inability to comprehend the opacity of language when, on arriving at Arthur's court, he comes up against Keu, the spiteful seneschal. Upon hearing Perceval's demand that Arthur give him the arms of the Vermillion Knight, Keu speaks out:

> "Amis, vos avez droit.
> Alez lui tolir orendroit
> Les armes, car eles sont vos.
> Ne feïstes mie que sos
> Quant vos por che venistes cha."
> (1003–7)

("How right you are, my friend! Go at once and take his arms, for they are yours! It is not the least bit foolish of you to come and ask!")

The seneschal is piqued by the impertinence of this stupid boy, and he means to mock him, but Perceval fails to hear in this sarcastic retort anything but what he wants to hear, the literal meaning, the permission to seize the arms. Arthur realizes that the naive youth will likely misconstrue Keu's words, and because he doubts it will be possible to secure the arms, he reproaches Keu, in essence, for making a promise that will not be fulfilled.

Arthur emphatically proclaims the duty of a worthy man not to promise anything that cannot be delivered or to raise undue expectations when there is no hope of fulfillment. The theme of Keu's outrageous tongue ("fole langue") is taken up again subsequently each time one of Perceval's vanquished foes is dispatched to the court as proof that the boy's foolish appearance masked a worthy knight. On the third occasion, the tale recounted by the Proud Knight sets Arthur to reminiscing about Perceval's first visit to court and the boy's reaction to Keu's ironic advice:

> "Cil qui ne sot le gab *entendre*
> *Cuida* que cil voir li deîst;
> Ala aprés et si l'ocist
> D'un gavelot qu'il li lancha."
> (4120–23)

("And the boy, not knowing how to *take* the joke, *thought* he'd told him the truth, and went after the knight and killed him by throwing a javelin at him.")

This is one of the many passages where the verb *entendre* refers to understanding rather than hearing; the sense is reinforced by the verb *cuidier,* which usually indicates mistaken belief. The function of Arthur's retrospective reading of the scene is to point up how differently the court interprets this entire exchange now that they know what happened directly afterwards. They had expected Perceval's misinterpretation to have disastrous consequences (and so had we), but his naiveté served him well, at least in this instance. It will not always be so.

Perceval applies the same blunt, unreflective manner of interpretation to the advice given him by his uncle, Gornemant, who tells him, among other things, not to talk too much:

> "Ne ne *parlez trop volentiers:*
> Nus ne puet estre *trop parliers*
> Qui sovent tel chose ne *die*
> Qui torné li este affolie,
> Car li sages *dit* et *retrait:*
> 'Qui *trop parole,* il *se mesfait.'*
> Por che, biax amis, vos *chastoi*
> De *trop parler* . . ."
>   (1648–56)

("Another thing: Don't *talk too much.* Anyone who *talks too much* is bound often to *say* things that make him look like a fool. For as the sage *says,* 'He who *speaks too much does wrong.'* That's why I *warn* you, dear friend, not to *talk too much.*")

Talking too much is seen as a "misdeed." This emphatically formulated verbal warning, which is supported by the authority not only of Gornemant's long experience but of humanity's collective wisdom (i.e., proverbs), is the source of Perceval's subsequent social problems both at Belrepaire and at the Grail Castle. When he is greeted by Blancheflor's subjects and led in to meet his hostess, his failure to greet her leads observers to wonder if he is not a mute. Fortunately, Perceval escapes complete censure because Blancheflor decides to take the intiative and breaks the silence.

Blancheflor is one of Chrétien's more perceptive creations. She has no trouble sizing up Perceval and manipulating him to her own ends. Anguished about the siege that is draining her fortress of supplies and manpower, she enters Perceval's room that night, scantily clad, kneels by his bed, and awakens the youth with her hot tears. When he asks why she has come, she prefaces her explanation with the prayer that he may not esteem her the less, though she is nearly naked! "Je n'i *pensa[i]* onques folie / Ne mauvestié ni vilonnie" (1987–88). She claims that her behavior does not spring from any vile or base motive. Here the verb *penser* is used to designate her intention, the construction she herself puts on her gesture, but she is mostly concerned with how her interlocutor will construe it. She is no fool; she knows he will accept her words at face value, but she also knows that her covert appeal to his sexual desire will do as much to convince him to help her as will her grim description of her situation.

If we have any doubts about Blancheflor's linguistic skill at the beginning of the speech, they are soon dissipated. After she has exposed her situation and her desire to kill herself and announced her intention to leave Perceval in peace, the narrator states that the youth will in time be able to gain fame, if he dares. For she has not come "to spill tears on his face" for any reason other than to make him want to fight to defend her land. This is her motive, no matter what she has tried to make him think: "que que ele entendant li face" (2042). Here the present participle of *entendre* denotes a continuing effort on the speaker's part to elicit a particular interpretation by the interlocutor.

Perceval's response is actually quite clever. He tells her to take comfort and stay with him that night, hinting (only hinting) that things may seem less hopeless in the morning. The next day, when Blancheflor is sure Perceval intends to fight, she tries to dissuade him, but the narrator observes that her implicit plea has been so effective that she can afford to pretend she does not want him to stay:

> Mais sovent avient que l'e[n] selt
> Escondire sa volenté,
> Quant on voit home entalenté
> De faire trestot son talent,
> Por che que mix l'en entalent.
> Ensi fait ele come sage,
> Qu'ele li a mis en corage
> Ce qu'ele li blame molt fort.
> (2130–37)

(But it often happens that one is wont to conceal one's wish when one sees a man well inclined to do one's will, so that he may be more inclined still. And so she acts wisely, for she has made him want to do what she reproaches him for wanting.)

At Belrepaire, Perceval makes good progress towards his socialization. But his behavior at the Grail Castle reveals that the process may have gone too far. He sits with his host, captivated by the wondrous spectacle which unfolds before his eyes, but he refrains from asking what it means. Three times, as the procession passes before Perceval, the narrator explicitly states that the boy remains silent because he remembers his uncle's advice and thinks it would be discourteous to ask. The second time, the narrator expresses his fear that the boy might suffer from it, adding:

> Por che que *j'ai oï retraire*
> Qu'ausi se puet on bien *trop taire*
> Com *trop parler* a la foie[e].
> (3249–51)

(For I have *heard* it *said* that a man can *remain too silent* just as he can *talk too much.*)

The narrator supports his fear by alluding to a proverbial saying which seems to contradict—or at least qualify—Gornemant's advice, itself supported by a proverb. But Gornemant can hardly be blamed. There is, among the proverbs collected by Joseph Morawski, one that expresses the folly of remaining mum (1542: "On se puet bien trop teire": "It is possible to remain too silent"). But there are many more which proclaim the virtues of saying little or of holding one's tongue, especially if one is likely to say things that are foolish (like Perceval) or malicious (like Keu). The following are especially eloquent: 1236: "Mieuz se vaut tere que folie dire": "It's better to remain silent than to say a foolish (or outrageous) thing"; and 1254: "Mieus vaut bons taires que fous parlers": "A good silence is better than thoughtless talk."[15]

Gornemant's advice does not seem particularly ambiguous, but Perceval's blunt interpretation makes it clear how much we take for granted when we communicate, i.e., how much we leave unsaid, assuming our interlocutors can fill in the gaps. By advising Perceval not to talk too much, Gornemant hardly expects him to remain completely silent. But, as we have seen, Perceval's limited scale of values jumps from black to white and admits no intermediate grays. Unfortunately, Perceval's dumb silence at the Grail Castle, unlike at Belrepaire, has disastrous consequences, as the boy learns from his cousin shortly after leaving. If only he had asked what the grail contained and whom it nourished, he would have restored to the crippled Fisher King both his health and the rule of his land.

But it is not Perceval's failure to speak *per se* that is at fault; unlike at Belrepaire, he has no trouble engaging in polite conversation with his host. The root of his trouble, curiously, and most significantly, is his failure to ask questions—the most elementary questions—about what unfolds before his eyes. He sees but does not understand. Chrétien seems to be saying that the greatest fault is the propensity to accept unquestioningly what one is told and what one witnesses. The truth will elude anyone who does not adopt a critical stance. What is needed is the curiosity of the young Perceval tempered by a more thoughtful approach to events, but not completely subdued by conventional standards of conduct.[16]

The folly of accepting things at face value and the necessity of weighing one's words (and one's silences) is demonstrated in Chrétien's first romance by the conduct of the heroine. Enide makes an interesting contrast to Perceval because she is much shrewder. But she is naive, too, in ways that are not at first apparent. Although she seems generally cognizant of the power of language and of silence, and demonstrates eventually a thorough knowledge of the uses and abuses of language, she suffers initially from a failure to recognize the persuasive impact of idle gossip (commonly held opinion) on her own ability to judge.

Enide's use of language and silence lies at the very heart of Chrétien's first romance. The crisis between the two protagonists is set off by Enide's bold decision to formulate the reproach that is on the minds (and lips) of Erec's subjects. Since their marriage, Erec has been so devoted to his wife that he has given no thought to bearing arms. Enide knows what people have been saying and feels she is partly to blame. One night while Erec is sleeping, she lies awake thinking, and her anguish is such that she gives voice to it:

> Tel duel en ot et tel pesance
> qu'il li avint par mescheance
> qu'ele dist lors une *parole*

> dom ele se tint puis por fole;
> mes ele n'i *pansoit* nul mal.
>
> (2481–85)

(Such was her grief and chagrin that by mischance she said a *word* for which she later considered herself most foolish, though she *intended* no malice.)

She begins to weep softly and to lament her situation. "Amis, con mar fus!": "My friend, woe is me!" (2503), she says aloud. This, then, is the "word" "parole" mentioned above and to which reference will be made repeatedly in the conversation which begins when Erec awakes and in the subsequent episodes. It is the *parole* that woke him up, and when he tries to find out why she is crying, she cannot deny having said anything (though she tries), for he plainly heard her *speak* ("bien ai la *parole* antandue" [2519]), and further, as he points out, her tears are a clear (nonverbal) sign that something is wrong. She has no choice but to tell him what she has heard said about him.

As she had foreseen, he reacts badly. Although he admits she was right (to be concerned?) and that the people who blame him are right to do so, he tells her to don her finest clothing and saddle up her best palfrey. From this point until the couple's reconciliation some 2300 verses later (fully one third of the romance), Erec will be as a stranger to his wife. Enide will have to depend entirely on her own judgment to interpret not only the individual adventures that come their way, but also the "aventure" that they are living as a couple in crisis.

The first mystery facing Enide is the meaning of Erec's order to prepare for a trip; she is convinced he means to send her off alone. Although she is reassured to see he will accompany her, her anguish returns when he instructs her unequivocally to refrain from speaking to him, no matter what she sees. In her first attempts to interpret this order, she remains at the level of appearances. She truly believes he does not want her to speak to him, come what may. She also believes this to be proof that he now hates her: "Anhaïe m'a, bien le *voi*, / quant il ne vialt parler a moi" ("He has turned against me, I *see* it clearly, since he will not speak to me" [2787–88]). The reader is better informed, having heard Erec's departing words to his father. These words, which reveal Erec's concern for Enide's welfare, are in direct contradiction to his harsh treatment of her.

Enide has had but a short time to reflect on the meaning of her unhappy situation when she sees coming towards them three robbers.

Though mindful of her promise to remain silent and of the possibility of incurring Erec's wrath, she feels bound to turn and warn him. Erec blames her, claiming that she clearly has little esteem for him: "Or me prisiez vos trop petit" (2846) and warning her that, though he will pardon her this once, she will not be so lucky the next time.

The narrator does not reveal Erec's real feelings, although in the second episode he does say that the hero sees five knights approaching and pretends not to notice. Enide's anguish is greater than before, though she comes to the same conclusion, and Erec's reaction is harsher still. He tells her in no uncertain terms that he is convinced she has no esteem for him and that he is not grateful for the warning; rather he despises her for it.

On the surface, Enide appears to believe him, but her repeated refusal to remain silent reveals that she knows, if only intuitively, how to interpret what he says. She senses what the narrator will explicitly reveal from the third episode on: that although Eric continues to demand silence, he considers every instance of disobedience as further proof of her love. As readers, we know from the start that everything Erec says has to be inverted. Or does it? Perhaps we, too, should be pondering the meaning of Erec's words. After all, if he really loves her, and actually knows she esteems him, and is truly grateful for her warnings, why must the testing go on so long? Is it simply, as some have suggested, that Enide's ordeal, like Griselda's, stems from some inexplicable quirk of cruelty on her husband's part; or could there possibly be some truth in Erec's assertions?[17]

Enide's own musings provide some insight into the problem. After Erec has defeated the second group of knights, Enide spends a wakeful night. Once again she chastises herself for having spoken out ("la *parole* qu'ele ot dite" [3098]), but this time she does not simply bemoan her fate; she blames herself for her pride and presumption:

> "*Savoir* pooie sanz dotance
> que tel chevalier ne meillor
> ne *savoit* l'an de mon seignor.
> *Bien le savoie. Or le sai mialz;*
> *car ge l'ai veü a mes ialz,*
> car trois ne cinc armez ne dote.
> Honie soit ma leingue tote,
> qui l'orguel et la honte dist
> dont mes cors a tel honte gist."
>   (3104–12)

("I might have *known* without doubt that there was no knight better than, or so good as, my lord. *I knew it well enough before. But now I know it better. For I have seen with my own eyes* how he has not quailed before three or even five armed men. Cursed be my tongue for having uttered such pride and insult as now compel me to suffer shame!")

Enide's emotion stems from her realization that when she recounted the opinion that Erec's subjects had of him, she was giving voice as well to her own feelings. Almost without realizing it, she had been swayed and won over by the opinion commonly held. There was, then, some truth in Erec's claim that she had no esteem for him; he has indeed had to prove himself to Enide.

In this light, the speech in which Erec finally forgives Enide becomes much more understandable. Just as she has been reassured concerning his prowess (she knew he was valiant, but now knows it even better), he is now reassured about her love for him and now loves her more than ever:

> "Ma dolce suer,
> bien vos ai de tot essaiee.
> Or ne soiez plus esmaiee,
> c'or vos aim plus qu'ainz mes ne fis,
> et je *re*sui certains et fis
> que vos m'amez parfitemant.
> Or voel estre d'or en avant,
> ausi con j'estoie devant,
> tot a vostre comandemant;
> et se vos rien m'avez *mesdit,*
> je le vos pardoing tot et quit
> del *forfet* et de la *parole.*"
>
> (4882–93)

("My sweetheart, I have tested you thoroughly. But now have no more fear, for I love you now more than ever I did before; and I am *once more* certain and reassured that you love me with a perfect love. From this time on for evermore, I offer myself to do your will just as I used to do before. And if you have *spoken ill of me,* I pardon you and call you quit of both the *offence* and the *word* you uttered.")

It is on *parole* that Erec ends the speech that closes this long, protracted misunderstanding between the lovers. It began because Enide dared to say the word that sowed doubt in Erec's mind (and revealed her own doubts); it was dissipated because Enide dared to speak when ordered to remain silent.[18]

The reliance which both Erec and Enide place on the evidence of deeds points up a fundamental mistrust of language. Language is suspect; ambiguous, or opaque at the very least, it must be supported by deeds which will either disclose its true meaning or reveal its vacuity. This attitude is illustrated not only in the central conflict between Erec and Enide, but in their encounters with others as well.

The couple's third encounter, one of the most elaborately developed episodes in the romance, underscores how skilfully language can be manipulated to achieve one's ends. When Count Galoen sets eyes on the handsome couple that his squire has led to the castle, he becomes instantly enamored of Enide. He asks Erec for permission as an act of courtesy and as a pleasure ("par corteisie et par deduit" [3288]) to sit next to her, so that he may offer her his service ("servise" [3293]). It is an ambiguous request, for it is couched in terms which are used in the context both of love service and simple courtesy. But Erec *senses* no trick ("n'i *pansa* nule boise" [3297]), partly because he is not jealous (as the narrator states), and partly because the Count interlaces his request with three different explicit assurances as to his good intentions.

As soon as he gains access to Enide, however, he informs her of his intention to make her his love. Enide's initial reaction is to recoil in disgust at the thought of betraying her lord; but when the Count threatens to have Erec killed then and there before her eyes should she refuse, she sees no recourse but to follow the Count's lead and manipulate him through language. She declares that she was only testing him and suggests that a more seemly solution would be for him to storm their room in the morning, take her by force, and slay Erec when he tries to defend her. Here we are no longer in the realm of ambiguity: Enide is giving the Count lie for lie. The narrator notes: "Ce panse cuers que ne dit boche": "The heart thinks what the mouth does not say" (3376).

Enide revels in her ruse, no doubt because she is no longer a victim of language; rather she is bending it to serve her own and Erec's interests. Gleefully she embroiders, asserting that she no longer loves Erec (and assuring the Count she has no desire to lie: "ja n'an quier mantir" [3389]), going so far even as to claim she can hardly wait to feel the Count's naked body next to hers. Having assured him thus of her love, she insists that he pledge to hold her forever dear. Once again, the narrator intervenes to underline the discrepancy between Enide's words and her intentions:

> Lors en a cele la foi prise;
> mes po l'an est et po la prise:
> por son seignor fu delivrer.
> Bien sot par *parole* enivrer
> bricon, des qu'ele i met *l'antante:*
> mialz est asez qu'ele li mante
> que ses sires fust depeciez.
>
> (3407–13)

(Then she took his plighted word; but little she values or cares for it, except therewith to save her lord. Well she knows how to deceive a fool [with *words*], when she puts her *mind* to it. Better it were to lie to him than that her lord should be slain.)

By forestalling the hour set for Erec's slaying, Enide manages to gain the time necessary for them to leave the castle next morning before the Count arrives. In spite of this proof of Enide's love, Erec continues to instruct her not to speak, and she is faced with the same dilemma as before when she sees the Count coming after them. Again she warns Erec, and again he complains of her lack of esteem for him. The Count, for his part, is entirely won over by Erec's prowess and Enide's loyalty. He, at least, needs no further proof of their worth.

Erec does not repeat his admonition, but when Enide hears another knight approaching, she once again weighs the pros and cons of speaking out. This time, though, she encounters a further obstacle to speaking: while her tongue moves to formulate her warning, her teeth, clenched tightly out of fear, keep the words enclosed within ("s'anclost la *parole* dedanz" [3720]). She begins a fresh argument with herself, and eventually manages to get the words out. Erec reacts as before, but the narrator assures us that his reproach has become formulaic:

> Ele li dit; il la menace;
> mes n'a talant que mal li face,
> qu'il *aparçoit* et *conuist* bien
> qu'ele l'ainme sor tote rien,
> et il li tant que plus ne puet.
>
> (3751–55)

(She speaks to him; he threatens her, but has no desire to do her harm, for he realizes and knows full well that she loves him above all else, and he loves her, too, to the utmost.)

If Erec is finally convinced, it is because Enide's actions have erased the hurt initially inflicted by her giving voice to the diminishing esteem felt by the populace (and by herself, apparently). In order to reaffirm her esteem and love of her husband, she had to prove, in essence, that there was no truth to what she and the others had said, that there was no congruence between that ill-fated *parole* and Erec's actual worth. This is curious, but more curious still is the fact that the acts which provide that proof are all "speech acts": Enide's repeated warnings of impending danger and her clever verbal manipulation of Count Galoen.

In the episodes that follow, Erec will continue to be obsessed with the relation of language to reality, but the emphasis is henceforth on the congruence of word and deed. For example, when Guivret can fight no longer and begs mercy, Erec insists that he *say* that he is vanquished. Later, when Guivret pledges his friendship and service, he receives the following cautious response:

> "Ja plus ne vos quier demander,
> fet Erec, molt m'avez promis;
> mes sire estes et mes amis,
> *se l'uevre est tex con la parole.*"
> (3896–99)

("I have nothing more to ask of you," says Erec; "you have promised me a lot. You are now my lord and my friend, *if your deed is as good as your word.*")

In the following episode Erec is pitted against two giants who tell him he is insane to think he can win against them. Erec answers them with a proverb: "tex vaut petit qui molt se loe": "many a man boasts loudly who is of little worth" (4410). Indeed, as it turns out, the giants are not able to live up to their boast.

The charge that a man often boasts of deeds he could not accomplish is frequently made by Keu. In *Yvain* he accuses the hero twice of being incapable of bringing his deeds into line with his boasts. In *Perceval* he goes further and actually claims that Gauvain's reputation for prowess is undeserved because he substitutes clever discourse for deeds. The seneschal has just failed in his attempt to convince Perceval to abandon his revery and accompany him to Arthur's camp. So far Perceval has fought off (literally) two rather rudely-formulated invitations extended by Sagremor and Keu, and now Gauvain is about to try his luck. Furious, Keu claims that Gauvain has won many a battle by waiting until his opponent was exhausted so that he could win him over with words:

> "Bien savez vos *paroles* vendre,
> Qui molt sont beles et polies.
> Grans oltrages, grans felonnies
> Et grant orgueil direz vos ja?
> Que dehés ait qui le quida
> Ne qui le quide, que je soie.
> Certes, en un blïaut de soie
> Porrois ceste besoigne faire;
> Ja ne vos i covenra traire
> Espee ne lance brisier.
> De ce vos poëz vous prisier
> Que se la langue ne vos faut
> Por dire: 'Sire, Diex vos saut
> Et il vos doinst joie et santé,'
> Fera il vostre volenté.
> Ne de rien por vos ensaignier;
> Bien le sarez aplaniier
> Si c'on aplanie le chat,
> Si dira l'en: 'Or se combat
> Mesire Gavains fierement.'"
> (4384–403)

("You're good at spinning fair and courteous *phrases*, aren't you? Are you going to assail him with hard and haughty words? A curse on whoever thinks so; I don't. You could do this job in a silk tunic! *You* won't need to draw a sword or break a lance. You can boast of this: that if you can just get your tongue round 'Sir, God save you and give you joy and health,' he'll do your will. Oh, far be it from me to give you lessons; you'll cosset and coax him like a cat, while everyone's saying 'Now Sir Gauvain's engaged in a mighty combat'!")

Gauvain, considering the source, chides Keu for his temper and sets out to bring Perceval back, which he manages to do by addressing him courteously. Keu rants and raves anew, but now that the battle has been won, no one much cares how it has been done.

Gauvain is indeed skilled with language, which accounts in part for his reputation as a flirt, but Keu's charges about his prowess appear unfounded, at least in this romance where he has ample opportunity to display his chivalric skills.[19] Still, as we have seen, he is accused a second time (at Tybaut's castle) of seeming to be what he is not, and towards the end of the romance, he is again charged with misrepresentation. This time, oddly enough, it is concerning a feat he has already accomplished! When Gauvain claims that he lay the night before on the Marvelous Bed, Guiromelant is incredulous, even though the two knights have just solemnly pledged to tell each other the truth:

> "Par Dieu, fait il, trop me merveil
> Des noveles que tu me dis.
> Or m'est il solas et delis
> De tes mençoignes escouter;
> Ausi orroie jou conter
> Un fableor que je faz toi.
> Tu iés jogleres, bien le *voi*,
> Et je *quidoie* que tu fuisses
> Chevaliers et que tu eüsses
> Dela fait alcun vasselage.
> Et neporoec or me fai sage
> Se nule proëce i *feïs*
> Et quel chose tu i veïs."
> (8674–86)

("By God," he replied, "I am astounded by what you tell me! But it's delightful listening to your lies: it's like being entertained by a story-teller. You're a minstrel—I *see* it clearly! And here I *thought* you were a knight and had done some feat of prowess yonder! But come now, tell me truly if you *did* any worthy deeds there and what you *saw*.")

This is an interesting variation, almost an inversion, of the custom of having a defeated knight return to court to recount verbally what has transpired, thereby offering testimony of the victorious knight's prowess. Perceval sends all his defeated foes back to Arthur's court, as does Erec when, having convinced Enide of his worth, he embarks on the second phase of his mission—proving himself to his peers. In the case in question, though, Gauvain endured a marvel, not a human foe: as he sat on the Marvelous Bed, the window opposite him flew open and he was assaulted first by arrows (which he managed to dodge) and next by a fierce lion which leaped at him and whose claws got stuck in his shield. Lacking the corroborating evidence of a human witness, Gauvain must rely on the physical signs of his victory:

> "Se vos *quidiez* que il n'i paire,
> *Vez* encore les ongles chi;
> Que la teste, la Dieu merchi,
> Li trenchai et les piez ensamble.
> Des ces *ensaignes* que vos samble?"
> (8708–12)

("If you *think* it's not true, *look* at the claws still hanging here. I cut off the head, thank God, and its feet, too. What do you think of these *signs of proof?*")

Authorial Commentary

Guiromelant's assimilation of Gauvain's story to the tales told by minstrels is most revealing. It provides some insight into the nature of Chrétien's own preoccupation with language, in particular, and with the misrepresentation (and misconstruing) of reality, in general. For in the prologues to both his first romance and his last, the poet alludes to the discrepancy between appearance and reality.

He prefaces his tale about Perceval with praise of Count Phillip of Flanders, who is worthier even than Alexander, because he pays more than lip service to justice, loyalty, and religion. He is more generous than any man known, for he gives according to the Gospel, without hypocrisy or guile. Citing the Gospel verse "Do not let your left hand know what your right hand does," Chrétien then proceeds to gloss the verse with reference to his patron, showing how Phillip is motivated by charity, not vainglory (which comes from false hypocrisy).

Chrétien's point about the opposition between appearance and reality (charity for show vs. heartfelt charity) is somewhat obscured here by his understandable desire to flatter his patron. But in the prologue to *Erec et Enide*, he is much more explicit about the problem and about the relation of the poet and his audience to it. The poem begins with an allusion to a proverb which warns about the failure of perception:

> Li vilains dit an son respit
> que tel chose a l'an an despit
> qui molt valt mialz que l'an ne *cuide*.
> (1–3)

(The rustic's proverb says that many a thing is despised that is worth much more than one *thinks*.)

Chrétien goes on to say that for this reason one should make the most of whatever intelligence one may possess and not remain silent when one can say something that might give pleasure (4–8). He himself will endow with a most beautiful structure ("molt bele conjointure") a tale of adventure which those who earn a living by telling stories are accustomed to mutilate and spoil (9, 13–22). Like Guiromelant, Chrétien gives little credence to the tales spun by minstrels. He implies that unlike his vulgar predecessors, he has the intelligence to structure the story in a way that will reveal its intrinsic worth.

The poet's duty to avoid misrepresentation is clear, but what of his audience? Can it sit back passively and expect the truth to be revealed to it as it is being entertained? It hardly seems so, for Chrétien has just underscored the duty of each ("chascuns") to use his intelligence, and it is not at all certain that he is speaking of himself alone. Let us examine carefully what he says in vv. 9–12:

> Por ce dist Crestïens de Troies
> que reisons est que totevoies
> doit chascuns *panser* et *antandre*
> a bien *dire* et a bien *aprandre*.

(For this reason Chrétien de Troyes says that it is right that everyone should always strive and apply oneself to speaking and teaching [learning?] well . . .)

Since Chrétien goes on to say what he intends to do, scholars have assumed that the activities described in vv. 11–12 referred to the poet.[20] *Dire* is clearly an activity of the "emitter," and *aprandre* can mean 'to teach' as well as 'to learn.' *Panser* and *antandre* are usually taken here to describe the poet's efforts.

But as we have seen, both *panser* and *antandre* (or *entendre*) can at different times refer to the receiving as well as the sending of a message. In fact, *antandre* most often refers to how a message is understood by the listener. With reference to the cognates, *antancïon* and *antante*, Marie-Louise Ollier notes that the former usually refers to the activity of the poet, while the latter, which is sometimes synonymous, can also refer to the activity of the reader/listener: "the three terms *antancïon, antante*, and the verbal form *antandre* are essentially dynamic, introduce a will, a directed endeavor, as much on the part of the author, who invests his text with meaning, as on the part of the reader, of whom the decoding effort is required."[21] To support her "micro-system," Ollier refers to the little prologue in *Yvain* with which Calogrenant prefaces his long tale: the knight-narrator asks for the hearts as well as the ears of his audience, claiming that words are wasted, meanings lost, if they are not understood by the heart:

> "Cuers et oroilles m'aportez,
> car *parole* est tote perdue
> s'ele n'est de cuer *antandue*."
> (150–52)

(Heart and ears bring to me/because words are utterly lost/if they are not heard with the heart.)

It is curious that Ollier does not question the traditional reading of *antandre* in the prologue of *Erec et Enide*, no doubt because the debate about the meaning of the key terms regarding Chrétien's composition (*sen, matiere, conjointure*, and *antancïon*) has generally revolved around the problematic interpretation of the prologue to the *Lancelot*. It is also odd that although Ollier cites the use of *antante* toward the end of *Erec et Enide* as denoting an author's efforts to *convey* a message (in this case it is Macrobius), she does not mention the use of *antandié* in the following verse, which refers to the author's *reception* of his source. The passage in question occurs when Chrétien's narrator is about to describe Erec's coronation robe:

> Lisant trovomes an l'estoire
> la description de la robe,

> si an trai a garant Macrobe
> qui an l'estoire *mist s'antante,*
> *qui l'antendié,* que je ne mante.
> Macrobe m'anseigne a descrivre,
> si con je l'ai trové el livre
> l'uevre del drap et le portret.
>
> (6674–81)

(Reading the story, we find the description of the robe, and to prove that I am not lying, I take as authority Macrobius, who *applied himself to the story and who understood it.* Macrobius teaches me to describe, just as I found it in the book, the work on the cloth and the design.)

Thus, Macrobius had to understand the story before he could apply himself to retelling it, just as Chrétien had to understand Macrobius before his narrator could relate it to us.

It is significant that there is no such description to be found in Macrobius's works. Several explanations have been offered recently by scholars who do not dismiss the citation as a simple error,[22] and it may well have been Chrétien's intention to set off just such an attempt to interpret this bizarre reference. Another narratorial intervention which occurs some 250 verses before this passage is illuminating in this regard. When Erec relates his adventure (his testing of Enide) to his father, the narrator interrupts to address Chrétien's audience:

> Mes *cuidiez* vos que je vos *die*
> quex acoisons le fist movoir?
> Naie; que bien savez le voir
> et de ice, et d'autre chose,
> si con ge la vos ai esclose.
>
> (6420–24)

(But do you *imagine* I'll *tell* you what his motive was? No, for you know the truth about this and other things, as I have revealed it to you.)

As Z. P. Zaddy claims, partly on the basis of this statement, it is up to the reader to figure out Erec's motivation by examining carefully Chrétien's text.[23]

In essence, then, Chrétien issues a double *caveat* throughout his entire work, both in the prologues and in the way he has composed his romances. The same careful attention must be applied to interpreting his *parole* as must be applied to deciphering the verbal and nonverbal signs which mediate reality.

Notes

1. There are many symbolic and allegorical interpretations of Chrétien's romances. This critical trend, initiated by Reto R. Bezzola's seminal study, *Le Sens de l'aventure et de l'amour (Chrétien de Troyes)* (Paris: La Jeune Parque, 1947), was largely influenced by D. W. Robertson, Jr. It is summarized by Peter Haidu (who advocates a less rigid approach to symbolism) in *Lion-Queue-Coupée: l'écart symbolique chez Chrétien de Troyes* (Geneva: Droz, 1972), pp. 11–17.

2. In a section devoted to "Perception and Illusion" in *The Craft of Chrétien de Troyes: An Essay on Narrative Art* (Leiden: Brill, 1980), Norris J. Lacy states: "The physical aspect of perception is one of the nearly constant themes running through [Chrétien's] romances" (p. 24). One of the first and most illuminating explorations of the illusion/reality theme was Peter Haidu's watershed piece, *Aesthetic Distance in Chrétien de Troyes: Irony and Comedy in* Cligès *and* Perceval (Geneva: Droz, 1968). See also Rupert T. Pickens's excellent study, *The Welsh Knight: Paradoxicality in Chrétien's* Conte del Graal (Lexington, Ky.: French Forum, 1977).

3. Yvain *dans le miroir: Une Poétique de la réflexion dans le* Chevalier au lion *de Chrétien de Troyes,* forthcoming in Purdue University Monographs in Romance Languages, vol. 25 (Amsterdam and Philadelphia: John Benjamins, 1988).

4. All references to *Erec et Enide* are to Mario Roques's *Classiques Français du Moyen Age* edition (Paris: Champion, 1952). References to *Le Roman de Perceval ou Le Conte du Graal* are to William Roach's *Textes Littéraires Français* edition, (Geneva: Droz, 1956). The English versions of the passages cited are my own fairly literal renderings which incorporate elements of the following translations: W. W. Comfort, *Erec et Enide* in *Arthurian Romances,* Everyman's Library (New York: Dutton, 1914); Robert White Linker, *The Story of the Grail* (1952; reprint, Chapel Hill: University of North Carolina Press, 1960); and Nigel Bryant, *Perceval: The Story of the Grail* (Cambridge: D. S. Brewer, 1982).

5. Pickens, p. 92, adds that "it is an indication of [Perceval's] intellectual development that he can deal effectively with the signs shown to him by his mentor."

6. See below, pp. 59–61 and 74–76.

7. This is beautifully illustrated in Eric Rohmer's screen adaptation: as the widow is speaking, Perceval breaks in to echo the few words (e.g., "kiss," "ring") that he will retain. *Perceval le Gallois, L'Avant-Scène Cinéma,* 221 (1er fév. 1979), p. 14.

8. On the persuasive authority of sententious discourse, see Marie-Louise Ollier, "Proverbe et Sentence: Le Discours d'autorité chez Chrétien de Troyes," *Revue des Sciences Humaines* 41 (1976): 329–57.

9. See Barbara Brend, "Le Développement de 'l'observateur à la tour' comme motif littéraire dans l'oeuvre de Chrétien de Troyes," *Le Moyen Age* 84 (1978): 443–77;

and Roberta L. Krueger, "Reading the *Yvain/Charrete:* Chrétien's Inscribed Audiences at Noauz and Pesme Aventure," *Forum for Modern Language Studies* 19 (1983): 172–87.

10. *Lion-Queue-Coupée,* p. 55.

11. As Pickens notes, p. 42, Gauvain "has no existence beyond his public persona."

12. Much later in the romance, Keu, coming upon Erec in the forest, fails to recognize him because his shield is damaged and Enide has drawn her veil across her face as if to protect herself from the heat and dust.

13. The first major study of Chrétien's monologues was by Alfons Hilka, *Die direkte Rede als stilistiches Kunstmittel in den Romanen des Kristian von Troyes* (Halle: Niemeyer, 1903). See also Peter F Dembowski, "Monologue, Author's Monologue and Related Problems in the Romances of Chrétien de Troyes," *Yale French Studies* 51 (1974): 102–14. Individual monologues are analyzed in the following: Jean Frappier, *Etude sur* Yvain *ou le* Chevalier au lion *de Chrétien de Troyes* (Paris: SEDES, 1969), pp. 166–76; Peter Haidu, *Aesthetic Distance,* pp. 70–78; F Douglas Kelly, Sens and Conjointure in the Chevalier de la charrette (The Hague: Mouton, 1966), pp. 227–33; Karl D. Uitti, *Story, Myth and Celebration in Old French Narrative Poetry 1050–1200* (Princeton, N.J.: Princeton University Press, 1973), pp. 159–73.

14. Dembowski, p. 113. He concludes that Chrétien learned to use the monologue after *Erec et Enide* but then realized its shortcomings in *Perceval* where he "relies upon a more indirect and far more subtle way of revealing his heroes to us" (p. 114).

15. Joseph Morawski, *Proverbes Français antérieurs au XVe siècle, CFMA* (Paris: Champion, 1925). There are at least six more: 105, 2046, 2254, 2276, 2278, 2428.

16. Pickens, pp. 81–91, offers an illuminating analysis of Perceval's use and misuse of language. Haidu's analysis is more diffuse, extending throughout the second half of *Aesthetic Distance.*

17. Ernest Hoepffner, "Matière et sens dans le roman d'*Erec et Enide,*" *Archivum Romanicum* 18 (1934): 443, thinks Erec's harshness is a cruel game that is nonetheless necessary to test Enide's love. But the general consensus is that Erec's testing was not totally unjustified. As Donald Maddox notes, "Enide herself seems to have been persuaded to some extent by the gossip she had heard"; see *Structure and Sacring: The Systematic Kingdom in Chrétien's* Erec et Enide (Lexington, Ky.: French Forum, 1978), pp. 63–65, and p. 198 n. 24. A similar view is held by Douglas Kelly, "La Forme et le sens de la quête dans l'*Erec et Enide* de Chrétien de Troyes," *Romania* 92 (1971): 345; and by Emmanuel J. Mickel, "A Reconsideration of Chrétien's *Erec,*" *Romanische Forschungen* 84 (1972): 27.

18. Maddox also remarks that it is Enide's voice which awakens Erec from his death-like swoon and prompts him to save her from Count Oringle (p. 65). Lacy, p. 79, notes that this scene echoes the one in which Enide's *parole* awakens Erec and precipitates the crisis.

19. However, as Haidu demonstrates, most of Gauvain's adventures are so ludicrous that they actually serve to humiliate him (*Aesthetic Distance,* pp. 194ff). On Gauvain's progressive "deheroicization," see Pickens, pp. 34–45.

20. Maddox's analysis of the prologue, pp. 14–24, shows that he espouses the traditional interpretation.

21. "The Author in the Text: The Prologues of Chrétien de Troyes," *Yale French Studies* 51 (1974): 32–33.

22. Claude Luttrell, *The Creation of the First Arthurian Romance* (Evanston, Ill.: Northwestern University Press, 1974), p. 21, thinks Chrétien deliberately tried to

obscure his real source. But according to Jeanne Nightingale Husemoller, Chrétien was alluding to the Macrobian tradition of *narratio fabulosa* which he followed in adapting fabulous elements of Celtic myth into his composition in a way that both embellishes the text and illuminates its deeper meaning. (Paper presented in May 1984 at the 19th International Congress on Medieval Studies, The Medieval Institute of Western Michigan University, Kalamazoo, Mich.).

23. *Chrétien Studies: Problems of Form and Meaning in* Erec, Yvain, Cliges *and the* Charrete (Glasgow: University of Glasgow Press, 1973), p. 2.

4

EMARÉ'S CLOAK AND AUDIENCE RESPONSE

ROSS G. ARTHUR

𝒯he starting point for this discussion, as is the case with most examinations of the problem of signification in medieval literature, is Augustine's *De doctrina Christiana*. Augustine's definition of the sign comes in the opening of Book Two: "A sign is a thing which *causes us to think* of something beyond the impression the thing itself makes upon the senses."[1] The importance of this formulation cannot be overemphasized. Something is a sign if and only if it has an effect on an audience. It follows that the meaning of a sign is in part determined by those who perceive it, and that if there are different audiences for the same sign, they will attribute different meanings to it.

A later passage in the *De doctrina* provides categories for distinguishing three types of responses to important signs. There are those who worship a sign without knowing what it means, those who use it and understand it, and those who know it is a sign without knowing its meaning:

> He is a slave to a sign who uses or worships a significant thing without knowing what it signifies. But he who uses or venerates a useful sign divinely instituted whose signifying force he understands does not venerate what he sees and what passes away but rather that to which all such things are to be referred. Such a man is spiritual and free, even during that time of servitude in which it is not yet opportune to reveal to carnal minds those signs under whose yoke they are to be tamed. . . . But just as it is a servile infirmity to follow the letter and to take signs for the things that they signify, in the same way it is an evil of wandering error to interpret signs in a useless way. However, he who does not know what a sign means, but does know that it is a sign, is not in servitude. Thus it is better to be burdened by the unknown but useful signs than to interpret signs in a useless way so that one is led

80

from the yoke of servitude only to thrust his neck into the snares of error.[2]

This triple categorization forms the basis of my examination of the varying audience responses to the gem-cloak worn by the heroine of *Emaré*,[3] a popular Middle English romance of the late fourteenth or early fifteenth century.

The poem is a version of the widespread Constance legend. It tells of Emaré, the beautiful and accomplished daughter of an emperor called Sir Artyus. Some years after his wife's death, Artyus is struck by an incestuous passion for Emaré, and manages to obtain a papal dispensation to marry her. When she refuses, he sets her adrift in the sea without food and drink. Her boat is driven ashore in the land of Galys, where she meets and marries the king, hiding her identity and calling herself Egaré. When her son Segramour is born, her mother-in-law changes the letter to the king announcing the birth, saying that Emaré has given birth to a monster. The king's reply is also changed, so that instead of looking after Emaré, his servants set her and Segramour adrift again. When they land near Rome, they are protected for several years by a kindly merchant. In time the king comes to Rome as a penance and happens to stay at the house where Emaré is lodged. He meets Segramour, and when he learns that the boy has the same name as his own lost son, he offers to make the boy his heir. Emaré finally reveals herself, reverts to her true name, and is even reconciled with her father the emperor.

Names as Signs

Several details in the elaboration of this narrative form a network of signs capable of conveying an underlying spiritual message. First, there are the names: the lady's name, "Emaré," means "purified," "gracious," or "adorned with all the rarest qualities"; whereas her alias "Egaré" means "outcast."[4] Since she begins in a condition of worldly grace, passes through a period of exile, and is ultimately reintegrated into society, the story could therefore be allegorized on the idea of the lost soul ultimately redeemed. Medieval allegorizations of the *Gesta Romanorum* tales often proceed to just such spiritual conclusions—and with just as little regard for the motives of their characters.

"Segramour" means "sycamore."[5] The most famous sycamore is that in Luke's story of Zachaeus:

And entering in, he walked through Jericho. And behold, there was a man named Zachaeus, who was chief of the publicans, and he was rich. And he sought to see Jesus who he was, and he could not for the crowd, because he was of low stature. And running before, he climbed up unto a sycamore tree, that he might see him; for he was to pass that way. (Luke 19:1–4).[6]

This passage, and especially the sycamore tree, can be understood in accordance with a homily by Bede: "Zaccheus" signifies the believing gentile. He is of little stature, which signifies low moral condition, and he is cut off from Christ by his faults and bad habits, symbolized by the clamoring crowd which prevents him from seeing Jesus. Nevertheless, he will be justified, Bede says, for he has the desire to escape from this crowd and rise above himself to a vision of Christ. The tree he climbs is the Cross:

Sycomorus namque, quae est arbor foliis moro similis, sed altitudine praestans, unde et a Latinis celsa nuncupatur, ficus fatua dicitur. Et eadem dominica crux, quae credentes alit ut ficus, ab incredulis irridetur ut fatua.[7]

(For the sycamore, which is a tree similar to the mulberry tree in its foliage, but remarkable for its height [whence it is also called *celsa*, "lofty," by the Latins], is called the "foolish fig." And the Lord's cross also, which nourishes the faithful as a fig tree, is mocked by unbelievers as foolish.)

Zaccheus, aware of his own infirmity, climbs the tree of the cross in his humility and, from a desire to display his faith in the Lord, is exalted by this "praiseworthy folly." In *Emaré*, Segramour is first slandered and rejected by an unbelieving queen mother, then is loved by his father for his name rather than for the reality which the name signifies, but finally effects a reconciliation between the emperor, the king, and Emaré, who earlier were separated by sinful loves and hates. He functions, therefore, as a kind of touchstone for faith. He is rejected outright by the unbeliever; he is desired without being truly recognized by the man sustained by hope; and he effects a passage to true love for the properly enlightened believer.

Beauty as Sign

In keeping with Augustine's three responses to important signs, Emaré's physical appearance also acts as a type of *signum,* revealing a major division among the other characters according to the way they respond to her beauty. Artyus's courtiers react to her outward beauty (and her talents as manifested in her outward behavior) with proper honour and reverence:

> She was curtays in alle thynge,
> Bothe to olde and to ʒyng,
> And whythe as lylye flowre;
> Of her hondes she was slye,
> Alle her loued þat her sye,
> Wyth menske and mychyl honour.
> (64–69)

Her father, on the other hand, looks on the same outward signs and reacts only with unnatural, unlawful passion:

> The mayden, þat was of sembelan swete,
> Byfore her owene father sete,
> The fayrest wommon on life;
> That alle hys hert and alle his powʒth,
> Her to loue was y-browght;
> He by-helde her ofte syþe,
> So he was an-amored hys þowʒtur tylle
> Wyth her he þowʒth to worche hys wylle
> And wedde her to hys wyfe.
> (220–28)

Later in the story, a similar division occurs. The king of Galys is attracted by Emaré's outward beauty (397–405), but he asks to marry her properly, and that only after he knows of her inward courtesy and wisdom (421–32). His mother, on the other hand, responds to her appearance in a diametrically opposed manner:

> The olde quene sayde a-non,
> 'I sawe neuer wommon
> Haluendale so gay!'
> The olde quene spakke wordus vnhende,
> And sayde, 'Sone, þys ys a fende,
> In þis worldly wede!'
>
> (442–47)

Thus, the good and evil characters in the story reveal their natures and even pass judgment on themselves by their responses to Emaré's beauty. The good see it as an outward sign of her inward personal worth (her talents, wisdom, and courtesy) and therefore honor her for it in a righteous manner; the bad see it as a thing in itself, and respond with either sinful love or sinful hate. Indeed, in other variants of the tale, the dying empress requires her husband to marry again only if he can find a woman exactly like herself, and after a worldwide search, their daughter is found to be the only woman who meets the requirements.[8] The emperor's error therefore consists in not recognizing that similarity between two *res* is not the same as similiarity between two *signa,* since the *signum* includes the response of the perceiver, which in this case is sinful.

Gem-Cloak as Sign

There are two passages in the poem, however, which by their unusual lengths suggest they carry special significance as to its meaning. First, the opening lines of the poem are an invocation to Christ. They constitute, as Rickert notes, the "longest introductory prayer in any English romance."[9] This lengthy opening supports the contention that the work has a fundamentally religious purpose. Second, and my primary subject here, is the lengthy description of Emaré's beautiful, gemmed cloak. The cloak is given to Emaré near the beginning of the story and accompanies her throughout her adventures. It has been argued that this description was "taken over more-or-less verbatim from a narrative poem on a much larger scale,"[10] perhaps a French romance or a longer *lai* of the thirteenth century. It is true that the English poem shows signs of compression and that there are numerous indications that the poet's understanding of his original and his mastery of the art of translation were less than complete. For example, although the proportion of French origin vocabulary is small for the period, the poet nevertheless imports a number of unusual words directly from his source rather than finding English equivalents. In addition, he is not above using French structures and even grammatical endings in places a more skillful translator would make modifications in line with the rules of the target language.[11] For these two long passages (the invocation and the description of the cloak) to have survived, therefore, their importance to the original work must have been great. Further, their survival provides us with evidence about the meaning of other sections of the poem which may have been weakened by the translation into English.

The cloak is introduced, somewhat clumsily, after an ambiguous description of Sir Artyus's life following the death of his wife:

> Aftyr, when hys wyfe was dede,
> And ledde hys lyf weddewede,
> And myche loued playnge,
>   (76–78)

These lines which suggest but do not directly assert that the king was promiscuous, are interrupted by the arrival of a certain Sir Tergaunte, the king of Sicily, who brings as a present a beautiful piece of cloth. It is a dazzling object, seven years in the making, embroidered by the daughter of the emir. It is adorned with gold, azure, and many types of precious stones, including topaz, rubies, toadstones, and agates. Each corner of the cloth is described separately, with detailed pictures of pairs of lovers and of more gems and plants. In the first corner, Amadas and Idoyne are depicted, accompanied by a true-love flower made of carbuncle, sapphire, chalcedony, onyx, and diamonds, all set in gold. In the second corner, Tristan and Isolde are presented, in topaz, rubies, toadstones, and agates. In the third corner are Floris and Blancheflour, again with a true-love flower of emeralds, diamonds, coral, chrysolite, crystal, and garnets. And finally in the fourth, the emir's daughter has embroidered a picture of herself, with a unicorn, and her lover, the son of the Sultan of Babylon, surrounded by birds and flowers made of more gemstones.

The gem–cloak plays no causal part in the narrative which follows. Sir Artyus becomes enamored of his daughter before she is given the cloak; her resistance to his passion and her exile proceed from purely natural motives; and her subsequent adventures are not influenced by it in any way. Yet the cloak is everywhere we look in the story. In addition to the long introductory description, we hear of it when she is first exiled (270), when she is rescued in Galys (350), when her husband falls in love with her (394–96), when she first meets her mother-in-law (439–47), when she is exiled again (590), and when she is reunited with her husband (933). Clearly such an omnipresent object—not functioning as causal *res* and too spectacular for decoration "for its own sake"—must be present in the poem as *signum*. By determining its function, we move a long way toward understanding the poem.

Previous attempts at interpreting this romance (except for those concerned with folkloric analysis) divide into two approaches. Some scholars, dealing with the functioning of the plot, reduce the poem to its underlying structure:

> *Emaré* has a basic structure that is curiously like that of *Horn Child*, which is unusually symmetrical for a romance plot. *Horn Child* begins in the country of the hero's father (A1); when this is overrun by the heathen, Horn takes refuge at the court of another king (B1); when a false accusation sends him once more into exile, he is welcomed by a third (C). Subsequently, he retraces his steps, first avenging himself on his calumniator (B2), and then winning back his father's kingdom (A2). This pattern is modified in *Emaré* to suit the different sex of the central figure. Since Emaré herself is a defenseless heroine, not an aggressive hero, she cannot seek out her former persecutors in their own lands; instead, they must be impelled by penitence to seek her out. Because of this, symmetry of the plot has more to do with personal relationships than with any geography. It begins in her father's land (A1); when she rejects his incestuous proposals, she is exiled and comes to the land of a king who courts and marries her (B1); from this, she is exiled by the contrivings of her mother-in-law, and at last finds shelter (with her new-born baby) at Rome (C). To this city there comes first her husband (B2), and then her father (A2).[12]

According to this view, the causes for the narrative action are to be found in simple narrative necessity bound by aesthetic choices based on the gender and status of the *dramatis personae*: there is no point in asking whether passivity of the leading character has any underlying meaning, since it is implied that she would have killed her wicked mother-in-law and father if only she had been a man. The historical critics, on the other hand, tend to focus on the Christian symbolism:

> . . . bietet auch diese auf dem erste Blick so wenig exemplarische Romanze ein Modell christlich-beispielhafte Tugend und einen anschaulichen Beleg für die bewahrende Macht Gottes und seine in das menschliche Leben hineinwirkende Liebe.[13]

> (This romance, at first glance so unexemplary, offers a model of perfect Christ-like virtue and manifest proof of the protective power of God and of the immanent operation of His love in human life.)

Thus, whereas Mills looks to narrative choices and the aesthetic structure to find the causes of events on the level of art, Schelp finds the same causes in the working out, through power and immanent love, of a divine plan. Because these two approaches are focusing on different things, they are bound to disagree on interpretation of an element as striking as the miraculous cloak. Nevertheless, they can be brought closer together by examining the semiotic aspects of the garment. In fact, there exist within the poem two different "audiences" for the cloak, one for whom the functionalist attitude is appropriate and one moved by its symbolic nature.

As Schelp has shown, many of the precious stones embroidered into the cloak were associated by the writers of medieval lapidaries with specific human virtues and with the type of life that leads to the knowledge of God. Concerning the topaz, the *London Lapidary* says:

> He that bereth þis stone shal þe more loue to leed his body in chastite, & þe more love to loke to the hevenly Ryal way . . . . All þei þat beholden my stones with sobrete more turne her sight up topace, þat signifieth þat we all shuld beholde þat life wherby a man myght se god in þe face.[14]

Concerning the onyx, we are told that

> Any onicle maketh a man bolde, hardy & courageful, & maketh hym to haue plente of spotel, & gederith plente of gode, & holdeth hym in heele þat bereth hit . . . [hit] betokeneth the holy men of this worlde þat be gode lyvyng ouercommen the temptacions of the deuel.[15]

And in regard to the ruby, that gem

> is of suche lordeshippe þat when he þat bereth hym cometh amonge
> men, all thei shul bere hym honour & grace & all shul bere hym joye of
> his presence. þe bokes seyn vs þat þe beestes þat drynken of the water
> where þe rubie hath been wette inne shul be hoole of þeir sekenes; & he
> þat is discomforted þat in gode beleue beholdeth þis stone, hit shal
> comforte & make hym to forgete his contrariousete be vertue þat god
> hath yeven þerto.[16]

Similar interpretations for the toadstone, the agate, the sapphire, and
the other stones in the poem may be found elsewhere in the lapidaries, or conveniently gathered by Schelp.

The major theoretical problem connected with belief in the virtue
of stones is the question of the nature of their efficacy. Belief in such
objects as charms was of course widespread in the ancient and medieval world, but there was always a concern that this tended toward
idolatry. Augustine discusses the matter in *De doctrina*, and makes the
following distinction:

> For it is one thing to say, "If you drink the juice of this herb, your
> stomach will not hurt," and quite another to say, "If you hang this herb
> around your neck, your stomach will not hurt." The first course is
> recommended as a healthful remedy, but the second is to be con-
> demned as a superstitious sign. Even though there are no incantations,
> invocations, or characters involved, the question often remains as to
> whether the thing which is to be tied or in any way attached to heal the
> body is valid because of the force of nature, in which case it is to be
> used freely, or is valid because of some signifying convention, in which
> case the Christian should avoid it the more cautiously the more it
> seems to be efficacious in doing good.[17]

The lapidarists skirted these difficulties by asserting the correctness of
the use of stones in two contradictory ways. Sometimes they speak as
if the power of the stones is purely natural, so that they may be used
in precisely the same ways as medicines. Other times they admit that
the stones have a signifying power but avoid the charges of witchcraft
and idolatry by insisting that this power depends on the "gode
beleue" of the user and the beholder.

In *Emaré*, however, any possibility that the cloak and its gems might operate in a purely natural fashion is denied. The robe does not cause the positive attitude of those who receive Emaré well when she is wearing it, and she is not honoured at all by those who seem to be most impressed by it. In this way, the poet directs us toward considering the cloak according to a theory of response to it as a sign. This may be done through reference to the three categories suggested by Augustine.

It is this distinction which allows us to confront and resolve the major disagreement over the cloak between the historicists, who read it as an emblem of the lady's inward virtues, and the functionalists, who read it as an emblem of her physical charms. Both points of view are presented by Mills in a note to his introductory description:

> The splendid cloth that is described in this passage is one of the most interesting and controversial features of the romance. . . . an attempt has been made by H. Schelp in his *Exemplarishche Romanzen* to give a predominantly moral sense to the passage (p. 105–13); his views are summarized by Dieter Mehl in his *Middle English Romance*:
>
> > 'The robe is an inseparable attribute, like her outward beauty. . . . [and] is in many ways symbolic of her inner perfections. The portraits of famous lovers can be seen as an allegorical representation of faith. . . . the precious stones, in particular, illustrate the virtues of the lady.' (p. 139)
>
> But we cannot overlook the fact that this cloth (which is in any case adorned with representations of wholly secular lovers) comes into the story just after the emperor has lost his wife and turned his thoughts to *playnge*; what is more, on two of the later occasions on which the heroine wears it as a robe, the man who sees her in it at once expresses his determination to marry her (247–9, 451–3). This makes it likely that one of its functions, at least, was to stand for the sexual attraction exerted by the lady; as French and Hale put it:
>
> > 'Though here rationalized, the cloth is a love charm—originally given to the fairy Emaré by supernatural well-wishers' (*Middle English Metrical Romances*, p. 428).[18]

Both approaches err, I believe, in focusing on what the robe itself "is" (or, in the case of the functionalists, on what it might have been in a hypothetical, mythical original version) rather than on how it *is interpreted*, and in focusing on the message and the sender to the exclusion of the receiver.

Returning again to the three categories of response, none of the participants inside the narrative falls into Augustine's first class, for no one venerates the robe idolatrously. There are no thieves who wish to possess it for its material worth and no misers who wish to own it for its own sake. There is no one in the second class either, for there is no one who gives an authoritative explication of its meaning. Emaré herself does not wear the cloak as if to say "I am virtuous" or even "I am sexually attractive"; it is imposed on her by chance (and aesthetic reasons), and it stays with her throughout the poem without any rational reflective choice on her part. Rather, all the characters in the poem belong, it would seem, in the third category, for without knowing its "meaning," they all "interpret" the cloak as a sign.

Everyone is astonished by the robe at first sight, startled by its glittering brightness (349–51, 394, 439–40, 697–99); everyone recognizes that it is an indication of something extraordinary about Emaré: "She semed non erthely wommon" (245), "She semed non erdyly thyng" (396), "And in his herte he thowgth ryght / That she was non erdyly wyght" (700–701). This state of wonder, however, leads to different responses in the story's different characters. The good characters either are slow to interpret the cloak or else respond positively and honorably toward the virtues it represents. The merchant who rescues Emaré is impressed by the cloak, but more so by Emaré herself, and his behavior toward her is above reproach. The king of Galys responds positively to the outward signs of her virtue, but is moved to marry her by her wisdom and courtesy. The bad characters, on the other hand, respond badly. Emaré's father treats the cloak as a further incitement to lust. The mother-in-law interprets unworldliness as unearthliness, and takes the cloak as token of a fiendish nature (445–47). Such bad interpretations are "useless" in the Augustinian sense, since they lead away from *caritas*.

There is a gradation among these characters regarding reconciliation with Emaré and with the virtues she embodies. The merchant is never really alienated from them, so needs no reconciliation. The husband is, in Augustine's terms, burdened by a sign which he does not fully comprehend. He is personally blameless, but he is subject to the danger of alienation because of the presence of evil in his kingdom in the person of his scheming mother. After an act of penance, however, which in this version is unmotivated because he has not acted sinfully toward Emaré or toward his mother, he is easily reconciled with Emaré. By keeping this motif of penance despite its narrative superfluity, the author signals us that the king is basically a good man. The father, of course, has further to go, since his incorrect interpretation of the sign was positively sinful; but his motivation was love, albeit a sinful love, so he too can be reconciled and can show that he has learned his lesson. The mother-in-law's interpretation was the most useless and most sinful, since it led to hatred and attempted murder. In the other versions she is executed for her duplicity and dies in her sin, but in *Emaré* even she is not totally excluded from the possibility of salvation. Further, her willingness to send the cloak with Emaré may indicate a spark of righteousness in her, for she does not destroy the sign nor does she keep it for its purely material value.

The poem is, therefore, as optimistic symbolically on the spiritual level, as it is literally. The plot allows its audience to participate vicariously in a story of adventure and undeserved hardship which culminates in a conventional happy ending. At the same time, and in the spirit of the lengthy invocation to Christ with which the poem is opened, responses to the central symbol of the gem-cloak assure us of the continuing presence of divine grace in human events and the enduring possibility of salvation for all human beings, no matter how sinful their first response to a divine message. The cloak, whatever its function may have been in earlier fairy-tale versions, is here a sign, a visible representation of that message. As such, it serves as a touchstone for determining the spiritual state and charting the spiritual progress of those who behold and respond to it.

Notes

1. Augustine, *On Christian Doctrine,* trans. D. W. Robertson, Jr. (Indianapolis: Bobbs-Merrill, 1958), p. 34 (emphasis added).

2. Ibid., pp. 86–87.

3. *Emaré,* ed. Edith Rickert, Early English Text Society (EETS), e.s. 99. All quotations are taken from this edition.

4. Frederic Godefroy, *Dictionnaire de l'Ancienne Langue Française* (Paris: Emile Bouillon, 1891–1902), entries for "esmaré" and "egaré."

5. Ibid., entry for "sagremore."

6. Translation form the Douai-Rheims version, as closest to the sense of the Vulgate.

7. Beda Venerablis, *Homilia* lxvi, *PL* 91, col. 440.

8. *Six Middle English Romances,* ed. Maldwyn Mills (London: Dent, 1973), p. 197.

9. Rickert, *Emaré,* p. 33.

10. Mills, *Six Middle English Romances,* p. 197; Rickert, *Emaré,* p. 38.

11. Rickert, *Emaré,* pp. xxii–xxvii.

12. Mills, *Six Middle English Romances,* pp. xiii–xiv.

13. Hanspeter Schelp, *Exemplarische Romanzen im Mittelengischen* (Gottingen: Vandenhoeck & Ruprecht, 1967), p. 113.

14. *English Medieval Lapidaries,* ed. J. Evans and M. Serjeanston, EETS 190, pp. 19–20.

15. Ibid., p. 27.

16. Ibid., p. 21.

17. Augustine, *On Christian Doctrine,* p. 65.

18. Mills, *Six Middle English Romances,* pp. 197–98.

PART III

CAVEAT LECTOR

Ambiguous Signs and
the Circular Semantics of Silence

EDITORS' INTRODUCTION

In the previous chapters, as we have traced the alternating discoveries of fullness or emptiness in the "husked" word, there has been a temptation to make the easy correspondence between what Peter Allen refers to as the "conventionalist theory" (names as conventions) and the postmodern theories of sign and signification. Indeed, it is not unusual to read of medieval authors' "surprisingly modern" attitudes toward the arbitrariness of sign. In his essay on the French *Le Roman de Silence*, Allen demonstrates such an awareness to be an important part of that poem's content, going so far as to note that the medieval manuscript allows some forms of ambiguity—such as the polysemousness resulting from abbreviations—that are not possible in modern writing.

Beginning with the manuscript itself as sign or text, Allen notes that the manuscript, as physical entity, is now breaking down—is metaphorically deconstructing, and hence is defying physical or intellectual categorization as either book or bundle of separate leaves. Moreover, the poem cannot really be read in the context of the other works in its manuscript or with other versions of the poem. Thus its meaning must be derived from the internal relationships inherent in the skein of its various parts rather than from external authoritative sources. And what is true of the whole is likewise true of its smallest parts. The editor, as metaphorical reader, has had to select meanings in a way that is clearly reductive, a necessity which serves to magnify our awareness of the absent presence of those meanings or readings that were passed over in favor of those which were chosen. Like Dante confounded at the final "showing" in Paradise or like Perceval bedazzled by incomprehensible brightness, we struggle to make sense of the editor's paradoxical subtitles.

Of course these observations and "metaphors" are ones which we as readers bring to the manuscript, and although they are intelligible characteristics of the present text, they are most certainly not a part of the intent of *Silence*'s author. Yet what Allen does find *within* the poem is a strongly felt theme of the vacuity of language, a medium that breaks down precisely because it enjoys no privilege and has no real core. As he points out, Silence's name is not a name at all, but is, instead, merely a "placeholder" giving the illusion of content where there is none. Instead of Joan Grimbert's "meaningful silence," we find only emptiness. And because there is no connection between signifier and signified, the characters' numerous attempts to control, manipulate, or alter reality through their manipulations of the names they use to describe it consistently come to nought. What we have is arbitrariness without the counterbalancing moral conventionality that other writers insisted was also part of language. Hence Silence's world is populated with liars, false accusers, linguistic deceivers, and a host of unsuccessful verbal manipulators whose failures result not from the restoration of the status quo through the reassertion of a positivist moral order, but rather from the inherent instability of the medium through which they work their deceptions.

As a result, far from being an abnormal state such as the product of *mis*reading or conscious manipulation, an ambiguity that confuses and deceives is seen as the natural state of language. Deceptiveness, as Edmund Reiss points out in the second essay in this chapter, is one of the most identifiable aspects of signs: "That language was implicitly deceptive and those who used it deceivers were common beliefs in the fourteenth century. . . . Throughout the Middle Ages fiction was commonly understood as synonymous with deceit, and its author viewed as no better than a liar." Such deception had its root in the fact that, whether empty or full, the sign was, in Grimbert's word, "opaque" at best.

In good medieval fashion, however, even such opacity has its purpose in the scheme of Creation. For both Allen and Reiss, albeit in two different fashions, ambiguity is linked with silence. For Allen, ambiguity ultimately hints at a lack of absolutes. It is the plenitude that points to profound emptiness. Silence—another name for linguistic emptiness, for lack of particularity or content—is simply a verbal mask for the logical but frightening extension of the nominalist rejection of the possibility of knowledge of the Absolute. Indeed, Professor Reiss—surveying works from England, France, Spain, and Italy—finds a widespread reaction to such unsettling intellectual currents:

> Responding to the developing nominalism of the time and the pervasive uncertainty of just what one could know, storytellers joined schoolmen in focusing not on truth itself but on such epistemological

matters as the essential ambiguity of signs and the inherent complexity of language.

The nature of that response, however, seems radically different. Ambiguity in the works studied by Reiss is an essentially attractive confusion, and one that might ultimately be of benefit to the reader in search of truth. For example, as Reiss notes in discussing the polyvalent term "love," ambiguity results from selecting from among the wealth of possible significations any single meaning *as opposed to* any other single meaning. Such reductive selections are, within the ordinary world, an intellectual necessity. But, like Virgil who leads Dante to the edge of Paradise, the attractive ambiguity of such signs can lead readers to the edge of truth. At the end, though, like Virgil, they too must be abandoned. Reduced to their "supplemental" status, they must be left behind. Ambiguity in signs is that which leads readers up to, but at the last minute becomes an obstacle in the way of, perceived truth. The void that such ambiguities mask is a translingual Silence, ineffable because it is beyond the finitude of sign which can only express partial meaning and, hence, lies. Interestingly enough, between the empty Silence of Allen and the full silence of Reiss, there lies, for both, the ambiguity of meaning that is their mutual starting place.

5

THE AMBIGUITY OF SILENCE
Gender, Writing, and Le Roman de Silence

PETER L. ALLEN

Texte de plaisir (text of pleasure): one that contents, fills, gives euphoria; one that comes from the culture, does not break with it, is tied to a *comfortable* practice of reading.
Texte de jouissance (text of sexual enjoyment): one that brings about a state of loss, one that causes discomfort (even a certain annoyance), shakes the historical, cultural, psychological bases of the reader, the consistency of his tastes, his values, his memories, causes a crisis in his relationship with language.[1]

Heldris de Cornüalle's thirteenth-century *Le Roman de Silence* is a *texte de jouissance*, a text that raises questions of sex and language by disconcerting its readers. Relatively new to the medievalist public, it confronts some of the major critical issues currently facing medieval studies. In studying it, we are forced to think about the claims of feminist criticism, the relationship between sexuality and literature, the role (and limitations) of the textual editor, the nature of the medieval "canon" of texts, and the modern reader's relationship with older literature. This paper will attempt to confront these issues through a discussion of the poem: by being forced to admit the inadequacy of our methods of understanding medieval writing, we will see what new possibilities of reading the text can offer us.

Heldris's poem, on the surface, seems unlikely to threaten anyone's notions of what medieval literature is all about. The text was apparently not particularly popular in the Middle Ages, since we have only one manuscript copy and the author is otherwise unknown. Even the modern (1972) edition is out of print,[2] and it is only quite recently that studies of the poem have begun to appear.[3] Furthermore, the text does not appear to challenge our ways of thinking: it does not explicitly call upon the support of such "serious" disciplines as phi-

losophy, theology, or politics. The absence of such "critical" problems is, however, in the eye of the beholder. In fact, the more closely
one looks, the more ambiguities one is likely to find. The title, whether
in Old French or modern English, is confusing: how can silence
provoke a poem, let alone a romance? The manuscript, Mi.LM.6 in
the library of the University of Nottingham, contains a number of
odd features that seem intimately related to the peculiarities of the
text. And Lewis Thorpe's editorial commentary, which seems to
present all the help a reader might wish or expect, is in fact riddled
with hypotheses and frustrations. These problems do not so much
make *Le Roman de Silence* unique as remind us of the special consideration medieval literature asks of us, its modern readers. Our models
of reading attempt to elucidate, pin down, and disambiguate medieval texts; *Le Roman de Silence* quietly, stubbornly, refuses to make
itself accessible to this kind of approach. We cannot remove the
ambiguities from the romance without breaking its silence—without
destroying the object we want to study. *Silence,* in fact, refuses to
permit itself to be studied as an "object." If we wish to read it, we are
obliged instead to make it the *subject* of our study: the text itself—
both as a poem and as a manuscript—tells us how to read. It informs
us when it will permit its meaning to be elucidated and when it will
not.[4] This kind of reading can be frustrating, if we use models
through which we attempt to master the text. If, however, we can
open ourselves up to the text and accept its ambiguities, the text will
free us to understand it better and to take pleasure in our readerly
role.

Since *Le Roman de Silence* is relatively unfamiliar, it will be useful to
begin this discussion with a summary of the plot.[5] Because of a
quarrel between two counts, King Ebain of England decrees that no
woman shall inherit property during his reign. Ebain marries one of
his retainers, Cador, to the daughter of the Count of Cornwall,
Eufemie (whose name recalls that of Ebain's queen, Eufeme). When
the Count dies, Cador accedes to his position, and, when the couple
gives birth to a daughter, the question of inheritance arises. The
parents decide to conceal the child's sex by naming her Silence,
reasoning that if she ever realizes that she is female, "Silenti*us*" can
always be changed to "Silenti*a*." Silence is brought up as a boy, but
when she reaches the age of puberty Nature and Nurture debate over
her gender. She runs away from home with a troupe of jongleurs; her
father, overcome with grief, kills all jongleurs who come to Cornwall. Silence, meanwhile, has mastered the art of poetry even better

than her masters, who threaten to kill her. She returns to Cornwall and escapes death there because she is recognized as the count's "son." Queen Eufeme, ignorant of Silence's sex, tries to seduce him (her), and, when Silence refuses, claims to have been his (her) victim. King Ebain exiles Silence to France; Eufeme substitutes for Ebain's *laissez-passer* a letter asking the King of France to execute the bearer; the fraud is revealed; and Silence is recalled. Eufeme repeats her accusation, and Ebain assigns Silence the penitential task of finding Merlin—a task only a woman can accomplish. Silence, of course, succeeds, and brings Merlin back to court, where he reveals such secrets as the heroine's true gender and the fact that Eufeme has a lover she disguises as a nun. Eufeme is executed; Silence is established as a woman; and Ebain makes her his queen.

A number of the romance's ambiguities emerge from this summary: the almost identical names of Silence's mother and her predecessor in Ebain's nuptial bed (i.e., the queen); the fact that both these names, unlike that of the heroine, valorize speech; the heroine's gender (and the Latin and French names that are used both to conceal and to reveal it to various "readers"—Silence herself, the king, ourselves); the presence of poets and poetry within the poem itself and their relationship to a poet (Silence) whose name implies the absence of all sound and, hence, poetry. The indeterminacies of this romance are not limited to details of plot, however, and it is best to begin our discussion at the beginning—namely, with an examination of the manuscript and the edition. What we find there will provide a fruitful introduction to the poem itself.

Manuscript as Sign: The Context of Silence

The manuscript that contains the unique copy of *Silence* also contains an interesting miscellancy of other literary works, including Benoît de Sainte Maure's *Roman de Troie,* Raoul de Houdenc's *La Vengeance Radiguel,* and ten fabliaux. It has, as Thorpe puts it, "been roughly used" (p. 1), and, as the binding weakens, the codex is in the process of separating into quires. Indeed, the condition of the manuscript makes it difficult for the reader to know which of the Nottingham University Library's Search Room Regulations to follow: #3, which states, "Whenever possible bound volumes should be read using a bookrest," or #5, "The arrangement of loose papers in a bundle should not be altered." MS. Mi.LM.6 totters between order and disorder, and the blue cord that ties it can only retard the speed at which this artifact of the Middle Ages obeys the law of entropy. Its content, too, seems in doubt. The case in which the manuscript is kept bears the inscription "'Le Roman de Troie,' etc.—Benoît de Sainte Maure," giving priority to the larger, more widely recognized works with which the manuscript begins; the fabliaux, which bear such intriguing titles as "D[ou] prestre ki perdi les colles" ("The Priest Who Lost His Balls"), are, however, ignored. Yet the large majority of those moderns who have edited the better-known romances were unaware that this copy existed (compare pp. 3–4), whereas the manuscript *has* been consulted by those editing the less canonical, more sexually explicit, fabliaux.

Yet even the fabliaux here are mutilated. "D[ou] prestre ki perdi les colles" is cut short, missing over two hundred of its 314 lines (compare p. 3 n.4). The last text in the manuscript, which is identified as Marie de France's "De la cugnie" (The Axe), stops after fifteen lines. But the strangest example is an anonymous fabliau that has no title in this copy but which is normally called "De la dame escolliée" (The Castrated Lady).[6] In this story a rebellious woman is cut open and two bull's testicles are produced by sleight of hand to show that her insubordination was due to inappropriate masculine characteristics: "Que ce sachiez, par ces grenotes / Sont les femes fieres et sotes" ("Know this: by these seeds / Women become proud and foolish").[7] The moral is that women must be kept in their place and must respect their rightful masters; "Dahet feme qui despit home!" ("Cursed be the woman who despises a man!").[8] This moralizing, however, ignores the fact that the fabliau's violence is completely unjustified: women cannot be "escolliées" because they have no "coilles" (balls). The dictionaries, of course, recognize this fact of physiology: they find no other occurrence of "escolliée" in the feminine. The extraordinary antifeminism of this fabliau is echoed in *Le Roman de Silence*. There Queen Eufeme is executed for expressing her sexual desire—a desire that makes her (like the classic queen of romance, Guenevere) not only an adulteress but a traitress, too, since her husband is the head of state. The outspoken woman is replaced by Silence, who gives up the male rôle (the bull's testicles) that had been attributed to her but was never truly hers. The manuscript reveals the violence men perpetrate on women, the source of whose sexual identity the fictions' men seem unable to understand.

The oddities of this manuscript are not limited to the literary

works that form a context for *Le Roman de Silence*. Fourteen illuminations illustrate the story of Silence, but they, too, leave room for
doubt. Of those that seem to be illustrations of the text, two now
have little gaps: the picture of Merlin has no face,[9] while that of
Silence, without her clothes at the point in the story when her true
gender is revealed, bears no features that distinguish the body as
female.[10] Furthermore, a series of illuminations which continues
throughout the manuscript seems to have no relation to any of the
stories. These are representations of animals and of mythical, half-
human beasts that seem to be present only to remind us that the texts
belong to the domain of fantasy.[11] Moreover, all the illuminations
replace initials in the text and force the adjacent lines of poetry to be
written as two half-lines: image and word thus compete for the
reader's attention.

To transform the text from its unruly manuscript state into an
accessible, socialized, printed work is the job of the editor. Lewis
Thorpe's work on *Silence* covers all the details that one could ask for
from an editor of a medieval text: Thorpe provides a summary of the
story, historical research, an introduction to the language, running
titles, an index of proper names and place names, and a glossary.
Despite all these efforts to make *Le Roman de Silence* a comfortable
texte de plaisir, however, the poem rejects, or, more precisely, undermines the editor's work: it demands our *jouissance* if we wish to read it
at all. Thorpe's wrestling with *Silence* illustrates the difficulties any
editor must face in attempting to move a medieval text from one
medium to another.

Medieval text production accepted many ambiguities which twen-
tieth-century editing does not. Modern conventions about language,
for example, require consistency in spelling and permit the use of
abbreviations only in a prescribed and limited number of cases. The
scribe of MS. Mi.LM.6, on the other hand, represents nasalizing
consonants indifferently by a tilde, *m,* or *n.* Thorpe writes that the
scribe "hesitates" between these choices (p. 235), but in fact, un-
disturbed by any need for consistency, the scribe blithely ignores the
idea that different spellings matter: it is the editor who hesitates. The
modern editor also finds that the text inhibits his (and our) attempts
to separate author from scribe. Thorpe's attempts to distinguish
francien forms from those that are *picard* are preceded by a caveat: "As
is true of so many other poems of the French Middle Ages, so here it
is only with the greatest difficulty that the language of the poet can be
distinguished from that of the scribe" (p. 56). The radical distinction

we moderns make between the inventor and the transmitter of texts is, for this manuscript, not a concern.

There is nothing unique about this conflation of dialects, of course, but—as with so many other features of Le Roman de Silence—it seems to echo the romance's refusal to behave according to our expectations, to fit into our categories. Distinctions between history and fiction, proper nouns and common ones, even text and absence are unsure: the editor must assume that a hole in the parchment is to be filled by *ne* (p. 236 n.1333), and the scribe changes "da Norwege" ("from Norway") into the meaningless "danor wege": the place we know as "Norway" was nothing but a linguistic fantasy to the copyist (p. 235 n.146). Moreover, our attempts to relate the characters to anything we recognize as history are fruitless (p. 26). Even the author, Heldris de Cornüalle, is named nowhere but in his poem, and the description Thorpe proposes is shadowy at best:

> If what I have written is accepted, then Heldris is established as a professional lay poet of the second half of the thirteenth century, who lived in all probability near to the present-day frontier between France and Belgium where Nord marches with Hainaut, but who had some connexion yet to be determined either with the Duchy of Cornwall or with Cornuaille or with the hamlet La Cornualle and who at the same time had some reason for featuring Château-Landon and Beaumont-en-Gâtinais in his poem. (p. 17)

Not only are Heldris's relations with the external world multiple and ambiguous, but he, like his poem, exists on the borders, between France and Belgium, between fiction and history.

Not only are we unable to distinguish between author and scribe and between historical characters and fictional ones, but we cannot even learn the history of the text as physical object from the inscriptions we can read in it. These notes, presumably made by the volume's owners, are inconclusive:

> F 244r, which is otherwise blank, has in the left-hand upper corner a scribbled note in what appears to be a northern French hand of the fourteenth century: *le ior de mardi / por donpere*. . . . It is ironic that we know the day in the week when something was to happen at Dompierre-du-Chemin, but not the month or year, or, indeed, what the event was! (p. 11)

By this point it is, no doubt, manifest that any attempt to relate *Le Roman de Silence* to the world outside its fiction is unlikely to succeed. Even our attempts to enter the text on strictly literary terms may be stymied if they try (consciously or not) to simplify the poem. Thus the running titles provided by the editor to guide the reader reduce Silence to a single gender (e.g. "Silence Considers Her Situation," p. 135), whereas the poet reserves the ungrammatical and unnatural but fictionally accurate privilege of calling his hero(ine) "le vallet ki ert meschine" (the youth who was a maiden [line 3704 and passim]).[12] Elsewhere the titles flirt with absurdity, as when they announce "Silence Has Great Success as a Minstrel" (p. 143) or "Cador Prepares to Execute Silence" (p. 153). These signposts are more likely to trip the reader up than to point him or her in the right direction: the poem refuses to be reduced to a single meaning.

Silence as Sign: The Limits of Language

That so much ambiguity should accrete around this text is not, I believe, entirely coincidental. It seems rather that the circumstances under which we meet the poem actually reflect the fundamental cracks and strains present in the romance itself—cracks and strains that affect the very materials out of which this piece of literature is constructed, namely words and gender. For writing about silence is an oxymoron, and the poem exists only because language exists at a second degree from the things it represents: if we had no word that meant "silence," we could not use the lack of a word to name a character. As it is, the titles of MS. Mi.LM.6 strain our means of communication; to add *"Le Roman de _____"* to "[De la dame escolliée]" would be too much—or not enough—for us to understand. Ambiguity promotes paradox, and it is within this gap, between language and meaning, between history and fiction, that this text exists.

Even writing, the means by which the romance is transmitted to us, is called into question on numerous occasions within the poem. The word *cartre* (paper) is used as a homophonic rhyme with *cartre* (prison) (lines 4959–60), and the word *gloze* is twisted in two different directions: rhyming twice with forms of *ozer* (to dare), it seems to mean once "jealous" (a form of *jalos/gelos* not otherwise recorded), and once "to dispute" (an extension of the more common "to criticize," itself an extension of "to gloss"). The greatest perversion of writing in the poem is Queen Eufeme's substitution of letters: for the letter from the king asking that Silence be welcomed at the French court, she exchanges one asking that the bearer be executed.[13] The Queen, however, knows that any definite charge is subject to disproof, so she uses a silent accusation to silence Silence:

> De par roi Ebayn, son segnor,
> Escrist al roi de France un brief
> Qu'il tolle al message le cief
> Qui les letres a lui enporte;
> Que il por rien ne l'en deporte,
> Car il a fait al roi tel honte
> Qu'il ne le violt pas metre en conte.
> (lines 4320–26)

(On behalf of Ebain, her lord, she writes the king of France a letter [saying] that he should cut off the head of the messenger who carries the letter to him; that he not spare him this for any reason, since he has caused such shame to the king that he does not want to recount it.)

[S]he who lives by the sword shall die by the sword, however, and Eufeme's accusation returns to persecute its maker: the count of Clermont advises the French king that he should not punish anyone whose crime he does not know, and eventually, as the plot is untangled, it is Eufeme who is executed—poetic justice for her abuse of writing.

Another key point in the romance's treatment of language is its discussions of the heroine's name, which is more a placeholder for a name than a real proper noun. Within this name, which seems to mean nothing, is contained Silence's whole story: it could be translated as "a-woman-whose-parents-had-to-give-her-a-name-that-doesn't-reveal-her-gender-because-the-king-had-forbidden-women-to-inherit-property-because-etc.-etc." This name, empty of significance but full of meaning, is the subject of much linguistic play. When the child is born, everybody gathers in the palace hall, wanting to know whether it is male or female. The child's aunt, who has been enlisted to keep its gender a secret, announces "Ma dame n'a mestier de noise!'" ("My lady has no need of noise!" [line 1998]). This announcement is a riddle that conceals its own answer, since the opposite of *noise* (in Old French or modern English) is *silence*. The

French name the child's parents choose for her masks with the genderless desinence *-e* the choice they would have been forced to make in Latin: "Silence" is a nominal zero, a placeholder for a name.

> "Sel faisons apieler Scilense
> El non de Sainte Paciense,
> Por cho que silensce tolt anse.[14]
> Que Jhesus Cris par sa poissance
> Le nos doinst celer et taisir,
> Ensi com lui est a plaizir!
> Mellor consel trover n'i puis.
> Il iert només Scilenscius;
> Et s'il avient par aventure
> Al descovrir de sa nature
> Nos muerons cest -us en -a,
> S'avra a non Scilencia.
> Se nos li tolons dont cest -us
> Nos li donrons natural us,
> Car cis -us est contre nature,
> Mais l'altres seroit par nature."
>   (lines 2067–82)

("So let us have her called 'Silence,' in the name of Saint Patience, because silence relieves all anxiety. May Jesus Christ by his power permit us to conceal it and keep it quiet! I can find no better plan. He will be named Silentius; and if it should happen that her nature is discovered, we will change the "-us" into an "-a", so she will have the name Silentia. So if we take this "-us" away from her, we will give her her natural usage, since this "-us" is against nature, but the other one would be natural.")

Silence's gender depends, then, not on nature but on custom or usage *(us)*. When she reaches puberty, Nature and Nurture debate the issue, but reach no resolution; and when Silence escapes with the jongleurs, she takes a pseudonym (Malduit) which, like her real name, reveals the confusion in which she finds herself: "Car il [i.e., Silence] se tient moult por mal duit, / Moult mal apris lonc sa nature" (For he [i.e., Silence] considers himself very badly taught, very badly instructed as to his nature [lines 3178–79]).

Names in this poem are not revealing: they hold back information, rather than expose it. Identity is hidden, or absent, or subject exclusively to the convenience of the text: one character's name, in fact, seems to have been invented simply to form a rhyme.[15] Queen Eufeme, whose name suggests that speech is positive, uses language for treacherous purposes and is finally silenced by death. Silence, too, is named to hide her identity, to conform to King Ebain's privileging of male over female. This submission of identity to convenience is an extreme statement of the "conventionalist" theory of naming, formulated early in Western literary tradition by Plato's character Hermogenes:

> "Whatever anyone calls anything, that is its correct name: and if one changes it for another, and abandons the former name, the new one is no less correct than the old—just as when we change the names of our slaves. For nothing has its name by nature, but only by usage and custom."[16]

The relationship of usage and custom to language is precisely what is at issue in *Silence*. Silence, by means of an evasive name, must try to escape the sentences of death and disinheritance which are laid down for her, but all her efforts to escape from the system only reveal her inability to do so. When she becomes a jongleur, she escapes silence, but nearly becomes the victim of her teachers when she surpasses them. All poets are banned from her native land, but nonetheless she returns. Her femaleness, which her parents attempt to cover up with language, is eventually reimposed on her by stripping away the male appendages (her clothes, the "-us" of her name) she had assumed. This reversion to femininity, however, means a new submission to the king's power—this time not legislative but sexual. King and parents exercise the power of the masters, the Cratylistic power to endow people with names, and to determine their destiny by speech. In fact, King Ebain explicitly exalts the ideal of the Silent Woman (often portrayed, of course, as a woman who has been decapitated):

> "Sens de feme gist en taisir.
> Si m'aït Dex, si com jo pens,
> Uns muials puet conter lor sens,
> Car femes n'ont sens que mais un,
> C'est taisirs."
>
> (lines 6399–6403)

("Woman's sense lies in being silent. So help me God, I think that a
mute could recount all their sense, since women have only one sense,
namely, being silent.")

Masculine speech is power; feminine speech (symbolized by Queen
Eufeme) is ripped apart, condemned to death (lines 6651–57).[17] All
the male characters the poem can imagine applaud the death of female
speech and the feminization and coronation of Silence:[18]

> Nus hom qui fust ne plaint Eufeme.
> Silence atornent come feme.
> Segnor, que vos diroie plus?
> Ains ot a non Scilensiüs:
> Ostés est -us, mis i est -a,
> Si est només Scilentiä.
>
> (lines 6663–68)

(No man alive lamented Eufeme. They dress Silence up as a woman.
Lords, what should I tell you? Before, her name was Silentius: the
"-us" is removed, an "-a" attached, and he is named Silentia.)

This removal of *-us* is reminiscent of nothing so much as the fictitious
castration of the "[Dame escoilliée]" of the fabliau: neither she nor
Silence ever really had any testicles, yet it is essential to the men in
their stories to "castrate" them.

That we should find Heldris performing surgery on suffixes is
hardly surprising in this text, where a disintegrating manuscript
encloses poems without titles and eunuch fabliaux. Confusion about
names and genders, however, is only a subset of the most important
ambiguity *Le Roman de Silence* confronts—that of language and uni-
valent discourse. Early in the romance the author admits that his
efforts towards artistry must at times distance his work from that
which he considers "true," but suggests that this distance, while
impermissible in Latin, is acceptable in *Romans*.

> Comence chi tels aventure
> C'ainques n'oïstes tele en livre.
> Qu'en latin escrite lizons,
> En romans si le vos disons.
> Jo ne di pas que n'i ajoigne

Avoic le voir sovent mençoigne
Por le conte miols acesmer:
Mais se jel puis a droit esmer
N'i netrai rien qui m'uevre enpire
Ne del voir nen iert mos a dire
Car la verté ne doi taisir.
(lines 1658–69)[19]

(Here begins an adventure such as you've never heard of in a book. That which we read written in Latin we will tell to you in *Romans*. I do not say that I do not often add lies to the truth in order to adorn the story: but if I can rightly judge, I will not put into it anything that will make my work worse, nor shall there be less of the truth to tell, since I should not keep the truth silent.)

Walter Ong and Sandra Gilbert and Susan Gubar have called Latin the "masculine" discourse of the Middle Ages and the vernacular languages the period's "feminine" mode of communication.[20] In this case, however, *Romans* is not so much a feminine language as a language that avoids definitions of gender. Thus the significant distinction between "Silenti*us*" and "Silenti*a*" (which the heroine's parents used to paper over the cracks in their daughter's identity [lines 2067–82] and which is reversed when Silence becomes queen) pertains only to Latin, the language Heldris and his audience *read (lisons);* it is irrelevant to *Romans,* the language they *speak (disons)*. *Romans* does not feminize communication: it simply tolerates certain ambiguities about gender that Latin does not. This is why Heldris uses it in composing his *roman,* a fiction that is all about ambiguity: Latin makes a useful source, but doesn't entertain. This association of the ambiguities of vernacular language with fiction recalls Jean Bodel's statement that "li conte de Bretaigne sont si vain et plaisant" ("the tales of Brittany are so meaningless, so pleasant"),[21] and Dante's "ambages pulcherrime Arturi regis" ("most beautiful ambiguities of Arthur the king").[22]

The ambiguity, the emptiness of the text: in these lacks lies the importance of *Le Roman de Silence.* The gaps in the work are what draw us to it: as Barthes enquires, "L'endroit le plus érotique d'un corps n'est-il pas là où le vêtement bâille?" ("Isn't the most erotic part of a body the place where the clothing parts?").[23] *Silence* is a text that refuses our violence but welcomes our *jouissance.* Its refusal can be read in various ways—as a characteristic of female writing (writing *about* women, if not *by* them) unwilling to accommodate itself to male readings; as a Marxist text refusing to accept capitalist modes of textual diffusion; as a medieval "other" that will not bow to modern assumptions; as a Freudian polymorphous perversity that our categories of thought about sex and gender cannot encompass, etc., all depending on our critical assumptions. These refusals share a common basis: they insist on the text's right to remain silent, to hold its ambiguity. To remove ambiguity from this text means to tear it, to falsify it, to lose its essence. Yet we can read the poem and enjoy it if we permit it, at the same time, to read *us*—to question the assumptions with which we teachers, students, readers, editors approach medieval literature. This literature cannot be forced to give up its secrets, if only for the reason that so many of these secrets are ambiguities or silences. We cannot recreate the historical context of the poem; all we can find is a Tuesday in a week and a year which can never be known. We cannot effectively summarize, we cannot completely translate. We cannot, in short, make our reading "comfortable"; we cannot subject the text to ourselves. Yet we can, and perhaps must, read and be read, enter into the world of *Romans,* of the *roman,* and see what we can experience of mute *-e* in the gap between *-us* and *-a,* in the ambiguity of silence.

Notes

1. "Texte de plaisir: celui qui contente, emplit, donne de l'euphorie; celui qui vient de la culture, ne rompt pas avec elle, est lié à une pratique *confortable* de la lecture. Texte de jouissance: celui qui met en état de perte, celui qui déconforte (peut-être jusqu'à un certain ennui), fait vaciller les assises historiques, culturelles, psychologiques, du lecteur, la consistance de ses goûts, de ses valeurs, et de ses souvenirs, met en crise son rapport au langage," Roland Barthes, *Le Plaisir du texte* (Paris: Les Editions du Seuil, 1973), pp. 25–26. This translation and all others in the essay are my own.

2. Paradoxically, however, it is not unavailable: as of this writing the publisher still has a few copies on its shelf: Heldris de Cornüalle, *Le Roman de Silence,* ed. Lewis Thorpe (Cambridge: W. Heffer & Sons, Ltd., 1972). All references to this edition will be given in the text: those to the romance itself will be given by line numbers, those to the editorial material by page number.

3. Articles on the poem are beginning to appear. See Kate M. Cooper, "Elle and *L:* Sexualized Textuality in *Le Roman de Silence"* and Michèle Perret, "Travesties et

transsexuelles: Ydes, Silence, Grisandole, Blanchandine," both in *Romance Notes* 25, 3 (Spring, 1985) and R. Howard Bloch, "Silence and Holes: The *Roman de Silence* and the Art of the Trouvère," *Yale French Studies* 70 (1986). I am indebted to Bloch's article for a number of ideas.

4. Barthes, *Le Plaisir du texte:* "Le texte est un objet fétiche et ce fétiche me désire" (p. 45). On the text's autonomy, compare also Robert S. Sturges, "Interpretation as Action: the Reader in Late Medieval Narrative," *DAI* 40 (1980): 5856A.

5. This summary is a reduction of that on pages 17–22 of Thorpe's edition.

6. "De la dame escolliée," in Anatole de Montaiglon and Gaston Raynaud, eds., *Recueil général et complet des fabliaux des XIIIe et XIVe siècles* (1890; reprint, New York: Burt Franklin [n.d.]), vol. 6, pp. 95–116.

7. "De la dame," vv. 602–3.

8. "De la dame," v. 618.

9. University of Nottingham MS. Mi.LM.6, fol. 221.

10. MS. Mi.LM.6, fol. 222v.

11. These figures occur on fols. 14v, 55v, 92v, 158v, 213, 217, 218v, 227, 232v, 239, 269, and 328. Fol. 157 contains the beginning of Gautier d'Arras's *Ille et Galeron* and an illumination of a ram bearing a staff with a cross and a flag. Thorpe suggests that the illuminations of animals are by a different hand from those illustrating the *Roman de Silence* (p. 6).

12. Questions of nature and gender abound in the romance, for the characters as well as for the readers. When Silence rejects Queen Eufeme's advances, the queen infers by this sign that the hero(ine) must be a (male) homosexual: "Certes, gel croi bien a erite / Quant jo li mostrai mes costés, / Que il me dist, 'Por Deu, ostés!' / Ene fu cho moult bone ensaigne / Qu'il despist femes et desdaigne?'" ("I certainly think he is a homosexual, for when I showed him my side, he said to me, 'For God's sake, take it away!' Wasn't this a very good sign that he despises and disdains women?") She uses the word *erites,* which derives its secondary meaning ("homosexual") from its primary meaning ("heretic"). Compare Bloch, "Silence and Holes," and Alain de Lille's *De planctu naturae* for further discussion of "right" religion, grammar, and sexuality. The *Roman de Silence* questions our concepts of sex rôles as much as it questions our concepts of language.

13. This passage is a reminiscence *avant la lettre* of the epistle Rosencrantz and Guildenstern bear in Shakespeare's and Stoppard's plays, as well as of the substitution in Poe's "Purloined Letter" and the literary-critical exchange of documents between Derrida, Lacan, and their readers over that short story.

14. Felix Lecoy changes this to "ance": "Corrections, *Le Roman de Silence* d'Heldris de Cornüalle," *Romania* 99 (1978): 117. Though it seems reasonable, I find no corroboration for Thorpe's gloss "anxiety" in either Godefroy or Tobler-Lommatzsch. I am grateful to Professor Michel-André Bossy for the reference to Lecoy's article, which revises Thorpe's edition of the poem thoroughly and should be used in any study of *Silence.*

15. "Ades," v. 583, and note, p. 241.

16. Plato, *Cratylus,* in *The Dialogues of Plato,* trans. Benjamin Jowett, 3rd ed. (Oxford: Oxford University Press, 1892), 384d.

17. Compare Monique Wittig, *Les Guérillières,* trans. David Le Vay (New York: Avon, 1973): "Unhappy one, men have expelled you from the world of symbols and yet they have given you names, they have called you slave, you unhappy slave. Masters, they have exercised their right to master. They write, of their authority to

accord names, that it goes back so far that the origin of language itself may be considered an act of authority emanating from those who dominate. . . . the language you speak is made up of words that are killing you," as cited by Sandra M. Gilbert and Susan Gubar, "Sexual Linguistics: Gender, Language, and Sexuality," *New Literary History* 16 (1985): 517.

18. Gilbert and Gubar (p. 521) cite Xavière Gauthier to similar ends: " 'as long as women remain silent'—that is, as long as women remain linguistically 'female'—'they will be outside the historical process. But if they begin to speak and write as men do, they will enter history subdued and alienated' " ("Existe-t-il une écriture de femme?", trans. Marilyn A. August, in *New French Feminisms,* ed. Elaine Marks and Isabelle de Courtivron [Amherst, Mass.: University of Massachusetts Press, 1980]).

19. Lecoy removes the period from line 1657, which reads, *"De Cador, de s'en-gendreüre,"* which, Lecoy states, *"se rapporte à ce qui suit,"* "Corrections," p. 116.

20. "It becomes necessary to speculate that since the thirteenth and fourteenth centuries male writers may have thought linguistic culture to be holding linguistic anarchy at bay because they have had to translate the 'high themes' of the classics into what they fear is a low language whose very accessibility might seem to vulgarize their noble subjects" (Gilbert and Gubar, p. 532); compare also Walter J. Ong, *Fighting for Life* (Ithaca: Cornell University Press, 1981), p. 37.

21. Jean Bodel, *Les Saisnes,* ed. F. Menzel and E. Stengel (Marburg, 1906), v. 9.

22. Dante, *Convivio,* 4.10.

23. Barthes, *Le Plaisir du texte,* p. 19.

6

AMBIGUOUS SIGNS AND AUTHORIAL DECEPTIONS IN FOURTEENTH-CENTURY FICTIONS

EDMUND REISS

Early in the *Libro de Buen Amor*, the Archpriest of Hita presents his audience with an amusing story showing the difficulty of understanding signs. This takes the form of a contest between the Greeks and the Romans.

Not wishing to teach laws to the ignorant Romans who have requested them, the Greeks propose a debate, ostensibly to determine if the Romans deserve to be taught laws. Since the Romans do not understand the Greek tongue, the debate must be in sign language. Each side chooses a representative, the Greeks a learned scholar and the Romans an ignorant lout, whom they tell to make whatever gestures he feels inspired to make. The debate begins with the Greek holding up his first finger. The Roman replies by holding up his thumb and first two fingers. The Greek then extends his open palm, and in response the Roman thrusts out his clenched fist. At this point the Greek ends the debate, saying that the Romans have indeed demonstrated their worthiness to receive laws.

Later, the Greek scholar is asked to translate the signs he and the Roman had used. According to him, his one finger indicated a belief in one God, and the Roman's three fingers affirmed that this God was One in Three Persons. The Greek's open palm suggested that all was by the will of God, and the Roman's fist acknowledged that God held everything in his power. Seeing the extent of the Romans' understanding, the Greek thus realized that the Romans were capable of receiving laws.

The Roman lout is then asked for his interpretation of the gestures. For him, the Greek's one finger indicated an intention to gouge the Roman's eye. By answering with two fingers and thumb, the Roman threatened to smash the Greek's two eyes and teeth. The Greek's open

113

palm signified his threat to slap the Roman, and the Roman's fist his punch in retaliation. At that point, seeing that the Roman would not be daunted, the Greek stopped making threats.[1]

By pointing to the ambiguity of signs at the very outset of his *Libro de Buen Amor*, the Archpriest alerts his readers to the difficulty of determining meaning in the work that follows. Notwithstanding the conventional medieval view that words are signposts offering guidance to man in his journey through life, by the late Middle Ages language was viewed as particularly susceptible to misinterpretation. Augustine had demonstrated not only that signs could not be taken at face value, but that they were often contrary or diverse.[2] And although the poets' *integumentum*, or enigmatic mode of expression, could serve to attract audiences to the truth within their words, it did not necessarily offer immediate or universal understanding. The shell containing the kernel of truth might well be tough to crack.

Moreover, the surface of a work might be purposely inaccessible. On the basis of Jesus' use of parables, Christian writers had long employed esoteric expression as a way of excluding the uninitiated.[3] When Boethius defended the difficult language of his tractates on Christian doctrine, he stressed that these *opuscula sacra* were to be "understood only by those who deserve to understand."[4] And on the authority of classical rhetoric, medieval writers consciously employed multiple meanings and ambiguity.[5] In the twelfth century, Marie de France, citing Priscian, traced her literary method back to the ancients who spoke obscurely in their books ("assez oscurement diseient") so that those who came after them might, through glossing the letter, supply additional meaning.[6]

The late Middle Ages knew well that everything was written, as Horace noted, for profit or entertainment ("aut prodesse, aut delectare"), or, as St. Paul affirmed, for our edification ("ad nostram doctrinam").[7] But by the fourteenth century, writers were less interested in restating moral and religious commonplaces than in investigating the possibilities and limitations of language. Responding to the developing nominalism of the time and the pervasive uncertainty as to exactly what one could know, storytellers joined schoolmen in focusing not on truth itelf but on such epistemological matters as the essential ambiguity of signs and the inherent complexity of language. Along with speculative grammarians, poets explored processes of signification and modifications of meaning. And, along with semioticians, fiction writers investigated modes of signifying ways in which language altered concepts of reality. For those involved with the word, the emphasis was on inference, equivocation, and various kinds of conundrums or *aenigmata*.[8]

The Sign Ambiguous

That language was implicitly deceptive and those who used it deceivers were common beliefs in the fourteenth century, as may be seen in one of the fabliaux in Chaucer's *Canterbury Tales*. Addressing the two students who have failed to prevent his deceiving them, the anti-intellectual miller in the *Reeve's Tale* scornfully derides school-men who employ words to twist reality. Responding to the students' request for lodging, he calls attention to the small size of his house and suggests they employ their "lerned art" and "by argumentes" make a place twenty feet wide seem like a mile. If his house is not large enough, he mockingly continues, they could make it roomier "with speche, as is youre gise" (I, 4122–26).[9] Although the miller is here commenting on the practices of logicians in particular, his criticism could be applied as well to poets and fiction writers.

Given the ambivalence of human signs, texts were understood in the fourteenth century as simultaneously concealing and revealing. We may see an example of this in Dante's *Paradiso*, when the narrator asks his ancestor Cacciaguida to tell what is in store for him. Cacciaguida responds not ambiguously ("né per ambage") but clearly and precisely ("per chiare parole e con preciso / latin," 17: 31–35).[10] While Dante's phrasing contrasts the ambiguous, enigmatic language of pagan oracles with plain, open speech, it also associates Cacciaguida with these oracles. Ancient prophecy, providing a context for Cacciaguida's speech, thus gives his words additional significance.

Moreover, as Dante presents him, Cacciaguida is simultaneously hidden and manifested by his own smile ("chiuso e parvente del suo proprio riso," 36). As his words contain what had been both hidden in pagan oracular "ambage" and manifested in Christian revelation, so is he himself at once concealed and revealed. That is, in Dante's rhetorically balanced phrasing, Cacciaguida speaks not obscurely but clearly; and he is both hidden and open. The apparent contradiction is purposeful.

Like Cacciaguida, late medieval works of literature may be re-garded as simultaneously concealing and revealing. The wisdom they contain goes beyond what Augustine had termed "this labor of words."[11] As defined by Nicholas of Cusa in the fifteenth century, wisdom (sapientia) is "utterly unknowable and unspeakable in all language." While being "unaffirmable in all affirmation" and "undeniable in all negation," paradoxically, because it is inexpressible, "there can be no limit to the means of expressing it."[12] Beyond knowledge and ordinary understanding, wisdom must be searched out and understood. And this, as late medieval authors frequently insisted, was the responsibility of the reader.

Following his account of the debate between the Greeks and the Romans, the Archpriest of Hita states that his work is subtle ("sotil") and cryptic ("encobierto," 65), and calls upon his reader to fathom out the true, or sure, meanings ("señales ciertas") of his veiled terms ("razones encobiertas," 68). Although his text speaks to everyone, those who are wise ("los cuerdos") will discern his wisdom ("cordura," 67). The Archpriest is not interested so much in teaching as in reaching those capable of using what he has to offer. In so doing, he is not alone.

The Archpriest's contemporary, Juan Manuel, offers much the same view when, in the prologue to his collection of tales, El Conde Lucanor, he admonishes readers who, unable to understand well, do not catch his subtle meanings ("las cosas sotiles").[13] Similarly, throughout his Commedia, Dante calls the attention of his perceptive readers, those "who have good understanding" ("li'ntelletti sani"), to "the teaching hidden beneath the veil" of his verses ("la dottrina che s'asconde / sotto 'l velame delli versi strani"). He warns them that they must sharpen their eyes in order to pass within the subtle veil of his allegory to truth.[14]

Medieval writers also ask their readers not to be taken in by the seemingly trivial surfaces of their work. In the Conclusione dell'Autore at the end of his Decameron, Boccaccio stresses that those who properly read his amusing tales will find them useful and virtuous ("utile e oneste").[15] And in his Canterbury Tales, Chaucer insists that his readers distinguish the doctryne he offers from the myrthe. In the words of his Nun's Priest, "Taketh the fruyt, and lat the chaf be stille" (VII, 3443). In making their point, however, both Boccaccio, who would ameliorate his improper novelle, and Chaucer, who would elevate his barnyard tale of the Cock and the Fox, employ voices quite different from those they used in the relevant fictions.

At other times when the medieval writer urges his readers to go beyond the appearance of trivia, his words take the form of the trivia. For instance, Chrétien de Troyes, at the beginning of his Erec et Enide, alerts his audience to the seriousness of what might otherwise be taken for a simple adventure story. But, incongruously, his authority for the point that many things are worth more than supposed is a folk saying.[16] As Chrétien emphasizes in his initial words, "li vilains dit," he is paradoxically employing a popular saying to show that his treatment of a popular story is not popular at all. He goes on to insist that the "molt bele conjointure" he derives from traditional material is the result of his speaking well and teaching the right (11–14).

Whatever its precise meaning, Crétien's "conjointure" represents his achievement, and, in pointing to it, he is in accord with later medieval writers who likewise call attention to the thing of value hidden beneath their fictions. It is no accident that the standard medieval collection of Aesop's fables, following Romulus's ninth-century Latin version, begins with the story of the cock who, searching for corn to eat, finds a precious stone. Unable to use this gem, the cock discards it. The glosses on this fable, though varied, typically have to do with understanding. As given by William Caxton in his fifteenth-century English translation, the gloss likens the cock to "the fool" who does not care about wisdom, and the precious stone to the "fayre and playsaunt book" at hand.[17] Showing that things may well be worth more than supposed, the fable demonstrates the need to discern true value. Like the popular saying invoked by Chrétien at the beginning of his *Erec et Enide*, this fable (the first in the medieval Aesop, and perhaps the basis of Chrétien's allusion), emphasizes that its readers must perceive better than the cock did.

The Sign Misunderstood

Whereas medieval writers could justify retelling the Aesopian fables by appealing to the passage in Job urging man to "ask the beasts, and they will teach you,"[18] the animals in their tales regularly misunderstand. In fact, fables, like fabliaux, usually turn on the misunderstanding of signs. Even the shortest of all extant fabliaux, Haiseau's eighteen-line "The Priest and the Sheep" ("Le Prestre et le Mouton")—which might be considered fable as well as fabliau—concerns the misunderstanding of a sign. While a priest is in bed with a lady, his sheep, seeing him raise his tonsured head, takes this as a sign to charge and butts the priest's head.[19] Haiseau's explicit *moralitas*, that one should watch out for everything ("il se fet bon de tot garder," 18), is unexpected. Hardly addressing the issues raised in the tale, it suggests that misunderstanding extends even to the gloss itself.

Without belaboring the pervasiveness of misunderstanding in these popular works, we may look at the fable of "The Priest and the Wolf" ("Del prestre e del lu"), ascribed to Marie de France. This fable is particularly pertinent in that it concerns not only misunderstanding but language. In attempting to teach the wolf his letters, the priest has him repeat each letter. After "C" the priest tells him to try by himself to say them, or at least what they seem to him ("di que te semble"). The wolf agrees, but what he says is "Aignel" ("Lamb"), not "ABC."[20] This, as the priest realizes, is what is actually on his mind. Notwithstanding the inadequate *moralitas*, which concludes that often one's thoughts are revealed through the mouth, the fable also suggests that there may be more to what one says than one admits or even knows. The full meaning of a sign lies beyond its obvious significance; and, furthermore, the full meaning of a work lies not only beyond the fictions it offers but any explicit interpretation of these fictions as well.

Recognizing the existence of meaningful signs and fictions and then understanding their complex signification is what much medieval literature is finally about. An inescapable point of the Grail story, even in its basic form as found in Chrétien and Wolfram von Eschenbach, is that one must avoid being like the *Dümmling* Perceval, who fails to ascertain the meanings of the mysteries he is permitted to witness.[21] As retold in the thirteenth-century *Queste del Saint Graal*, the story serves as a guide to these mysteries. In the steps of Augustine, who had insisted that man both recognize signs and know their significance, the Cistercian author of the *Queste* effectively reiterates the need for man to read the signs offered him.[22] To be the successful Grail quester, one must learn to discern and comprehend ambiguous and apparently contradictory signs. Only after passing through ambiguity and perplexity to wisdom—what Wolfram represents as the passage from *tumpheit* to *wisheit*—is one able to experience the mystery of the Grail. Like the Beatific Vision at the end of Dante's *Commedia*, it is only for those able to see clearly.

Most frequently, medieval writings showing man on his journey through this world focus not on the vision that is the result of insight, but on the difficulties of comprehension. In accord with the thirteenth-century *Roman de la Rose*, dream allegories depicting the narrator in a never-never land peopled by ambiguous and contradictory allegorical figures tend to conclude with the narrator failing to profit from his vision or with the dreamer awakening bewildered.[23] And literary dialogues and debates, in the tradition of Abelard's *Sic et Non*, not only offer alternatives as equivalents but also end inconclusively. Frequently, where the debate is left unresolved, as in the twelfth-century *The Owl and the Nightingale*, the sense is that neither of the views offered is preferable and even that both views are inadequate.[24]

Although the Grail questers and Dante succeed in breaking through the complexities and ambiguities facing them in their journeys, most often in later medieval narrative the struggle of man to understand is presented as an end in itself, with no obvious victory. In William Langland's *Piers Plowman*, one vision leads to another, and at the end, especially in the B and C versions, the narrator is still searching for that which will take him to Truth. Rather than slough off meanings, signs in this complex poem tend to accumulate them. The figure of Piers Plowman becomes more symbolically intricate the further one reads in the poem; and the ideals represented by Dowel, Dobet, and Dobest accrete significances each time they are mentioned, much like the Kingdom of Heaven in the parables offered in the Gospel of Matthew.

At the end of *Piers Plowman*, the narrator, Will, still searching for Truth, is in a real sense no closer to it than he was at the outset when he asked Holy Church for instruction about Truth and Falsehood. In Langland's view, this world, the "fair feeld ful of folk" that is the setting of his poem, is peopled with "Fals and Favel, and hire feeres manye."[25] Falsehood and Fable (that is, Deception), together with their many companions, are so much the way of this world that the narrator is unable to be free of them.

Similarly, in the *Queste del Saint Graal*—notwithstanding the success of Galahad, Perceval, Bors, and, to a lesser extent, Lancelot in viewing the Grail—the emphasis is not on success but on frustration, waste, even failure. Not only is the Grail taken away from the world, which has been unable to use it properly, but the quest for it has not changed the world. Only the successful few, who have sampled the joys beyond the ambiguities of this world, are any different; and two of these, Galahad and Perceval, prefer not to continue living in this confused world. Moreover, as incorporated in the so-called Vulgate Cycle of Arthurian romances, the *Queste* leads to the *Mort Artu*, where, after returning to Arthur's court, Lancelot falls back into his old sinful ways. Even with the example of these knights who have experienced the reality of the Divine Mysteries, the court fails to move beyond confusion, and the fall of Camelot is imminent. In the realm of fortune and change, where ambiguity is the norm and definitive signification is impossible, the truths of the Grail lack point and purpose.

The Sign Deceptive

Even when offered Truth, one still may not know it or know what to do with it, and the Archpriest of Hita thus calls upon the reader to understand his words and ponder their significance ("Entiende bien mis dichos e piensa la sentencia," 46). Doing so, the reader may thus avoid what happened to the wise man from Greece. By this the Archpriest apparently means that understanding will keep one from being deceived. But the deception in the sign contest is even more complex than it first appeared to be.

On the one hand, although the Archpriest implies that the Romans were perpetrators of the deception, is this really so? Were not the Greeks, who proposed the debate knowing that the Romans were incapable of debating, actually the ones who intended to deceive? The Romans, realizing that they themselves were unlearned and unable to compete with the Greeks, merely told their representative to make whatever gestures ("signos") God might inspire him to make (51). If anything, they showed faith that God would turn these signs to good. More accurately, the deception of the wise man from Greece may have actually been self-deception. Though both he and the Roman lout interpreted the gestures according to their individual systems of values, the Greek, by announcing that the Romans had proved they deserved laws, assumed that his individual interpretation was both true and correct for everyone.

On the other hand, as presented by the Archpriest, law is synonymous with learning or knowledge (46–47), and this is precisely what the Romans lack. Though accidentally successful in getting the Greeks to transmit laws to them, may the Romans not have deceived themselves in thinking that they were capable of understanding or using this knowledge? Moreover, as the Middle Ages learned from Aristotle, law could exist only among those possessing a sense of right and wrong. The Romans' subterfuge in the contest may well demonstrate their implicit inability to comprehend law, whose basis must be a desire for justice, defined by Aristotle as "complete virtue."[26]

What we see in the debate between the Greeks and the Romans is a tour de force of deception. While actually showing problems of signification, the contest also reveals the failure to see clearly. And while functioning as an object lesson in the perils of misinterpretation, it also suggests that even misinterpretation may operate for the good. Deception, that which the Archpriest warns against, is paradoxically his method and a pervasive theme of his work. In its ambiguity of signs and complexity of interpretation, the *Libro de Buen Amor* is similar to several other important fourteenth-century texts.

For instance, the fifty-one stories told by Juan Manuel in his *El Conde Lucanor*, while presented as "enxiemplos" designed to give one better understanding, are very much concerned with deception. The first story is of a king who, deceived into distrusting his favorite, decides to test him. The favorite passes the test, but only because he is warned of the king's trickery. His success is actually due to his deceiving the king, the intended deceiver. Interestingly, this story of deception is told to Count Lucanor by his own favorite, Patronio, who wants the count to see that a wealthy friend is testing him in a similar way. In this account of craftiness involving a triple, or perhaps quadruple, deception, no one is as he seems to be, and no one's words can be taken at face value.

Similarly, in the middle tale (no. 26) of *El Conde Lucanor*—or, more exactly, that which begins the second group of twenty-five tales (each group ends with an account of the noble Saladin)—the narrative is about Falsehood's deception of Truth. Although in this tale Truth is finally triumphant, the lies and deceptions of Falsehood are shown to be the way of the world. We are introduced not only to the single and the double lie, but also to the triple lie, which deceives by telling the truth ("la quel miente et le engaña diziéndol verdat").[27] Along with breaking down the assumption that truth and falsehood are simple dichotomies, this triple lie also raises the possibility that if truth can be a means of lying, why cannot lying be a way to truth?

As the subject of the first and middle tales in Juan Manuel's collection, deception may provide a context for comprehending the other tales. The focus on deception also suggests that *El Conde Lucanor* should not be taken as simply a series of obvious moral lessons. The understanding that the work seeks to give is more complex than the lesson explicitly drawn by the Count at the conclusion of each tale.

Inadequate *moralitates*, as well as deceptions, are also offered in John Gower's book of good love, the *Confessio Amantis*. The glosses given by Genius, Venus's priest, to the tales he tells are frequently misapplied or ridiculous. The need to understand is pointed up when, in an analysis of hypocrisy early in the work, Genius notes that one should not believe everything he hears ("men scholde noght / To lihtly lieve al that thei hiere," 1:1062–63).[28] This advice follows the first extensive tale in the *Confessio*, the story of how the false Mundus, by impersonating a god, deceives the innocent Paulina (1:761ff). Though Genius's words specifically represent a comment on hypocrites such as Mundus, they may offer an indication of how we should view the entire work, which is designed, Gower states, to be "wisdom to the wise" and "pley" to those desiring play (Prol:84–85).

Another work begining with an intricate account of deception is Boccaccio's *Decameron*. The first story of the first day of tale-telling concerns the great sinner Cepparello, who on his deathbed makes a false confession and gives the impression that he is a saint.[29] After his death he is revered by the townspeople and becomes the means by which God performs a series of miracles. The immediate irony of the inveterate sinner being worshipped as a saint is obvious. The further miracle, wicked Cepparello transformed into a vehicle for doing good and bringing people to God, is less striking but no less important. Though apparently in hell after his death, Cepparello, like the devil, becomes a means of divine justice.

In this tale of deception, the consummate deceiver is not only totally successful, but, inasmuch as his evil is finally turned to good, he may be seen as deceived too. Successful in his deception, and apparently damned because of it, Cepparello becomes through his deception an agent for good. The triumphant sinner is likewise the vanquished one, and, ironically, the sinner Cepparello is reborn as the saint Ciappelletto. In Boccaccio's paradoxical tale, where fabliau becomes saint's life, nothing can be taken at face value. Indicating the ambiguity of the words to follow in the *Decameron*, as well as suggesting the pervasiveness of deception, the tale provides a fitting introduction to Boccaccio's ten days of tale-telling.

Among the several accounts of deception in Chaucer's *Canterbury Tales*, the Pardoner's Prologue offers a situation comparable to Boccaccio's paradox. Acknowledging his hypocrisy in preaching against avarice when in fact covetousness is his principal concern, the Pardoner is anything but contrite. He even boasts that, in spite of being "a ful vicious man," he can still tell "a moral tale" (vi, 459–60), and that, notwithstanding his own sinfulness, his preaching is effective in making others repent (vi, 429–33). Realizing that this lecherous eunuch is a living lie, we are forced to consider the distasteful possibility that someone who delivers venomous words "under hew / Of hoolynesse" (vi, 421–22) may actually function as God's means of bringing salvation to mankind.

The notion that deception, like evil, is not only a part of God's plan but a way of effecting divine justice may be strikingly seen in *Inferno* 23, after Dante and Virgil realize that they have been deceived by the devils who have supposedly been leading them to safety. Aware of the devils in pursuit, they hurriedly slide down to the next ditch, that of the hypocrites. It is not accidental that the deception occurs at this point in their journey, for the devils' action provides a context for the hypocrisy at hand. At the same time, given the tendency of Dante the poet to join apparently unrelated traditions and images, we should examine the opening and closing details of the canto.

In the initial lines, having just witnessed two devils fighting over an escaped quarry, Dante the narrator notes that he was reminded of the fable of the frog and the mouse (23:4–6). In this a frog deceives a mouse into being tied to him as they cross a river, but when the frog tries to drown the mouse, both are caught by a hawk. Though Dante applies this fable to the preceding episode of the devils fighting over their prey, inasmuch as in its standard form the fable is of the deceiver deceived, we should recognize that it provides an ironic context, an encompassing gloss, as it were, for understanding the devils' deceptive actions in the adventure at hand.

A further gloss is offered at the end of the canto. A friar, one of the "painted people" in the ditch of hypocrites, commenting on the devils' deception, notes that he once heard it said in Bologna that the devil is "a liar and the father of lies" (23:142–44). The irony here is not only that the source of the quotation is the Gospel of John (8:44), not the people of Bologna, but also that this truth is being uttered by a condemned hypocrite whose very nature, like the devil's, is to lie. In having his liar utter an apparent (though suspect) truth about lies, Dante joins Boccaccio and Chaucer in offering variations on that favorite medieval conundrum, the liar saying that what he says is a lie.[30]

Without multiplying examples, we may see that in late medieval narrative, deception frequently goes beyond particular episodes. Like the sign contest in the *Libro de Buen Amor,* a single episode should be taken to suggest the purposely ambiguous nature of the work of which it is part, and, furthermore, to reveal the point and method of its author. Whatever else these masters of fourteenth-century narrative may be, they should be understood as liars and tricksters par excellence. Not content with simply deceiving, they even tell their audiences what they are doing and warn them to beware.

The Author as Trickster

Throughout the Middle Ages, fiction was commonly understood as synonymous with deceit, and its author was viewed as no better than a liar.[31] For instance, Favel, the name of the figure created by Langland in *Piers Plowman* as a variant of *fable* (from Latin *fabula,* meaning "fiction") became in late fourteenth-century England a generic term for one whose words deceive.[32] But, given the important distinction made by Augustine between the *fallax* (fallacious) and the *mendax* (mendacious), deception was understood to have a positive as well as a negative side. Although both terms involve feigning and deceiving, the *mendax,* through employing lies like those found in comedies and fables, aims primarily to delight. According to Augustine, feigned narratives like fables may give true significations.[33] Of this sort are the fictions of late medieval writers, which, while purporting to deceive, actually serve to teach wisdom.

Something of what this means may be seen in the *Canterbury Tales,* where fraud and deception are everywhere, and where the reader must be constantly vigilant. At the end of the *Friar's Tale,* Chaucer's pilgrim narrator addresses his audience: "Waketh," he charges them. "Beth war" of the "temptour" Satan, who, he notes, quoting Psalm 10 (Vulgate 9), sits in his lair waiting to seize the unwary (III, 1654–58). Ironically, the passage in Psalms actually refers not to the devil but to the wicked man who seeks to trap the unwary. Like the Pardoner, Chaucer's Friar uses Scripture to mislead, and the passage he misapplies may well refer back to him. He, as well as the fiend, should be the object of man's vigilance. Good as the Friar's counsel may seem, it illustrates a major point of his tale, that words can be purposely misapplied and are frequently misunderstood. As the devil in the tale contemptuously points out, man is easily deceived, even by "a lowsy jogelour" (III, 1467).

In his writings, Chaucer often casts himself in the role of "jogelour," a word which, besides suggesting "trickster," is a variant of "jangler," or false speaker. In this role he is not one of the "japeres and jangeleres" criticized in *Piers Plowman* for their foolishness

(B.Prol:35–36). Rather, like the juggler who is able to keep in motion several objects simultaneously, Chaucer challenges the appearance of things. His design is to stimulate, tease, and provoke, even by confusing and startling, and thus involve his audience in the process of understanding that may be seen as the dominant experience of his book. Something of this "play" is to be found in the work of other fourteenth-century writers of fiction who, in their search for understanding, routinely go beyond traditional literary distinctions and practices and offer their audiences something not only new but challenging.

Purposely creating intellectual puzzles, dilemmas, and conundrums, these late medieval poets and storytellers may be seen delighting in *numerositas* and *varietas,* the multiplicity and diversity of creation celebrated by such authorities as Thomas Aquinas.[34] The inherent connection of things, even those that seem most dissimilar (the idea of the *connexio rerum* that Aquinas took from Pseudo-Dionysius), might well lead to the harmonizing of opposites, as in Nicholas of Cusa's *concordantia oppositorum,* but it also encouraged juxtaposition and contradiction.[35]

Unable to say anything new or to grapple meaningfully with the age-old problems of mankind, late medieval secular writers may well have felt condemned to insignificance. From the point of view of moralist and theologian, the manipulation of words by the poet and storyteller was not only an incidental activity but even a form of folly. And Tertullian's 1200-year-old assessment of secular literature as "foolishness in the eyes of God" represented more than a minority view in the fourteenth century.[36] Recognizing that along with being trivial, they were necessarily ludic, poets and fiction writers, instead of hiding their play, often gloried in it. Rather than simply restating conventional morality, they frequently preferred to offer ambiguity and conundrum. Since theirs was necessarily a ludic craft, storytellers made their works into what might be termed *specula stultorum,* or mirrors of fools.

Along with being the actual title of a twelfth-century narrative poem by Nigel Wireker about the folly and misadventures of Dan Burnel the Ass (a work quite popular in the fourteenth century), the *Speculum Stultorum* may be considered a generic term for that kind of composition that employs folly as its *modus operandi.* In a letter about his poem (often printed as a prologue), Nigel acknowledges the absurdity of his narrative and urges his readers to find instruction beneath its dissembling words. Explaining a few of his hidden meanings ("de absconditia meis"), he notes that his title, *Speculum Stul-torum*—which will seem ridiculous to those lacking understanding ("legentibus et non intelligentibus videtur esse ridiculosus")—was designed to suggest that the work, in relating folly for the instruction of the foolish, is simultaneously a mirror about fools and one for fools.[37] In the hands of fourteenth-century writers, the *speculum stultorum* also came to be a mirror ostensibly *by* fools. Donning the motley garb of Chaucer's "lowsy jogelour," the writers of such *specula* played the fool to the extent of purposely misstating, garbling, and misapplying conventional language, traditional forms, and standard doctrina.

The narrators of these *specula* resemble the "mased thyng" found throughout Chaucer's dream visions, who responds to his vision by thinking how "queynt" it is.[38] When offered Truth, they apparently do not know what to do with it. They are like Langland's narrator, Will, who at the beginning of *Piers Plowman* ignores Holy Church's repeated instruction, "When alle tresors arn tried, Truthe is the beste" (B.1:135), and asks instead "to knowe the false" (B.2:4).[39] The result of such blindness is a fall into error, what Langland appropriately terms "the lond of longynge and love" (B.11:8), where confusion is the normal condition of man, marking his perception and his art.

Bewildering hodgepodges of traditional forms and styles, and cacophonous minglings of religious and secular concerns thus mark the work of such storytellers as the Archpriest of Hita, Gower, Boccaccio, and Chaucer. The Archpriest, using sermon as framework for amorous escapades, compiles a Book of Good Love that is about seduction. Gower creates a parodic confession in which the priest of Venus instructs by twisting and misapplying the signification of classical and biblical stories. Boccaccio reports, as respite from the plague that many considered the result of human sin, an amorous sojourn in the countryside, where tale-telling functions as the equivalent to love-making. And Chaucer, after offering in the *Legend of Good Women* the lives of Cupid's saints as though they were martyrs in a legendary, presents a pilgrimage that is an excuse for mirthful fictions. Beginning (and ostensibly ending) in a tavern, and overseen by a tavern keeper who strives to insure that *myrthe* prevails, the intended pilgrimage to the holy shrine at Canterbury is more accurately a holiday in "the lond of longynge and love."

These narratives also ignore distinctions between autobiography and fiction. The Archpriest is both author and protagonist of his *Libro de Buen Amor,* as may be seen in the many headings within the work.

One introduces us to "the prayer that the Archpriest made to God when he began his book," and another announces its subject as "how the Archpriest fell in love."[40] At the beginning and end of the *Decameron,* Boccaccio not only talks about what he is doing but interrupts his narrative to tell a tale in his own voice. His incomplete story of Filippo Balducci is, he insists, a poor effort, to be distinguished from the other tales which are told by his illustrious company.[41] Whereas Boccaccio and the Archpriest never come into their works as actual characters, Chaucer acts in the *Canterbury Tales* as both author and pilgrim. And unlike Boccaccio, he even tells a tale that is part of the work, though his effort is rudely interrupted and evaluated as "drasty rymyng . . . nat worth a toord" (vii, 930).[42]

Sometimes, when fourteenth-century authors put themselves in their work, it is as protagonist. The figure who finds himself alone in the dark wood of error at the beginning of the *Inferno* is not merely Dante's narrator, or the central figure in the *Commedia.* He *is* Dante. And in witnessing his journey to understanding, we are well aware of his several flaws, including his inadequate perception of the events he experiences. What Dante the author termed "the Comedy of Dante Alighieri, a Florentine by birth but not in character," may not inaccurately be seen as a "comedy" *about* Dante, a real-life Florentine who, while meaning well, tends to bumble through the otherworld making mistakes and acting foolishly.[43]

Although, significantly, Dante does not name himself until he no longer requires the guidance of Virgil[44]—identity being the result of self-understanding—other medieval writers do not hesitate to name themselves in their work. When near the end of his *Confessio Amantis* John Gower tells his full name to Venus, it is not so much Gower the author signing his poem as Gower the protagonist identifying with the folly that is the subject of the work (8:2321–22).[45] And when Venus addresses him in reply as "John," the incongruity is much like that in the *House of Fame* when the giant eagle, lecturing Chaucer whom he is carrying in his claws, addresses him as "Geffrey."[46] In such instances, the writer purposely identifies himself with the subject of his *speculum stultorum.*

From the point of view of late medieval audiences, a large part of the pleasure of reading and listening to poets and storytellers may have been in recognizing the intentional play and in avoiding being deceived. Understanding is the means of avoiding deception, but deception is the means of provoking understanding. So, in the *Libro de Buen Amor,* following the sign contest, the Archpriest insists that where his reader thinks he is lying, that is where he is speaking the greatest truth; and where the reader thinks he is most appealing, that is where he is actually most ugly (69). Like Wolfram von Eschenbach, who interrupts his *Parzival* to make the startling assertion that his work is no book and he himself not literate ("ich enkan deheinen buochstap," 2:116),[47] the Archpriest challenges his reader, bringing him into his work as a participant in a contest in which he must avoid being deceived. But, thinking again of the sign contest, we may wonder which participant is the reader and which the Archpriest.

The answer would seem to be that each is both. As purposeful deceiver the Archpriest functions as the Romans, but as the one trying to instill wisdom, he is like the Greeks. Similarly, as he who is being tested, the reader is like the Romans, but as the one who must avoid being deceived, he is like the Greeks. Thus the Archpriest's audience should be regarded as active participant in the work. To make this clear to the audience, the Archpriest changes metaphors and, speaking in the first person as his book, notes that the *Libro de Buen Amor* should be viewed as a musical instrument, whose effectiveness depends wholly on the ability of its player (70). Responsibility for arriving at truth is thus the reader's, even more than the author's.

Since signs—including words—are neutral, no word, the Archpriest insists, is bad if it is not taken badly; conversely a word is well said if it is well understood ("si bien es entendida," 64). Boccaccio makes the same point about his fictions. Like everything else, stories may be harmful or useful depending on how their audience takes them ("avendo riguardo all'ascoltatore").[48] It is up to the reader and hearer of these narratives to understand and to beware of being deceived. Though on the one hand, the audience may be seen as the writer's partner, finally giving the work its meaning, on the other hand, the audience may appear as a nuisance the writer prefers to ignore. Thus, in the Prologue to his *De doctrina Christiana*, Augustine asserts that he is not to blame if readers do not understand him ("me non esse reprehendendum, quia haec non intellegunt").[49] He cannot supply the vision for others to understand the meaning of his words.

The topos of *caveat lector*, common in late medieval literature, suggests an adversarial relationship between writer and reader. "Blameth nat me," Chaucer tells his audience if, in choosing among his *Canterbury* tales, they "chese amys" (I, 3181) and find "harlotrie" instead of "moralities." His words amount to a forewarning. "Avyseth yow," he says, "and put me out of blame." And, he adds, "men shal nat maken ernest of game" (i, 4355). Chaucer is not being whimsically self-contradictory here. While "game" should not necessarily be viewed as "ernest," the two together may be the way to truth. Wisdom, if not ambiguous itself, is, as we have seen Nicholas of Cusa insisting, at least composed of ambiguities.

Again, "blameth me nat," says Chaucer the pilgrim to those about to hear his *Tale of Melibee*, if they find it a bit different from the narrative familiar to them (vii, 961). The familiar and the unfamiliar are to be joined in his retelling, and although the result will be something new and different, the "sentence," or meaning, will, he insists, be the same. He is challenging his audience; it is up to them to respond to the challenge. Even though Chaucer seems to take pains to explain his literary method, we should understand that his words here may be suspect—does his retelling of a French version (one of four) of a Latin treatise necessarily mean the same as all the other versions?— and also that they represent one of three contradictory theories of narrative offered in the *Canterbury Tales*.[50] Although Chaucer is not so blunt as Boccaccio, who asserts that his tales will run after no one asking to be read ("elle non correranno di dietro a niuna a farsi leggere"),[51] he is clearly demanding reader response and responsibility.

Beyond the Word: From the Ambiguous to the Ineffable

What Chaucer says about his particular *Tale of Melibee* may apply to all of his tales. While resembling narratives that are familiar and typical of various genres, each of his tales must finally be understood *sui generis,* as a unique creation, not as representative of a standard genre. If one is searching for examples of medieval narrative forms, Chaucer is not the author to look in. Each of his offerings complicates the simple preexisting genres by bringing in matters that confuse, issues that obfuscate, details and allusions that perplex. Instead of neatly delimiting and separating "ernest" and "game," the *Canterbury Tales* purposely mingles them. And rather than instruct through conventional morality or entertain through repeating tried-and-true narrative, Chaucer is more concerned with twisting and garbling familiar material, distorting it, altering its essential nature, and blending it with apparently inappropriate material.

Such may also be said of the *Libro de Buen Amor.* In a prose

prologue added in his second (1343) redaction, the Archpriest emphasizes understanding, along with will and memory ("entendimiento,
voluntad e memoria"), as what is necessary to bring comfort to the
soul.[52] In accord with Psalm 31:8 (Vulgate), beginning "Intellectum
tibi dabo," the Archpriest is eager to give his readers understanding.
But, as he presents it, good understanding ("buen entendimiento")
depends on good love ("buen amor"). Whereas in this prologue
(actually a *sermon joyeux*) good love is distinguished from the mad
love of this world, the two loves are soon blurred, with the result that
venereal love is cited as "buen amor."[53] Incorporating love of God,
paternal and filial love, married love, and friendship, as well as
venereal lust, amoral, sensual, and illicit, this "buen amor" is simultaneously ideal Christian love and a skillful technique for seduction. In
the tradition of *Le Roman de la Rose* and the various medieval versions
of Ovid, the *Libro de Buen Amor* (the title dates from 1898), while
ostensibly praising love, actually condemns it. And, as the Archpriest
presents love, it defies both meaningful definition and the "good
understanding" of the reader.

Though purporting to be an account of how "buen amor" may
make the uncouth man subtle and the silent man eloquent (156), the
Libro de Buen Amor is, as the Archpriest simultaneously insists, not
what it seems to be ("lo que semeja non es," 162). This may be seen
early in the narrative when we meet Love, described as a tall, handsome, well-mannered man named "Amor tu vezino" (181). This
figure may be "Love, your neighbor," as he is commonly presented in
the standard editions, or "Love-your-neighbor," an allegorical representation of the Great Commandment. Or he could be both simultaneously. Although in appearance and name "Amor tu vezino" might
well be a manifestation of Christian love, the narrator takes him for
venereal love, and in some 240 stanzas angrily berates him as deceitful, false, and destructive to man (182–422). Likening him to the
devil, he tells the fable of the frog and the mouse (here mole) to
demonstrate Love's treachery (407–16). When Love responds (423–
575), it is not to correct the narrator or to distinguish between the two
loves, but to state how one should behave if he is to be a successful
lover of women. That is, notwithstanding his initial appearance or
name, "Amor tu vezino" becomes precisely the pander of venereal
love that the narrator has accused him of being.

Rather than simply distinguish between Christian and venereal
love, the Archpriest purposely mixes the two, producing a confusion

of the sort seen in the next episode, where we are told that the narrator has fallen in love with a woman who is his neighbor ("vezina," 582). Even though the narrator has insisted that he does not want Love as his neighbor (261), he literally comes to love his neighbor. This lady may initially suggest another manifestation of "Amor, tu vezina," perhaps more spiritual than the previous one; but, inasmuch as she is described as the narrator's death and life ("mi muerte e mi salud," 582), she likewise suggests venereal love and, in fact, anticipates the goddess Venus, who is described two quatrains later as *our* life and death: "Ella es nuestra vida e ella es nuestra muerte" (584).

Along with being a book of love (good and otherwise), the Archpriest's work—like Boccaccio's verbal substitute for love-making, Chaucer's pilgrimage of wrong loving, and Gower's confession of a lover—is a study of the ambiguity of language and its constructs. As such it is again related to *Le Roman de la Rose,* particularly to the discussion of language and meaning near the beginning of Jean de Meun's continuation, where Raison points out to Amanz the need to look for the sense behind the letter. The "paraboles" that one learns in school are not to be taken literally (7124). The "cloudy fable" ("fable occure," 7134) needs clarification, for in "their games and their fables" the poets hide ("covrirent") their thoughts (7145–48). Although Amanz is not interested in exploring the possibilities of significances, fables, and metaphors ("les sentances, / les fables et les methaphores," 7160–62), Jean de Meun certainly is, and so were subsequent fourteenth-century poets and storytellers.

Rather than think that these "sentances," "fables," and "methaphores" represent three kinds of veiled writing, we should recognize that these terms of medieval fictions are inclusive, not exclusive. Like one of the French versions of Aesop that speaks of its narrative in terms of parables, examples, and frivolities ("ces paraboles, / ces exsemples et ces frivoles"),[54] *Le Roman de la Rose,* as well as other medieval fictions, may be understood as all of these at once. In like manner, when Boccaccio in the proemium to the *Decameron* says he will narrate "a hundred stories, or fables, or parables, or histories, or whatever we wish to call them" ("cento novelle, o favole o parabole o istorie che dire le vogliamo"), he is clearly giving possible names for his compositions; and apparently to his mind no one name is preferable to any other.[55]

The separation of name and thing is the subject of the only tale in the *Decameron* told by Boccaccio in his own name. In this story

Filippo Balducci, to preserve the innocence of his son, who has just seen women for the first time, tells the boy that they are called geese. By avoiding saying their real name ("lo proprio nome"), the father hopes to prevent the boy from feeling desire.[56] At the same time, he knows that his wit ("ingegno") is no match for nature. Breaking off the story at this point, Boccaccio emphasizes that words do not finally matter. The term the father chooses to use will not alter his son's feelings, any more than the clerks' terms in Chaucer's *Reeve's Tale* would alter the size of the miller's house.

Like the dispersion following the Tower of Babel and the *regio dissimilitudinis* of the Neoplatonists, the world of the late Middle Ages was without certainty or clear meaning. Because of the fourteenth century's increasing sense that all of creation was inherently uncertain, the dominant question came to be, What can be known in a contingent world? Schoolmen fretted that since God's power *(potentia absoluta)* was unlimited, He could deceive man into taking as true that which was false and believing as real that which was unreal. Stemming from this worry are various *impossibilia* like the proposition of Siger of Brabant, that since everything appearing to us is but semblance and dream, we cannot be certain of the existence of anything ("omnia quae nobis apparent sunt simulacra et sicut somnia, ita quod non simus certi de existentia alicuius rei").[57]

Only God's existence was certain, and He was absolutely unknowable. While language and its constructs offered the possibility of bringing order out of confusion, the order might be more apparent than real. For some fourteenth-century thinkers, increasingly frustrated by the traditional study of Aristotle, as well as by the more recent manipulations of language by speculative grammarians and new logicians alike, the answer was to turn away from grammar, rhetoric, logic, and even metaphysics. If, as Jean Gerson emphasized, all wisdom lay in repentance and belief in the Gospel (the lesson of Mark 1:15, "poenitemini, et credite Evangelio"), then, as Nicholas of Autrecourt affirmed, it was best for one to devote oneself to the study of Scripture and to the state of one's soul.[58]

For some fourteenth-century writers, therefore, real wisdom lay beyond the word. For all of the intellectual pleasures possible through language, its manipulation, range of significations, and play of ambiguities often led one beyond it. Dante's vision in the *Commedia* is finally too great to be revealed in language ("il mio veder fu maggio / che 'l parlar mostra"), and his speech too inadequate and feeble to express his conception ("O quanto è corto il dire e come fioco / al mio concetto"). [59] When he enters the hot white light of the Empyrean, his power fails and his work simply ends. The conclusion of his journey to understanding is silence.

Chaucer in the *Canterbury Tales* likewise moves beyond the word, but to repentance rather than a vision of Truth. In the last tale—that which, notwithstanding the incomplete state of the *Tales,* was apparently designed to be last—the Parson focuses on the "ful noble way" of Penitence (x, 80). Transforming the worldly journey at hand to the "parfit glorious pilgrymage" called "Jerusalem celestial" (x, 50–51), the *Parson's Tale* shows what can take man to God. And in the so-called Retraction that follows, Chaucer applies the Parson's admonitions to himself and contritely confesses his sins, specifically his worldly writings ("enditynges of worldly vanitees," [x, 1085]). With the Parson having nothing to do with verse or with "fables and swich wrecchednesse" (x, 34), the Canterbury pilgrims move beyond poetry and fiction to explicit "moralitee and vertuous mateere" (x, 38). And when in the Retraction the author of the work likewise moves beyond tale-telling, wishing only "to bewayle my giltes, and to studie to the salvacioun of my soule" (x, 1090), he in effect offers his own repentance as *exemplum* of the proper activity of man.

But, obviously, both Dante and Chaucer recognize that language and its constructs are what enable them to reach the point where they can go beyond the word. Inasmuch as the last line of his poem links the *Paradiso* to the previous *Purgatorio* and *Inferno,* [60] Dante indicates that the process through ambiguity and confusion is necessary for one seeking truth. Even when one knows truth and goes beyond the word, language—its play and its fictions—may still offer a way to other readers and hearers. Similarly, though Chaucer in his Retraction shows that he has reached a point where he no longer values his fictions, his "entente" all along was that these serve for "oure doctrine" (x, 1083). Moreover, the *Canterbury Tales* was apparently designed by Chaucer to make just the point of this Retraction, and in fact the *Parson's Tale* and Retraction may have been written at the same time as the *General Prologue,* as the frame for the entire *Tales.* [61]

The Archpriest of Hita likewise goes beyond his work, but in a way different from either Dante or Chaucer. At the conclusion of his *Libro de Buen Amor,* along with repeating his initial assertion that it offers more than his audience might at first think (1631–32), he also makes the surprising pronouncement that anyone able to write poetry should feel free to add to his narrative or even to emend it wherever he wishes ("puede más añedir e emendar lo que quisiere," 1629). As the Archpriest views his book, it is not a finished work of art that should be left alone but an ongoing composition designed to be passed from hand to hand. He insists that although he is putting a period to his book, he is not closing it ("faré / punto a mi librete, mas non lo cerraré," 1625–26). It remains open and open-ended, with its words constantly demanding glosses and with all of its contradictions and ambiguities gloriously unresolved.

Like the debate between the Greeks and the Romans with which it began, the entire *Libro de Buen Amor* is concerned with the difficulty of determining meaning. But this difficulty should not be viewed as necessarily negative. For the Archpriest, the ambiguities of the initial sign contest represent the promise of more ambiguities to come, and at the end of the book he in effect reaffirms this promise. Conundrum remains, for in his work, as in other fourteenth-century narratives, wisdom comes about through recognizing complexity, not through insisting that it be removed; through realizing that apparent signification is not necessarily final or total signification; and through acknowledging that *myrthe* and *doctryne* remain intertwined to the end.

Notes

1. Juan Ruiz, *Libro de Buen Amor,* ed. and trans. Raymond S. Willis (Princeton: Princeton University Press, 1972), stanzas 46–63. Subsequent references are to this edition.
2. Augustine (*De doctrina Christiana,* 3.25.36) discusses the lion, for example, as both devil and Christ, and water as both people and the Holy Spirit; in *Sancti Aurelii Augustini Opera,* 6.6, ed. William M. Green, Corpus Scriptorum Ecclesiasticorum Latinorum, 80 (Vienna: Hölder-Pichler-Tempsky, 1963), pp. 100–101.
3. See, e.g., Matthew 13:13.
4. Boethius, *Quaemodo substantiae,* prologue; in *Boethius, The Theological Tractates,* ed. and trans. H. F. Stewart and E. K. Rand, Loeb Classical Library, 74 (London: Heinemann, 1921), pp. 38–41.
5. See, e.g., Quintilian on ambiguity *(amphiboliae); Institutio oratoria,* 7.9.1; in *Quintilian,* ed. and trans. H. E. Butler, Loeb Classical Library, 126 (London: Heinemann, 1921), 3:152–53.
6. Marie de France, *Lais,* ed. Jean Rychner, Les Classiques Français du Moyen Age, 93 (Paris: Champion, 1971), prologue, 11.9–16. For Priscian, see *Institutionum*

grammaticarum, preface; in *Grammatici Latini*, ed. Henricus Keil (Leipzig: Teubner, 1855), 2:1.

7. Horace, *Ars poetica*, l.333; in *Horace, Satires, Epistles and Ars Poetica*, ed. and trans. H. Rushton Fairclough, Loeb Classical Library (London: Heinemann, 1929), p. 478. Paul, Romans 15:4.

8. See Gordon Leff, *The Dissolution of the Medieval Outlook: An Essay on Intellectual and Spiritual Change in the Fourteenth Century* (New York: New York University Press, 1976); also the discussion in Edmund Reiss, "Chaucer's Fiction and Linguistic Self-Consciousness in the Late Middle Ages," *Chaucer and the Craft of Fiction* (Rochester, MI: Solaris Press, 1986), pp. 97–119; and Reiss, "Medieval Irony," *Journal of the History of Ideas* 42 (1981): 209–26.

9. Chaucer, *The Canterbury Tales*, I, 4122–26; in *The Works of Geoffrey Chaucer*, ed. F. N. Robinson, 2nd ed. (Boston: Houghton Mifflin, 1957). Subsequent references are to this edition.

10. Dante, *Paradiso*, 17:31–35; in *La Divina Commedia*, ed. Natalino Sapegno, 2nd ed., Scrittori Italiani (Florence: 'La Nuova Italia,' 1968), 3 vols. Subsequent references are to this edition.

11. "Hoc opere sermonis," Augustine, *De doctrina Christiana*, 4.4.6; ed. Green, p. 121.

12. Nicholas of Cusa, *De Sapientia*, 1; in *Unity and Reform: Selected Writings of Nicholas of Cusa*, ed. John P. Dolan (Notre Dame: University of Notre Dame Press, 1962), p. 106.

13. Juan Manuel, *El Conde Lucanor*, Prologue, ed. Antonio Martinez Menchen, Biblioteca de la Literatura y el Pensamiento Hispanicos (Madrid: Editora Nacional, 1977), p. 71.

14. Dante, *Inferno*, 9:61–63; *Purgatorio*, 8:19–21.

15. Boccaccio, *Decameron*, Conclusione dell'Autore; ed. Vittore Branca, Nuova Universale Einaudi, 169 (Turin: Einaudi, 1980), p. 1257.

16. Chrétien de Troyes, *Erec et Enide*, 11.1–3; in *Les Romans de Chrétien de Troyes*, I ed. Mario Roques, Les Classiques Français du Moyen Age, 80 (Paris: Champion, 1970), p. 1.

17. Caxton, *Fables of Esope*, 1.1; in *Caxton's Aesop*, ed. R. T. Lenaghan (Cambridge, MA: Harvard University Press, 1967), p. 74. Phaedrus (first century) applies the moral to those who do not understand him ("qui me non intelligunt"; *Fabulae Aesopiae*, 3.12, in *Babrius and Phaedrus*, ed. Ben Perry, Loeb Classical Library [London: Heinemann, 1965], p. 278). Later Romulus applies the moral to those who do not understand in general ("qui non intelligunt"; Aesop, in *Les fabulistes latins depuis le siècle d'Auguste jusqu'à la fin du Moyen Age*, ed. Léopold Hervieux, 2nd ed. [Paris, 1893–99; reprint, New York: Franklin, 1965], 2:195).

18. Job 12:7. See, e.g., the application by Nicole Bozon in his early fourteenth-century *Contes moralisés*, proemium; ed. Lucy Toulmin Smith and Paul Meyer, La Société des Anciens Textes Français (Paris: Firmin Didot, 1889), p. 8.

19. Haiseau, "Le Prestre et le Mouton"; in *Recueil général et complet des fabliaux des XIIIe et XIVe siècles*, ed. Anatole de Montaiglon and Gaston Raynaud (Paris, 1895; reprint, New York: Franklin, 1964), 6:50.

20. Marie de France, "De presbytero et lupo," 11.11–12; in *The Fables of Marie de France*, ed. and trans. Mary Lou Martin (Birmingham, Ala.: Summa Publications, 1984), p. 212.

21. See Chrétien de Troyes, *Le Roman de Perceval, ou le Conte du Graal,* ed. William Roach, Textes Littéraires Français, 71 (Geneva: Droz, 1956); Wolfram von Eschenbach, *Parzival,* ed. Albert Leitzmann, 7th ed., Altdeutsche Textbibliothek, 12–14 (Tübingen: Niemeyer, 1961–65).

22. Augustine, *De doctrina Christiana,* 3.9.13; ed. Green, pp. 87–88; *La Queste del Saint Graal,* ed. Albert Pauphilet, Les Classiques Français du Moyen Age, 33 (Paris: Champion, 1949), especially the testing of Bors, pp. 162ff.

23. See Guillaume de Lorris and Jean de Meun, *Le Roman de la Rose,* ed. Félix Lecoy, Les Classiques Français du Moyen Age (Paris: Champion, 1965–70), 3 vols.; also, e.g., Chaucer's several dream visions.

24. *The Owl and the Nightingale,* ed. E. G. Stanley (Edinburgh: Nelson, 1960); see also Edmund Reiss, "Conflict and Its Resolution in Medieval Dialogues," *Arts libéraux et philosophie au moyen age: Actes du quatrième congrés international de philosophie médiévale* (Montreal: Institute d'Etudes Médiévales, 1969), pp. 863–72.

25. Langland, *The Vision of Piers Plowman,* ed. A. V. C. Schmidt (London: Dent, 1978), B. Prol:17; B.2:6.

26. Aristotle, *Nichomachean Ethics,* 5.3.1129b.

27. Juan Manuel, *El Conde Lucanor,* tale no. 26; ed. Martinez Menchen, p. 168.

28. John Gower, *Confessio Amantis;* in *The English Works of John Gower,* ed. G. C. Macaulay, EETS, e.s., 81–82 (London: Oxford University Press, 1900–1901). Subsequent quotations are to this edition.

29. Boccaccio, *Decameron,* 1.1; ed. Branca, pp. 49ff.

30. See, e.g., its use in Albert of Saxony's *Sophismata;* cited in Philotheus Boehner, *Medieval Logic: An Outline of Its Development from 1250 to c.1400* (Chicago: University of Chicago Press, 1952), p. 13.

31. John Lydgate considers "ficcion" as synonymous with "symulacioun" and "deceyt" (*The Pilgrimage of the Life of Man,* 11.6057–58; ed. F J. Furnivall, EETS, e.s., 77 [London: Kegan Paul, Trench, Trübner, 1899]). Guido Almansi's critical study of Boccaccio's narrative technique is titled *The Writer as Liar* (London: Routledge & Kegan Paul, 1975).

32. *Piers Plowman,* B.2:6ff.; Hoccleve, *La Mâle Règle,* vv. 247–48; in *English Verse Between Chaucer and Surrey,* ed. E. P. Hammond (Durham, N.C.: Duke University Press, 1927), p. 63.

33. Augustine, *Soliloquia,* 2.9.16 (*PL,* 32:882); *Contra mendacium,* 13.27 (*PL,* 40:537); see also *De doctrina Christiana,* 2.25.39 (ed. Green, p. 62); and Isidore of Seville, *Etymologiae,* 1.40; ed. W. M. Lindsay (Oxford: Clarendon, 1911).

34. Thomas Aquinas, *Summa contra gentiles,* 2.45.

35. Ibid., 2.68; Ps.-Dionysius, *De divinis nominibus,* 7; Nicholas of Cusa, *De docta ignorantia,* 3.1.

36. Tertullian, *De spectaculis,* 17. The Middle Ages found echoes of this view in the writings of such authorities as Jerome, Augustine, Boethius, and Gregory the Great.

37. Nigel Wireker, *Speculum Stultorum,* prologue; in *The Anglo-Latin Satirical Poets and Epigrammatists of the Twelfth Century,* ed. Thomas Wright, Rerum Britannicarum Medii Aevi Scriptores, 59 (London: Longman and Trübner, 1872), 1:3. See also Nigel's verse epilogue, where he notes that the reader must carefully examine what his words mean ("quicquid mystice signant," vv. 3881–82; ed. Wright, 1:145; also ed. John H. Mozley and Robert R. Raymo (Berkeley and Los Angeles: University of California Press, 1960), p. 116.

38. See especially *The Book of the Duchess*, ll. 12, 1330; ed. Robinson, pp. 267, 279.

39. See also *Piers Plowman*, B.1:207.

40. *Libro de Buen Amor*, ed. Willis, pp. 3, 30.

41. See *Decameron*, 4.introduzione; ed. Branca, p. 462.

42. See also *Canterbury Tales*, II, 2109ff., and the criticism of his work that Chaucer earlier puts in the mouth of the Man of Law, II, 46ff.

43. See Epistola 10, to Can Grande della Scala, sect. 10; in *Literary Criticism of Dante Alighieri*, ed. and trans. Robert S. Haller, Regents Critics (Lincoln: University of Nebraska Press, 1973), p. 100. The identification of character with author may exist notwithstanding Dante's earlier assertion in his *Convivio* that it is not fit for one to speak of himself ("parlare alcuno di sè medesimo pare non licito," 1.2)

44. *Purgatorio*, 30:55.

45. See also *Confessio Amantis*, 8:2908.

46. *House of Fame*, l. 729; ed. Robinson, p. 289.

47. *Parzival*, ed. Leitzmann, 1:90.

48. *Decameron*, Conclusione dell'Autore; ed. Branca, p. 1256.

49. *De doctrina Christiana*, Prologue.3; ed. Green, p. 4.

50. Besides *Canterbury Tales*, II, 2133–54, see I, 725–42 and X, 31–41. Also Edmund Reiss, "Chaucer's Fiction and Linguistic Self-Consciousness in the Late Middle Ages," in *Chaucer and the Craft of Fiction*, pp. 97–119.

51. *Decameron*, Conclusione dell'Autore; ed. Branca, p. 1258.

52. *Libro de Buen Amor*, prologue; ed. Willis, p. 5; also p. 7. The Archpriest refers to the passage as Ps 31:10.

53. Ibid., prologue; ed. Willis, pp. 7, 9. See also, e.g., stanza 443.

54. *Isopet II de Paris*, Prologue; in *Recueil général des Isopets*, ed. Julia Bastin, Société des Anciens Textes Français (Paris: Champion, 1929–30), 1:35.

55. *Decameron*, proemium; ed. Branca, p. 9. Similarly, writers of fables could call their works fabliaux and writers of fabliaux say they wrote fables. See the discussion in *Fabliaux*, ed. R. C. Johnston and D. D. R. Owen (Oxford: Blackwell, 1957), pp. xvi–xvii.

56. *Decameron*, 4.introduzione; ed. Branca, p. 465.

57. Siger of Brabant, *Impossibilia*, 2; ed. Clemens Baeumker, Beiträge zur Geschichte der Philosophie des Mittelalters, 2.6 (Münster: Aschendorff, 1898), p. 7.

58. Gerson, e.g., *De modis significandi* and *Contra curiositatem;* see Etienne Gilson, *History of Christian Philosophy in the Middle Ages* (London: Sheed and Ward, 1955), p. 531; Nicholas of Autrecourt, *Exigit ordo executionis;* cited in Armand A. Maurer, *Medieval Philosophy* (New York: Random House, 1962), p. 289.

59. *Paradiso*, 33:55–56, 121–22. A variant of "parlar mostra" ("speech shows," 33:56) is "parlar nostro" ("our speech").

60. Compare *Paradiso*, 33:145; *Inferno*, 34:139; and *Purgatorio*, 33:145, all of which employ the word "stelle" ("stars").

61. See Edmund Reiss, "The Pilgrimage Narrative and the *Canterbury Tales*," *Studies in Philology* 67 (1970): 295–305.

PART IV

LANGUAGE REDEEMED
The Filling of the Void

EDITORS' INTRODUCTION

N ature," as the saying goes, "abhors a vacuum." The same might be said of human nature as well, and, in fact, the two essays contained in this chapter both begin with Chaucer's recognition of the void that is concomitant with the "conventionalist" view of language and end with him attempting to fill that void with the substantive language of the Word. For Liam Purdon, *Lak of Stedfastnesse* is a product of the poet's "anxiety over the mutable condition of language"; for Phillip Pulsiano, "*Troilus and Criseyde* functions, among other things, as Chaucer's moral and philosophical workshop for exploring the breakdown of language as a vehicle for truth and the acquisition of knowledge." Yet despite Chaucer's awareness of the "crisis of the free-floating sign" which both authors find to be at the center of the poet's perception of language, both Purdon and Pulsiano agree that Chaucer ultimately insists on a positivist core at the heart of the linguistic medium, that as the world collapses, the Word, or Logos, emerges.

Lak of Stedfastnesse, as Purdon points out, begins as complaint over the abuse or debasement of language, a theme also seen in the essays by Professors Arthur, Allen, and Ashley. There is, for example, the people's inability to hold to fixed principle, especially in regard to oaths and pledges—a problem symptomatic of the legal practice, both canon and secular, of the period and evidenced as well in the literature, as we shall see in Edith Joyce Benkov's discussion of the false oaths of Isuet and Guinièvre. Such abuse of language, as Augustine notes in regard to lying, constitutes a deviation from the original purpose for which language was created. Indeed, Chaucer's *Lak of Stedfastnesse* links moral being and fidelity in the use of language. Corrupted language affects moral being; the corrupted or unsteadfast soul produces corrupted, unreliable language. This corruption of language takes place on both the individual and the societal level. The Fall of Man—and of his language—repeats itself in the fall of the individual and of society as well. History, the unfolding of God's originating words in the act of Creation, reveals the ongoing debasement of language, the widening distance between word and deed, between God's word and man's. And it is to History that

Chaucer returns, in Heideggerian fashion, to invoke a Golden Age that, like Dante's Eden, might serve as the repository of the "archival deposit" of the "Originating Proper." In language, Purdon argues, there is for Chaucer hope for redemption, much as there was for Dante hope for redemption in prayer. The Word redeems man's fallen nature and hence his fallen words. Language—as the medium between abstract and concrete, between idea and object, and even between sacred and secular—holds a privileged place. It remains the closest thing to a transcendental that man has of his own making.

If man's word is fallen, it still holds traces of the fullness from which it fell, and this is a point that Pulsiano, picking up where Purdon leaves off, develops at length. As he notes in regard to Dante, once one recognizes the fallen nature of language (the perception of the *Inferno*), the question becomes how to create a new form of expression in language (the work of *Paradiso*).

Pulsiano has Chaucer facing not the collapse of his own society (although that is perhaps implicit in the collapse of Troy) but rather the "unmaking of his verbal art," a recognition of his medium's radical instability made clear in the famous "Go little Book" passage at the end of the last book of *Troilus and Criseyde*. Given this recognition, the question for Chaucer becomes, How, then, might language be redeemed? The poet's answer, Pulsiano suggests, is that "through language, and more specifically as a result of the Incarnation, man is able to enter into a dynamic relationship with God. . . . Human speech is thus redeemed through Christ the Word, allowing for words to function as accurate though incomplete signifiers of God." In a subsequent essay, David Hiscoe's discussion of the Augustinian answer to the same question, we will encounter a similar response: "The gift of the Incarnation, when the Word reenters the world of the flesh, returns to us the possibility of speaking, listening, and understanding properly."

If, as Glenn Arbery argues, in Adam's Eden language was "supplementary," Pulsiano is quick to remind us that Eden became part of history, inextricably bound up in the Divine Word, and in history the human word is an absolute necessity. Citing Augustine's argument that "Christ made use of external words to remind us that He dwells within us," Pulsiano notes that "if God can proceed from transverbal to verbal communication, man should be able to use language as a springboard to nondiscursive modes of communication." As with Arbery, the verbal act of prayer becomes the means to redemption and transcendence. Language, being neither object nor idea, becomes the gateway or medium for commerce from one realm to the other, reflecting both the mutability of the one and the permanence of the other. No matter that oaths might be broken, that literary skeins might unravel, or that texts might be mismetered by later tongues. Through their congruence with the medium of the Creation and with the Word itself, verbal signs reflect, if not possess, enough substance to satisfy the would-be positivist, to fill the void.

7

CHAUCER'S *LAK OF STEDFASTNESSE*
A Revalorization of the Word

LIAM O. PURDON

Recently, renewed interest in Chaucer's role as poet and administrator[1] has prompted scholars to reinvestigate the aesthetic sophistication of Chaucer's minor lyric poetry. One poem to have received considerable attention as a result of the desire to understand the historical Chaucer is his *Lak of Stedfastnesse*, a work whose date of composition F. N. Robinson indicates falls somewhere between 1386 and 1399.[2]

This *ballade* has been variously described and interpreted. Haldeen Braddy, for example, concludes it is "an occasional balade [*sic*] skilfully and diplomatically worked out, rich both in poetic and political meaning."[3] A. Brusendorff claims it is a shrewd Machiavellian compliment.[4] J. E. Cross, comparing it to the Old Swedish *Trohetsvisan*, contends it is a moralizing *planctus*.[5] John Gardner asserts it is a diatribe against political pluralism.[6] Donald R. Howard maintains it is a work of secular pragmatism which pleads for social justice through the pursuit of reason.[7] In the variorum edition of Chaucer's minor poems, George B. Pace and Alfred David characterize it as a " 'morale ballade' with a political slant,"[8] arguing it is less Boethian than B. L. Jefferson and F. N. Robinson maintain.[9] Rossell Hope Robbins categorizes it as a "jeremiad" having much in common with other "evils-of-the-age" works.[10] D. W. Robertson, Jr., considers it a work of moral instruction whose tone is pessimistic.[11] And, finally, Margaret Schlauch indicates it is a theoretical political statement about the limitations of absolute monarchy.[12]

Though these scholars' assessments of *Lak of Stedfastnesse* are based primarily on internal evidence of the *topoi* and the language Chaucer uses, none of their interpretations examines the poem's evident thematic concern about the nature of language itself. This omission is remarkable, not because it indicates these scholars have overlooked the obvious, but rather because it reveals that their examinations of the poem's language have consistently led them away from the issue of language to considering the influences and historical circumstances affecting the poem's composition. Why has this happened? One answer is that this may actually be the intended effect of the poem's veil of abstractions and diplomatic vagueness.[13] But it may also be the effect that Chaucer's felt—and in this case, expressed—anxiety about the mutability of language has on the critical suppositions we bring to Chaucer's lyrics and to his treatment of the subject of language in general.[14] While we do hear the "Grant translateur" express concern over the impermanence and abuse of language, we usually take his concern for granted because it is always expressed so persuasively and elegantly.

History makes it clear that Chaucer and others had to act (and no doubt write and speak) prudently and diplomatically under the watchful eyes of Bussy, Bagot, Green, and others during the waning years of the House of Plantagenet.[15] Yet in this poem Chaucer is anything but vague when he expresses his concern over the mutable condition of language. He calls our attention, for example, to a number of elusive concepts and quasi-legal terms such as "obligacioun," "dissensioun," and "extorcioun." He also refers explicitly to the relationship between words and deeds, a relationship pilgrim-Chaucer articulates as narrative method in the *General Prologue*, a relationship poet-Chaucer explores in his treatment of the pilgrims and the tales they tell in the *Canterbury Tales*,[16] and a relationship poet-Chaucer also evidences interest in in his discussions about the translator's art in the *Prologue* to the *Legend of Good Women*. Here, in *Lak of Stedfastnesse*, Chaucer not only identifies the supreme evil of the age as loss of belief in the life of principle,[17] he also demonstrates how the mutability and debasement of language are responsible for and encourage that evil.[18]

Fallen Language in a Fallen World

The expression of concern over the condition of language appears in the first stanza of the poem, as Chaucer distinguishes the current medieval use and abuse of words from the former, proper employment of language in an unspecified linguistic Golden Age ("Somtyme"). By using the same method of comparison between present and past he employs in *The Former Age*,[19] Chaucer immediately defines the fundamental linguistic problem he and other sensitive translators of language face in the "newe world" of the latter part of the fourteenth century. In that former linguistic Golden Age, Chaucer points out, "mannes word was obligacioun" (2). A man's word, that is to say, was a bond or a contract, and, implicitly, a man was either as good or as bad as his word.[20] In that former age, then, there was no divergence between sign and signified. In the present moment of the late fourteenth century, however, a man's word, Chaucer laments, is, like the world itself, "fals and deceivable" (3). The result of this condition, Chaucer adds, is that words and deeds, " . . . as in conclusioun,/ Ben nothing lyk" (4–5). The sign and the signified, in other words, are no longer the same, are noticeably divergent. Moreover, language itself, the former nature of which once mirrored the stability of creation and social order, now is distorted, as is revealed in Chaucer's use of "turned up-so-doun" (5), an explicit idiomatic hyperbole.

While Chaucer's initial expression of concern about the mutable condition of language is conspicuously contrived, insofar as it presumes the existence of a former linguistic Golden Age and naively denies the possibility of evolution of linguistic forms to accommodate the complexity of communication within a sophisticated bureaucracy, his second expression of anxiety over the current treatment of language is reasonable and persuasively logical. In the second and third stanzas of the poem, Chaucer indicates that abuse of words not only distorts reality but also eventually engenders further linguistic and moral abuse. Linguistic abuse is already evident in the "turned up-so-doun" trope. Truth, we are then told, is "put doun" (15). What Chaucer means here is that truth is silenced, attacked, or denied. But because the verb phrase "put doun" is an idiomatic rather than a literary expression, Chaucer's use of the phrase signals a second intrusion into the poem of mutable language, another example of a potential distortion of reality. The distortion implicit in this example is also apparent in the second half of the same line. Here Chaucer states that "resoun," the means by which humankind perceives truth, is now "holden fable" (15). What Chaucer is suggesting here is that people consider reason to be a deception, a lie. But Chaucer's reportorial account of the people's expression of mistrust toward reason also reveals a conspicuously inappropriate term to describe the complexity of inductive and deductive thinking. Reason may be something the people denigrate, as Chaucer laments, but the actual verbal means they use to denigrate it ironically signals a further distortion of rational process. The people neither consider nor contemplate the conceptual; rather, they view it in concrete terms, as the first element of the colloquialism "holden fable" suggests.

The obvious result of the mutable and debased state of language and thought, according to Chaucer, is that vice reigns, while virtue and pity and mercy, the aspects of morality which support social order, are either relegated to a state of insignificance or exiled: "Vertu hath now no dominacioun; / Pitee exyled, no man is merciable" (16–17).

But the abuse of words, Chaucer points out, has yet another effect, one as insidious as the distortion of reality. Language abuse gives rise to further linguistic and moral abuse. The world, Chaucer says, is "variable," for example, because people now enjoy engaging in "dissensioun" (9). Whether Chaucer had in mind the etymology of dissension, which is to separate or dissociate oneself from feeling or thinking, is debatable; but that this desire, according to Chaucer, is further encouraged by the erroneous belief that one is deemed capable if and only if one can harm another or one's neighbor by engaging in "collusioun" (11) would seem to indicate he had such an idea in mind. Furthermore, Chaucer's choice of the term "collusioun" introduces yet another, far more dangerous, kind of linguistic abuse. Quarrels and disagreements are not productive. But the secret agreement or understanding between two or more parties for fraudulent or treacherous purposes represents the subversion of language itself, the effect of which has moral as well as legal implications.

Though the poem convincingly demonstrates that language abuse leads to further debasement of thought and behavior, Chaucer repeatedly underscores the fact that the apparent cause of the world's "permutacioun" (19) is people's inability to remain steadfast to a "fixed principle."[21] This weakness of humanity, he adds, has created, on the one hand, the desire to distort, cheat, and defraud for "mede" (6) and, on the other, a "wilfulness" (6) and "wilful wrechednesse" (13), both of which engender the covetousness that blinds "discrecioun" (18), the condition of mind evidenced not only by the discernment of what is judicious or expedient but also by the prudent use of language. Chaucer's repetition of the line, "That al is lost for lak of steadfastnesse," identifies the cause of the present social disorder in a lack of moral certitude and fortitude. However, it also implies that the world's "permutacioun / Fro right to wrong, fro trouthe to fikelnesse" (19–20) has come about through the abuse and mutability of language. To be steadfast to a fixed principle in the post-lapsarian world implies an understanding of some general law or truth. To comprehend a general law or truth implies the command of a symbolic means whereby that truth or law may be both known and verified. The most accurate means for such kinds of verification is command of the symbolic medium of language. Thus, while the world's "permutacioun" has, according to Chaucer, resulted from humankind's innate weakness, Chaucer's references to the nature of this "permutacioun" reveal, in an oblique way, that human weakness is correlated with the mutable condition and improper use of language.

Christ's Word

The poem starts by distinguishing between linguistic ages, by contrasting humankind's present linguistic deficiency to an earlier and opposite condition of linguistic perfection. Chaucer's envoy, addressed to a "prince," continues to develop the idea of the mutable inheritance of language. Knowing that the abuse of language and language's mutable nature itself are chief factors in the loss of the former linguistic Golden Age, Chaucer addresses the final words in the poem to the linguistic and moral ideal. When he exclaims "O prince," he may be referring to Richard or extolling the idea of princeps in general. But it is equally likely he is exhorting the condition theoretically practiced by all medieval Christians of living or continuing in Christ's word, which Christ in John 8:31 indicates is the only way true freedom is attained.[22] As Chaucer suggests in the previous stanzas, the act of continuing in Christ's word is now a difficult task, especially since the world has undergone a "permutacioun." But, as he points out, it is not impossible. The pursuit of honor or moral probity is one way of turning things around. Hating "extorcioun" (23) is another and, within the moral-linguistic context of the poem, an important one since it presupposes a respect for language. Doing nothing that is "repreuable" is yet another way, while dreading God, upholding law, and loving truth and worthiness allow one also to see what the Pharisee cannot comprehend. The effect of this rigorous linguistic-moral behavior results in, as the last line of the envoy indicates, the wedding of the people to "stedfastnesse," the act of which can be taken as a synonym for continuing in Christ's word.[23] Further, this interpretation of the line explains what Chaucer means at the ends of the previous stanzas when he states: "al is lost. . . ." For the medieval Christian, not continuing in Christ's word was tantamount to experiencing the death of the soul.[24] Moreover, the significance of being wed to steadfastness or continuing in Christ's word also sheds light on the meaning of Chaucer's choice of the *topos* of the sword of "castigacioun" (26). While the image of the sword creates a vigorous conclusion,[25] especially after Chaucer has urged the "prince" to "Cherish thy folk" (23), this *topos*, the combination of a thing—the sword—and an idea—"castigacioun"—offers a metaphor of the condition of being wed to "stedfastnesse," of continuing in Christ's word, since discipleship implies belief, the act of perceiving agreement, and God, the concept of the Supreme Being.[26] In addition, unusual as the *topos* is, it is not thematically inconsistent with the idea of cherishing the people, since it spiritually nurtures the individual who appreciates the significance of being wed to steadfastness. Comprehension of Chaucer's rhetorical strategy in the poem offers the same conceptual reward. The strategy, which consists of presenting and repudiating a sense of hopelessness through the relationship between the envoy[27] and the last lines of each preceding stanza, rhetorically demonstrates, on the one hand, the principle that a belief engendered by language can be altered by the same process and, on the other, its corollary that the proper use of language as well as moral probity leads to the perception of the truth. Reformation, Chaucer therefore indicates, is not only ethical but also linguistic.

Chaucer's idealistic view of language and moral reform expressed in the envoy of *Lak of Stedfastnesse* ends the poem on an optimistic note. But the intended optimism is not as reassuring as it might be, not because it is threatened by the presence of irony, but rather because it follows a persuasive lament over the mutable condition of language and the effect that condition can have on social, intellectual, and political stability. It is no doubt for this reason that Chaucer employs the imperative mood consistently throughout the envoy. By using this mood, he begins the process of reform that is his subject both rhetorically, by means of a mood to alter opinion, and linguistically, by means of the impression of inflectional consistency. Whether such reform is ultimately achievable Chaucer neither says nor indicates. But one thing is certain as the *ballade* ends. Unlike the *General Prologue* or the *Canterbury Tales,* there is not a magnificent presence of a Harry Bailly in this poem to hold in check the powerful debasement of language which can eventually make "word and deed

. . . nothing lyk." As a result, the burden of responsibility rests on the shoulders of the reader, who must decide whether to be a Pharisee[28] or a prince wedded to the word.

Notes

1. See, for example, Patricia J. Eberle, "Commercial Language and the Commercial Outlook in the *General Prologue*," *Chaucer Review* 18 (1983): 161–74; and Sigmund Eisner, "Chaucer as Technical Writer," *Chaucer Review* 19 (1985): 179–201.

2. *The Works of Geoffrey Chaucer*, ed. F. N. Robinson, 2nd ed. (Boston: Houghton Mifflin, 1957), p. 862. All references will be to this edition. For a complete, brief history of the scholarly debate over date of composition of *Lak of Stedfastnesse*, see Haldeen Braddy, "The Date of Chaucer's *Lak of Stedfastnesse*," *Journal of English and German Philology* 36 (1937): 481–90, especially p. 481 n. 1; and George B. Pace and Alfred David, *A Variorum Edition of the Works of Geoffrey Chaucer*, vol. 5, *The Minor Poems*, Part I (Norman: University of Oklahoma Press, 1982), pp. 77–78.

3. Haldeen Braddy, "The Date of Chaucer's *Lak of Stedfastnesse*," p. 490.

4. Aage Brusendorff, *The Chaucer Tradition* (London: Oxford University Press, 1925), p. 274.

5. J. E. Cross, "The Old Swedish *Trohetsvisan* and Chaucer's *Lak of Stedfastnesse:* A Study in Medieval Genre," in *Saga-Book* 16 (1965): 274.

6. John Gardner, *The Life and Times of Geoffrey Chaucer* (New York: Knopf, 1977), p. 277.

7. Donald R. Howard, *The Idea of the Canterbury Tales* (Berkeley: University of California Press, 1978), pp. 129–33.

8. Pace and David, *The Minor Poems*, p. 77.

9. B. L. Jefferson, *Chaucer and the Consolation of Philosophy of Boethius* (Princeton: Princeton University Press, 1917; reprint, New York: Gordian Press, 1968), pp. 106–7; Robinson, *The Works of Geoffrey Chaucer*, p. 862.

10. Rossell Hope Robbins, "The Lyrics," in *Companion to Chaucer Studies*, ed. Beryl Rowland, 2nd ed., rev. (New York: Oxford University Press, 1979), pp. 380–402.

11. D. W. Roberston, Jr., *A Preface to Chaucer* (Princeton: Princeton University Press, 1962), pp. 13, 461.

12. Margaret Schlauch, "Chaucer's Doctrine of Kings and Tyrants," *Speculum* 20 (1945): 137. For several general, introductory studies of Chaucer's lyric poetry and *Lak of Stedfastnesse*, see Thomas H. Carter, "The Shorter Poems of Geoffrey Chaucer," *Shenandoah* 11 (1960): 48–60; George B. Pace, "Chaucer's *Lak of Stedfastnesse*," *Studies in Bibliography* 4 (1951–52): 105–22; Pace and David, *The Minor Poems*, pp. 3–9; and Edmund Reiss, "Dusting off the Cobwebs: A Look at Chaucer's Lyrics," *Chaucer Review* 1 (1966): 55–65.

13. Pace and David, *The Minor Poems*, p. 78.

14. See R. A. Shoaf, "Notes towards Chaucer's Poetics of Translation," in *Studies in the Age of Chaucer*, ed. Roy J. Pearcy (Norman, Oklahoma: New Chaucer Society, 1979), p. 65.

15. May McKisack, *The Fourteenth Century: 1307–1399* (Oxford: Clarendon Press, 1959), pp. 477–96.

16. For a bibliographical discussion of the Platonic source for this distinction, see Robinson, *The Works of Geoffrey Chaucer*, p. 668.

17. Pace and David, *The Minor Poems*, p. 79.

18. Several scholars have begun to examine Chaucer's treatment of language in the minor poems. Among recent studies are R. T. Lenaghan, "Chaucer's *Envoy to Scogan:* The Use of Literary Conventions," *Chaucer Review* 10 (1975): 46–61; Charles D. Ludlum, "Heavenly Word-Play in Chaucer's 'Complaint to His Purse,'" *Notes and Queries* n.s. 23 (1976): 391–92; and Edward Vasta, "'To Rosemounde': Chaucer's 'Gentil' Dramatic Monologue," in *Chaucerian Problems and Perspectives: Essays Presented to Paul E. Beichner, C.S.C.*, ed. Edward Vasta and Zacharias P. Thundy (Notre Dame, Ind.: University of Notre Dame Press, 1979), pp. 97–113.

19. For comparisons between the poems, see Jefferson, *Chaucer and the Consolation*, pp. 91–92; and John Norton-Smith, "Chaucer's *Etas Prima*," *Medium Ævum* 32 (1963): 117–24, esp. 123–24.

20. *Middle English Dictionary* (Ann Arbor: University of Michigan Press, 1982), vol. 10, 25 s.v. "obligacioun," entries A and B.

21. Pace and David, *The Minor Poems*, p. 79.

22. While the debate over the identity of "prince's" referent seems to have ended in a stalemate between those who view the poem as an occasional piece and those who view it as a theoretical political or moral statement, another interpretation is possible. Since "prince" is the title given to the son of the sovereign and since the sovereign designated in the stanza is not Edward but God ("Dred God"), it would appear that the referent of "prince" is Christ. While it would be illogical to presume the son of God needs such admonishing or that Chaucer would engage in such a foolish act, it is not so illogical to read in place of the word "prince" or even the name "Christ" the term "word." According to the New Testament the word is made flesh through the incarnation of Christ. This process continues in history, as John 8:31–32 indicates, by the transformation of the flesh back into the word. To continue in Christ's word does not simply involve the reading alone of Christ's words. Rather, it requires the understanding and application of Christ's words to life. Thus, the condition of continuing in Christ's word, as well as the act of maintaining the value of Christ's word, implies a linguistic treatment of the word which exalts the word's importance and also allows the word to nurture spiritually. This attitude is evident, for example, in *The Sowdone of Babylone* as the poet states: "God . . . that all things made in sapience / By vertue of woorde and holy goost" (Emil Hausknecht, ed., *The Sowdone of Babylone*, EETS, e.s. 38 [London: Kegan Paul, Trench, Trubner and Company, 1881], p. 3).

23. The Matthaean parable of the Wedding Feast validates this association. The individuals in the parable who are invited to the celebration do not heed the significance of the invitation; they lack steadfastness, in this case a proper respect for their lord, and return home to their chattel. The individual who does comprehend the significance of the invitation or message presented obliquely in all of the Matthaean parables of the Kingdom, on the other hand, will not appear poorly attired at the

feast. To be wed to "stedfastnesse" is to be prepared to work toward an understanding of the eschatological significance of Christ's words. To gain access to those words, one has to continue in Christ's word.

24. In Book XIII of *The City of God,* Saint Augustine argues that the soul of one who ceases to continue in Christ's word is bereft of the life it derives from God. This is an eschatologically perilous condition, for were one to die in this state of being, one would, according to Saint Augustine, experience the horror of the second death or the death that does not die (*The City of God,* trans. Henry Bettenson, ed. David Knowles [New York: Penguin, 1972], pp. 510–46).

25. John N. Fisher, *John Gower* (New York: New York University Press, 1964), p. 249.

26. The image of the sword, though associated with violence, is frequently representative of human authority (see Heinrich Zimmer, *The King and the Corpse: Tales of the Soul's Conquest of Evil* [Princeton: Princeton University Press, 1948], p. 146). In Matthew 10:34 the sword, according to Christ, is also the agent of purification, or a sword of castigation which sets father against son, mother against daughter, for the purpose of the offspring's salvation.

27. While Earle Birney, "The Beginnings of Chaucer's Irony," *PMLA* 54 (1939): 639, does not mention Chaucer's *Lak of Stedfastnesse* in his discussion of irony in the lyrics, irony nevertheless is present in the thematic reversal which occurs in the envoy. It is not a trenchant irony; rather, it is a delicate, intellectual irony which softens the insistently imperative mood characterizing the final stanza. Whereas the first three stanzas express hopelessness in the fictionalized world of the poem—that is, in the world where hope and wish fulfillment are usually achieved—the envoy, which etymologically is associated with the actual world, ironically is the part of the poem offering the sense of hope and encouragement.

28. The decision may also consist of the distinction between being a Hebrew or a Christian. The exhortation in the envoy involving the twofold condition of being wed to steadfastness and being intellectually committed to belief ("Dred God, do law, love trouthe and worthinesse") parallels the twofold exhortation in Hebrews which emphasizes the need to "hold fast" (3:6) and the need to "go on to maturity" (6:1).

8

REDEEMED LANGUAGE AND THE ENDING OF *TROILUS AND CRISEYDE*

PHILLIP PULSIANO

haucer's fascination with exploring the limitations of language as a mediating element between man and universal truths has been commented upon most aptly by Paul Ruggiers. Speaking of Chaucer's exploitation of language in the *Canterbury Tales,* he writes:

> But in the *Manciple's Prologue* and in that of the Parson, Chaucer faces up to rules and to their limitations: there are some truths that words cannot convey. It is not so much that poetry fails finally to be. expressive, but in the largest sense, there are some truths that escape the net of language: we know in ways other than by verbal signs. Failing to tell the larger truth because of the inadequacy of language, poetry, in Chaucer's charter, yields to something larger.[1]

Although Chaucer nowhere directly addresses the leading language theorists of his day, his poetry reflects an intense awareness of the moral and philosophical dimensions of language, an awareness which gave shape to his own developing poetics. And while one cannot say with any certainty whether Chaucer allied himself with the realists or the nominalists on the issue of verbal epistemology,[2] clearly his ideas on language are compatible with those of a wide range of writers: from Macrobius he would have had access to Neoplatonic ideas on hypostasis (the World-Soul). From Ockham and the fourteenth-century philosophers he influenced, Chaucer would have been familiar with the nominalist theories of conceptualism, signification, and supposition; that is, with the problem of universals, the limitations of cognition, and the question of truth. And from Augustine, perhaps the most influential language theorist from the patristic period through the Middle Ages, he would have inherited the concepts of the Stoics. For Augustine, verbal signs have the potential to adumbrate universal truths and, to a limited extent, thus serve to signify God. As a result of the Incarnation, through the Word made flesh, language, now redeemed from the fetters of abuse in the classical conception of language, has the potential to bridge the gulf between God, the origin of truth, and humanity. It is this unique function of language as both cognitive intermediary and avenue toward truth that can serve to illuminate Chaucer's purpose in constructing the ending to *Troilus and Criseyde,* an ending which one earlier critic regarded as "detachable at will" and unnecessary to the interpretation of the work, but which most modern critics view as a profound, though not expressly clear, philosophical message.[3]

Troilus and Criseyde functions, among many other things, as Chaucer's moral and philosophical workshop for exploring the breakdown of language as a vehicle for truth and the acquisition of knowledge. In a world where words continually belie intent, where speaking in 'amphibologies' is too often the norm, the problem becomes how one can know with certitude the truth of individual utterances, especially in the absence of any objective criteria against which words and actions can be measured and judged. Indeed, the more a character makes protestations of truth, the further away from truth we are left; "by my trouthe" and "have here my trouth" become Chaucerian signposts that something is amiss, that what we have in actuality is rift between word and thought. Even when a character does stand at the threshold of truth, as when Cassandra utters her majestically concise, "This Diomede is inne, and thow art oute" (v, 1519),[4] it is more often than not rejected in favor of maintaining an illusion of subjective truth. Troilus wants to believe that Criseyde will return, wants desperately to see her approaching the gates of Troy: "Have here my trouthe," he says to Panderus, "I se hire! Yond she is!" (v, 1158). But we know it is only a "fare-carte" (1162) that he sees.

Nor can we with all confidence look to the narrator as a guide consciously leading us to the discovery of a reality behind the veil of fiction. As a sorrowful devotee to the God of Love (Proem I), he has his own problems to contend with. And as a narrator, he is far from remaining omniscient: he freely interjects himself, his passions, his sentiments, into the drama he unfolds. At times his own ability as poetic craftsman verges perilously on the edge of disaster; one need only recall the often discussed Proem to Book II:

> For in this see the boot hath swych travaylle,
> Of my connyng, that unneth I it stere.
> This see clepe I the tempestous matere
> Of disepeir that Troilus was inne.
>
> (3–6)

While the narrator struggles with the rags and bones of his fiction, he must also wrestle with maintaining the stability of his poetic medium, language itself: "Ye knowe ek that in forme of speche is chaunge . . . (II 22ff.). Not only do the characters of this drama not suffice as guides to truth—the reality of their own fiction—but the narrator himself is continually in danger of proving inadequate, leaving his readers to find their own ways through the darkness. It is precisely for these reasons that the conclusion of the poem comes as something of a shock: our narrator stumbles, and from the mouth of a naif springs wisdom.

Stanzas 253–57 (lines 1765–99) betray a narrator in search of an ending, of a fitting conclusion which will at once provide a necessary consolatory note in anticipation of Troilus's fate and yet affirm the poem's validity. The result, as many critics have commented, is comic disorder. A poem invoking the trappings of epic seemingly demands a conclusion consonant with epic conventions. But, as our narrator understands, battles and warlike deeds are properly found in Dares (1770–71), whereas the *Troilus* requires a conclusion of a different sort altogether. So he turns instead to absolving Criseyde of guilt (1776): he is, after all, only a translator, not the poetic wellspring. Yet the task of ending this poem is not a responsibility our narrator can let pass completely from his shoulders. He takes a different stance: "Beth war of men, and herkneth what I seye!" (1785) he cautions. Yet his bald attempt at playing the moralist with *exempla* ready at hand is not satisfactory either. Perhaps a simpler approach will suffice:

> Go, litel bok, go, litel myn tragedye,
> Ther God thi makere yet, er that he dye,
> So sende myght to make in som comedye!
>
> (1786–88)

However, following safely in the footsteps of those who had employed the "Go, litel bok" *envoi* before him, and solemnly entreating his book to "kis the steppes, where as thow seest pace / Virgile, Ovide, Omer, Lucan, and Stace" (1791–92), unfortunately also conveys an air of feigned humility mingled with outright arrogance.[5] Yet, use of this convention inadvertently gives rise to new direction and serious purpose in the following stanza. Here our narrator is unexpectedly confronted by the prospect of "unmaking" his poem at the same moment he hopes to bring it to conclusion; for if our language is constantly changing due to the "gret diversite / In Englissh and in writyng of oure tonge" (1793–94), how can he be assured that his poem will be understood, its meaning secure?[6] The answer, though at this point only dimly perceived, is nevertheless at hand, and it is signaled by the double reference to God, the "makere" of both poem and narrator. Having stumbled upon it, the narrator now abruptly breaks off to begin his conclusion once again: "But yet to purpos of my rather speche" (1799).

Whatever sphere Troilus ascends to, whatever place he is escorted to by the psychopomp Mercury,[7] whatever his "fyn," Troilus does condemn those that follow the "blynde lust" (1824) of worldly appetites. This need not reduce his love to mere vanity and illusion, though it is certainly unstable, for, if anything, it is a human love, fraught with pain and joy, fear and comfort. More important for the audience of the poem is that they are not consigned to follow in Troilus's uncertain path, since for them the theological realities of the Christian "comedy" provide direction, purpose, and stability in a transient world:

> O yonge, fresshe folkes, he or she,
> In which that love up groweth with youre age,
> Repeyreth hom fro worldly vanyte,
> And of youre herte up casteth the visage
> To thilke God that after his ymage
> Yow made, and thynketh al nys but a faire
> This world, that passeth soone as floures faire.
>
> And loveth hym, the which that right for love
> Upon a crois, oure soules for to beye,
> First starf, and roos, and sit in hevene above;
> For he nyl falsen no wight, dar I seye,
> That wol his herte al holly on hym leye.
> And syn he best to love is, and most meke,
> What nedeth feynede loves for to seke?
>
> (1835–48)

These stanzas present two crucial theological truths: that man is made in the image of God, and that Christ, the Son of God, became incarnate in order to redeem mankind. These doctrines have important ramifications for the creation of poetry and for its efficacy as a medium which, though it engages in the craft of fiction-making, goes beyond the slipperiness of words to reveal universal truths. Here Chaucer looks beyond the secular vision of Boccaccio's *Filostrato* to Dante's *Divine Comedy,* and, ultimately, he enters the arena of verbal epistemology.

Augustine and Language Redeemed

In his life of Dante, Boccaccio asserts "that not only is poetry theology, but also that theology is poetry."[8] Properly viewed, the nature of poetry is not incompatible with that of theology. Both employ *fabulae;* and while theology consistently draws man towards truth, poetry always has the potential at least to do so:

> Holy Scripture—which we call theology—sometimes under the form of history, again in the meaning of a vision, now by the signification of a lament, and in many other ways, designs to reveal to us the high mystery of the incarnation of the Divine Word, his life, the circumstances of his death, his victorious resurrection and wonderful ascension, and his other acts, so that, being thus taught, we may attain to that glory which He by his death and resurrection opened to us, after it had been long closed through the sin of the first man. In like manner do [pagan] poets in their works—sometimes under fictions of various gods, again by the transformation of men into imaginary forms, and at times by gentle persuasion, reveal to us the causes of things, the effects of virtues and of vices, what we ought to flee and what follow; in order that we may attain by virtuous action the end that they, although they did not rightly know the true God, believed to be our supreme salvation.[9]

Yet, for Boccaccio and Dante, as indeed for Augustine, that poetry which takes as its end the telling of diverting fables about pagan gods and men is ultimately a form of sterile rhetoric, for in their lack of moral content, such fables draw man away from divine truth. The point is made a number of times by Augustine. In his discussion of

Greek and Latin grammar in the *Confessions,* for instance, he speaks of the "sweetly deceptive" poetic fictions ("dulcissime uanus," 1.14.23) of the *auctores* as draping a cloak of error over men's eyes rather than leading them to an understanding of some "honored mystery" ("honorem secreti," 1.13.22). [10] Where man should understand permanent truths, he hears patent untruths, untruths which bring him the precarious security of a false morality and in doing so abuse the function of language itself. In themselves, words are merely transient sounds that take on meaning only when they bring to mind the realities which they signify. [11] Thus Scripture is justified in using fictions "with the intent that one may get to the thing which is intended, by a feigned narration indeed, yet not a lying one, but with a truthful signification." [12] When, however, the supposed realities are untrue or an author's nonexistent creations, then man's progress towards permanence, towards an understanding of theological realities, is hindered. As a consequence, it must end in failure. Such indeed is the world of Chaucer's *Troilus,* where virtually all weave fictions, even the narrator.

How, then, can language be redeemed? The answer for Augustine rests in the Incarnation. Through Christ, the "poverty of human language" ("penuria sermonis humani") is overcome; [13] the Word was made flesh so that man can take on divinity, can know in a limited way the permanence of the divine nature. Augustine explains this central idea in *De civitate Dei:*

> And that Mediator in whom we can participate, and by participation reach our felicity, is the uncreated Word of God, by whom all things were created. . . . God himself, the blessed God who is the giver of blessedness, became the partaker of our human nature and thus offered us a short cut to participation in his own divine nature. [14]

And again, more pointedly, in his commentary on the Psalms:

> Before you perceived God, you believed that thought could express God. Now, you are beginning to perceive Him, and you think that you cannot express what you perceive. But, having found that you cannot express what you perceive, will you be silent, will you not praise God? . . . "How," you ask, "shall I praise Him?" I cannot now explain the small amount which I can perceive, in part, through a glass darkly. . . . All other things may be expressed in some way; he alone is

ineffable, Who spoke, and all things were made. His Word, by Whom we were spoken, is His Son. He was made weak so that he might be spoken by us, despite our weakness.[15]

In God's unfolding the Word before man, we are drawn to participate in the Trinity, and so "arrive at those realities in which we believe, and which we can still in some small measure comprehend."[16]

Cognition through language becomes the key, in Augustine's linguistic epistemology, for perceiving and comprehending the truth. But, as Augustine explains in De magistro, words themselves are merely signs which point to a reality behind their thought or expression; they make sense only when they correspond in some way to the realities which we suppose they signify.[17] Understanding is thus an act of recollection; for unless we perceive something of what the word signifies, the sound itself remains an incomprehensible utterance. It is not the outward sign which we consult, "but the truth which presides over the mind itself from within, though we may have been led to consult it because of words."[18] In speaking, Augustine maintains, "we merely call something to mind, since, in turning over the words stored therein, memory brings to mind the realities which have words for their signs."[19]

Augustine expands his discussion in De doctrina Christiana to define more specifically the distinctions among the different types of signs (conventional vs. natural; literal vs. figurative) and to consider also the problem of Scriptural ambiguity. As in De magistro, he holds that "a sign is a thing which causes us to think of something beyond the impression the thing itself makes upon the senses."[20] Yet, a wrong understanding of the realities behind the words is possible, thus negating the function of language and, more importantly, impeding our understanding of Scripture and, consequently, our progress towards knowledge of God.

The language problem remains unanswered in De doctrina but finds its most complete illustration in the Confessions. This work opens with an expression of Augustine's burning desire to praise God linked at the same moment with a realization of the inadaquacy of language as an expressive, cognitive medium: "But how does one who does not know you call upon you?"[21] As Augustine notes in De magistro, in order for langauge to accurately signify its referent, there must be established a correspondence between the sign and the reality toward which it points. The problem, then, becomes one of how to bridge the gap between transient acoustic signs and nondiscursive theological realities. It is to the Incarnation that Augustine turns for the solution. Christ, the Interior Teacher, as he states in *De magistro,* "made use of external words to remind us that He dwells within us."[22] Immediately a potentially reciprocal relationship is established between God and man; for if God can proceed from transverbal to verbal communication, man should be able to use language as a springboard to nondiscursive modes of communication.

Augustine gives the point concrete illustration in Book 9 of the *Confessions,* in his conversation with Monica. The discussion centers on the truth of the Lord and on imagining what everlasting life with the saints would be like. They strain, as Augustine says, "with the heart's mouth for those supernal streams flowing from your fountain. . . ."[23] Implicit here is the struggle of the conversants to transcend the boundaries of human language, to realize in the spoken word ideas and concepts which surpass the limitations imposed by verbal expression. Augustine describes at length the process by which they are able to transcend these boundaries:

> When our discourse had been brought to the highest delight of fleshly senses, in the brightest corporeal light, when set against the sweetness of that, life seemed unworthy not merely of comparison with it, but even of remembrance, then, raising ourselves up with a more ardent love to the Selfsame, we proceeded step by step through all bodily things up to that heaven whence shine the sun and the moon and the stars down upon the earth. We ascended higher yet by means of inward thought and discourse and admiration of your works, and we came up to our own minds. We transcended them, so that we attained to the region of abundance that never fails . . . where life is that Wisdom by which all these things are made. . . . [A]nd we turned back again to the noise of our mouths, where a word both begins and ends.[24]

The conversants begin and end with the transient word; yet it is paradoxically through human speech that they are able to transcend language itself and so arrive through inward thought at "the food of truth" ("ueritate pabulo," 9.10.24). The transverbal journey ends with a question posed by Augustine in reflection: "But what is there like your Word, our Lord, remaining in himself without growing old, and yet renewing all things?"[25] The riddling question receives an immediate response. If the natural world were to fall silent, and if man also should fall silent, he would hear everything in the created universe proclaim that God is Lord and Creator. The universe becomes a multitude of signs, all proclaiming God's divinity. But language itself takes a special place among all signs, for, as Augustine writes in *De magistro,* "I have learned that He alone teaches who made use of external words to remind us that He dwells within us."[26]

Thus, through language, and specifically as a result of the Incarnation, man is able to enter into a dynamic relationship with God. He does so, not by ignoring the transient acoustic sign, but by using language (which includes meditation as a form of language) as an avenue for approaching and understanding divine truth. Human speech is thus redeemed through Christ the Word, allowing for words to function as accurate, though incomplete, signifiers of God.[27]

Dante, Chaucer, and Language Aspiring to Truth

This central importance of the Incarnation for redeeming language brings us once again to stanzas 263 and 264 of the *Troilus* and the narrator's injunction to call to memory the transience of this world against the steadfast truth of God, Who will "falsen no wight" (1845). Whereas only a few stanzas earlier the poem had edged its way toward collapsing into romance, toward becoming what Augustine would call a "poetic fable," now it aspires beyond fable to Christian truth. According to Augustine, man sees within himself a distant parallel to the Trinity; and though it is not an adequate image, it is nevertheless a reflection of the image of God (*De civitate Dei,* 11.26). In calling to mind the Supreme Trinity, Chaucer affirms the Trinity within man; and in doing so in his role as poet, he also affirms the validity of the Word. For if we recognize in ourselves a reflection of the Trinity ("To thilke God that after his ymage / Yow made," 1838–39), we recognize also that in giving voice to this truth we accept the Incarnation and the efficacy of language as a means of participating in the divine wisdom. As Donald Rowe puts it: "Chaucer sought to incarnate the Word in his poem as the Word is incarnated in the time and place of this world. . . ."[28] Both man and the poem itself, in effect, mirror the Word.

This idea of language as a mirror of the divine is further enforced by the devices Chaucer uses in constructing these stanzas. "Repetition," as Joan Ferrante writes in her study of Dante's *Paradiso,* "is a mirroring in language—like the heavenly mirrors, the words are apparently but not perfectly identical."[29] Within these three stanzas, for example, forms of the word "love" are repeated throughout; yet as the stanzas progress they differ substantively in meaning. Stanza 262 speaks of Troilus's carnal love for Criseyde, or, as the narrator calls it, his "lust" (1831). The following stanza equivocates as to whether the poet is referring to earthly love or to a love that should be directed elsewhere, "to thilke God." This ambiguity is resolved in the third stanza of this group. Here, forms of the word "love" appear three times, and always in reference to God. Thus, as the narrator grows in his understanding of love, a growth reflected in changes in the meaning of the word "love," so too does his audience grow to understand a love which surpasses earthly bounds. So too does the poem as a whole shift to an entirely different plane of meaning, one which must now be viewed in terms of Christian truth.

Other forms of repetition exist. The "Swich fyn" stanza, for instance, balances the later repetition in the "Lo here" stanza (265). And perhaps we are intended to view them as forming a sort of envelope, one which opens with praise for Troilus's love and, after moving to an understanding of a greater, divine love, ends with a condemnation of "payens corsed olde rites" (1849) and "thise wrecched worldes appetites" (1851). On the one hand is a love that is changeable; on the other is a truth that is unchangeable. As God expresses his love through the Word, so the poet expresses his understanding of that love through the incarnation of his poem. Within this envelope, then, are set ideas and words in opposition, the type of antithesis which, as Augustine writes, "gives beauty to a poem" ("pulcherrimum carmen," De civitate Dei, 11.18). As the opposition of contraries is harmonized in the Trinity, so does the poem, as a mirror of the creating Word, "bring added beauty to speech" ("sermonis pulchritudinem reddunt") through the paradox of contraries harmonized (De civitate Dei, 11.18). Chaucer is not denying the earthly love of Troilus and Criseyde; but the Christian has available to him a love that is greater, that is everlasting. And it is to this love that we should ultimately turn. We can, if we choose, look to "the forme of olde clerkis speche / In poetrie" (1854–55). But there is a greater poetry that proceeds, as Boccaccio writes, "from the bosom of God."[30] It is the poetry of Christian love made possible through the Word and made available by way of paradox through the poem itself.

In ending his poem with reference to the Trinity, Chaucer does more than simply bow to the ineffable in a gigantic leap of faith; such an interpretation of the poem's closure could hardly do justice to all that has preceded. Rather, we must see the narrator as making an ascent analogous to that made by Troilus. In his discussion of ambiguous signs in Scripture, Augustine delineates the steps by which one comes to an understanding of the Truth beyond the obscurity of language. He begins with recognition of the love of God, and thence proceeds to the discovery that man "has been enmeshed in the love of this world, or of temporal things, a love far remote from the kind of love of God and of our neighbor which Scripture itself prescribes."[31] Such knowledge of the limitations of earthly, transitory love leads to "the love of eternal things, specifically . . . [of] that immutable unity which is the Trinity."[32] At this stage, the mind protests against "the appetite for inferior things" ("appetitu inferiorum") and so arrives at the "counsel of mercy" ("consilio misericordiae," De doctrina Christiana, 2.17[11]). It is at this stage that we find the narrator of Troilus and Criseyde, and it is in this light that we must view the triple reference to 'mercy' in the last two stanzas. Chaucer and narrator, now no longer distinguishable, stand in the presence of the Trinity, both having ascended from the transitory, ambiguous world to a point where, for the first time, language truly and unambiguously signifies its referent. The outward sound, as Augustine writes in De Trinitate, "is a sign of the word that shines within."[33] And when the inward and outward sign are in harmony, "then there is a true word, and truth such as is looked for from man."[34]

The question of the relationship between theology, language, and the poem as a whole moves towards a resolution in the well-known prayer to the Trinity. To understand the impact of Chaucer's decision to end his poem with this passage, the prayer must be considered within its proper context in the Paradiso and within Dante's own views on language. Like Augustine, Dante recognizes the limitations of speech and conceptualization in signifying completely theological realities. At the conclusion of St. Peter Damian's speech in canto XXI, for example, we are told that the whirling flames "uttered a cry of such deep sound that nothing could be likened to it; nor did I understand it, so did the thunder overcome me" (140–42: ". . . e fero un grido di sì alto suono, / che non potrebbe qui assomigliarsi; / né io lo 'ntesi, sì me vinse il tuono").[35] Further, upon seeing the "hosts of Christ's triumph" (XXIII, 19–20: "le schiere / del trïunfo di Cristo") and the ever-increasing radiance of Beatrice's smile, Dante pauses to comment again on his craft's limitations:

Se me sonasser tutte quelle lingue
che Polimnïa con le suore fero

> del latte lor dolcissimo più pingue,
> per aiutarmi, al millesmo del vero
> non si verria, cantando il santo riso
> e quanto il santo aspetto facea mero;
> e così, figurando il paradiso,
> convien saltar lo sacrato poema,
> come chi trova suo cammin riciso.
> (xxiii, 55–63)

(Though all those tongues which Polyhymnia and her sisters made most rich with their sweetest milk should sound now to aid me, it would not come to a thousandth part of the truth, in singing the holy smile, and how it lit up the holy aspect; and so, depicting Paradise, the sacred poem must needs make a leap, even as one who finds his way cut off.)

And later, as he approaches his final canto and the culmination of his vision, Dante again and repeatedly reminds his readers of the inadequacy of speech to encompass all that he has experienced:

> Da quinci innanzi il mio veder fu maggio
> che 'l parlar mostra, ch'a tal vista cede,
> e cede la memoria a tanto oltraggio.
> (xxxiii, 55–57)

(Thenceforward my vision was greater than speech can show, which fails at such a sight, and at such excess memory fails.)

> Omai sarà più corta mia favella,
> pur a quel ch'io ricordo, che d'un fante
> che bagni ancor la lingua a la mammella.
> (106–8)

(Now will my speech fall more short, even in respect to that which I remember, than that of an infant who still bathes his tongue at the breast.)

> Oh quanto è corto il dire e come fioco
> al mio concetto!
> (121–22)

(O how scant is speech, and how feeble my conception!)

Expression is a serious problem for Dante, the poetic craftsman, as he attempts to describe divine wisdom and truth within the limitations imposed by a fallen, transient language. But as problematic as this juncture is for the poet, he is far removed here from the contrasting failure of speech in the *Inferno*.

In Hell are heard "Strange tongues, horrible outcries, utterances of woe, accents of anger, voices shrill and faint . . ." (III, 25–27: Diverse lingue, orribili favelle, / parole di dolore, accenti d'ira, / voci alte e fioche . . .). Here the words of the condemned degenerate into groans and curses, or tumble in unchecked confusion from their mouths: the councilors of fraud are depicted as flaming tongues in a parody of the tongues of fire bestowed on the Apostles by the Holy Ghost (XXVI); clerics bark (VII, 43); the Minotaur, unable to voice its hate and pain, bursts with inward rage (XII, 15: l'ira dentro fiacca); and suicides, metaporphosed into trees, speak in hisses like escaping wind (XIII, 40–44). Such babelic pandemonium serves to underscore the inutility of language as a communicative medium in man's unredeemed state. When inhabitants of Hell do speak, it is in a corrupted form of language which acts more as a mirror of their depraved moral conditions than as an avenue to truthful discourse. What these sinners have lost, Dante tells us in *De vulgari eloquentia*, is the understanding of the proper function of language: "[God] wished that the man should speak, in order that in the unfolding of so great a gift, He Himself who had freely bestowed it might be glorified."[36] Whereas in the prelapsarian state every utterance commenced with joy, as a consequence of the Fall every speech, we are told, begins with "Alas." Man is left to await the time when Christ will disperse the language of confusion with that of grace.

But the obstacle confronting Dante as he approaches Paradise is not at base unredeemed rhetoric. Rather, the problem is one of how Dante the poet can mold language—if need be, create a new language—capable of expressing the Divine. In *De vulgari* Dante suggests that, as language is the externalization of thought, it has a specific moral dimension. Great poetry demands "men who excel in genius and knowledge" . . . ; and since, as man is, above all other earthly creatures, a rational being, "he seeks for what is right."[37] But a correct moral view of poetry must also have as its corollary the ability of the poet to express accurately the relationship between words and images and their *significata*. Disjunctive yoking of things inferior with things perfect, as in describing "an ox with a saddle or a swine with a belt,"[38] can degrade the art of poetry-making. However, when poetry possesses what Marcia Colish terms an aesthetic of rectitude, that is, "a correspondence to realities as they are" combined with a right moral attitude on the poet's part toward those realities, then poetry is capable of providing a sensible medium for understanding theological truths.[39] It does so by casting spiritual realities in concrete terms, in images drawn from life and expressed in the vernacular. Thus, words are capable of signifying truth accurately, though they do so incompletely.

It is therefore not surprising that Dante uses metaphors of writing and sculpture as he approaches the vision of the Trinity beginning in canto XIII and culminating in canto XIV, the source for the prayer in the *Troilus*. Whereas in the *Inferno* "God and truth are absent [and] speech has lost the power to communicate in a normal way," in the *Paradiso* Dante attempts to create a new form of expression in language, to push it to its limits.[40] God manifests himself in man much like an imprint made in wax (*Paradiso* XIII, 52–78). Whatever imperfections arise are due not to God, but to Nature "working like the artist who in the practice of his art has a hand that trembles" (similemente operando a l'artista/ ch'a l'abito de l'arte ha man che trema, XIII, 77–78). A singular moment in history had occurred, however, when the ideal of God found its perfect expression in one of mankind, namely through the Incarnation:

> Così fu fatta già la terra degna
> di tutta l'animal perfezïone;
> così fu fatta la Vergine pregna.
> (XIII, 82–84)

Thus was the dust made fit for the full perfection of a living creature; thus was the Virgin made to be with child.)

Because of the Incarnation—because the Word was given concreteness in the flesh—the divine image within man can be expressed in correspondingly concrete terms, though with the trembling hand of an artist, in this case Dante. As Colish writes: "The Incarnation, for Dante no less than for Augustine, transforms the sensible world. As a result, concrete, material things, individual persons as moral ends, and earthly beauties as objects of authentic aesthetic experience become means by which God chooses to descend to man, in and through the conditions of human life."[41]

Dante's prayer to the Trinity in canto XIV becomes a perfect expression not only of the paradox of the Trinity, but of Dante's own poetic techniques. It recalls the image of the circles of water that begins the Canto:

> Dal centro al cerchio, e sì dal cerchio al centro
> movesi l'acqua in un ritondo vaso,
> secondo ch'è percosso fuori o dentro.
>
> (1–3)

(From the center to the rim, and so from the rim to the center, the water in a round vessel moves, according as it is struck from without or within.)

The simple image of ripples of water in a vessel provides the concrete metaphor for explaining the paradox of the trinity:

> Quell' uno e due e tre che sempre vive
> e regne sempre in tre e 'n due e 'n uno,
> non circunscritto, e tutto circunscrive.
>
> (28-30)

(That One and Two and Three which ever lives, and ever reigns in Three and Two and One, uncircumscribed, and circumscribing all things.)

Here the imagery is also that of writing ("non circunscritto, e tutto circunscrive"), as though bearing witness to the fact that God gave expression of himself to man through language, speech—the Word— and in doing so opened the way for communication with the Divine. Yet, we must recall that it is Beatrice who interprets Dante's question for Solomon and so opens the way to the vision of the Trinity and later of the Cross. It was her love that initially brought forth Virgil to guide the poet (*Inferno*, II, 72), and it is the vision of her in this canto that " 'empowers' him to rise to the next heaven"[42] and to a vision of the Cross. Human love is thus drawn into relationship with divine love, and that relationship can only be expressed as a result of the Incarnation.

Within this context we can now assess the importance of the concluding lines of *Troilus and Criseyde*. Dante's trembling hand as it shapes through the Word becomes the narrator's tremulous voice as he approaches the ineffable:

> Thow oon, and two, and thre, eterne on lyve,
> That regnest ay in thre, and two, and oon,
> Uncircumscript, and al maist circumscrive,
> Us from visible and invisible foon
> Defende, and to thy mercy, everichon,
> So make us, Jesus, for thi mercy digne,
> For love of mayde and moder thyn benigne.
> Amen.
>
> (1863–69)

By redirecting the poem's purpose in this way, by leading his audience to consider the moral implications of the tale he has related, Chaucer becomes, in effect, a poet of rectitude. The verbal signs he has called to mind—the Trinity and the Incarnation—propel him beyond the restrictions of ambiguous language: here, then, for the first time in the poem, a true correspondence is established between signs and their *significata*, and between word and intention. The prayer is preceded by a reference to "that sothefast Crist, that starf on rode" (1860) and ends with a reference to Jesus and Mary. As though in preparation for the verbal icon of the Trinity, Chaucer reminds his audience that Christ the Word "became a partaker of our human nature," as Augustine writes, "and thus offered us a short cut to participation in his own divine nature";[43] for, by having available a Mediator between God and man, man can, however imperfectly, give expression to the divine nature. The paradoxical "Uncircumscript and al maist circumscrive" reminds us that God wrote his image in man, and, as a result of the Incarnation, man is able to reciprocate by writing in praise the truth of God's divinity.[44]

The final two lines of the poem, however, in calling to mind Jesus and Mary, cast us back into the world of the poem, back to the world of human love. As Dante's love of Beatrice led him to the next heaven, so the very real human love of Troilus and Criseyde empowers our narrator to consider a higher love. Colish observes that Dante does not seek "to transcend human existence by using the world as a vehicle to God and then leaving it behind. Rather, [his] motive is to infuse the world and human existence with divine wisdom, power, and love, to transform it from within."[45] Indeed, the same can be said of Chaucer. The poet is not asking us to leave behind the world of human experience; rather he is asking that we transform it by refocusing our perspective.[46] For to perceive the world exclusively in terms of the physical is to deny the efficacy of signs as avenues to spiritual cognition. It is this confusion of the carnal with the spiritual that pulls humankind away from *caritas*; on the contrary, the *res* must be viewed as a means to the *signum*.[47] In the most minute ways, this world is a reflection of the Trinity and God's love, and Chaucer presses us to acknowledge the source of this love in our own world. Thus he ends his poem reminding us of Mary, reminding us of human love directed to God.

By ending his poem on a distinctly Christian note, Chaucer is not finally asking that we judge pagan Troy in light of Christian ethics, though certainly the one comments upon the other.[48] Rather, the abruptness of the poem's ending serves to pluck us from the seductiveness of a world of romance and courtly love, a world whose very distance in time and setting is as alluring as the intrigues and emotions of its characters. For Troilus, the Paradise that stands in Criseyde's eyes (v, 817) is a worthy goal toward which he can aspire. For the reader, however, that Paradise is one of limited earthly joys. The reader at this point is much like Dante the pilgrim, who, as he turns to behold the splendor of Beatrice's eyes, is confronted instead by the benign eyes of St. Bernard, and is directed to lift his eyes to the "thousand angels making festival" (xxxi, 131: *mille angeli festanti*). Where earlier we too might have sought Paradise in Criseyde's eyes, now, as we approach the verbal icon of the Trinity, we are admonished to turn our gaze upward toward God:

> And of youre herte up casteth the visage
> To thilke God that after his ymage
> Yow made.
> (v, 1838–40)

Like Dante, Chaucer provides his readers with a complex, yet concrete metaphor by which we can comprehend in some measure Divine Love within the context of human experience. From the Christian ethical perspective, the world of Troilus and Criseyde, of Pandarus and Diomede, is essentially a sterile one; but within that world of lust, deceit, and self-centeredness is found a purer, more enobling love in Troilus. It is here that Christian love converges with pagan; as Elizabeth Kirk writes, " . . . God loves not as Criseyde loved Troilus, but as Troilus loved Criseyde. So it is that Troilus, of all the characters, enters Heaven."[49] Like the pilgrim Dante, we have only to turn our eyes to the true path to behold "the height and breadth of the Eternal Goodness, since it has made itself so many mirrors where it is reflected, remaining in itself One as before":

> Vedi l'eccelso omai e la larghezza
> de l'etterno valor, poscia che tanti
> speculi fatti s'ha in che si spezza,
> uno manendo in sé come davanti.
> (xxix, 142–45)

Armed with a new understanding of the relation between language and truth, and with fresh insight into the relationship between love, man, and the divine, we can reenter the poem better prepared to evaluate the world of Troilus and Criseyde. Like Troilus, however, we may be tempted to laugh; for in locating the core of truth, and in seeing "The blynde lust, the which that may nat laste" (1824), we must ask ourselves "And syn he best to love is, and most meke, / What nedeth feyned loves for to seke?" (1847–48). Like Dante, Chaucer has taken us on a journey from doubt to certitude, from ambiguity to truth. He becomes our guide through the world, so that "by means of corporal and temporal things we may comprehend the eternal and spiritual."[50] In doing so, he explores the limits of language itself: where once we could never be certain of the truth of words, nor could ever express in them anything beyond themselves, now language has the potential to signify an eternal truth; and, as a consequence, language allows us to participate in the divine nature of the Trinity.

Notes

1. "Platonic Forms in Chaucer," *The Chaucer Review* 17, no. 4 (Spring 1983): 379.

2. See, for example, P. B. Taylor, "Chaucer's *Cosyn to the Dede*," *Speculum* 57, 2 (1982): 315–327; Russell A. Peck, "Chaucer and the Nominalist Questions," *Speculum* 53 (1978): 745–60; David C. Steinmetz, "Late Medieval Nominalism and the *Clerk's Tale*," *The Chaucer Review* 12 (1977): 38–54.

3. Walter Clyde Curry, *Chaucer and the Medieval Sciences* (New York: Barnes & Noble, Inc.; revised and enlarged ed., 1960), p. 298. Prof. Curry writes further: "What follows in the Epilog to the completed drama (v, 1807–69) is dramatically a sorry performance. From one point of view one may lament the fact that an enlightened artist, who has held himself with admirable courage to the composition of a stirring tragedy, should have in the end deemed it expedient to drop into the role of an extraordinary moralist, pointing out to his contemporaries that earthly joy is but false felicity" (p. 294).

Discussions of the ending of the poem are numerous; see, for example, John S. P. Tatlock, "The Epilog of Chaucer's *Troilus*," *Modern Philology* 18, no. 12 (April 1921): 113–147; Peter Dronke, "The Conclusion of *Troilus and Criseyde*," *Medium Ævum* 33 (1964): 47–52; P. M. Kean, "Chaucer's Dealings with a Stanza of *Il Filostrato* and the Epilogue of *Troilus and Criseyde*," *Medium Ævum* 33 (1964): 36–46; Anthony E. Farnham, "Chaucerian Irony and the Ending of the *Troilus*," *The Chaucer Review* 1 (1966–67): 207–16; Ida L. Gordon, *The Double Sorrow of Troilus: A Study of Ambiguities in Troilus and Criseyde* (Oxford, The Clarendon Press, 1970), esp. pp. 53–59; E. Talbot Donaldson, *Speaking of Chaucer* (London: The Athelone Press, 1970), ch. 6; Murray F Markland, "*Troilus and Criseyde* and the Inviolability of the Ending," *Modern Language Quarterly* 31 (1970): 147–59; Bernard F. Huppé, "The Unlikely Narrator: The Narrative Structure of the *Troilus*," in John P. Hermann and John J. Burke, Jr., eds., *Signs and Symbols in Chaucer's Poetry* (Tuscaloosa: The University of Alabama Press, 1981), pp. 179–94, esp. pp. 192–94; Bonnie Wheeler, "Dante, Chaucer, and the Ending of *Troilus and Criseyde*," *Philological Quarterly* 61 (1982): 105–23; Gerald Morgan, "The Ending of *Troilus and Criseyde*," *Modern Language Review* 77 (1982): 257–71; David Lawton, "Irony and Sympathy in *Troilus and Criseyde*: A Reconsideration," *Leeds Studies in English* 14 (1983): 94–115, esp. 190f. See also the important recent study by Winthrop Wetherbee, *Chaucer and the Poets: An Essay on Troilus and Criseyde* (Ithaca: Cornell University Press, 1984), esp. ch. 8 (pp. 224–43).

4. All quotations from Chaucer are from *The Works of Geoffrey Chaucer*, ed. F. N. Robinson, 2nd ed. (Boston: Houghton Mifflin, 1957). Stanza numbering refers to R. K. Root's edition (Princeton, N.J.: Princeton University Press, 1926; reprint, 1952).

5. See Donaldson, *Speaking of Chaucer*, p. 95; see also Wetherbee, *Chaucer and the Poets*, p. 227f, who sees the naming of the *auctores* as implying (though still somewhat comically) an emerging of the poet's own identity.

6. Wheeler, "Dante, Chaucer," p. 108.

7. On the question of Troilus's ascent and the apotheosis tradition, see E. J. Dobson, "Some Notes on Middle English Texts," *English and Germanic Studies* 1 (1947–48): 61–62; Jackson L. Cope, "Chaucer, Venus, and the 'Seventhe Spere'," *Modern Language Notes* 67 (1952): 245–46; Forrest S. Scott, "The Seventh Sphere: A Note on 'Troilus and Criseyde'," *Modern Language Review* 51 (1956); 2–5; Morton W. Bloomfield, "The Eighth Sphere: A Note on Chaucer's 'Troilus and Criseyde'," *Modern Language Review* 53 (1958): 408–10; "On the Tradition of Troilus's Vision of the Little Earth," in Alfred L. Kellogg, *Chaucer, Langland, Arthur: Essays in Middle English Literature* (New Jersey: Rutgers University Press, 1972), pp. 199–211; John M. Steadman, *Disembodied Laughter: Troilus and the Apotheosis Tradition* (Berkeley: University of California Press, 1972).

8. *The Earliest Lives of Dante*, trans. James Robinson Smith with an introduction by Francesco Basetti-Sani (New York: Frederick Ungar Publishing Co., 1963), p. 54.

9. Ibid., p. 51.

10. John Gibb and William Montgomery, eds., *The Confessions of Augustine* (Cambridge: Cambridge University Press, 1908).

11. *De magistro*, 2.6.: "[S]imul enim te credo animadvertere, etiamsi quisquam contendat, quamvis nullam edamus sonum, tamen, quia ipsa verba cogitamus, nos intus apud animum loqui, sic quoque locutionem nihil aliud agere quam commemorare, cum memoria, cui verba inhaerent, ea revolvendo facit venire in mentem res ipsas, quarum signa sunt verba" (CSEL 77).

12. *Contra mendacium*, 13.28: "[Q]uod totum utique fingitur, ut ad rem, quae intenditur, ficta quidem narratione, non mendaci tamen, sed ueraci significatione ueniatur" (CSEL 41). Translated in *Seventeen Short Treatises of S. Augustine, Bishop of Hippo* (London: Walter Smith, 1885), p. 455.

13. *De civitate Dei*, 9.16 (CCSL 47); the translation is that of Henry Bettenson (Middlesex, England: Penguin Books, Ltd., 1972).

14. "[S]ed mediator, per quod homo, eo ipso utique ostendens ad illud non solum beatum, uerum etiam beatificum bonum non oportere quaeri alios mediatores, per quos arbitremur nobis peruentionis gradus esse moliendos, quia beatus et beatificus Deus factus particeps humanitatis nostrae compendium praebuit participandae diuinitatis suae" (9.17).

15. *Ennarationes in Psalmos*, 99.6; quoted and trans. by Marcia L. Colish, *The Mirror of Language: A Study in the Medieval Theory of Knowledge*, rev. ed. (Lincoln: University of Nebraska Press, 1983), p. 26.

16. *De civitate Dei*, 10.29: "[S]ed incarnationem incommutabilis Filii Dei, qua saluamur, ut ad illa, quae credimus uel ex quantulacumque parte intellegimus, uenire possimus, non uultis agnoscere." See also 9.15: "Neque enim nos a mortalitate et miseria liberans ad angelos inmortales beatosque ita perducit, ut eorum participatione etiam nos inmortales et beati simus; sed ad illam Trinitatem, cuius et angeli participatione beati sunt."

17. *De magistro*, 11.36.

18. *De magistro*, 11.38: "De universis autem, quae intelligimus, non loquentem, qui personat foris, sed intus ipsi menti praesidentem consulimus veritatem, verbis fortasse ut consulamus admoniti." The translation is that of Robert P. Russell, O.S.A. (The Fathers of the Church, vol. 59; Washington, D.C.: The Catholic University of America Press, 1968).

19. *De magistro*, 1.2: "[S]ic quoque locutionem nihil aluid agere quam commemorare, cum memoria, cui verba inhaerent, ea revolvendo facit venire in mentem res ipsas, quarum signa sunt verba."

20. *De doctrina Christiana*, 2.1: "Signum est enim res praeter speciem, quam ingerit sensibus, aliud aliquid ex se faciens in cogitationem uenire . . ." (CCSL 32). The translation is that of D. W. Robertson, Jr. (Indianapolis: The Bobbs-Merrill Co., Inc., 1958).

21. *Confessions*, 1.1: "[S]ed quis te inuocat nesciens te?" The translation is that of John K. Ryan (New York: Image Books, 1960).

22. *De magistro*, 14.46: "[U]trum autem vera dicantur, eum docere solum, qui se intus habitare, cum foris loqueretur, admonuit."

23. *Confessions*, 9.10.23: "[S]ed inhiabamus ore cordis in superna fluenta fontis tui. . . ."

24. *Confessions*, 9.10.24: "Cumque ad eum finem sermo perduceretur, ut carnalium sensuum delectatio quantalibet in quantalibet luce corporea prae illius uitae

iucunditate non conparatione, sed ne conmemoratione quidem digna uideretur, erigentes nos ardentiore affectu in id ipsum perambulauimus gradatim cuncta corporalia et ipsum caelum, unde sol et luna et stellae lucent super terram. et adhuc ascendebamus interius cogitando et loquendo et mirando opera tua et uenimus in mentes nostras et transcendimus eas, ut attingeremus regionem ubertatis indeficientis . . . et ibi uita sapientia est, per quam fiunt omnia ista . . . . [E]t remeauimus ad strepitum oris nostri, ubi uerbum et incipitur et finitur."

25. *Confessions*, 9.10.24: "[E]t quid simile uerbo tuo, domino nostro, in se permanenti sine uetustate atque innouanti omnia?"

26. See note 22 above.

27. *De civitate Dei*, 11.26.

28. *O Love O Charite! Contraries Harmonized in Chaucer's* Troilus (Carbondale: Southern Illinois University Press, 1976), p. 152.

29. "Words and Images in the *Paradiso:* Reflections of the Divine," in Aldo S. Bernardo and Anthony L. Pellegrini, *Dante, Petrarch, Boccaccio: Studies in the Italian Trecento in Honor of Charles S. Singleton*, Medieval and Renaissance Texts and Studies 22 (Binghamton: State University of New York at Binghamton, 1983), p. 121.

30. *Geneaologia deorum gentilium libri*, 14.7; the translation is that of Charles G. Osgood, *Boccaccio on Poetry*, The Library of Liberal Arts 82 (New York: The Liberal Arts Press, 1956).

31. *De doctrina Christiana*, 2.7.10: "Necesse est ergo, ut primo se quisque in scripturis inueniat amore huius saeculi, hoc est, temporalium rerum, implicatum, longe seiunctum esse a tanto amore dei et tanto amore proximi, quantum scriptura ipsa praescribit."

32. Ibid.: "Hoc enim affectu ab omni mortifera iucunditate rerum transeuntium sese extrahit et inde se auertens conuertit ad dilectionem aeternorum, incommutabilem scilicet unitatem eandemque trinitatem."

33. *De Trinitate*, 15.11.20: "Proinde uerbum quod foris sonat signum est uerbi quod intus lucet . . ." (CCSL 50a).

34. Ibid., 15.11.20: "Quando ergo quod est in notitia hoc est in uerbo, tunc est uerum uerbum et ueritas qualis exspectatur ab homine. . . ."

35. All quotations are from Charles S. Singleton, ed. and trans., *The Divine Comedy*, Bollingen Series 80 (New Jersey: Princeton University Press, 1970–1975).

36. The translation is that of A. G. Ferrers Howell, *Dante: De vulgari eloquentia* (London: Rebel Press, 1973), p. 22.

37. Ibid., pp. 49 and 52.

38. Ibid., p. 50.

39. Colish, *The Mirror of Language*, p. 206 passim.

40. Joan M. Ferrante, "The Relation of Speech and Sin in the *Inferno*," *Dante Studies* 87 (1969): 34.

41. Colish, *The Mirror of Language*, p. 192.

42. Singleton, *The Divine Comedy*, vol. 2, p. 247.

43. *De civitate Dei*, 9.15; see note 14 above.

44. Of interest is R. Allen Shoaf's discussion of language and coinage imagery in "Dante's *Commedia* and Chaucer's Theory of Meditation: A Preliminary Sketch" in *New Perspectives in Chaucer Criticism*, Donald M. Rose, ed. (Norman, Okla.: Pilgrim Books, Inc., 1981), pp. 83–103.

45. Colish, *The Mirror of Language*, p. 192.

46. Wetherbee offers a compatible view. He sees the final prayer as "a plea for the

reintegration of human life, for the redemption of the imagination of that psychological schism that has allowed Troilus to invoke love in the language of Dante's Saint Bernard, praying to Mary at the summit of the *Paradiso,* yet allowed him also to believe that Paradise is the love of Criseyde" (*Chaucer and the Poets,* p. 243). Similarly, this idea of what Wetherbee calls "human community," a community made palpable through "the continuum of poetic experience and poetic tradition" (p. 226), is discussed by Stephen Manning in "*Troilus,* Book v: Invention and the Poem as Process," *Chaucer Review* 18, 4 (1984): 288–301: "The poet's love binds together his universe and enables him to see the Love which binds together the larger universe. It is this creative love which provides the transition between his earlier view and his later reformulation of it, between worldly and divine love. Moreover, the analogy between the poet and the Divine Artist is what extols and simultaneously limits his poetry. Finally, if the human love of Troilus and Criseyde exemplifies humanity at its noblest and necessarily at its most finite, then the poet through the process of his poem illustrates the same humanity perhaps even more perfectly" (p. 301).

47. For a compatible approach to the study of language in the thirteenth century lyric, "Nou goth sonne under wod," see James P. Hala, "*Signum et Res:* Wordplay and Christian Rhetoric," *Michigan Academician* 16, no. 3 (1984): 315–28.

48. See Elizabeth D. Kirk, "'Paradis Stood Formed in Hire Yen': Courtly Love and Chaucer's Re-Vision of Dante," in *Acts of Interpretation: The Text in Its Context, 700–1600: Essays on Medieval and Renaissance Literature in Honor of E. Talbot Donaldson* (Norman: Pilgrim Books, 1982), pp. 257–77.

49. Ibid., p. 271.

50. *De doctrina Christiana,* 1.4.4: " . . . ut de corporalibus temporalibusque rebus aeterna et spiritalia capiamus."

PART V

REWRITING THE TEXT
The Privatization of Signs

EDITORS' INTRODUCTION

If words are not exact—if there exist both difference and identity between signifieds and signifiers—then the anxiety that Dante feels at the end of the *Paradiso* in regard to the painted figure is relieved by the realization that such *signa* are only fictions, reflections rather than the substantive phenomena themselves. This realization comes partly through the understanding of the common trope of language as *speculum,* as a mirror that reflects only one side of a given object at any given time, while the others exist *in potencia.* Indeed, such a relationship was demonstrated, in the last chapter, by Phillip Pulsiano in discussing the different, singular meanings of the polysemous term "love" at the end of *Troilus,* and was equally evident in R. A. Shoaf's discussion of "mewe."

Far from being a source of anxiety, however, this "interpretive anarchy," to borrow a phrase from the first of the following two essays, can be like the creative and creating Word or, like Dante's multileveled text, something to be celebrated. Thus, instead of a society painfully aware of its broken oaths and fractured texts, Judith Ferster speaks of "a period [that] saw increases in literacy and increased interest in the use and misuse of texts," and, as a result, of a society which was increasingly aware of the privatization that occurs in private as opposed to public reading of texts.

Much of what we have seen in earlier chapters simply explores the essential dynamic inherent in language, which by its nature is both arbitrary *and* conventional, both fluid *and* fixed. Until recently, our tendency, as Shoaf points out, has been to assume that medieval views of language, like modernists, stressed the latter. The essays in this chapter, however, stress the medieval awareness of the fluidity of language. Ferster's essay graphically demonstrates the two polar yet complementary positions, first the fixed in the story of Simeon and secondly the fluid in the account of the woman taken in adultery. In the play of Simeon, we witness repeated unsuccessful attempts to place the ultimate authorized text under physical erasure. Through the invisible hand of a guardian angel, the old priest's alterations in the miraculous prophecy repeatedly disappear, finally to be replaced by the convincing letters of gold. In the story of the woman taken in adultery, on the other hand, we are shown just the opposite. In what Ferster notes is the only scriptural account of Jesus writing, we witness an account that would seem to confirm the playwright's perception that "the fate of the text [is] to be appropriated by its readers, who interpret it according to their needs." Although seemingly the product of the very appropriation to which it alludes, the idea is not far from the Augustinian argument, cited by Pulsiano, that Christ used words to remind us of what is written in us, nor from the Augustinian principle, cited by Ross Arthur, that the fate of the text is to be read (or misread) according to fixed principles of the human psyche. The difference here, of course, is that the truths pointed to by the writing on the ground are private, individualized sins rather than universal virtues. These are more of those "discriminating signs," discussed earlier by Arthur, which actually reveal the nature of their perceiver. Thus, far from resulting in "interpretive anarchy," the polysemousness in this story, like the fixedness in the story of Simeon, is the stuff of miracles, a demonstration of "God's plenitude" rather than a sign of His absence. In the end, however, there are limits, and although the reader can read with self-interest, he or she must, to read truthfully, select from among truths, self-interested though they be.

The same positivist combination of "plenitude" and "truth" is at the heart of Julian Wasserman's discussion of fate and language in Chaucer. God, through grace, allows us authorized individuality, that is, free will—a freedom that is exercised linguistically. For Palamon and Arcite, reading is unwittingly (re)writing the text. Much like the partial readers described by Jean Grimbert, each reads according to his nature, choosing the part for the whole, whether aspects of Emelye or conditions of success in the tournament's outcome. Yet what each reads is part of the fixed truth, a truth fixed "with that word." Here as in Ferster, meaning results from an interplay of what is fixed in the sign, its wealth of potentialities, and what is fixed in the reader, his habitual ways of interpreting signs.

9

WRITING ON THE GROUND
Interpretation in Chester Play XII

JUDITH FERSTER

In Play XI of the Chester Mystery Cycle, the righteous old priest Simeon, who expects the coming of a savior but does not know that he has already been born, is startled to read that Isaiah predicts the birth of "Emanuell" to a virgin. He not only refuses to believe that a virgin could bear a child, but also insists that the book is "wronge written."[1] After he speaks briefly with a woman named Anna, he takes up the Bible again and is amazed to see that the words he has substituted for those of Isaiah are gone and that in their place stands "a virgin" in red letters. He reveals this "miracle" (61) to Anna and decides to test it by erasing the text again and substituting his own version, "that soother ys" (69). Indeed, the miracle is repeated: when he opens the book again, his words are now replaced with golden letters that reaffirm Isaiah's prophecy. He at last declares his willingness to believe the prediction (94–95), and the angel who has been miraculously restoring the text appears to him and tells him that he will live long enough to meet his savior, the miraculous child.

This story of the contest between manipulative misinterpreter and the guardian angel of the text must have had great resonance for late medieval writers because of the increases in literacy and resulting increased interest in the use and misuse of texts. Simeon is a blatant misuser, for whom the Bible is a book to be corrected and appropriated to reflect his own opinion of what is true. He demonstrates that not only may texts fail to win acceptance for the beliefs they advocate but they may prompt revisionary interpretation as well. The angel who guards the integrity of the Bible in Play XI is one solution to the problem of the vulnerability of texts.

Another supernatural solution appears in the very next play of the Chester Cycle, which includes the episode of the woman taken in adultery. The story, which comes from the Gospel according to John (8:1–11),[2] is the only account we have of Jesus writing. It solves the problem of the text's vulnerability to interpretation not by preventing misreading but by describing a special correspondence between the intentions of author and audience. I want to focus on the extraordinary story of Jesus' writing on the ground and the Jews' interpretation of his text. Why does he write when he could speak to them? Why does he write on the ground? What is the significance of the Jews' responses to his text? I believe that the work of Paul Ricoeur can help to illuminate this episode, its relation to some of the other plays in the cycle, and its significance for late medieval ideas about interpretation.

The Semantic Autonomy of the Written Text

The Chester version of the story seems to try to explain some of what is left obscure in the Gospel. John does not explain the content or the function of the writing. An undisclosed number of scribes and Pharisees bring an adulteress to Jesus, citing the Old Testament law about stoning adulterers and asking him for his judgment. They hope "that they might be able to accuse him" (8:6).[3] He writes on the ground with his finger, but they are not deterred from their questioning. He speaks—"Let him who is without sin among you be the first to cast a stone at her" (8:7)—and writes again. The scribes and Pharisees depart "one by one, beginning with the eldest" (8:9), leaving Jesus and the woman alone. He asks her who accuses and condemns her. When she replies, "No one," he says, "Neither will I condemn thee. Go thy way, and from now on sin no more" (8:11). In this story, the first writing seems to have no effect.[4] When the questioning persists, his speech supplements the writing, and either the speech alone or the speech and the second writing together cause the Jews to abandon the scene. The medieval plays specify the number of Jews at two (Chester), three (N-Town), and four (York). The number of Jews was surely influenced by the exigencies of production—how many actors were available, how many could fit on the set, etc. But a result of the small number of Jews is that they can all *see* the writing, as they could not in a large crowd. The speech comes first and has no impact: in the Chester play, Primus Pharaseus repeats the case to Jesus—"shall shee be stoned or elles naye . . . ?" (246)—as though he had not heard Jesus' moral principle. Only after the Jews read the writing do they flee, each one chastened by what he has read, each one claiming that he does not dare to stay and accuse the woman. The first fears worldly shame, and (in the Harley text) says he must leave because "I see my synnes so clearly" (after 255). In the Gospel, the writing is ineffective (the Jews may not even read it) and must be bolstered or explained by the speech. In the play, by contrast, the speech is insufficient and the writing chases the Jews away by showing them not merely a moral principle about the fitness of judges and executioners, but their own sins.[5]

The importance of the writing in the Chester play is clear if we compare the Chester version to the two other cycles. In the N-Town, the woman enters asking for mercy; in the York, Jesus asks her to repent, and she does. Although penitence is not the focus of the story in John, these two plays make the story into an *exemplum* of repentance.[6] In the Chester play, however, there is no mention of repentance. The woman converts when she recognizes Jesus as God because his writing displayed a supra-human knowledge of her accusers:[7]

> For godhead full in thee I see
> that knowes worke that doe wee.
> (277–78)

The writing is what frees Jesus from the trap set by the Jews and what makes the woman abandon sin for his sake.

Thus, the writing, undisclosed and almost nonfunctional in John, is turned in the Chester play into a magic text that discloses to each man his own sin. This is an extremely interesting kind of text in the late Middle Ages. Medieval narratives are full of stories of people seeing themselves in a text as if in a mirror. The most famous example is perhaps Augustine, who converted when he read a portion of the Bible "as if addressed to himself."[8] The insomniac narrator of Chaucer's *Book of the Duchess* finds Ovid's story of Ceyx and Alcyone memorable chiefly for its reference to a god of sleep, of whom he was previously unaware. The narrator focuses on the part of the story that addresses his self-interest. In Chester Play xi, Simeon interprets according to his preconceived notions of what is possible in nature.

This is the fate of any written text—to be appropriated by its readers, who interpret it according to their own needs. They can interpret it as they like, just as they can control the experience of it by reading it in the wrong order, skipping, or skimming at will. Even the freedom not to read is a part of the license a reader has that a listener does not, and this license must have been growing clearer in the late Middle Ages as more and more people could read and could afford books.[9] Conditions of reception in the late Middle Ages highlighted the reader's role as a shaper and interpreter of the text, and the reader's role often became part of the subject matter of the work.[10] This is to say that the late Middle Ages was paying more and more attention—was being forced by the changing conditions of reception to pay attention—to what Paul Ricoeur would call the semantic autonomy of the text. With writing, says Ricoeur,

> the author's intention and the meaning of the text cease to coincide
> . . . . Inscription becomes synonymous with the semantic autonomy
> of the text, which results from the disconnection of the mental inten-
> tion of the author from the verbal meaning of the text, of what the
> author meant and what the text means. The text's career escapes the
> finite horizon lived by its author. What the text means now matters
> more than what the author meant when he wrote it.[11]

The increasing reading audience, and the increasing likelihood that readers would have access to a text they could read alone, meant that writers were becoming especially conscious of the likelihood that their works might be subjectively interpreted by private readers. I do not mean to suggest that works read aloud in groups or for that matter conversation cannot be misinterpreted. I do mean that the situation of texts was changing enough to bring the question of interpretation to consciousness as subject matter for late medieval writers. For example, the Church's anxieties about access to the Bible by readers untrained in authorized exegetical methods[12] indicates ecclesiastical awareness of the power of those who could read for themselves.

Active Readers

In the Chester cycle, the Expositor is an example of an active reader. In Play xii, he applies the commentary of St. Gregory to the first episode, the story of the temptation of Christ, interpreting the three sins to which he was tempted as gluttony, avarice, and vainglory (calling the opportunity to eat after forty days of fasting "gluttony" is

very medieval). After the episode of the adulterous woman, he interprets in several ways. For instance, he decides a point not perfectly
clear from the play by saying of the Jews that

> . . . non of them wiser was,
> but his synnes eych man knewe.
> (307–8)

In Play v, the Expositor is an even more obtrusive reader in that he
acknowledges that the story he takes from the Bible is cut:

> But all that storye for to fonge
> to playe this moneth yt were to longe.
> Therfore moste fruitefull ever amonge
> shortly wee shall myn.
> (45–48)

The story that is too long to tell is the central one of the giving of the
Law to Moses. At the end of the play the Expositor acknowledges
that the Balaam and Balak episode from Numbers has been short-
ened:

> Lordings, mych more mattere
> is in this storye then yee have hard here.
> (440–41)

He claims that the cuts destroy none of the meaning:

> But the substans, withowten were,
> was played you beforen.
> (442–43)

His claim that God's book can be condensed without loss is striking, especially in light of his great busy-ness in this play. He not only
notes cuts in the story; he narrates an important event (the rewriting
of the tablets of the Ten Commandments) instead of letting it be
dramatized, and he intrudes (in the Harley manuscript) after every
prophet in the prophets' procession to interpret the prophet's speech

(usually typologically, with reference to Christian history). He interrupts even where he asserts that no interpretation is necessary:

> Lordinges, these wordes are so veray
> that exposition, in good faye,
> none needes; but you know may
> this word "Emanuell."
> "Emanuell" is as much to saye
> as "God with us night and day."
>
> (H305–10)

Despite his claim here of the transparency of the prophet's meaning, the claim undermines itself: transparency that needs labelling isn't transparent, and besides, the word "Emanuell" needs translating. At the end of the procession, during which, with his help, Old Testament prophets predict the events of the New Testament, he himself predicts (444–55) the events of two of the next plays, Play vi (the Nativity) and Play viii (the Magi). Several of the Expositor's comments explicitly address the shaping power of interpretation—both his own as a reader and that of his audience of playgoers. He labels his role as reader ("as reede I," 53) and acknowledges the importance of the interpreter's will when he interprets Ezekiel's gate as a reference to the conception of Jesus:

> By this gate, lords, verament
> *I understand in my intent*
> that way the Holy Ghost in went
> when God tooke flesh and bloode
> in that sweet mayden Mary.
>
> (H321–25; emphasis mine)

Although this is certainly a traditional reading of the gate, it is important that he mentions neither the tradition nor the writer's intention, but instead his own, the *reader's* intention. He may be meant as a guide to interpretation of the material the plays present. But his activities as reader call attention to the ways in which readers are independent.

The Expositor explicitly refers to his audience when he predicts what will be played next ("played as yee shall see," 57; "as yee shall played see," 445), and acknowledges his hearers' power to decide for themselves when he exhorts, "leeve yee mee" (444, H81). This emphasis on the audience's interpretation is consonant with the theme of belief in the Christian story. In a number of places in the Gospels, Jesus' miracles depend on the belief of the person they affect. For instance, in Mark, a woman's belief allows her to be cured when she touches Jesus, even though Jesus does not notice her or intend her to be cured (Mark 5:25–34; this episode also occurs in Luke 8:43–48 and Matthew 9:20–22). The Chester cycle registers the importance of belief in Play XIII, which contains two miracles, the curing of the blind man and the raising of Lazarus from the dead. When the Jews curse the blind man and ask Jesus if he is the Christ, Jesus tells them that he has already answered the question:

> That I spake to you openlye
> and workes that I doe verelye
> in my Fathers name almightie
> beareth wytnes of mee.
>
> But you beleeve not as you seene,
> for of my sheepe yee ne beene . . .
>
> (239–44)

The discussion of belief becomes more intense in the second half of the play because it becomes more specific. Now the issue is kinds of belief among members of the fold. When Jesus arrives at the home of Mary and Martha, who are grieving for their brother, Martha speaks first:

> And this I leeve and hope aright:
> what thinge thou askest of God almight,
> hee will grant yt thee in height
> and grant thee thy prayer.
>
> (377–80)

Martha affirms her belief *before* Jesus promises to help her, but her belief is limited to trust that Jesus could have prevented the death of Lazarus had he been present at the time:

> A, lord Jesu, haddest thou binne here leade,
> Lazar my brother had not binne deade . . .[13]
>
> (373–74)

All she wants from Jesus now is advice ("but well I wott thou wilt us reade," 375), and when he promises that Lazarus will rise, she assumes that he refers to the resurrection of the dead on Judgment Day:

> That leeve I, lord, in good faye,
> that hee shall ryse the last daye;
> then hope I him to see.
>
> (382–84)

When she shows Jesus the body and its advanced state of corruption (435–37), he must reemphasize the importance of her belief:

> Martha, sayd I not to thee
> if that thou fullye leeved in mee
> Godes grace soone shalt thou see?
> Therfore doe as I thee saye.
>
> (438–41)

Ironically, Martha's profession of faith reveals the limit of her faith.

Jesus reiterates the importance of faith in his lyric in Play XVIII, "De Resurrectione":

> And that bread that I you give,
> your wicked life to amend,
> becomes my fleshe through youre beleeffe
> and doth release your synfull band.
>
> (174–77)

In the raising of Lazarus, Martha's belief did not have to be total or precise. Here in the resurrection lyric, however, Jesus speaks as if transubstantiation depended absolutely on the faith of the communicants. The intentions of the "audience" are necessary to the meaning of the event. The "author's" intentions do not suffice. Interpretation is crucial.

Many Meanings from One Text

We are now more prepared for questions about why Jesus wrote at all and why he wrote on the ground. To answer the first question, we may look at the two other cycles' versions of the episode of the woman taken in adultery because they highlight the important issue of privacy even more than the Chester, and the issue of privacy highlights the oddity of Jesus' writing. To communicate to the Jews, Jesus need only have spoken. As we saw, in the Gospel according to John the number of Jews was unspecified: possibly not all the Jews could have heard him. In the plays, however, there are only a few, and speaking is easier and faster and requires no bending. However, when one speaks, all who are present hear, and the peculiar effect of Jesus' writing is to prevent that. In all the plays, each Jew seems not to have learned the sin(s) of the other(s) from reading the writing. For instance, the Pharisee in the N-Town Cycle is afraid because

> If that my fellowes that did espy
> They will tell it both far and wide.
> (219)

Others voice similar fears.[14] In the N-Town play, the woman herself has special horror of *public* humiliation:

> I pray you kill me here in this place
> And let not the people upon me cry.
> If I be slandered openly
> To all my friendes it shall be shame.
> I pray you kill me privily!
> Let not the people know my defame.
> (216–17)

Ironically, writing, the instrument that bridges distance, mediates absence, and publishes, is here an instrument of privacy.[15] This means not only that the Jews read silently to themselves and not out loud (reading out loud was common in the Middle Ages), but also (unless each Jew did the same foul deed) that the same text (Jesus does not write again after the first Jew reads) means different things to the different men.

One text with many meanings can sometimes be a formula for chaos. In Chaucer's *Squire's Tale,* the people of Cambyuskan's court are puzzled by the brass horse brought by the "strange knight." They speculate about it, and

> Diverse folk diversely they demed;
> As many heddes, as manye wittes [opinions, minds] ther been.

They murmureden as dooth a swarm of been,
And maden skiles aftir hir fantasies,
Rehersynge of thise olde poetries,
And seyden it was lyk the Pegasee,
The hors that hadde wynges for to flee;
Or elles it was the Grekes hors Synon,
That broghte Troie to destruccion,
As men in thise olde geestes rede.[16]

This passage is interesting both for its identification of the source of ideas as fantasies shaped by "olde poetries" and for its reduction of a crowd of individual speakers into an inarticulate swarm of bees. Furthermore, nothing is settled about the horse until the king asks the knight who arrived on it to explain it. The knight explains how to work it, but not how it works, but this seems to satisfy the king. Judgment is deferred until authority steps in with instruction and evasion. The moment is emblematic of the structure of the *Canterbury Tales* as a whole, a chorus of voices each presenting a world view in a contest never finished and never judged, but closed by the instructions and evasions of the *Retraction,* and by its deference to God.

The particular interest of the late Middle Ages in the multiplicity of interpretations is reflected in the scene of Jesus' writing but in a problematic way. The chaos is part of Jesus' tactic of divide and conquer. Because the Jews fear each other, they flee each other as well as Jesus. Their plot to force Jesus to violate either Moses' teaching or his own, fails. Their reading is self-interested; that is, each seems to read his own sins into the text, and yet the interpretive anarchy that results seems to be exactly Jesus' purpose, a way not of solving but of dissolving the double bind into which the Jews have placed him. Jesus' magic polysemous writing, which mirrors each man's sin, disperses the conspiracy.

The best analogue for this positive version of interpretive anarchy is Scripture as Augustine speaks of it in the *Confessions.* Augustine insists that Scripture is polysemous and that no one interpretation is exclusive. He praises Moses' style specifically for its openness to interpretation from many points of view, by hypothesizing that if he, Augustine, had been "commissioned" by God to write Genesis, he would have prayed for "such skill in writing and such power in framing words, that . . . those who can should find expressed in the few words of your servant whatever true conclusions they had reached by their own reasoning; and if, in the light of truth, another man saw a different meaning in those words, it should not be impossible to understand this meaning too in those same words."[17] Interpretive anarchy is not a disaster; it is a divine miracle, testimony to the plenitude of God's meaning. Scripture is a spring with many channels, an orchard with hidden fruit.[18] However, it is also true that Augustine's system has some safeguards. Scripture cannot mean just anything; it can only mean something that is elsewhere revealed "in the light of truth," that is, by other passages or Church doctrine. What each interpreter sees in Scripture can correspond to his own personality and preoccupations; that is, it can be self-interested. But it must also be true.

The story of the woman taken in adultery does not provide such theoretical statements about interpretation, but in the light of Augustine it is perhaps possible to see Jesus' writing on the ground as an analogue to the safeguards in Augustine's system. Of course, the commonsense explanation is that Jesus writes on the ground because it is handy; it eliminates the need for tools—writing surface, writing implement, a means of support. If the purpose of the writing is to make the audience go away, the text can be temporary, erasable by a foot or a breeze. And what better place than earth to write about human sin? But to write on the ground is also to keep the audience from physically controlling the text. If one writes on the ground a message designed to disperse the audience, one is separating audience and text, keeping them from gaining mastery over it. They cannot, like Chaucer's reading audience for the *Canterbury Tales*, "Turne over the leef and chese another tale . . ." (I, 3177). They cannot fold, spindle, or mutilate; they cannot reread. Jesus' choice of writing surface enforces a kind of control over the audience's use of the text.[19]

Writing on the ground is a way to control—even if only symbolically—what is usually uncontrollable, an audience's uses of texts. The only way to achieve absolute control over a text is to refuse to publish it, and the cycle plays usually include the story of Moses' temporary censorship of the Ten Commandments. When God chooses a human agent to transmit the Commandments, he risks having the message interpreted, transformed in some way. There is no hint that when Moses wrote the tablets himself, he did not write them exactly as God had first written them (Exodus 34:4),[20] but Moses' action upon God's first version, written by his own finger, is radical; and it assures that the audience will never see it, never interpret it, and never use it for their own purposes. Of course he does finally give the Commandments to the people, but the moment of refusal to give the text away is an interesting analogue to the later episode.[21]

The fact that Jesus both speaks and writes reinforces the idea that the episode—especially in the medieval versions—is about control of a reader's interpretation by an author's intention. In the Chester version, Jesus' oral statement of the impropriety of sinners' judging other sinners has no impact until the Jews read the writing about their own sins. General principle means nothing until it can be applied to the individual, until each one, in Augustine's formulation, takes it as a counsel "addressed to himself." Jesus provides both aphorism and application, both (oral) text and (written) gloss.

In his retelling of the story, the Expositor implies that the Jews' interpretation of the writing is correct, that is, accords with Jesus' intention. He says

> [t]hat wyst Jesu full well their thought,
> and all theire wyttes hee sett at nought—
> but bade which synne had not wrought
> cast first at her a stonne;
> and wrote in claye—leeve yee mee—
> their owne synnes that they might see,
> that ichone fayne was to flee,
> and they lefte hir alonne.
>
> For eychon of them had grace
> to see theire sinnes in that place . . .
> (297–306)

Thus the miraculous nature of this text: each reader sees himself in it, yet this idiosyncratic, even selfish reading occurs through grace and is in an important way "authorized." According to Ricoeur, what I have called idiosyncratic interpretation is not necessarily self-enclosed, because reading can be the occasion for learning about the self:

> Far from saying that a subject already mastering his own way of being in the world projects the *a priori* of his self-understanding on the text and reads it into the text, I say that interpretation is the process by which disclosure of new modes of being—or if you prefer Wittgenstein to Heidegger, of new forms of life—gives to the subject a new capacity

for knowing himself. . . . The reader . . . is enlarged in his capacity of self-projection by receiving a new mode of being from the text itself.[22]

Jesus' writing is an ideal case. The readers' self-recognition (not particularly pleasant or welcome, but true) coincides precisely with the author's intentions.

The issues of interpretation I have discussed here show how Play XII fits into the Chester cycle. They also show how the play, along with the story of Simeon's book in Play XI, addresses late medieval concerns about the dangers of interpretation. In the Middle Ages, Jesus as writer has the power many writers, medieval and modern, must have wished for: the power to touch readers individually and with force, but without being misunderstood.[23]

Notes

1. R. M. Lumiansky and David Mills, eds., *The Chester Mystery Cycle, Vol. I, Text*, Early English Text Society, Suppl. Series 3 (London: Oxford University Press, 1974), ll. 30–31. All quotations from the Chester cycle are taken from this edition. References to the Harley manuscript are from their textual notes (for Play V, discussed below, found in appendix IB, pp. 466–81). For the York cycle, I have used the edition of Richard Beadle, *The York Plays*, York Medieval Texts, 2nd Series (London: Edward Arnold, 1982). For both cycles, references appear in the text and are by line numbers (in Harley Play V preceded by an "H"). For the N-Town, I have used the edition of R. T. Davies, *The Corpus Christi Play of the English Middle Ages* (Totowa, N.J.: Rowman and Littlefield, 1972), with references by page numbers.

2. In fact, the incident is not found in the best manuscripts of John. It is included in one group of Luke manuscripts, but is commonly found in John; medieval writers treat it as authentic. See *The Interpreter's Bible* (Nashville: Abingdon, 1982) 8:592.

3. Unless otherwise indicated, Biblical quotations are from *The Holy Bible Translated from the Latin Vulgate with Annotations, References, and an Historical and Chronological Table*, The Douay Version of the Old Testament, The Confraternity Edition of the New Testament (New York: P. J. Kennedy, 1950).

4. According to some interpreters, the writing is not necessarily even verbal: "Probably the author meant no more than that Jesus idly traced figures on the ground to indicate his disinterest in the proceedings." Raymond E. Brown, S. J., et al., eds., *The Jerome Biblical Commentary* (Englewood Cliffs, N.J.: Prentice-Hall, 1968), 2:441.

5. The order in the N-Town version is closer to that of John. Jesus writes during 32 lines of dialogue. There is no response from the Jews until he states the general

principle orally and then writes again (Davies, *Corpus Christi Play*, pp. 217–18). The writing scene is unfortunately lost from the York play; a leaf is missing from the manuscript.

6. For a comparison of the repentance theme in all three English versions, see Eleanor Prosser, *Drama and Religion in the English Mystery Plays: A Re-evaluation* (Stanford: Stanford University Press, 1961), chapter 6. For an explication of Prosser and the particular slant of the Chester version, see Peter W. Travis, *Dramatic Design in the Chester Cycle* (Chicago: University of Chicago Press, 1982), pp. 154–56.

7. Travis, *Dramatic Design in the Chester Cycle*, p. 155.

8. The phrase, actually written about St. Antony, applies equally to Augustine himself. He is imitating Antony's use of the Bible. R. S. Pine-Coffin, trans., *The Confessions of St. Augustine* (Baltimore: Penguin, 1961), 8.12, p. 177.

9. On the effects of cheap paper, book ownership, and increasing literacy, see Janet Coleman, *Medieval Readers and Writers: 1350–1400* (New York: Columbia University Press, 1981).

10. For example, see Judith Ferster, *Chaucer on Interpretation* (New York: Cambridge University Press, 1985).

11. Paul Ricoeur, *Interpretation Theory: Discourse and the Surplus of Meaning* (Fort Worth: Texas Christian University Press, 1976), pp. 29–30.

12. Coleman, *Medieval Readers and Writers*, pp. 209–11.

13. Even a Jew believes that much, saying that if Jesus could make the blind man see, he could probably have prevented Lazarus's death if he had arrived in time (430–33).

14. In the York play (61–62), the second Jew voices the same concern.

15. As I have already noted, the Expositor in the Chester play confirms that each Jew's privacy has been preserved:

> yett non of them wiser was,
> but his synnes eych man knewe.
> (307–8)

In the Harley version this is even clearer: "other" and "owne" replace "them" and "synnes".

16. *Riverside Chaucer*, ed. Larry D. Benson, 3rd ed. (Boston: Houghton Mifflin, 1987), V, 202–11). Subsequent references to the text are from this edition and appear in the text.

17. Augustine, *The Confessions*, 12.26 Pine-Coffin, p. 303.

18. Ibid., 12. 27–28, pp. 303–4.

19. In conversation, Geoffrey Harpham was quick to suggest that Jesus' writing literalizes a common metaphor and actually grounds the text in a specific social context from which it cannot be removed.

20. In Exodus 34:1 God says that he will write the second version of the Ten Commandments. Who did the writing is unclear in the Latin, but probably it was Moses: "Fuit ergo ibi cum Domino quadraginta dies et quadraginta noctes: panem non comedit, et aquam non bibit, et scripsit in tabulis verba foederis decem." *Biblia Sacra iuxta Vulgatam Clementinam*, Nova editio logicis partitionibus aliisque subsidiis ornata a R. P. Alberto Colunga, O.P., et Laurentio Turrado (Madrid: 1953), 34.28. The simplest explanation is that all four of the parallel verbs ("Fuit . . . comedit . . . bibit . . . scripsit") have Moses as their subject. In Deuteronomy 10:2–4, Moses says that God wrote the second tablets himself.

21. In the Gospel and in the N-Town play (217), Jesus writes with his finger, which reinforces the parallel between his writing and God's writing of the Ten Commandments. See "digito" in Exodus 31:18 and John 8:6 (*Biblia Sacra*).

22. *Interpretation Theory,* p. 94. See also Hans-Georg Gadamer, "On the Problem of Self-Understanding," in his *Philosophical Hermeneutics,* trans. and ed. David E. Linge (Berkeley: University of California Press, 1976), pp. 44–58.

23. My interest in Chester Play XII was sparked by Cindy Weinstein's unpublished paper on the way the two halves of the play (the episodes of the temptation of Christ and the woman taken in adultery) are united by their concern with language. While writing this paper, I had helpful conversations with Ms. Weinstein. I am also grateful for the comments of Geoffrey Harpham, Robert C. Lane, and Stephen Spector. I also had helpful discussions with the late John Hazel Smith, who read several drafts and commented with his customary verve on matters ranging from literary theory to textual problems.

10

BOTH FIXED AND FREE

Language and Destiny in Chaucer's Knight's Tale
and Troilus and Criseyde

JULIAN N. WASSERMAN

Aventure . . . is the moder of tydynges"—or so we are paren-
thetically told in Chaucer's *House of Fame* (III, 1982–8).[1] And, indeed,
the matter seems simple and straightforward enough: the curious
twists of fortune often set tongues to wagging. Beyond the case of
simple rumor, "aventure, or sort, or cas" initially determines the
speaking order of the Canterbury pilgrims. Yet there is within the
works of Chaucer a sense in which just the opposite is true:
"tydynges" seem just as often to be the source of "aventure." The
decree of fortune with which the pilgrims' tales commence is undone
or at the least begun anew by the vocal interjection of the drunken
Miller; the written "tydynges," or books, read by Geoffrey at the
beginnings of the *Book of the Duchess,* the *Parlement of Fowls,* and the
House of Fame are the first causes of fortuitous dreams; and it is true
that it is merchants, the "fadres of tydynges," who set in motion the
events of the "Boethian" tale told by the Man of Law. The "moth-
erhood" which stands between "aventure" and "tydynges" is, then,
no more clearly drawn than the supposedly Platonic "cousinage"
between word and deed to which the poet frequently refers.

No doubt, one of the reasons for the ambiguous relationship
between "aventure" and "tydynges" is that the two halves of the
equation—fortune and language—are themselves two of the most
richly complex and frequently examined concepts in an age which
was itself given over to the convolutions of philosophical speculation.
Of course complexities of the Boethian theme of Fortune have long
been the subject of critical scrutiny, and until recently, the first half of
the equation, "aventure," was apt to receive a great deal more attention and glossing than the "tydynges." However, as recent studies
have shown, Chaucer demonstrates a surprisingly theoretical

awareness of and concern with the nature of language as a symbolic medium and especially with the problem of linguistic ambiguity.[2]

Despite the recent interest in the semiotic attitudes which underlie much of the work of this poet, what has remained unexplored is the relationship between "aventure" and "tydynges" addressed in the *House of Fame*—between the poet's interest in language and what is widely recognized as one of his most frequently explored themes: Fortune or Providence and, in particular, the conflicting "necessitiees," to borrow a Boethian term, of divine prescience and individual free will. As we shall see, both the Chaucerian concepts of language and Fortune are comprised of a seemingly fixed absolute capable of being fulfilled in many ways by freely choosing individuals.

Fixed Fate and the "Eterne Word"

Written within approximately five years of each other, *Troilus and Criseyde* and the *Knight's Tale* share a Boethian cosmos where the traditional conflict between Providence and Free Will lies at the center of any assessment of human affairs.[3] In the classical world evoked by both poems, divine foresight is an active force in shaping the fates of men. Yet if, as the knight so frequently reminds us, "Al is . . . reuled by the sighte above" (I, 1672), the medium through which men's fates are fixed is language—in particular, the "eterne word," the creative medium through which God brought and perpetually brings the world into being.[4] As a result, the poet consistently presents the metaphorical gods as resolving the conflicts of men with the "worde eterne."[5] Indeed, within the *Knight's Tale,* this principle is confirmed by both mortals whose fortunes comprise the action of the tale and the various gods who fix those fates. For example, Palamon first conditions his prayer for the love of Emelye by stating, "If so be my destynee be shapen / By *eterne word*" (I, 1108–9, emphasis mine), and later, complaining of Arcite's release, he cries,

> "O crueel goddes that governe
> This world with byndyng of youre *word eterne,*
> And *written* in the table of atthamaunt
> Youre parlement and youre eterne graunt,

What is mankynde moore unto you holde
Than is the sheep that rouketh in the folde?"
(I, 1303–8, emphasis mine)

For their part, the gods also confirm that language is the medium through which fortunes are made, as when Diana assures Emelye that her fate will be fixed according to her prayers:

"Doghter, stynt thyn hevynesse,
Among the goddes hye it is affermed,
And by *eterne word writen* and conidered . . ."
(I, 2348–50, emphasis mine)

Despite this agreement that words are the means by which destinies are determined, knowledge of fate remains elusive. A person's fate may be written with "eterne word," but no one may with certainty know all of the separate and possibly contradictory meanings, or fates, which those words may signify. From the point of view of those whose fates are fixed in such fashion, "the goddes," as Criseyde points out, only seem to "speken in amphibologies, / And, for o sooth, they tellen twenty lyes" (IV, 1406–7). Similarly, Diomedes, too, speaks of the ambiguous language of prophecy, of being deceived by "ambages—/ That is to seyn, with double wordes slye,/ Swiche as men clepen a word with two visages" (V, 897–99). Fortune, it seems, is a text, written in signs which are undecipherable to mortal minds. The same sentiment is echoed by the Man of Law whose use of metaphor specifically emphasizes the role of language as medium through which fates are fixed:

Paraventure in thilke large *book*
Which that men clepe the hevene *ywriten* was
With sterres, whan that [a man] his birthe took,
That he for love sholde han his deeth, allas!
For in the sterres, clerer than is glas,
Is writen, God woot, whoso koude it *rede,*
The deeth of every man, withouten drede.
(II, 190–96, emphasis mine)

Yet the seemingly superfluous "whoso koude it rede" in the second to the last line becomes the very point of the entire excursus as the narrator goes on to lament: "but mennes wittes ben so dulle / That no wight kan wel *rede* it *atte fulle*" (II, 202–3, emphasis mine).[6] To be sure, the problem is just that: no one can read that book *atte fulle*—at least from an earthly prospective, and the source of that inability is the nature of language as a set of verbal signs and the nature of destiny as a set of possibilities.[7]

The Bodily Ear and the Circumscription of the Word

Language embraces both the abstract, transcendental medium of thought and the particular, phenomenalized speech act occurring in time and space. Because they are neither the idea of an object nor the object itself, verbal signs mediate between the purely ideal or essential realm of forms and the purely phenomenal realm of things, partaking of both but accepting complete identity with neither.[8] In discussing the verbal act through which all things were brought into being, Augustine, in the *Confessions,* makes just this point concerning the contrast between the infinite variety which exists in the language of the intellect and the finitude of the language of the "bodily ear":

How did you make heaven and earth? . . . It must be that *you spoke and they were made.* In your word alone you created them.

But how did you speak? Did you speak as you did when your voice was heard in the clouds saying: *This is my beloved son?* At that time your voice sounded and ceased. It was speech with a beginning and an end. Each syllable could be heard and then died away, the second following after the first and the third after the second, and so on in sequence until the last syllable followed all the rest and then gave place to silence. From this it is abundantly clear that your speech was expressed through motion of some created thing, because it was motion subject to the laws of time, although it served your eternal will. These words, which you had caused to sound in time, were reported by the bodily ear of the hearer to the mind, which has intelligence and inward hearing responsive to your eternal Word ["aeternum Verbum"]. The mind compared these words, which it hears sounding in time, with your Word, which is silent and eternal, and said, 'God's eternal Word is far, far different from these words that sounded in time . . .'[9]

The Augustinian concept of creation is that of an ongoing process, an unfolding in time and space of all that exists *in potentia* in the Word. In this conception, language is the medium through which those things willed by God are confirmed and wrought. Augustine's "aeternum Verbum" (perhaps suggestive of the "eterne word" of Chaucer's classical gods) and its range of meaning are, however, set against the related though distinct language of the "bodily ear." It is little wonder, then, that men cannot read the book of fate "atte fulle," for theirs is the language of the phenomenalized parts and not of the transcendental whole.[10]

Augustine notes that we cannot read history—the working out of all that is implicit in the Divine Word with which creation was wrought—for the very reason that we are a part of the very Whole we are trying to read (*De vera religione* xxii.43).[11] History is conceived of as an expression of language; the "course of ages" is likened to an "exquisite poem" composed of language made "beautiful" by its multiplicity; that is, its resolved "contraries" (*De civitate Dei,* ii.xxiii).[12]

This same contrast between transcendental wholeness in the mind of God and the multitudinous parts phenomenalized in time and space is also the point of the prayer with which the poet takes his leave in *Troilus and Criseyde*. Referring to the Divinity as "Uncircumscript and al maist circumscrive" (v, 1865), the poet casts his prayer in terms which at least implicitly evoke the trope of writing as the medium through which Divine Will is worked. The uncircumscript knowledge of God is, as the Knight terms it, His "pryvetee," a term which emphasizes its unknowability, its unreadability. Of course, it is the Miller's subsequent scatological punning on that very term which sets the meaning of "the bodily ear" against that of the eschatological language of the divine intellect:

> An housbonde shal nat been inquisityf
> Of Goddes pryvetee, nor of his wyf.
> So he may fynde Goddes foyson there,
> Of the remenant nedeth nat enquere.
> (i, 3163–66)

The Miller's wordplay makes us aware of the multiplicity of meanings that are possible to any term. It also makes us aware of just how much the "goliardyes" of a Miller has dealt away in choosing the meaning he has assigned to the word in question.[13] In fact, the linguistic act which this Miller has performed reflects the very content of his speech. He is happy so long as he has *his part* of the "foyson" and cares not a straw for the rest, whether that "foyson" be God's "pryvetee," his wife's favors, or the denotations of words. This, of course, is circumscription of the severest kind—from the infinite to the scatological, from theology to fabliau, in the shift of a single term. Such movement makes plain the limits under which any speaker, not just the deliberately wrong-headed one, must labor.

How, then, may such circumscriptions be made? By what means, we may ask, does the single word "pryvetee" become the property of both the Knight and the Miller, and how are we to know when to accept one "meaning" as opposed to the other? Citing Geoffrey of Vinsauf's dictum that every word has both a "mind" (a range of potential meanings) and a "face" (its phenomenalized form), Margaret Nims observes that to medieval rhetoricians, "A word standing alone has an element of un-definedness analogous to that of prime matter. It is, to be sure, a unit of meaning, but much of its meaning is held in suspension, in potency, until its position in discourse stablizes its grammatical form and elicits the relevant areas of meaning.[14] Implicitly, Nims's remarks set forth the two dynamic, perhaps even contradictory properties which both medieval and modern linguists believe to be inherent in all true signs and, hence, languages: arbitrariness and conventionality. First, the set of signs which compose any language are arbitrary; there is no implicit connection between a given signifier and that which it signifies.[15] Such arbitrariness in the application of signs or names has, in fact, already been seen in the words of the Man of Law's assertion that the fates of men are written in the book "Which that men clepe hevene." Men simply *call* it such; that is not its absolute name, and any other term would do as well. The arbitrariness of the association is underscored by the figurative use of "book" as a name for the same referent. The second property of language derives from the first; language is, by definition, conventional.[16] As a matter of habit arising from lexical convention, we regularly call the "book" of the stars by the arbitrarily chosen sign "hevene." Language requires public agreement, agreement between speaker and listener, in order to prevent a recurrence of Babel, a situation where each speaker chooses his own private set of signs for a given referent. Arbitrariness and conventionality are, thus, properties through which the wholeness of mental language is circumscribed into Geoffrey of Vinsauf's "faces," into Augustine's language of "the bodily ear."

Interestingly enough, the fact of semantic arbitrariness, of multiple expressions of a single abstraction, surfaces repeatedly in the works of Chaucer. For example, in the proem of the second book of *Troilus and Criseyde,* the narrator describes the different ways in which men speak of love. Despite the fact that they denote the same thing, the words used by men from the past differ in "forme" and seem "wonder nyce and straunge" (II, 22, 24) in regard to those used in the present. Moreover, the poet goes on to observe that men in England speak differently from men in other countries. And, even among contemporary Englishmen, no three speak in the same fashion, for as the narrator notes, "every wight which that to Rome went/ Halt nat o path, or alwey o manere" (II, 36–37). The same trope concerning the many paths to Rome also occurs in the much later *Treatise on the Astrolabe,* again in connection with the multiplicity of expressions given to a single idea, as Chaucer argues that English suffices as as true a medium of expression as Latin, Greek, Hebrew, or Arabic: "And God woot that in alle these languages and in many moo, han these conclusions ben suffisantly lerned and tauht, and yit by diverse reules; right as diverse pathes leden diverse folk the righte way to Rome" (36–40).[17] Put another way, no man may know *all* the roads to Rome. Although a man's fate may be written with "eterne word[es]" no man may know "atte fulle" all of the separate, and possibly contradictory, meanings, or fates, which those words may signify. A single idea finds many distinct expressions or "faces" which are dependent on context—"position in discourse" or "diverse reules" of diverse tongues,[18] and that multiplicity is the very reason that, in the Man of Law's words, no one can read the book "at fulle."

From the point of view of the Bishop of Hippo, the multiple figurative meanings in a given sign as well as the ambiguity they engender are part of the infinite creativity of the Divinity. They are signposts which point to higher truths.[19] From the point of view of Criseyde, such multiplicity is merely a means of divine equivocation. What both Criseyde and Diomedes mistrust in prophecy is the multiplicity which Augustine praises as an inherent property of language. As a result, the solutions which both Criseyde and Diomedes propose consist not in the transcendence of multiplicity or the reconciliation of opposites but, rather, in a resolution brought about through championing the one *against* the many[20]—in the case of Criseyde, the "oon sooth" against the "twenty lyes" which are really not lies but merely other paths to Rome; that is, roads not taken, meanings or visages not perceived—possibilities, events existing *in potentia.*

Language and Fortune: From "Purveaunce" to "Destyne"

Significantly, Criseyde's semantic championing of the one over the many is the same habit of mind which Boethius says leads men to place themselves in the hands of Fortune. This is the process by which men create "destyne," the outcome of events in the earthly sphere, out of "purveaunce," or divine foresight:

> . . . thilke devyne thowht, that is yset and
> put in the towr (that is to seyn, in the
> heyte) of symplicite of God, stablyssheth
> many manere gyses to thinges that ben to
> done; the whiche manere, whan that men
> looken it in thilke pure clennesse of the
> devyne intelligence, it is ycleped
> purveaunce; but whanne thilke manere is
> referred by men to thinges that it moeveth
> and disponyth, than of olde men it was
> clepyd destyne. . . . For purveaunce
> enbraceth alle thinges to-hepe, althogh that
> thei ben diverse, and althoughe thei ben
> infinite. But destyne, certes, departeth
> and ordeyneth alle thinges singulerly,
> and devyded in moevynges, in places, in
> formes, in tymes.
>
> (IV, Prose vi, 50–72)

In short, "purveaunce" is associated with the abstract and intangible. It is characterized by the transcendence of opposites: "it knytteth alle thinges in her ordres" and "enbraceth alle thinges to-hepe." In contrast, "destyne"—which "departeth and ordeyneth alle thinges singulerly and devyded in moevynges, in places, in formes, in tymes"—belongs to the world of time and space and is associated with multiplicity—the unresolved opposition of one form, or place, or time against another. And, of course, the traditional sign of the making of "destyne" out of "purveaunce" is a verbalization, a speech act whereby an attitude vis-à-vis fortune is objectified in the world of phenomena by being made apprehensible to the "bodily ear." In Boethian tragedy, characters circumscribe their lives and place themselves on the Wheel of Fortune by explicitly thanking or cursing Fortuna for the temporal particulars of their lives.

An example of the distinction between prescience and destiny which is set forth by Boethius is best seen in Theseus's final speech at the end of the *Knight's Tale* wherein the Duke of Athens first notes that it is foreordained that every man owes God a death, "the kyng as shal a page" (I, 3030), but then goes on to note the diverse ways in which the preordained debt can be paid:

> "Som in his bed, som in the depe see . . .
> Ther helpeth noght; al goth that ilke weye."
> > (I, 3031 . . . 33)

The simple truth that men die is "purveaunce." Their individual deaths, the separate interpretations of that decree, constitute "destyne." While "purveaunce" can contain many opposing elements "enbrace[d] . . . to-hepe," destiny is the result of reading those elements "singulerly," which is the way that mortals read in temporal affairs. In the end, all do, indeed, go "that ilke weye," but as with the journey to Rome, the paths differ. What is true of language is true of fate.

The relationship between the range of potential meanings which exist in the abstract for a given word and the singular meaning created by the particulars of grammatical form and context is markedly similar to the relationship between the range of potential events contained in God's general "purveaunce" and the individual "destyne," or events which occur in time and space. The various meanings exist in dynamic harmony within the contextless ontological and exist "singulerly" in regard to the context of "moevynges" in which they find their phenomenal expression. The earthly context of "moevynges . . . places . . . formes . . . [and] tymes" isolates an individual destiny much like "position in discourse" and "grammatical form" generates a "singuler" meaning from the range of potential ones which are bound "to-hepe" in the abstract.

If we return briefly to a consideration of the two essential properties of language, we will see that the relationship between arbitrariness and conventionality likewise reflects that between "destyne" and "purveaunce." Arbitrariness in language allows for the free exercise of the will in a "singuler" context; contrarily, conventionality restricts the use of the same faculty in favor of predetermined structures of infinite potential, with the result that the essential tension in the linguistic act is that which lies at the heart of the debate over divine providence.

The reconciliation of these two properties exists on both the syntactical and the lexical levels. From a generative point of view, the "rules of grammar" dictate the structure of the as yet unrealized elements of discourse. In short, from one point of view, a Chomskian "deep structure" plays the role of providence in predetermining the structures of the theoretically infinite number of sentences which exist *in potentia*—"to-hepe" as it were—in the generative model.[21] At the same time, the speaker is, within the limits of other rules, allowed the freedom to insert words at will, thereby generating "singuler" sentences which may never have been constructed before.

Linguistically, the reconciliation of these two properties is seen on yet another level. Through conventionality, the denotative meaning of a sign is essentially fixed—that is, predetermined—by the speech community. At the same time, each sign has a connotative association based on personal experience. When we hear the verbal sign "dog," we summon up an image of the animal conventionally signified by the sign. At the same time, the image may be personalized into the benign pet we knew as a child or the Doberman Pinscher which chased us home from school.[22] What one finds here is a type of circumscription which provides idiosyncratic, singular meanings on the connotative level. Arbitrariness results in our ability to make words our own, to personalize meanings on the sematic level much as fortune (the manner of the death we owe) is individualized. The full potential for the interplay of these elements in regard to both language and fate is, I believe, evident in an example of semantic ambiguity of which Chaucer was most likely unaware but which illustrates the point so well that it is worth noting even by way of analogy. In Gottfried Von Strassburg's *Tristan*, Isolde undergoes a trial by ordeal wherein she will seize a hot iron in order to test the validity of her oath of fidelity. As the ordeal takes place, Isolde swears that she has lain with no man save the King, but then, to the amusement of all, she thoughtfully adds, "with the exception of the 'poor pilgrim'" into whose arms she had accidentally fallen as she was being publicly assisted in coming ashore on the way to face the ordeal. Unbeknownst to the court which has witnessed the fall, the pilgrim was, in fact, the disguised Tristan. Of course her oath is now technically true, and she remains unscathed from the hot iron.

Two points become clear in this incident where private language,

connotation, determines an individual's fate. The first is that Isolde
has within the conventionally defined denotation of "the poor pilgrim" provided a connotation which is unknown to society which, in
turn, misreads the meaning of her remaining unscathed. In her act of
verbal circumscription, Isolde is clearly dealing in "ambages, / That is
to seyn with double wordes slye / Swich as men clepen a word with
two visages." Characterized throughout the poem by a kind of myo-
pic literal-mindedness—conventionality in the extreme—society is,
on the other hand, clearly aware of only one of those faces.23 The
second point concerns Isolde's similar circumscription of fate. It was
preordained that anyone speaking the truth would remain unscathed,
yet it is the semantic flexibility built into both "truth" and her oath
which allows her to exercise her will within the limits of her pronounced—that is, foreordained—destiny.

What, then, is foreordained? The events of Isolde's ordeal might
well be thought of as a syllogism, the first part of which is a general
statement of purveyaunce or absolute necessity: "All persons speaking
the truth remain unscathed." Linguistic circumscription, or Free Will,
operates at the second level of the syllogism: "Isolde spoke the
truth"—although it is a "private" truth of letter rather than of spirit—
thereby creating the final part of the syllogism: "Isolde remained
unscathed." Thus, Gottfried concludes his narration of the events of
the ordeal with an observation which is perhaps unique in medieval
literature:

> da wart wol goffenbaeret
> und al der werlt bewaeret,
> daz der vil tugenthafte Crist
> wintschaffen alse ein ermel ist:
> er vueget unde souchet an,
> da manz an in gesuochen kan,
> alse gevuoge und alse wol,
> als er von allem rehet fol.
> erst allen herzen bereit,
> ze durnehte und ze trugeheit.
> ist ez ernest, ist ez spil,
> er ist ie, swie so man will.
>
> (And so it was made manifest
> and proved to all the world by test,
> that Christ's law can be made to strain
> like any windswept weathervane.

It can be twisted to any bent,
whatever may be man's intent,
to be as friendly and respected
as is by human kind expected,
assisting all men vying
in virtue or in lying.
In serious or if in jest,
it's always ready at thy behest.)[24]

Despite the narrator's assertion, the law has, in fact, been upheld and, hence, confirmed. Gottfried's quarrel is not with the law but with the medium, the words which can be "twisted to any bent / whatever may be man's intent" by speaker and listener alike.

Returning briefly to the Man of Law's lament, concerning the book of heaven, what is, in fact, lamented is the semantic distance between writer and reader—the distance between the author of the sign of Isolde's "truthfulness" and society as the all too limited receiver of that "text"—that is to say, or the distance between the "intellectual" language of God and that of the "bodily ear." In regard to any book, no reader may know the text completely because no reader may know the subtext—that is, the connotative meaning—of another.

As regards the book of heaven, its Writer has, as part of His "pryvetee," indicated all possible denotations and connotations of His terms, whereas the earthly reader's understanding is "circumscribed" by his or her own time, place, experience, and identity and, for that matter, his semantic categories. In other words, a churl will not only tell a churl's tale but will hear one as well, regardless of whether the tale is of God's "pryvetee" in the most eschatological of senses. As we shall see, in Chaucer the qualities which make for the productive and intelligent reading of signs are the same as those which help men eschew the snare of fortune. So long as fate is fixed with language, which is of necessity ambiguous and delimited in an earthly context, the multiplicity of expression which results from that ambiguity allows for the free exercise of will which selects only partial, singular meanings and converts them into "destyne."

Reading in Private: Palamon, Arcite, and the Distorted Sign

The *Knight's Tale* as a whole clearly demonstrates this very point concerning the linguistic operation whereby the exercise of will creates "destyne" out of "purveaunce." To be sure, neither Palamon nor Arcite reads signs very well. Each reads selectively, defining his part as the whole, shaping his destiny through such readings—the difference between the two Theban knights and Isolde being that her circumscriptions are both deliberate and conscious while theirs are neither. In essence, the entire action and resolution of the *Knight's Tale* may be seen to spring from a semantic debate in which each of the knights attempts to define Emelye in his own terms and to the exclusion of those of his rival. In the midst of their debate, it is easy to take Emelye not as a character but as an emblem for the type of ambiguous sign which Augustine describes in *De doctrina*.[25] The semantic gamesmanship begins as Palamon spies Emelye in the garden and declares, "I noot wher she be womman or goddesse, / But Venus is it soothly, as I gesse" (I, 1101–2). In the debate which follows, Arcite defends his right to love Emelye by claiming

> For paramour I loved hire first er thow.
> What wiltow seyen? Thou woost nat yet now
> Wheither she be a womman or goddesse!
> Thyn is affeccioun of hoolynesse,
> And myn is love as to a creature . . .
>
> (I, 1155–59)

Clearly this is above all else a semantic debate, a matter of categorization, an argument over which term best describes the woman in question, a contest whose futility is underscored by the narrator's own use of the rhetorical device of *occupatio* (I, 1188)—the denial of one's ability to describe the subject at hand. The ability of such verbal constructs to define reality is made clear in the Knight's *demande d'amour* with its semantic games of defining the tower in which Palamon remains captive as either a heaven or a hell, depending on one's very relative point of view. Each character's view of reality and especially his future actions and, hence, destiny is dependent on these semantics. Both knights create a verbal reality upon which all their subsequent deeds and, hence, fates are grounded, and from that point on, all actions taken are literally prefaced with the phrase, "with that word."[26]

As the question of Emelye's status as a woman or goddess (or that of the tower as Heaven or Hell) indicates, the semantic exercise in which the knights engage is essentially a divisive one with each knight choosing one category at the expense of the other. Each of the knights, in the act of reading Emelye, performs an act of circumscription, an act of differentiation that reflects his own faculties as a perceiver.[27] Knowledge is not a function of the known but, rather, the knower or, better still, the semantic categories which the knower brings to the known.[28] Indeed, Lady Philosophy notes in the *Boece*:

> For al that evere is iknowe, it is rather/
> comprehended and knowen, nat aftir his/
> strengthe and his nature, but aftir the/
> faculte *(that is to seyn, the power and the nature/)*
> of hem that knowen.
>
> (v, prose iv, 140–44)

Thus, Palamon views Emelye with an eye toward "hoolynesse" and sees a "goddesse" while Arcite views her with an eye toward the "creature" and sees a "womman." Yet assuredly, the word "love" can mean both otherworldly *and* fleshly affection, and Emelye is both woman *and* goddess.

The young knights' proclivity for championing the part at the expense of the whole is seen in the opposing banners of red (Arcite) and white (Palamon) with which the two represent themselves in their tourney.[29] When Emelye enters the love garden in which she is first seen by the two knights, she not only combines the traditionally complementary lily and the rose (i, 1036–38) but also "gader[s] floures, party white and rede, / To make a subtil gerland for hire hede" (i, 1053–54). Moreover, the tandem use of the two colors embodied in Emelye and demonstrated in her act of weaving is also evident in Theseus's banner with its "rede statue of Mars" on a "white banner large" (i, 975–76). In choosing their respective banners of white *or* red, Palamon and Arcite are again separating those parts of Emelye which, in the words of Boethius, exist "to-hepe, although that they been diverse." Moreover, the process is at least on one level a semiotic operation, for the heraldic banners are themselves signs— concrete, apprehensible figures which serve as emblems for things other than themselves. What Palamon and Arcite demonstrate in their choosing of those emblems is a mistrust, already seen in Criseyde and Diomedes, of the complexity embodied in both the compound floral/ color symbols associated with Emelye and with the heraldic banner of Theseus, as well as an attempt to circumscribe or delimit the multiplicity inherent in signs. White and red, taken separately as singular signs, do, to be sure, take on separate significations distinct from those found in their traditional tandem use as the colors associated with the perfection of lovers, and as with the Miller's pun on "privetee," we are made aware of how much is lost in that process, a meaning which is the sum of the parts of the sign which the two knights violate with their singular vision.

In defining Emelye as they do by considering her qualities "singularly," the two knights thus create a juxtaposition or tension between the formerly harmonious parts of a natural unity. That, of course, is the essence of the folly which Boethius points out as a reliance on "destyne" rather than "purveaunce." Interestingly enough, the knights first set forth their conflicting views in a tower— Chaucer's addition to the poem—reminiscent of Boethius's metaphor of the "heye towre of [God's] purveaunce" (IV, prose VI, 219) in which oppositions are held "to-hepe althoghe that thei ben diverse." When the oppositions are no longer held in dynamic harmony, the two knights leave the tower and fight out the conflict in the world of "moveable" things as symbolized by the arena with its carvings that emphasize the worldly manifestations of the three separate deific principles to whom the protagonists pray.[30]

It is in those prayers that one most readily sees the linguistic principles which underlie the tale as a whole. The world of the *Knight's Tale* is a world in which prayers are answered in literal fashion, so that in exercising their free wills and speaking their prayers, both Palamon and Arcite shape the individual destinies which will befall them. Their prayers to the deities reflect the same linguistic tendencies as their original treatment of Emelye as sign. Each persists in taking the part for the whole, and because each sees only a fraction of the truth, whether it be the nature of Emelye or the facts of his own situation, each asks for only a partial solution. Although each is responsible for the outcome of the contest, neither is truly in control of his fate because neither understands the language of his own prayer "atte fulle."[31] Palamon pleads to Venus, "Yif me my love" (I, 2260) and thinks he is asking for victory in the tournament. Arcite asks that Mars "Yif me victorie, I aske thee namoore" (I, 2420), thinking that victory will assure his possession of Emelye. Interestingly enough, the subject of these orisons, Emelye, makes a prayer of her own, and the difference between her prayer and those of her suitors is worth noting. Whereas the two knights pray for their singular outcomes, Emelye prays for either of two destinies. Her first prayer is that there be "love and pees betwixe hem two" (I, 2317) so that she might remain a "mayden" (I, 2305). The second prayer is that if she "shal nedes have oon of hem two," it be "hym that moost desireth" her (I, 2324–25). For Emelye, reconciliation is preferable to conflict. Both of her prayers seek unity rather than diversity, as is befitting a woman in whom diverse qualities, such as the red of the rose and the white of the lily, exist in harmony.

Even more significantly, each of the three characters receives a direct answer, a "signe," in response to either his or her prayer, and again the inherent connection between an individual's fate and his ability to interpret signs becomes apparent. For Palamon the response to his prayer is the shaking of the statue of Venus:

> But atte laste the statue of Venus shook,
> And made a signe, wherby that he took,
> That his preyere accepted was that day
> For thogh the signe shewed a delay,
> Yet wiste he wel that graunted was his boone.
> (I, 2265–69)

The language here is revealing. The narrator moves from "tooke" to "wiste," from "supposed" to "knew," so easily that we hardly notice that there are no logical grounds for the increase in certainty. More- over, reduced to the concessive clause between "tooke" and "wiste" occurs the unnoticed fact of the delay in the appearance of the sign, a delay that is part of the sign's meaning. For his part, Arcite receives a sign in the form of the ringing of the armor on the statue of Mars and a disembodied voice crying "Victorie!" (I, 2433), but because he has not understood the parameters of his own semantic circumscription of the term "victory" in his original prayer, he does not understand its meaning when the same word is given to him as a sign portending his future. The passage, like that devoted to the prayer of Palamon, ends with a decided emphasis on the certainty that the prayer has been received and granted with a Croesus-at-Delphi certainty which rests entirely on interpretation and a belief that such signs have but one meaning and can be read "atte fulle." Emelye, as we might expect, does just the opposite and emphasizes her uncertainty as to the meaning of signs. When she first receives the sign of the two flames, "she ne wiste what it signyfied" (I, 2343). And even after receiving a gloss directly from Diana in which she is told that her fate has been sealed by the "eterne word," she asks "What amounteth this?" (I, 2362).

It is obvious, then, that neither Palamon nor Arcite reads these signs very well, and in each case the misreading—actually a partial reading or circumscription mistaken for a whole—shapes the reader's destiny by singling out one destiny from the range of potential outcomes. The dangers of such delimiting vision constitute the matter of Theseus's final speech in which he once again returns to the problem of "purveaunce" and its relationship to free will by painting a picture of the Neoplatonic chain of being beginning in the "eterne" (I, 3004) and descending to the successions of the "nat eterne" (I, 3315), so that

> Every part derryveth from his hool,
> For nature hath nat taken his bigynnyng
> Of no partie or cantel of a thyng.
> (I, 3006–9)[32]

Troilus and the Fate of Fiction

If, as in the *Knight's Tale,* linguistic circumscription can bring about one's downfall, we might well ask if one can shape his fate for the better by deliberately shaping the form through which his fate is fixed, by selectively (mis)reading the "eterne word" through which events are set.[33] When Palamon and Arcite make a "cantel of a thyng" out of the "hool" which is "parfit" and mistake the "nat eternal" language of the bodily eye for the multifaceted "eternal," they surely do so unwittingly because they lack the knowledge that words, or even a woman, may, to quote Diomedes, have "two visages." Yet as the words of both Diomedes and Criseyde indicate, *Troilus* is a work in which almost all of the characters not only understand the ambiguity inherent in language but deliberately exploit that multiplicity of meaning in order to change or manipulate events within the poem by misinterpreting the signs which portend them. Deliberate manipulation of events through language is a way of life within *Troilus,* which is literally filled with language which is willfully ignored or manipulated, at the least deliberately delimited.[34]

The love affair is something of an illusion. Like the dumb show created by the magician in the *Franklin's Tale,* it is brought into being, made substantive, through the verbal brokering of Pandarus, the greatest of verbal manipulators, the master of the double entendre and verbal puppeteer who speaks for, through, and about almost all of the other characters in the poem.[35] In the first part of the poem, it seems as if love spoken of automatically becomes love possessed. In advising Troilus on the ways of love, Pandarus argues in Book One for the necessity of speech. Without speech, he says, nothing can be accomplished. In the third book he advises the would-be lover when not to speak. By not speaking, tragedies may be prevented and, perhaps, ill fortune might be avoided.[36]

For her part, Criseyde is a true niece of her uncle and from the very start shows herself only slightly less capable than her uncle at manipulating words. For Criseyde, words exist to mask reality.[37] Because we are privy to the thoughts which precede her words, we know her words to be illusion-creating equivocations. This device is most readily seen in Criseyde when she devotes some seventy lines (II, 694–763) to reasons for and some thirty-five lines (II, 771–805) to reasons against accepting the love of Troilus, only to announce her decision in a terse two-line speech which borders on a cliché: "He which that nothing undertaketh, / Nothying n'acheveth, be hym looth or deere" (II, 807–8).[38] Language for Criseyde ceases to be a mediating force between the abstract and the concrete but is, rather, a mask used to create an illusion that is taken for reality. She is, after all, a woman who makes a vow concerning the future just after condescendingly noting the "amphibologies" inherent in prophetic language. Significantly, she breaks that vow for the sake of a man who from the outset speaks knowingly of "ambages" and words with "two visages."[39]

Within the poem, Troilus plays the linguistic innocent. Despite the fact that his fate rises and falls on a virtual sea of words, he seems woefully ignorant of the medium which all other characters seem so adept at manipulating to their own advantages. And again that verbal ignorance, as in the case of Palamon and Arcite, consists largely in mistaking the part for the whole, as the Trojan warrior begins his ill-fated love with Criseyde by trying to place her in a familiar dichotomy: "But wheither goddesse or womman, iwys, / She be, I not" (I, 425–6).

In the end, it is the goddess he comes to love. His problem is that he cannot reconcile the visage of the goddess with the visage of the woman who betrays him later in the tale. At the "colde dores" of Criseyde's abandoned house, the broken-hearted Troilus laments her absence in terms which combine both the eloquence of the lover's complaint and a vulgar sexual pun, a combination perhaps significant of the doubleness of Criseyde, the duplicity of her vow, and perhaps even of Janus, who is, after all, not only the twin-visaged god of doors but of gates, the site at which Troilus learns of Criseyde's duplicity.[40]

Criseyde, it seems, is both goddess and woman, both true and false, and as in the *Knight's Tale,* the division of the whole into its subparts leads to tragedy. In the beginning Troilus achieves such circumscription unintentionally. As he is slowly tutored in the linguistic arts, however, the misreadings, as in the case of his dream of the boar, become intentional and desperate.[41] In order to prevent Criseyde from breaking her vow to return, he pathetically attempts to redefine the vow (v, 1186–90). The search for ambiguity becomes a search for a saving grace through which the facts of the phenomonal world might be denied. Love for Troilus is described as the fixing of a mental image deep within the recesses of his heart. And immediately upon fixing the "ymage," his first question regards the manner in which he should speak in order to "arten hire to love" (I, 388). Later, as his idealized image of Criseyde is threatened by the fact of her betrayal, he attempts to revive her fading image by reading old love letters:[42]

> The lettres ek that she of olde tyme
> Hadde hym ysent, he wolde allone rede
> An hondred sithe atwixen noon and prime,
> Refiguryng hire shap, hire wommanhede,
> Withinne his herte, and every word or dede
> That passed was.
>
> (v, 470–75)

When Criseyde still does not return, Troilus demands that she objectify her love in the form of a letter (v, 1387–1400). Indeed, throughout the poem, such letters have been used as a tool to objectify feelings. But the letters, like the vows made right after discussing "amphibologies," have been used to hide as much as to reveal, or at least to shape a revelation which is a part rather than a whole. The tactic is most clear in Pandarus's famous advice on the writing of love letters (II, 1023–43).

In the Neoplatonic world of the poem, trying to manipulate foresight through phenomenal language is like attempting to affect an object by altering its shadow. Of course, to do so would be to establish an explicit identity between a signifier and its referent and would violate the arbitrariness of sign. The idea should generate the words which create or describe the reality. This is in keeping with the Neoplatonism of Theseus's fair chain of Love and with the speech in the fifth book of the *Boece* wherein lady Philosophy advises Boethius that "every signe scheweth and signifieth oonly what the thing is, but it ne maketh nat the thing that it signifieth" (prose iv, 64–67). Within the world of *Troilus*, words are, instead, used in circular fashion to generate what should be the informing idea which lies behind them. True seers see first and then speak, with their prophetic words acting as mediators between phenomena and the visions which portend them. The lovers attempt to speak first in order to create a foreseeing, a mental image, and to create self-fulfilling prophecies. For Troilus, as well as for all of the characters in the poem, the attempt to order a world by bringing his mental images into being by concretizing them in language becomes a pale, almost parodic, version of the creative act described by Augustine.[43] In the end, the love between Troilus and Criseyde is based on ambiguities, double entendres. In the end, all are undone by the linguistic vagaries that they hope to exploit just as surely as they are earlier brought to bliss through them, but they are undone not because they, like Palamon and Arcite, did not know such vagaries exist but because they think such vagaries are capable of being manipulated. As Pandarus himself observes, a man often carves the rod with which he is later beaten.

Yet for all the tears shed by Troilus, Criseyde, and Pandarus throughout the tale, the real tension within the poem resides not in the struggle of the characters caught in this web of words, nor is their linguistic determinism even the source of the poem's ultimate resolution of the problem of language, fate, and will. The problem of events fixed by divine foresight becomes, for the narrator, the literary problem of an inherited plot previously set out by the "auctors" whom he so frequently says that he must follow.[44] All of the as-yet-unrealized events of the poem are foreknown to the narrator, who has read previous versions of the legend. The literary question which naturally arises concerns the degree of freedom—that is, free will—the narrator has in telling his tale. Foresight—the reading of Boccaccio's *Il Filostrato*, for instance—demands a betrayal on the part of Criseyde and a tragic ending for the earthly lovers. The narrator's free will desires the heroine's acquittal from the most damning charges or, at the least, a measure of consolation at the poem's conclusion. Like Troilus, the narrator tries to manipulate one part of the whole at the expense of the other, as is seen in the narrator's idealized, perhaps even goddess-like, portrait of Criseyde in Book ɪ (99–105). The idealized portrait is the equivalent of the idealized "ymage" which Troilus attempts to protect throughout the poem. And like Troilus, the narrator is ultimately at a loss for words to manipulate fate in order to protect his partial image of the same woman. Indeed, it is the failure of that verbal manipulation with which the poet demonstrates the limits of verbal manipulation, so that the poem self-consciously falls back upon itself as a series of signs twice removed from their significations, a story about the stories that others have told.[45] In the end, despite his personal feelings, the narrator can no more change the events of which he has read than the seer can change the events he foresees. Both must report what they have seen, and failure to do so denies the definitive function of either the writer or the visionary. In the end, the narrator provides the second visage of Criseyde in the "flawed" portrait of Book v (806–26). Significantly, the second portrait, unlike the first, is not original and is taken directly from one of his "auctors."

Yet there is also free will—even for an "instrument," as the narrator defines himself in the poem's beginning. If fate is fixed with the "word eterne," we may no more change that fate than the narrator of Troilus may change the outcome of his tale; but, like that narrator, we may color it within the bounds of the ambiguity built into the words with which that fate is fixed, imparting an informing spirit to the letter which he has inherited. Like Hester Prynne, whose fate is circumscribed by a letter imposed from without, the narrator may embroider—that is, interpret—his own tale of a woman who "In beaute firste so stood . . . makeles . . . Right as oure first lettere is now an A" (ɪ, 172, 171), perhaps even exploring its ambiguity to discover the Angel as well as the Adulteress implicit in its decree. But in the end, free will exists only within the bounds of that ambiguity, and the letter must be lived with. Thus, although Chaucer's narrator may not change the ending of his source, he has not exactly told that tale either. He has produced *Troilus and Criseyde,* not *Il Filostrato.* As the narrator says in the second proem, what he has to tell is history, but, as he notes, history is language, and language is infinite in its variety, with many forms and faces. Therein lies the solution not only for his own narrative dilemma but for the question of providence and free will.

Notes

1. All textual citations to the works of Chaucer are taken from *The Works of Geoffrey Chaucer*, ed. F. N. Robinson, 2nd ed. (Boston: Houghton Mifflin, 1957).

2. The extent of recent critical interest in "semiotic" aspects of Chaucer's thought and work is probably best illustrated by the amount of attention devoted to such studies in the published papers from the 1980 International Congress of the New Chaucer Society in *New Perspectives in Chaucer Criticism,* Donald M. Rose, ed. (Norman, Oklahoma: Pilgrim Books, 1981). Particularly noteworthy in that volume are Morton W. Bloomfield's "Contemporary Literary Theory and Chaucer," especially pp. 27–30, and Florence Ridley's "A Response to 'Contemporary Literary Theory and Chaucer'," especially pp. 37–41, 43–45—both of which essays place the recent semiotic interest in Chaucer in the larger context of Chaucer studies. Without question, the study which has had the most impact on Chaucer in regard to linguistics and semiotics has been Eugene Vance's study of *Troilus* as a poem about the abuse of signs: "Mervelous Signals: Poetics, Sign Theory, and Politics in Chaucer's *Troilus,*" *New Literary History* 10 (1979): 293–337, which both Bloomfield and Ridley treat as indicative of a new direction in Chaucer criticism. Given the importance of Vance's study, of particular interest is Winthrop Weatherbee's cautionary article—"Convention and Authority: A Comment on Recent Critical Approaches to Chaucer" contained in Rose, *Perspectives,* pp. 71–81—which while generally favorable in regard to Vance's "Mervelous Signals" and R. Allen Shoaf's "Notes on Chaucer's Poetics of Translation," *Studies in the Age of Chaucer* 1 (1979): 55–66, criticizes both critics for "treating Chaucer exclusively as a poet of *courtoisie*" (p. 73). Also included in Rose's volume is a study by R. Allen Shoaf which considers the work of both Dante and Chaucer in regard to the "problem of referentiality"—"Dante's *Commedia* and Chaucer's Theory of Mediation," pp. 83–103. Other semiotically oriented discussions of Chaucer range from Piero Boitani's very recent "Chaucer's Labyrinth: Fourteenth-Century Literature and Language," *Chaucer Review* 17 (1983): 197–220, which considers the *House of Fame* in regard to what the poem reveals about the poet's concept of signs, to that of Peter Elbow, *Oppositions in Chaucer* (Middleton, Connecticut: Wesleyan University Press, 1973), pp. 152–58—who in his final chapter provides a short consideration of the relationship between speech and action by providing a very brief but suggestive application of J. L. Austin's theory of speech acts to the works of Chaucer. Also see Stewart Justman, "Literal and Symbolic in the *Canterbury Tales,*" *Chaucer Review* 14 (1980): 199–214, as well as Charles Dahlberg, "The Narrator's Frame for *Troilus,*" *Chaucer Review* 15 (1980): 85–100 and Donald W. Rowe, *O Love O Charite! Contraries Harmonized in Chaucer's "Troilus"* (Carbondale: Southern Illinois University Press, 1976). Of special note, although not specifically "Chaucerian," are two studies of medieval symbolism and allegory: Gerhart B. Ladner, "Medieval and Modern Understanding of Symbolism: A Comparison," *Speculum* 54 (1979): 223–56 and Margaret F. Nims, I.B.V.M, "Translatio: 'Difficult Statement' in Medieval Poetic Theory," *University of Toronto Quarterly* 43 (1974): 215–230. Finally, an excellent general survey of medieval linguistic theory is to be found in pp. 66–93 of R. H. Robins, *A Short History of Linguistics* (Bloomington, Indiana: Indiana University Press, 1967).

3. As Troilus notes in his Boethian speech of Book IV, the problem of Divine prescience and free will has been taken up by "clerkes grete many on" without any

agreement. So it is with the poem's critics by whom the Boethian elements have, in Donald Howard's words, been "endlessly remarked" [*The Idea of the "Canterbury Tales"* (Berkeley, California: University of California Press, 1976), p. 228.] Most recently, Edward C. Schweitzer, in "Fate and Freedom in *The Knight's Tale*," *Studies in the Age of Chaucer* 3 (1981): 13–46, has examined the poem in light of the disturbing sense of the arbitrariness and hence injustice of its ending, finding the two knights responsible for their own ends (29–30) despite the pervasiveness of planetary influences (16). Also see J. O. Fichte, "Man's Free Will and the Poet's Choice," *Anglia* 93 (1975): 335–60 for a survey of critical treatments of Boethian themes in the *Knight's Tale.*

Joseph S. Salemi provides an excellent summary of the role of fortune and our sense of the reconciliation of free will and determinism in *Troilus*—"Playful Fortune and Chaucer's Criseyde," *Chaucer Review* 15 (1981): 209–23—seeing in the three major characters the three possible responses to fortune. Martin Stevens presents a useful survey of critical treatments of the theme of destiny in *Troilus*, beginning with the work of Walter Clyde Curry, as a preface to his discussion of the "recurrent figure" of the "winds of fortune" as part of the "ubiquitous presence of destinal forces" within the poem—"The Winds of Fortune in *Troilus*," *Chaucer Review* 13 (1979): 285–307.

4. The concept of language, specifically the Word, as the medium of creation is, of course, ubiquitous in medieval thought and is naturally an important reason for the period's preoccupation with linguistic theories upon which this paper draws so heavily. See Augustine, *De genesi ad litterarum* IX.x. 17 (*PL* XXXIV, 398–99), as well as Hugh of St. Victor, *De arca Noe morale* II, xiii (*PL* CLXXVI, 644 B).

5. For a discussion of the role of the gods in affecting human events, see John Frankis, "Paganism and Pagan Love in *Troilus and Criseyde*," in *Essays on "Troilus and Criseyde,"* ed. Mary Salu (Cambridge: D. S. Brewer, 1979), pp. 57–72. As Frankis points out, the gods obviously "cannot be dissociated from the influence of the planets which bear their names" (p. 59). Also see Chauncey Wood, *Chaucer and the Country of the Stars: Poetic Uses of Astrological Imagery* (Princeton, N.J.: Princeton University Press, 1970), pp. 69–78.

6. The emphasis found here on the explicitly linguistic nature of Creation is a virtual commonplace in patristic thought. For example, Peggy A. Knapp—"The Nature of Nature: Criseyde's 'slydyng corage'," *Chaucer Review* 13 (1978): 133–40— cites Augustine's *Sermonum mai* 126.6 (*PL* XXXVIII, 699–702) in support of Augustine's belief that nature is a "book in which God's purposes can be read, and yet of all books the most difficult to interpret rightly" (p. 133). Also see Hugh of St. Victor, *De eruditione docta* VII, iii (*PL* CLXXVI, 814 B): "Universus enim mundus iste sensibilis quasi quid om liber est scriptus digito Die," as well as Alanus de Insulis's oft-quoted lines:

> Omnis mundi creatura
> Quasi liber et pictura
> Nobis est et speculum
> Nostrae vitae, nostrae mortis
> Nostrae status, nostrae sortis
> Fidele signaculum.
> *Rhythmus alter* (*PL,* CCX, 579 A–B)

7. For Augustinian thought on the nature of signs, see Tzvetan Todorov, *Theories of the Symbol,* trans. Catherine Porter (Ithaca, N.Y.: Cornell University Press, 1977),

pp. 36–59. and Eugene Vance, "St. Augustine: Language as Temporality" in *Mimesis: From Mirror to Method, Augustine to Descartes,* ed. John D. Lyons and Stephen G. Nichols, Jr. (Hanover, N.H.: University Presses of New England, 1982) and Ronald H. Nash, *The Light of the Mind: Augustine's Theory of Knowledge* (Lexington: University Press of Kentucky, 1969). Also see Ladner, "Symbolism," and Nims, "Translatio," and "The Symbolist Mentality" in M.-D. Chenu, *Nature, Man, and Society in the Twelfth Century: Essays on New Theological Perspectives in the Latin West,* ed. and trans. Jerome Taylor and Lester K. Little (Chicago: University of Chicago Press, 1968), pp. 99–145. Concerning the multivalent nature of signs, Chenu notes that "the most constant characteristic" of the medieval symbol is its "polysemousness" (p. 136). Also see Shoaf, "Mediation," p. 90 and Boitani, "Labyrinth," p. 214. It is this particular property of language which from an earthly point of view requires delimiting properties of context in order to fix singular or particular meanings. Moreover, what is true for an individual sign is likewise true for larger blocks of language or ideas which also depend on the delimiting fact in context in order to create meaning. See Weatherbee, "Convention," who discusses Chaucer's "misappropriation" of texts as the poet's "own way of representing the dislocation of literary language from its primal sources" (p. 79). For discussions of such "misappropriations" and their effects on the "meaning" of the material taken out of context, see Robert R. Burlin, *Chaucerian Fiction* (Princeton, N.J.: Princeton University Press, 1977), pp. 95–96 and Ida L. Gordon, *The Double Sorrow of Troilus: A Study of Ambiguities in "Troilus and Criseyde,"* (London: Oxford University Press, 1970), p. 24. For a treatment of the Man of Law's "misuse" of Bernard Silvestris's trope concerning the "book of heaven," see Chauncey Wood, *Stars,* 209ff. However, the Man of Law's misappropriation of Silvestris may serve to confirm the validity of the passage's contents: namely, the inability of men to read texts.

8. For the mediating role of language, see Shoaf, "Mediation," who finds in the poet's early works a "theory of mediation responding to the problem of referentiality—a theory that, while transformed in them, nonetheless informs the *Canterbury Tales*" (p. 84). Also see Vance, "Mervelous Signals" (pp. 297–98), who notes Dante's assertion that language is necessary because of man's medial position between angels and beasts in *De vulgari eloquentia,* lii and iii.

9. Quomodo autem fecisti caelum et terram, et quae machina tam grandis operationis tuae? . . . *Ergo dixisti, et facta sunt,* atque in verbo tuo fecisti ea. . . . Sed quomodo dixisti? Numquid illo modo quo facta est vox de nube, dicens: *Hic est Filius meus dilectus?* . . . Illa enim vox acta atque transacta est, capta et finita. Sonuerunt syllabae atque transierunt, secunda post primam, tertia post secundam, atque inde ex ordine, donec ultima post caeteras, silentiumque post ultimam. Unde claret atque eminet, quod creaturae motus expressit eam, serviens aeternae voluntati tuae ipse temporalis. Et haec ad tempus facta verba tua nuntiavit auris exterior menti prudenti, cujus auris interior poita est ad aeternum Verbum tuum. At illa comparavit haec verba temporaliter sonantia, cum aeterno in silentio Verbo tuo, et dixit: Aliud est, longe aliud est. . . .
Confessionum, xi.5–6; (*PL* xxxii, 811–12)

The translation quoted in the text is that of R. S. Pine-Coffin (Baltimore, Maryland: Penguin Books, 1961), p. 257–8. For the difference between divine and human "words," also see *De doctrina Christiana,* 2.i.1–2 (*PL* xxxiv, 35–37) as well as *Confessionum,* II.vii.7 (*PL* xxxii,). Also see Vance, "Mervelous Signals," p. 296. Also see Eugene Vance, "St. Augustine," p. 20.

10. See *Confessionum,* xiii.xv.18 (*PL* xxxii, 852–53), where the fragmentary, multiplistic nature of human thought is reflected in enigma-filled human language which is broken up into syllables and syntactical parts as opposed to the unified spiritual discourse of angels. The effect of multiplistic consciousness on linguistic utterance is also seen in the earthly necessity of separating the Trinity into three distinct entities with names, or signs, that require three separate utterances (*De Trinitate* iv.xxi.30).

11. *PL* xxxiv, 440. Cited in Vance, "St. Augustine," p. 31.

12. *PL* xli, 70. Cited in Vance, "St. Augustine," pp. 31–32.

13. See Justman, "Literal," who argues that punning "reduces language to the verbal equivalent of counterfeiting" (p. 210).

14. Margaret Nims, "Translatio," p. 216.

15. For a discussion of arbitrariness as an essential element in signs, see *De doctrina Christiana,* 2.ii.1 (*PL* xxiv, 37). Also see Donald W. Rowe, *O Love,* pp. 59–60 as well as R. Allen Shoaf, "Mediation," p. 91 and Robert B. Burlin, *Chaucerian Fiction,* p. 103.

16. For a discussion of the conventional aspect of language, see *Confessionum,* i.xviii.29 (*PL* xxxii, 673–74). Although the focus of his study is on the "structure of usage" (strategies, idioms, groupings, habits of association, and register), John Burnley's observations concerning the conventionality of grammatical structure are concise and helpful (*Chaucer and the Philosopher's Tradition.* [Totwa, N.J.: Rowan and Littlefield, 1979], pp. 1–2). Also see Robins, *Linguistics,* pp. 17–20, 137–38 as well as John P. Hughes, *The Science of Language: An Introduction to Linguistics* (New York: Random House, 1968), pp. 38–39, for a discussion of both conventionality and arbitrariness.

17. Chaucer's statement concerning the multiplicity of tongues should be given special note here because, as Chauncey Wood notes in regard to Chaucer's attitude towards astrology, the *Treatise on the Astrolabe* is one of the few places where the poet speaks directly, without benefit of a mask or persona. Vance states, "Augustine believed that the meaning of the language of the Scriptures is strictly autonomous from the temporal, verbal signs by which it is experienced and such temporal meaning must be grasped by the reader in a direct process of illumination from within. For this reason, the Scripture may be translated from one historical language to another" ("St. Augustine," p. 26). Chaucer's sentiment, here as well as elsewhere, concerning the abilities of different languages to express similar if not identical content would, then, seem congruent to that of Augustine in regard to the translation of Scripture into the vernaculars.

18. The multiple, contextually evoked meanings of "hende" in the *Miller's Tale* certainly attest to Chaucer's appreciation of this fact. For a very readable discussion of the fixedness of meaning in medieval English, see Norman Blake, *The English Language in Medieval Literature* (London: Dent, 1977), who repeatedly demonstrates the semantic flexibility found in Middle English. Also see J. D. Burnley, *Tradition,* who cites Blake in contradicting H. S. Bennett's assertion of the "clear-cut and limited meanings" of the language of Chaucer's day (p. 4). Instead, Burnley points to the linguistic complexity inherent in a multi-linguistic, multi-cultural community such as that of fourteenth-century London (p. 8).

19. See D. W. Robertson, Jr., *A Preface to Chaucer: Studies in Medieval Perspectives* (Princeton, N.J.: Princeton University Press, 1962), p. 15 as well as p. 57ff.

20. The thematic and structural use of oppositions and *concordia discors* has received

a great deal of attention in the last decade. See Peter Elbow, "How Chaucer Transcends Oppositions in the *Knight's Tale*," *Chaucer Review* 7 (1970), as well as his longer study *Oppositions in Chaucer.* Also see Donald W. Rowe, *O Love,* whose thesis is that "Chaucer imitated the *concordia discors* conception of universal order in forming *Troilus and Criseyde* from the matter of Boccaccio's *Il Filostrato*" (p. 39), adding "that literature which most insistently presents the *concordia discors* conception is by and large literature which it is generally agreed Chaucer knew" (p. 7).

Ladner, "Symbolism," discusses the principle of unity in multiplicity as an essential element of medieval symbolism (p. 225), as does Nims, "Translatio," who cites Geoffrey of Vinsauf in noting that "metaphor introduces a *concors discordia,* harmonious contradiction" (p. 222). The oft contradictory "*In malo*" and "*In bono*" denotations of a single symbol also illustrate the point.

21. See Justin Leiber, *Noam Chomsky: A Philosophic Overview* (Boston: Twayne, 1975), pp. 94–108, for a discussion of Chomsky's *Syntactic Structures* as well as pp. 109–34 for a discussion of generative structures in *Aspects of the Theory of Syntax.* Also see pp. 63, 96. In regard to the generation of structures, see Elmer Holenstein, *Roman Jakobson's Language of Phenomenological Structuralism,* trans. Catherine Schelbert and Tarcisus Schelbert (Bloomington, Indiana: Indiana University Press, 1976), pp. 81–83.

22. For a discussion of the constituents of meaning, see Leonard Bloomfield, *Language* (New York: Holt, Rinehart, and Winston, 1933), pp. 42ff, 425–43, as well as Holenstein, *Jakobson,* pp. 76–81; Hughes, *Science,* pp. 8–14; and Todorov, *Theories,* pp. 37ff.

23. Mark, himself a man unable to distinguish brass from gold or Brangaene from Isolde on his wedding night for that matter, may be seen as an unconcerned abuser of signs. For a discussion of Mark's proclivity towards literalism, see S. L. Clark and Julian N. Wasserman, *The Poetics of Conversion: Numerology and Alchemy in Gottfried's "Tristan"* (Bern: Peter Lang, 1977), pp. 60ff. The dangers of such literalism, especially in regard to language, is a common theme in Chaucer as well, for instance in the Friar's and Pardoner's tales.

24. Gottfried von Strassburg, *Tristan und Isold,* ed. Fredrich Ranke (Zurich: Weidemann, 1968), vv. 15733–44. The translation is that of Edwin H. Zetdel, *The "Tristan and Isolde" of Gottfried von Strassburg* (Princeton, N.J.: Princeton University Press, 1948), ll. 15737–48.

25. Emelye might be taken as an ambiguous sign, much like Criseyde who, because of her "slyding" heart, that is, her mutability, has been treated as something of a multivalent sign to be read by both characters and reader alike. Knapp ("Corage," pp. 133–40) associates Criseyde with nature which, in turn, is ambiguous and argues that the key to understanding the forces at work in the poem is understanding Criseyde. Michael E. Cotton—"The Artistic Integrity of Chaucer's *Troilus and Criseyde,*" *Chaucer Review* 7 (1972): 44–66—notes that Criseyde is explicitly identified with the changeable moon upon which she makes her oath to return in ten days' time. Shoaf, "Mediation," in a study specifically concerned with the multivalence of signs, notes "Chaucer supplements the image of Criseyde as coin with numerous suggestions that she is also like a sign or text" (p. 85).

26. Concerning the verbal tactics of the two knights, Peter Elbow, "*Knight's Tale,*" notes,

Arcite and Palamon sometimes engage in what might look like thinking: making logical distinctions and drawing inferences (1152–86, 1223–74, and in particular 1280–1333). But in every case they are using words and thoughts to justify a mood and point of view they already hold. . . . They use the ingredients of thought not for flexibility but to avoid flexibility. Theseus is significant because he uses words and thoughts to arrive at a new mood and point of view, and thereby call into question some of the things that were formerly taken for granted. (p. 108)

The linguistic assumptions concerning the nature and function of language in Elbow's observation are worth noting. Palamon and Arcite demonstrate a linguistic rigidity which denies what Chenu described as the "polysemousness" of the signs which fill their world. Theseus, on the other hand, repeatedly demonstrates a willingness to redefine or modify his words, thereby avoiding the type of bondage to a rashly given vow which occurs so frequently on the parts of medieval literary kings and especially King Arthur.

27. For the most part, critics have seen the two knights as essentially identical. For example, see Schweitzer, "Freedom," p. 13 and Robert B. Burlin, *Chaucerian Fiction*, pp. 100; 262 n. 6. However, for an opposing view, see Peter Elbow, *"Knight's Tale,"* p. 98. In a paper delivered at the 1982 New Chaucer Society, "Palamon and Arcite: Rival Theories of Human Nature in the *Knight's Tale*," as well as in a forthcoming book-length study, Lois Roney makes a very convincing argument for the distinction between Palamon, who represents Augustinian/Franciscan points of view and Arcite, who represents Aristotelian/Thomist positions.

28. That language, i.e. semantic categories, directs thoughts, is today commonly known as the "Sapir/Whorf Theory." Eugene Vance, although not citing the theory explicitly, notes that "poetic language does not express, by its conventions, the consciousness of the desiring individual, but determines the operations of that consciousness" ("Mervelous Signals," p. 306). In short, our linguistic boundaries may become the boundaries of our actions, shaping rather than reflecting our actions, and this, in effect, is exactly what happens to the characters in both poems.

29. For a detailed discussion of the poet's use and manipulation of the conventional joining of red and white in regard to the theme of unity and multiplicity in the *Knight's Tale,* see Robert J. Blanch and Julian N. Wasserman, "The Red and the White: Chaucer's Manipulation of a Convention," in *Chaucer in the Eighties,* ed. Julian N. Wasserman and Robert J. Blanch (Syracuse, N.Y.: Syracuse University Press, 1987), pp. 175–91.

30. See Schweitzer, "Freedom," pp. 35–36.

31. Georgia Ronan Crampton, *The Condition of Creatures: Suffering and Action in Chaucer and Spenser* (New Haven: Yale University Press, 1974) argues that the gods resolve the conflict through use of a "shabby technicality" by taking advantage of a "verbal slip" (p. 70). This, however, seems, at least to me, to seriously miss the point, which is that the two deliberately choose the words of their prayers. The fact that there are two prayers indicates that there is a choice, just as the two earlier choose between the categories of "woman" and "goddesse." It is their fault if they choose either rashly or without fully knowing the choices, a common trope in medieval folklore and literature, as is seen in Arthur's rash vow in *Sir Gawain and the Green Knight.*

32. See Knapp, "Nature," for an analysis of Theseus's final speech which points to Chaucer's understanding of the Bonaventurian concept that "sensible things, rightly seen, carry the mind to the principle of order which gives them their beauty and

worth, 'as if by signs to the signified'" (p. 133). Estimations of Theseus vary from Elizabeth Salter, *Chaucer: The "Knight's Tale" and The "Clerk's Tale"* (Great Neck, New York: Barron, 1963), who sees Theseus's attempts to impose Boethian order on the events of the tale as raising more problems than they solve, to J. D. Burnley, *Philosopher*, who sees in the duke the person of the ideal philosopher-king. Peter Elbow, *"Knight's Tale,"* sees in Theseus's changes of mind and revision of his word both a flexibility and a concommitant verbal ability which separates him off from the more rigid Palamon and Arcite (p. 108). For a survey of reactions to Theseus, see Crampton, *The Condition of Creatures*, pp. 47–49.

33. Chaucer's works are, of course, filled with characters who either willfully or unknowingly misread signs, ranging from Chaunticleer and his dream to the fatally literal-minded rioters of the Pardoner's sermon. Consider, for example, Robertson's treatment of "Chaucer's exegetes" (*Preface*, pp. 317ff). Stewart Justman, "Literal," finds that the *Canterbury Tales* "abound with mock signs, false exemplifications, allegory that fails" (p. 199) as part of the poet's skeptical attack on the authority or absolute referentiality of conventional signs. In a similar although slightly different vein, Eugene Vance notes, "In Chaucer, the 'rhetor' came to be seen as a powerful and dangerous figure who subverts the well-being of society; such is the case with the Summoner, the Pardoner, and the Wife of Bath, all of whom are answered by the Nun's Priest, a paradigm of Christian eloquence, not in the high, but the 'mixed' style" ("Mervelous Signals," p. 299). Finally, see Shoaf, "Mediation," who explores the metaphor of the counterfeit coin in regard to "the issue of corrupt or fraudulent referentiality" (p. 85).

34. Part of what makes *Troilus* of peculiar interest is that while all of the major characters play fast and loose with signs, the two characters who do read accurately are the traitor Calkas and Cassandra, both of whom are greeted with disbelief in Troy. See Justman, "Literal," for a discussion of the dire threat to social order that counterfeiting, that is, the abuse of symbols or signs, poses to social order (especially p. 204). Eugene Vance, "Mervelous Signals," maintains much the same position (p. 295) applying it to *Troilus* and noting that within the poem "we encounter strategical designs by which Chaucer underscores the vitiation of social order that attends decadence in the use of language. . . . Troy is a city where people have forgotten how to use signs properly, and as a result their erotic discourse of love is ornamented with figurative violence of the most extravagant sort" (p. 313).

35. Eugene Vance sees Pandarus as a dealer in equivocal signs ("Mervelous Signals," p. 312) and an "abuser of *sermonacio*" (p. 313). Also see pp. 321–22 as well as Shoaf, "Mediation," pp. 96–98.

36. Pandarus's initial argument that Criseyde can only be won by speaking and his subsequent advice that love can be lost through speech in some ways seems a parody of the argument of *De magistro* in which Augustine first argues that nothing can be taught without signs and then demonstrates that nothing may be taught with signs.

37. As Augustine notes, the purpose of language is communication (*De ordine* II.xii.35 [*PL* XXXII, 1011–12]). Hence the use of language to dissemble is in Augustinian terms a clear instance of "abuse."

38. Here is one place where one might take exception to Eugene Vance's otherwise insightful reading of the poem. By including thought as well as spoken language as part of the discourse which he notes composes at least half of *Troilus* ("Mervelous Signals," pp. 303–4), Professor Vance ignores the distinction between linguistic competence and linguistic performance, which in turn lessens the emphasis on the mediat-

ing function of signs. The point is that language is *not* mediating between the two and has an existence separate from thought.

39. Of Criseyde's new lover, Vance says, "In Diomedes we glimpse the potentiality of conventional signs to become vehicles of the most despicable cruelty" ("Mervelous Signals," p. 329).

40. See Boitani, "Labyrinth," pp. 46, 83.

41. Shoaf sees Troilus, with the aid and encouragement of Pandarus, as intentionally falsifying Criseyde, arguing that "Criseyde is *already* gold and minted; she is already a sign ("Mediation," p. 94).

42. The obviously linguistic allegory, *The House of Fame,* demonstrates the process by which spoken words generate such an image in the House of Rumor which serves as a metaphor for human consciousness. Interestingly enough, language in the form of books was seen to be the first cause of dreams—that is, mental images—in Chaucer's first two dream visions.

43. The ability of words to affect material things is parodied in the *Reeve's Tale,* as the miller taunts the students by asking them,

> Myn hous is streit, but ye han lerned art.
> Ye konne by argumentes make a place
> A myle brood of twenty foot of space,
> Lat se now if this place may suffise,
> Or make it rowm with spech as is your gise.
> (I, 4122–26)

the *Miller's Tale* has long been seen as a parody of that told by the Knight. Consider how Absolon's selective reading of signs—"My mouth hath icched al this longe day— / That is a signe of kissyng atte leeste" (I, 3682–83) parodies the selective reading of signs by Palamon and Arcite in the respective temples of Venus and Mars. To be sure, the sign is read correctly, although the kissing is not what the Absolon has in mind. Nicholas, on the other hand, is a willful misreader of signs, though he fares no better.

44. The dilemma felt by the narrator has been well remarked. Most comments have their basis in E. Talbot Donaldson's "Criseyde and her Narrator," in *Speaking of Chaucer* (New York: W. W. Norton, 1970), pp. 65–83. For a discussion of the problem posed by the "auctors" in regard to the "limitations under which a poet must operate," see Rose A. Zimbardo, "Creator and Created: The Generic Perspective of Chaucer's *Troilus and Criseyde," Chaucer Review* 11 (1977): 284. Zimbardo extends this creative dilemma both in the direction of the characters and in the direction of the poet who stands behind the narrator: "Although Pandarus is a maker of sorts, he is also a character, a character within the design of a poem the scope of which he has only dim intimations of. He is subject to the designing will of a creator beyond himself, Chaucer the narrator, and he is subject to the facts of the story, the given substance which the poet-narrator has been required to forge into new forms" (p. 287).

45. See Shoaf, "Mediation," p. 90.

PART VI

LAUGHING AT THE VOID
The Comic Possibilities of Semantic Chaos

EDITORS' INTRODUCTION

For the most part, the problem of the distance between word and deed, signifier and signified, and an author's intention and reader's response have been treated seriously, even in those essays which see in the chaos of such "cracks" evidence of God's plenty rather than emptiness. But such discrepancies, such violations of expectations— whether philosophical, social, or even spiritual—can also be the stuff of comedy. In her discussion of the Miller's wit, Peggy Knapp notes, "According to Freud, wit entails a psychic shortcut. Something is used where it is unexpected but not unfamiliar." In his discussion of Gower's intentions, David Hiscoe points out that since "signification is fundamentally linked to memory," the comic possibilities of the gap between what is recalled and what is present or appropriate are real and exploitable. Thus the two essays in this chapter explore the use of those gaps and shortcuts for comic purposes—the first in regard to "moral Gower" (a violation of our expectations in itself), the second in regard to a more traditional source of medieval humor, the French fabliaux.

David Hiscoe begins with the now familiar assertion that "the process of assigning meaning mirrors the spiritual condition of the humans who engage" in such activity. He points out that the use of the first person plural in Augustine's definition of sign—"Something that allows *us* to think of something else" explicitly brings the reader into play—a point similar to R. A. Shoaf's observation that Dante's letter to Can Grande implies that the reader supplies the supplementary allegorical meanings. But what if the interpreter's "spiritual condition," rather than courtly ardor, as in the case of Arcite and Palamon, or spiteful pettiness, as in the case of the Chester Pharisees, is, instead, comic denseness?

Accordingly, Hiscoe presents a reading of the *Confessio* suggesting that the inappropriateness of Genius's tales to Amans's condition is a discrepancy whose comic implications were recognized and exploited by Gower. Hiscoe, like Professors Pulsiano and Purdon, grounds his argument in the "purpose" of language, which is to represent/(re)present, arguing that the sign forces us to recall that which

225

has already been 'written' on our consciousness by experience. Spiritual language should point to spiritual truths that are prewritten, that pre-exist. The argument, then, somewhat parallels Glenn Arbery's discussion of Derridian "good writing" in Dante, although, rather than Dantean angst, the fact that the new writing is shown to be empty generates the tale's "comic design." An underscoring of prewritten truths, as we are shown through an examination of the tale of Bardus, is exactly what Genius's signs should but do not do. Rather, Christian language is grafted onto very unchristian tales, and the result of this violation of expected recall is "comic hollowness"—a sophisticated and subtle joke told deadpan but a joke nonetheless. In Gower, Hiscoe suggests, expectations generated by the moralizing subject matter and confessional situation are so strong they blind us to the comedy of their violation, even though the basic, comic disparity is the same as that in the fabliau.

In essence, Gower's Genius is comic because his "Christianized" tales are unfaithful to their sources. The same kind of infidelity is the cornerstone of the fabliau. But if the infidelity of spouses is a constant theme in the fabliaux, so too is the infidelity of language, of signs that betray their usual denotations, signs whose "false seeming" seduces. A word is wedded to its signification somewhat as a wife, in medieval thinking, is wedded to her husband, and it is the breaking of the former bond that leads to the breaking of the latter, as in Nicholas's prophecy in the fabliau told by Chaucer's Miller. As Edith Joyce Benkov notes, Iseut's manipulation of the oath, her deliberate creation of a gap between what the audience perceives and what she actually says when renaming Tristan as "that beggar," is the means through which she continues, and even seems to receive divine sanction for, her infidelity. Such verbal manipulations are, of course, stock in trade for Tristan's and Iseut's less royal counterparts.

Another standard fabliau theme is power, the attempt to control a wife or daughter, usually through words (Arthur, Allen, Ashley) but also through silence (Grimbert). Language, as has often been noted, is associated with creation, birth, and fecundity. In medieval texts, words are often described as "seeds." The generative medium of Creation is achieved through the "speech act" of the Divinity. And thus the creative potential of words poses the same dangers as the fecundity of women. Words are, in Shoaf's terms, capable of "promiscuous coupling." On the human level, the danger of such coupling in a patrilineal society is the loss of paternal identity, a clouding of "origin" that threatens the foundation of male hierarchy. Since the cuckoo lays its eggs in other birds' nests, to be cuckolded is to doubt the origin of one's offspring. On the linguistic level, the result of such coupling is likewise the loss of origin, what Pulsiano has described as the danger of the "free-floating sign." Male/female relations, are, then, as Benkov demonstrates, a constant battle for the power to control language, to appropriate origin. Language is the means used to attempt to control behavior because in the world of fabliau language is itself a behavior, a set of manners that defines selfhood, as is evident from the models of socially based discourse provided by Andreas in *The Art of Courtly Love*.

In the end, as with Purdon and the others, language is a moral issue. In a fallen world, there is fallen language. The fabliau deals with that part of the Fall with which man has the least quarrel, sex, and often with the comic loss of the innocence that results from ignorance of the gap between signifier and signified. As Benkov notes, "*Escuiruel* does not mean *vit*," a fact unknown to the innocent. Her point is that the prelapsarian state of the beguiled, both male and female, is their lack of awareness of semiotic arbitrariness. Language is conventional, and to be ignorant of the conventions is to court disaster. Romance and fabliau alike, as Benkov notes, demonstrate the danger to both marriage and the social order of the privatization of language, be it the monologue of Enide or the private, and hence unconventionalized, dialects between maidens and their keepers.

11

HEAVENLY SIGN AND COMIC DESIGN IN GOWER'S *CONFESSIO AMANTIS*

DAVID W. HISCOE

Medievalists have reacted to semiotics in the same way we once responded to the work of D. W. Robertson, Jr.: with tittering scepticism, self-satisfied indignation, bellowing outrage—and with a growing sense that we have been given a lens that can for the first time focus clearly much in medieval literature that in the past seemed diffuse or vaguely puzzling. After all, if Eugene Vance is even partially correct in arguing that "sign theory . . . is the most singular feature of the intellectual coherence of the Middle Ages,"[1] then we can undoubtedly expect medieval authors to be concerned with the subject. Further, if Jonathan Culler is right when he suggests that "the advent of semiotics has helped to reveal . . . that what had previously been sneered at as medieval scholasticism was in many respects a subtle and highly developed theory of signs,"[2] then a good deal of what we have regarded as inordinately pointless and insignificant in medieval intellectual life is up for rescue. And surely few artifacts from the Middle Ages are in more need of deliverance than *Confessio Amantis,* a poem ravaged by Chaucer's characterization of its author as "moral" Gower. Expecting a pedantic schematization of the virtues and vices, we not surprisingly have found just that when we have gone to Gower's collection of moral tales. However, when the *Confessio* is placed beside even the most commonplace medieval speculation on the uses and abuses of verbal signs, it begins to look less like a compulsively scholastic gathering of ethical lore and more like a tour de force of comic skill and audience engagement. As we begin to appreciate the implications of medieval sign theory for the practice of medieval literature, we can begin to value properly the comic design behind this, the most significant poem of Chaucer's closest literary acquaintance.

Memory and Representation

The comic strategy of *Confessio Amantis* is built on the medieval assumption that the process of assigning meaning mirrors the spiritual condition of the humans who engage in the process. The bedrock on which the *signum* rests during the period is Augustine's definition of a sign as "a thing which causes us to think of something beyond the impressions the thing makes upon the senses."[3] Though such a definition in large part echoes those developed by countless predecessors, including Aristotle and the Stoics,[4] Augustine, as R. A. Markus points out, radically rearranges the stress that was traditionally placed on the various agents of the process.[5] Between the *signans* and the *signatum*, Augustine allows to fall the interpreter of the transaction: signs cause *us* to think; and as the place where the signifier becomes the signified, *we* become the central actors in all transfers of meaning. Since the essential link in the process of establishing significance is thus a member of fallen humankind, signification is necessarily implicated in the larger Christian drama of Fall and Redemption. Signification thus becomes a moral and spiritual act.

Man's ability to signify correctly, therefore, reveals his willingness to accept the sacrifices by which Christ redeems both humankind and human language. In the prelapsarian existence, the Word manifested itself clearly and unambiguously in a universe where, as Augustine argues in *De doctrina Christiana* and *De Genese contra Manichaeos,* men knew God completely and inwardly.[6] In such a state, "Omnis mundi creatura," as Alan of Lille's popular school lyric proclaims, are a faithful "signaculum" in which, "quasi liber, ut pictura / . . . et speculum," we can read "Nostrae vitae, nostrae mortis, / Nostri status, nostrae sortis."[7] The Fall and its babelic consequences, however, fracture the Word and place postlapsarian man in a world of painfully equivocal significations. The gift of the Incarnation, when the Word reenters the world of the flesh, returns to us the possibility of speaking, listening, and understanding properly. Redeemed signification, Marcia Colish points out, "becomes a mirror through which men may know God in this life,"[8] and the willful refusal to participate in this redemption of language reveals a parallel refusal to show the proper appreciation for Christ's corresponding Redemption. "Words," as Dante says, "are like seeds of actions":[9] their eloquent use reveals the user's wisdom and piety; their misuse both reveals and sows discord and confusion.[10]

The way in which medieval theorists imagined this semiotic re-

demption to work in the individual Christian helps to construct the
backdrop against which Gower plays out the comic strategy of *Confessio*. In a world where mankind is at once fallen and yet able to
participate in redeeming that fall, the ability to remember the possibilities of one's proper nature becomes a spiritual necessity. As
Augustine makes clear in the famous Book x of the *Confessions*,
signification is yoked to memory. Words themselves remain empty of
any significant content unless transformed by a speaker's awareness of
how verbal signs gain ultimate authority solely from their capacity to
call up Christian truths to their speakers and to their audiences.[11] The
signa Dei which permeate the spiritual universe become meaningful
only when the human mind allows the signs to point mankind toward
the Creator.[12] By definition then, words are, in Marcia Colish's
terms, "instrumental, not heuristic."[13] Signs, Augustine would say,
exist only to cause us to think of something else not present to the
senses. "The utmost value I can attribute to words is this," explains
the Saint: "They bid us to look for things [*res*], but they do not show
them to us so that we may know them."[14] "If we know a thing,"
concludes Augustine, "we recall rather than learn."[15]

By the time Gower arranged the comic design of his poem around
such a theory of recall, the importance of remembrance in medieval
speculation about language had received re-emphasis from the
Ockhamist teaching that all signs merely "present again to the
knower what he formerly had known."[16] For Ockham, continuing
on in the Augustinian tradition, words, in their attempt to represent
an idea, truly do re-present. Language gains its only meaningful
significance from its ability to remind speakers and listeners of spiritual realities that exist prior to and independent of the verbal instruments we use to call them up.

Such a signification theory has obvious implications for the practice of literature. First and foremost, if literary language is to be
significant, it must refer to the sacred background against which all
meaning shows itself. Our sense, therefore, that even the most secular
of medieval literature presses in some sort of allegorical fashion
toward things beyond the senses is easily justified when we realize
that the medieval understanding of allegory, as the trope in which
"one thing is sounded while another is meant,"[17] is almost exactly
Augustine's definition of signification in general. Standing behind or
under all medieval stories is always the Story—God's Word which
makes all words meaningful.

Recent attempts to establish a semiotics of poetry give us a theoretical position which, in its key tenets, nicely parallels its medieval precursors. Michael Riffaterre, for instance, argues that the essence of literary language is determined by what he calls "hypogrammatic derivation": language becomes "poeticized when it refers to . . . a preexisting word group"—the previously established "thematic complex," the "past semiotic and literary practice," against which individual literary works create themselves.[18] All literature by definition is "a departure from a norm," what Jonathan Culler calls a "transformation of past poetic discourse."[19]

The role of the reader in the theory of literary practice shared by Riffaterre and the Middle Ages is to detect the originating story behind the poetry at hand. As Culler explains, the audience "interprets a poem by recognizing references to hypograms . . . and reconstructing the original matrix."[20] Thus, the function of the reader has become central to contemporary semioticians, who, in Umberto Eco's phrase, see many modern works as "Opera Aperta," open works, which invite readers, again to quote Culler, "to play a . . . fundamental role as constructor of the work," rather than just to interpret it.[21] Such recent theories, of course, neatly spell out the same aesthetics that one would expect to develop from Augustinian sign theory. Given the decisive importance the medieval period placed on the interpreter as the agent that relates the *signans* to the *signatum,* it follows that perhaps the most characteristic act of medieval literature should be the poet's creation of works that ask the audience to become actively involved in creating their meaning.[22] And if for Riffaterre the constant discovery of matrices and hypograms makes poetry "more of a game than anything else,"[23] then the game that medieval readers are asked to play is one that exercises and measures their ability to understand, use, and enjoy the doctrines that give their lives significance.

The largest body of evidence that literary theorists in the Middle Ages understood the implications of medieval sign theory for poetic making is the massive quantity of energy medieval commentators devoted to finding the sacred hypograms standing behind Ovid's *Metamorphoses.* With a single-mindedness that has struck some modern readers as bizarrely inappropriate, the moralizers of Ovid reveal just how seriously medieval readers practiced what their semiotics preached. If poetry, like all signification, causes us to think of something else, and if the only meaningful reference is finally to sacred story, then the Ovidian tales, like all fictions, must of necessity be holy signs that point in the directions indicated by Pierre Bersuire and the *Ovide Moralisé*.

Holy Signs and Gower's Comic Strategy

The desire to see Holy Scripture behind all writing need not, however, be reductive. In another essay, I have tried to show how the organizing comic strategy of *Confessio Amantis* is a playful manipulation of the mythographic impulse that required medieval readers to have their Ovidian mythologies recall Christian truths.[24] Gower can assume that both the Ovidian tales he presents and the allegories demanded of them are well-known to his original audience. But instead of dishing out the expected significations, he puts his mythological revisions into the mouth of Genius, a supremely unreliable narrator, who shrinks and stretches his holy *exempla* to clothe narrative purposes for which they are often superbly ill-fitted. By detecting the comic inadequacies of Genius's presentation, the audience obtains the pleasure of watching a jangler as he wreaks erratic havoc on the world of holy signs. And even more importantly, the readers of the *Confessio* can signal with their laughter their ability to perceive and evade the moral and spiritual distortions Genius inadvertently inflicts on stories that a medieval audience would regard as pointers toward more explicitly sacred tales.

Perhaps, though, an even stronger indication of the way Gower transforms his audience's impulse to look for heavenly signs into the comic design of his poem can be found in those stories not drawn from the mythographic tradition. Almost without exception, the non-Ovidian tales in the *Confessio* are ones whose traditional details beg for exactly the sort of sacred recall Gower's readers would have brought to his Ovidian reworkings. The principle of inclusion for stories not centered on classical mythography seems to require that the tale teem with particulars of plot, theme, and structure that would demand allegorical attention from an audience already expecting secular fiction to point toward anagogic truth. Such stories enable Gower once again to metamorphose the readers' desire for holy signs into a comic strategy. The evocative details of Genius's stories urge readers to expect heavy spiritual weight; instead they are entertained with the spectacle of a storyteller comically unable to understand or control the inherent significances of the tales he himself chooses to tell.

Since Genius specifically offers the tale of Adrian and Bardus as an example of "unkindness" and "unkindeschipe," this story provides a convenient place from which to watch the skill with which Gower creates the comic strategy of the poem by arousing his audience's allegorical impulse.[25] Though the story does not bring with it the established tradition of spiritual interpretation an audience would bring to an Ovidian myth, it is clearly the sort of tale that would, as Augustine might say, cause medieval readers to think of something beyond the impression it makes upon their fiction-reading senses. The story as it exists before Genius is turned loose on it contains insistent parallels to the Christ story, especially as it was understood in the Middle Ages. Gower's principle source, as Macaulay notes, is probably the *Speculum Stultorum, The Book of Burnel the Ass*.[26] Yet Nigel's account is itself a substantial reworking of his oriental sources, probably some version of the Sanskrit *Panchatantra* or the Arabian *Kalila and Dimna*. The merest outline of some of the plot details of these works suggests how a medieval audience would have inevitably responded to them. In the Sanskrit version, the crucial episode of the tale centers on the earth-wrenching death of a king's son, a tragedy that ends, however, in triumphant resurrection when the story's Brahman, the equivalent of Bardus in Gower's version, restores the life of a queen whose death has been brought on by the attack of a serpent.[27] In the Arabian analogue, such allegorically alluring details are reinforced by making the story a crucial episode in Burzoe's search for the Kalilah, the fabled life-giving herb of renewal and rebirth.[28]

The largely unsifted evidence that we have about late medieval uses of oriental material suggests that, by the time of Nigel and Gower, a European reader might well expect the same sort of spiritual manipulation from his Arabian tales as from a reworking of Ovid. According to Dorothee Metlitzki, for example, the preaching of the period commonly employed such tales "not only as moral *exempla* but as allegories of the life of the soul;"[29] and one need only turn to recent Chaucer criticism to see how a contemporary might fulfill such expectations by using oriental motifs such as the Blind Man in the Fruit Tree or the eastern elements transmitted by Aesopean animal tales. A good deal of Chaucer's oriental material has analogues in popular moralized collections such as Petrus Alphonsi's *Disciplina clericalis* or John of Capua's *Directorium vitae humanae*,[30] both of which share most of the plot motifs of the Adrian and Bardus story. In the extremely well-circulated *Gesta Romanorum,* even the scurrilous *Dame Sirith,* whose "weeping bitch" motif is from the same well of tales as those of Nigel, Chaucer, and Gower, becomes an allegory in which the "miles est Christus" rebuking his wife, an "anima per baptismum lota," for misdirecting her free will towards "carnalem concupiscenciam."[31]

The temptingly allegorical overtones in the oriental beginnings of the Adrian and Bardus story would surely not have been overlooked by medieval readers, a fact Nigel counts on when he chooses the tale as the climactic ending for the *Speculum.* When Gower adopts the story as his culminating *exemplum* of "kindness," he adopts the primary concern of Nigel's story: the adventures of Burnal the Ass as he roams about the world in his pseudo-epic attempt to correct what he sees as "Nature's deficiency." In introducing the donkey's comic quest to restore "kinde," Nigel explicitly directs attention to how he wishes his tale to be perceived: the reader, one with "a wise, reflecting mind," must "forget the verse's outward sound, / And keep the inward sense with them upbound," if he or she is to find the "Great mysteries" hidden in the author's fable.[32] In late medieval culture, in which Christ is constantly seen in verse, drama, and exegesis as the "kynd lord" who redeems Nature from the deficiencies drawn down on it by the Fall, the great mysteries Nigel demands that his audience discover behind his *integumentum* would have been easy to recall. Burnel becomes the comic mirror in which we watch a foolish speaker turn "up-so-doun" the spiritual certainties of the Middle Ages.

The ludicrous insufficiency of Burnel's conception of what constitutes Nature's deficiency is revealed in the calamitous deficiency the donkey finds at the heart of the universe's imperfections: his tail is too short. In the story, the call for Nature's delivery fairly screams for spiritual interpretation; the ass meanwhile is concerned exclusively with his hindmost member. Nigel's asinine hero undertakes a journey to seek the magical herbs that will lengthen his tail and thus set the universe right again. Once more introducing elements into the text that would surely ask the original audience to recall Christian spiritual commonplaces, Nigel introduces a character who forcefully reminds the audience of the proper way to participate in straightening out the disorders present in the natural scheme of things. Galen the Physician, after explaining that an all-wise God is the true creator of all that is natural, warns that a meaningful reformation of the donkey's condition will come only if he will "return himself" to his proper place and "change his state" from the disarray into which it has fallen (4). Burnel stubbornly sets out nevertheless and, after much expected foolishness and failure, is returned (minus even his stub of a tail, of course) to his master Bernard, whom the donkey, not having learned anything from the parodic pilgrimage, sees as the source of all his problems.

The unreformed nature that has directed his errant wanderings is indicated by the principle that organizes his approach to the supposed injuries done both to himself and his much-prized tail:

> Give limb for limb, the ancient law doth say,
> And tooth for tooth, and for foot foot repay,
> So will I do to Bernard.
>
> (122)

Since Bernard presumably lacks the limb which might requite Burnel's tail, the ass's moral imperatives seem doomed from the start. The Christian audience, of course, would bring to such a botched solution of Burnel's problem a New Law that would allow them both on the one hand to enjoy the comic blunderings of the *stultus* and on the other to imagine a more successful resolution to the deficiencies of nature. Thus when Nigel ends the *Speculum* with the gratitude the beasts show their rescuer in the Adrian and Bardus story, he is providing in their charitable response a clear remedy to the donkey's beastly behavior as well as a sign that points to the *caritas* that extends in importance far beyond the comic affairs of the animal kingdom.

Gower brought to his poem, then, a tale that was ripe with archetypal resemblances to important elements of the Christ story, and one which had already been used, by an immensely popular predecessor, as just the sort of holy sign on which he rests his own comic strategy in *Confessio Amantis*. Genius is quickly made to turn a story that would call up his readers' most fundamental religious assumptions into a mind-teasing set of equivocal contradictions. Gower's audience is asked to show, by their laughter, that they can control a more substantial understanding of man's nature even in the midst of narrative situations created to mirror the shiftiness and obscurity of the fallen world itself.

Genius's Garbled Signs

In the long preface to the Adrian and Bardus tale, Gower first allows Genius to undermine his own credibility as a proper perceiver, much less teacher, of the human "kinde"—of the nature that leaves us at once fallen and yet desirous of regeneration. The priest's formal introduction to the concept is, to begin with, a delightfully garbled mixture of accepted doctrine and incredible insipidity. "God of his justice / Be weie of kinde and nature" has created all creatures with an instinctive moral sense (4928–32). This is, of course, admirably sound Boethian wisdom.[33] Such natural inclinations compel mankind "with kind" (4925) to practice the Golden Rule (4926–27). Yet Genius's learned preparation for his story abruptly climaxes in a pedagogical dead-end when he concludes, with marvelous circularity, that "to seie unkinde" is to name a "thing which don is ayein kinde" (4923–24). Proper medieval signs function to point the reader elsewhere; Genius's signs—quite literally here—point only to themselves. If one's language mirrors one's essential spiritual self, the priest who will lead us through his tale will do so from a strangely unformed and unreliable moral and linguistic perspective.

As the *exemplum* that is to flesh out Genius's conception of "kindnesse," the Adrian and Bardus story disastrously reflects the moral chaos that provides the only underpining for the priest's sign-making. Although almost every addition the tale brings to Nigel's version is one that cries out for allegorical attention, Genius consistently fails to appreciate the sacred truths to which his fiction insistently directs his audience. The story begins as Adrian "fell lowe" (4947) into a pit, "his fall" leaving him asking "For socour and deliverance" (4953). Here, one might expect, is mankind's predicament, the pit being a universal as well as specifically Christian archetype for the grave[34] and "deliverence" the potential for rebirth. The language Genius has grafted onto Nigel's tale is clearly the language of Christian redemption. Yet, the language points nowhere. Adrian's salvation comes, for example, most inappropriately with "Eve" (4954), a detail that requires from us quite a bizarre rethinking of the Christian scheme of atonement. The agent of that salvation, Bardus, initiates Adrian's deliverance by riding into the scene on an ass and carrying—again Genius's addition—green and dry sticks for "who that wolde hem beie" (4959–60). The dry twig that is transformed into or replaced by the living green branch is one of the central typological motifs with which Biblical tradition prepares for Christ's bringing of life through the cross.[35]

Genius, however, cannot seem to grasp the pattern. Not bothering to distinguish between the two conditions, he casually throws the dead and fallen kind in with the restored and living. While these sticks buy Bardus his "lifode" (4961), Genius's rider of the ass will save Adrian if a "covenant" (5032) is made between the two (4976–78), a pledge that Adrian will amply reward Bardus for delivering him to safety. That agreement solemnly completed, Bardus goes about trying to fish the man out of his deadly hole, a detail that Russell Peck, although he does not bite at Genius's carelessly baited allegorical hooks, suggests is suspiciously like the "familiar icon of Christ the fisherman with his staff (cross) tied to a line drawing men's souls from the pit."[36] The serpent that he soon drags out of the pit is a blatantly loaded detail. When he next fishes up an ape, a familiar emblem of man's fallen nature,[37] our expectation for some sort of salvation allegory is clearly being whetted. And, given mankind's penchant for unnatural behavior, it is no surprise when, even after the "lord of Rome" blesses Bardus on "the thridde time" (5017–22), Adrian breaks the covenant by refusing to repay Bardus for his deliverance.

Readers who are upholding their end of the medieval semiotic covenant, who are honoring their responsibility to allow the details of the tale to direct them toward the larger reality to which such signs point, have surely by this time noticed the insistent if a little uncomfortable parallels to the Christ story that form the bulk of Genius's additions to the *Speculum Stultorum*. As the *exemplum* moves toward its happy ending, however, Genius's allegory slides even further out of his already tenuous control. Though Adrian has abrogated his promises to his savior, Bardus is magically rewarded—"be grace" Genius tells us—with an invaluable jewel that always returns to its master. Christ's gift of unmerited grace clearly lies somewhere behind this puzzling plot detail. Yet the details with which Genius effects the joyful redemption of the broken covenants clash mightily with their apparent allegorical significations. Bardus, who up to this point has consistently suggested Christ, may be justifiably upset when "the mannes Son hath failed to requite his kindness" (5075). After all, "he hadde most travailed" and finally "putte himself in goddes hand" (5076) in behalf of the man in the pit. One has to become a bit uncomfortable on being told, though, that should the phrase be emphasized differently, the Son of Man has failed. Further, one can only wonder why Genius should insist on having the tale's everyman accept his precious stone, presumably some sort of pearl of great price, from a serpent (5061–69). It might also appear to be a somewhat revealing allegorical *faux pas* to name one's savior *bardus*—Latin for *stupid*. By this point, clearly, Genius has wandered into quite different integumental regions. As the broker who confounds the expectations of his "jueler" (5086) when he repeatedly "profreth to the sale" (5083) his precious stone, Bardus has now unaccountably come to represent fallen mankind. And Genius, of course, grants the sale his solemn approval. Though the priest cannot seem to speak without babbling in the language of traditional allegories of redemption, holy signs become, in his mouth, only dangerously garbled nonsense.

Even if we ignore the anagogical bait that Genius has strewn throughout his tale and consider the story purely on an ethical level, the *moralitas* to which he wants to direct us curiously ignores even the most obvious implications of the tale itself. One can decide that the point is, as Peck argues, "that kindness, no matter how often spent, is never diminished; rather, it grows with use,"[38] only if one winks at Bardus's rather unseemly behavior towards the merchants to whom he repeatedly sells the stone. Genius, however, cheerfully brings the tale to its happy denouement by conferring upon its hero a sus- piciously unearned and very material wealth in a wildly inappropriate reward for an *exemplum* whose stated function—and Genius himself has done the stating—is to expose and decry Avarice. Thus, the priest of love simultaneously expects us to censure greediness and to ap- plaud Bardus as he cheats others out of their goods. One of the pleasures to which the audience is entitled is the discovery that, in fact, Genius's story confounds itself at all possible planes of interpreta- tion.

Gower's priest, quite unaware of the willy-nilly wedges he drives between the letter and the spirit of his story, explains meanwhile that it is "fortuen and the grace" (5122) that gives "the vertu of the Ston" (5111) around which his plot revolves. Genius again makes no at- tempt to distinguish between the two realms. As Amans's confessor, he is tied to the world of *amor* where fortune holds complete sway and grace concerns itself only with the lady's favors. In his fictional world, grace becomes merely another form of the concupiscent power of love, from which "may nothing ben hid" (5123). Lacking the direction confirmed by the grace toward which all medieval signs tend, his story has become a narrative version of Fortune's wheel, on which fictional details spin madly toward no apparent end.

This humorous lack of moral and fictional acuity on Genius's part is brought to a fitting climax in the "Court of juggement" (5143) held to determine the proper punishment for "unkindnesse" (5141). From the perspective of last things, Bardus has sold his precious stone and attempted to dupe his jeweler; from the moral perspective that seeps into the tale despite Genius's blithe unconcern for such issues, Bardus is somewhat of a greedy cheat. When the wheel governing the priest's fictional world turns, however, it is Adrian who is sentenced for his "unkind blod" (5156). Missing from Genius's story and from his conception of "kinde" is, as always, an understanding of the reformation offered by Christ's kind blood,[39] a reformation that gives order to Nature and that might have done so for Genius's tale. Instead, the priest wanders into the story's Last Judgment only out of a sort of literary version of curiosity—to watch the "gret wondringe among the press" (5149).

The final comic spin of the wheel comes when Genius gives a parting summary of the tale's *moralitas* and then teaches Amans how to apply it to his own amorous pursuits. Quite surprisingly, he begins by invoking exactly the doctrinal explanation of "kinde" to which his audience would have been expecting the story to point all along. The "unkinde" man (5170) is one who "his feith / Foryat for worldes covoitise" (5166–67), the man who accepts for his "kinde" only the fallen nature manifested in the misdirected love of worldly things. The whirl from proper signification to chaos occurs with the usual rapidity, however. From Augustine on, sexual love provided a favorite medieval metaphor for the *cupiditas* that attaches one too closely to things of this world. Marvelously avoiding the point of his own moral, Genius glibly assures Amans that the love he pursues is absolved from any suspicion. Since the lover guarantees his confessor that he hoards all his cupidity for use on one woman only, the priest proclaims that all is fine. Amans, after all, does not forget his faithful pursuit of cupidinous delight to go coveting after each lady who presents herself. After Genius has larded his story with details that continually call up the Christian history of the Fall and the faith that redeems that Fall, he concludes that loss of fidelity is only worrisome when one avariciously seeks out more than one source of worldly pleasure: "Here love is after sone ago" (5174). Genius's constant referral to his charge as "mi Sone" in this passage directs the audience, by way of pun, toward the connection that the priest himself is unable to keep clearly in mind. The proper kind of love will do just what Genius warns Amans to avoid: it will follow the Son. Once again, Genius can speak the right words while at the same time having comically little idea what they might mean to one less "astoned" than Gower's priest of love.

Amans as Misdirected Student

Genius begins his misdirected *moralitas* by assuring Amans that the Adrian and Bardus story will "stant the memorie" of time as long as wise men can use it as the example that will recall proper behavior (5157–60). The lover's ensuing defense of his amorous integrity shows that he has learned and can remember his lessons well: he too can now reduce speech to garbled equivocation. Amans's rhetorical task is to convince his pastoral guide that he is faithful in his virtuous practice of love, but each attempt at justification only serves to dramatize to Gower's audience the lover's inability to make his signs point in the direction he desires. He assures us, to begin his argument, that he has never taken his lady's love and then sought further "profit elles where" (5186). He has never, in short, pledged his troth and then pursued other loves. Yet even while proclaiming his innocence, he ensnares himself with his own choice of metaphor. As readers, we are surely to bring our own memory into play at this point. It has been only a few verses, after all, since we have listened to Genius wax eloquent in praise of Bardus's ability to find profit at every opportunity. If Bardus's ability to profit from his stone signifies the reward for his faithful adherence to charitable values, Amans's declared refusal to show a profit here seems a bit odd. Something, at any rate, is out of joint between the *signa* the master and his pupil are trying to exchange. Even in declaring his truth, Amans can only succeed in arousing our doubts as the chaotic signs of Genius's story begin to tangle around both the lover and his priest.

Amans's second testimony of his faithfulness entangles him even more tightly in a web of ludicruously misdirected speech. His love for his lady, he assures Genius, is an ideal one, a meeting of true souls. Yet, as he himself soon reveals, his would-be lover seems to show no interest. Amans's attempt to gloss over the gaping distance between his rhetoric and the uncomfortable reality of his amatory failure comically reveals the essential duplicity of his own sign-making. Of course, with impeccable courtly decorum, he will retain his dignity and never presume to confront or blame the woman he sees as the perfect repository of his desires. As an ideal lover, he surely would "dar noght speke it out" (5190) if he felt that his lover's stubborn refusal to love should put him in a somewhat uneasy position. No words of blame, he solemnly assures us, will ever escape his lips. Having just presented himself as the protector of proper speaking, Amans next shows, however, exactly how far his linguistic integrity goes. Militantly insisting that he will not *speak* poorly of his lady, he meanwhile discloses that it seems perfectly suitable that he "wel thenken all about" (5189) the inevitable conclusion that his true love is at least somehow at fault for his distress. Amans's words comically lack accord with his cognitive deeds. Language here is merely the mask behind which his self-justification hides.

As he presses the matter further, his equivocal use of speech becomes even more humorously apparent. Proud that he will not cast aspersions on his lady, he firmly insists that "for to sai sche is unkinde, / That dar I nought" (5192–93). Though his repeated insistence that he does not dare cross his lady perhaps makes us wonder if he does not fear the woman herself more than any violation of courtly conduct, his refusal to call her unkind is, at least on the surface, a noble one. On the very suspicious other hand though, he also will not allow himself to go so far as to "say that sche is kinde" (5196). In Amans's mouth, speech, as the recurring emphasis on *saying* suggests, has become an ambiguous ploy that allows one to direct attention away from one's vicious accusations while simultaneously making those charges abundantly clear to all.

The disreputable intent of the lover's sign-making allows him to career comically close to blasphemy during his last assurance that his *amor* is an ideal one. While Amans boasts that he will never speak against his lady, he is equally sure, as he tells his confessor, that "god above, / Which demeth every herte" (5199–200) is solidly "on myn oghne side" (5201). The Lord, he is sure, will have the last word; God will take care of his servant's verbal dirty work. Having carefully fortified his case with the supreme prejudice, he then escapes with his oral integrity sufficiently intact in his own mind: "dar I no more telle" (5204). In the process of not speaking poorly of his sweetheart, Amans has thus managed to find a plenitude of ways to cast a variety of articulate stones. Unmoored from its responsibility to point toward truth, the lover's language, like Genius's, carries only moral and spiritual befuddlement.

Amans's rhetorical strategy is, in fact, a finely ironic, comic reversal of the medieval understanding of allegory and of signification in general. When he makes a sound, something altogether different is usually meant, but I doubt Isidore of Seville would approve. On the other hand, when readers laugh at his confusion and the confusion of Gower's other characters, they are demonstrating their own ability to direct themselves toward the sacred truths that Genius and Amans can only comically misspeak. Whereas the priest and his charge violate the holy signs, Gower uses their violations to encourage his audience to recall the spiritual realities beyond the senses, the things to which speech can only point. It is no accident, then, that Chaucer calls on "moral Gower" to correct his words at the end of *Troilus,* since the Middle Ages assumed that moral behavior included the capacity to see the spiritual implications of language. The skill with which Gower both calls attention to and manipulates the literary implications of medieval sign theory is surely responsible for some of the respect he was accorded by his contemporaries. And, I suspect, the presently growing interest in both medieval and modern semiotics will do a great deal to restore that reputation.

Notes

1. Eugene Vance, "Mervelous Signals: Poetics, Sign Theory, and Politics in Chaucer's *Troilus,*" *New Literary History* 10 (1979): 293.

2. Jonathan Culler, *The Pursuit of Signs: Semiotics, Literature, Deconstruction* (Ithaca: Cornell University Press, 1981), pp. 21–22.

3. "Signum est enim res, praeter speciem quam ingerit sensibus, aliud aliquid es se faciens in cogitationem venire." *De doctrina Christiana* 2.i.5–7; *PL* 34, 35; *On Christian Doctrine,* trans. D. W. Roberston, Jr. (Indianapolis: Liberal Arts Press, 1958), p. 34.

4. For the place Augustine holds in the history of sign theory, see John Deely, *Introducing Semiotic: Its History and Doctrine* (Bloomington: Indiana University Press, 1976), pp. 13–46; Sten Ebbesen, "The Odyssey of Semantic from the Stoa to Buridan," in Achim Eschbach and Jurgen Trabant, *History of Semiotics* (Amsterdam: John Benjamins, 1983), pp. 67–86; Marcia Colish, *The Mirror of Language: A Study in the Medieval Theory of Knowledge* (Lincoln: University of Nebraska Press, 1983), pp. 7–54; and R. A. Markus, "St. Augustine on Signs," *Phronesis* 2 (1957): 60–83.

5. Markus, "St. Augustine on Signs," pp. 71–73.

6. See B. Darrell Jackson, "The Theory of Signs in St. Augustine's *De doctrina Christiana,*" *Revue des etudes augustiniennes* 15 (1969): 27.

7. *PL* 210, 579.

8. Colish, *The Mirror of Language,* pp. 27, 222.

9. Dante, *Convivio* iv.ii.8.

10. See Joan Ferrante, "The Relation of Speech to Sin in the *Inferno,*" *Dante Studies* 87 (1969): 33–46. For the topos in medieval literature as a whole, see John Alford, "The Grammatical Metaphor: A Survey of Its Use in the Middle Ages," *Speculum* 57 (1982): 728–60, esp. 744–45.

11. See Markus, "St. Augustine on Signs," p. 81.

12. See Donald E. Daniels, "The Argument of the *De Trinitate* and Augustine's Theory of Signs," *Augustinian Studies* 8 (1977): 57 and Colish, *The Mirror of Language,* p. 125.

13. Colish, *The Mirror of Language,* p. ix.

14. "Hactenus verba valuerunt, quibus ut plurinam trihuam, admonent tantum ut quaeramus res, non exhibent ut noverimus." *De magistro* xi. 36: *PL* 32, 1215; *Augustine: Earlier Writings,* vol. iv, trans. John H. S. Burleigh (London: SCM Press, 1953),

p. 94. See also Edward G. Ballard, "An Augustinian Doctrine of Signs," *New Scholasticism* 23 (1949): 207–211, especially 209.

15. "Si scimus, commemorari potius quam discere." Augustine, *De magistro*, XI. 36. See also Etienne Gilson, *The Christian Philosophy of St. Augustine*, trans. L. E. M. Lynch (New York: Random House, 1960), pp. 68–69.

16. Philotheus Boehner, "Ockham's Theory of Signification," in *Collected Articles on Ockham* (St. Bonaventure, New York: The Franciscan Institute, 1958), p. 209.

17. "Allegoria est alieniloquium. Aliud enim sonat, et aliud intelligitur." Isidore of Seville, *Etymologiarum sive originum*, ed. W. M. Lindsay (Oxford: Oxford University Press, 1911), I, xxxvii, 22.

18. Michael Riffaterre, *Semiotics of Poetry* (Bloomington: Indiana University Press, 1978), p. 23.

19. Culler, *Pursuit of Signs*, p. 83.

20. Ibid.

21. Jonathan Culler, *On Deconstruction: Theory and Criticism after Structuralism* (Ithaca: Cornell University Press, 1982), p. 37.

22. For such a view of the role of the audience in medieval literature, see, for instance, Edmund Reiss, "Chaucer and his Audience," *Chaucer Review* 14 (1980): 390–402 and "Medieval Irony," *Journal of the History of Ideas* 42 (1981): 209–26.

23. Riffaterre, *Semiotics of Poetry*, p. 12.

24. David W. Hiscoe, "The Ovidian Comic Strategy of Gower's *Confessio Amantis*," *Philological Quarterly* 64 (1985): 367–85.

25. See John H. Fisher, *John Gower: Moral Philosopher and Friend of Chaucer* (New York: New York University Press, 1964), p. 160; J. A. W. Bennett, "Gower's 'Honest Love,'" in *Patterns of Love and Courtesy: Essays in Memory of C. S. Lewis*, ed. John Lawlor (London: Oxford University Press, 1966), p. 112; and Kurt Olsson, "Natural Law and John Gower's *Confessio Amantis*," *Medievalia et Humanistica*: 11 (1982): 229–62.

26. *The Works of John Gower*, vol. II, ed. G. C. Macaulay (Oxford: Oxford University Press, 1901), p. 502.

27. *The Panchatantra*, ed. and trans. A. W. Ryder (Chicago: University of Chicago Press, 1956), pp. 112–19.

28. See Alexander Honeyman, "The Mission of Burzoe in the Arabic *Kalilah and Dimnah*." Ph.D. diss., University of Chicago, 1936, p. 12.

29. Dorothee Metlitzki, *The Matter of Araby in Medieval England* (New Haven: Yale University Press, 1977), p. 10.

30. See Metlitzki, *The Matter of Araby*, p. 97; and Robert Pratt and Karl Young, "The Literary Framework of *The Canterbury Tales*," in *Sources and Analogues of The Canterbury Tales*, ed. W. F. Bryan and Germaine Dempster (Chicago: University of Chicago Press, 1941), p. 7.

31. *Gesta Romanorum*, ed. Hermann Oesterley (1872; reprint, Hildesheim: Georg Olms, 1963), p. 327.

32. *Speculum Stultorum*, ed. and trans. J. H. Mozley (1961; reprint, Notre Dame, Ind.: University of Notre Dame Press, 1963), pp. xvi, 1. All line numbers refer to this edition.

33. See, for instance, *The Consolation of Philosophy*, II, prosa 2, 22–23.

34. The *MED* cites a common figurative meaning of "hole" as "a grave" and "the pit of hell." See Isidore of Seville, *Etymologiarum* XIV, ix; and the "wicket well" which the *moralitas* of Henryson's "Fox and the Wolf" explains is the way to the "pane of

hell" (*The Poems and Fables of Robert Henryson,* ed. H. Harvey Wood [Edinburgh: Oliver and Boyd, 1933], p. 84). See also Jung's discussion of caves and pits in *The Archetypes and the Collective Unconscious,* trans. R. F C. Hall (New York: Pantheon, 1959), pp. 135–47; and Russell Peck, *Kingship and Common Profit in John Gower's Confessio Amantis* (Carbondale: Southern Illinois University Press, 1978), p. 118.

35. See Esther Casier Quinn, *The Quest of Seth for the Oil of Life* (Chicago: University of Chicago Press, 1962), pp. 8–67; and esp. 102–31.

36. Peck, *Kingship and Common Profit,* p. 117.

37. See H. W. Janson, *Apes and Ape Lore in the Middle Ages and the Renaissance* (London: University of London Press, 1952), p. 166, especially his chapter "The Ape and the Fall of Man," pp. 107–44.

38. Peck, *Kingship and Common Profit,* p. 118.

39. The connection between "kindness" and Christ's sacrifice on the cross as well as that between "unkindness" and the men and women who reject or ignore the results of the Passion is ubiquitous in late medieval literature and theology. See, for instance, the Virgin's meditation in "Ihesu, þi swetness" (*The Minor Poems of the Vernon Manuscript,* ed. Carl Horstmann, EETS, e.s. 98:

> þat bi-foren my burþe to me tok hede,
> And siþen wiþ Baptym wesche þat kynde
> þat suyled was þorwh Adam dede;
> Wiþ noble mete he norsched my kynde,
> ffor wiþ his flesch he dude me fede.
>
> (25–30)

Wyclif reminds his charges, "þy kynd lord, specialy for his kyndeness . . . made vs first of nouȝt and siþen bouȝt vs fro þe fendes prisoun. . . . þe gretness of þis lord and of his kyndenesse shuld meue us to sorow for oure synnes" ("On Confession," in *The English Works of Wycliff,* ed. F D. Matthew, EETS, o.s. 74, p. 338). The narrator of the Harley lyric "God, þat al þis myhtes may" (*The Harley Lyrics,* ed. G. L. Brook [Manchester: Manchester University Press, 1948], p. 68) resolves to the Redeemer of Nature to "do by wille":

> In herte ne myghte y neuer bowe,
> ne to my kunde Louerd drawe;
> my meste vs ys loues trowe,
> Crist ne stod me neuer hawe.

Though Christ is never unkind, the narrator of Chaucer's "ABC" confesses to being, like most of humankind, "fals and eek unkynde" (166) to his Savior. The coupling of "kindness" and Christ is such a common one that the poet of the Easter poem from Digby 102 can use it as the organizing device for the entire work ("Wiþ god of loue ond pes, ȝe trete,") in *Twenty-Six Political and Other Poems,* ed. J. Kail, EETS, o.s. 124.

12

LANGUAGE AND WOMEN
From Silence to Speech

EDITH JOYCE BENKOV

To trust what a woman says is folly, or so the majority of medieval French writers would seem to have us believe. In their eyes, women's facile manipulation of language and their skillful ways of blending truth and lies appear as constant sources of worry and even danger in both romance and fabliau alike. Indeed, so genuine is the fear of the creative power of language as a weapon in women's arsenal in regard to the battle of the sexes, that much of medieval literature seems to have as its subtext that women's speech must either be carefully controlled or in some cases violently suppressed. In short, female discourse, like female sexuality, could be a genuine threat to established order (whether of husband or king) and was often as closely guarded in the male-dominated world of medieval French fiction. Yet, as any reader of Jean de Meun is aware, overseers are seldom successful, often themselves falling victim to the carefully manipulated word. Spread throughout the literature of the period, failures at such "close keeping" are, by turns, comic and serious, and at times even tragic. Cutting across lines of genre and class, such failures, as we shall see, tell us a great deal about medieval society: the relations between genders, the role of women, and especially the deep-seated medieval belief in the affective power of the word and its ability to shape not only one's perceptions but the everyday reality of the world in which one lives. And in the last lies the danger as well as the comic possibilities so well exploited by medieval writers.

Moderation, Propriety, and Silence: The Female Ideal in Language

An enterprise such as the education of women in their socially accepted forms of speech must be undertaken at an early age, presumably by those in charge of a young woman's upbringing. What a girl may or may not say in polite company might well have occupied the thoughts of a governess, a parent (more likely a mother than a father), or a simple servant in whose hands a female child was left. Perhaps such tutors would seek out authorities, lay or ecclesiastic, for guidance in this project. Indeed, proscriptions and prescriptions designed to instill virtues and dictate acceptable comportment in a lady form the stuff of books of manners, and for sources of moral judgment, one could also refer to the Church Fathers.

Not surprisingly, ecclesiastic writers such as Tertullian, St. Ambrose, or St. Augustine are most likely to be concerned with the more spiritual aspects of female behavior and development and with questions of virginity and marriage. Pauline precepts send a woman home from church to learn from her husband (I Cor. 14:35) but do not consider the instruction of the young girl. References to language among these writers are rare, perhaps because churchmen have simply interpreted Saint Paul's admonition—that "women keep silence in church" (I Cor. 14:34)—as a more general rule that silence should be the natural state for women. Saint Jerome, however, does make a point of the dangers of some women's speech when he warns that mothers should protect their daughters from the nefarious influence of woman-servants' chatter: "tibi est proviendum ne ineptis blanditiis feminarum dimidiata dicere verba filia conuescat."[1] He relies upon mothers to guide their daughters and to ground them in the traditional Christian virtues. We should note, though, that implicit in his advice is a distinction of class rather than gender: female servants can say nothing of value; rather, their words will have a corrupting influence.

Medieval didactic treatises and courtesy literature address the question of a woman's proper practice of the art of discourse with far greater frequency than the writings of the Fathers and, in the main, stress two points: a) the less a woman talks, the better she will be viewed and b) that when a woman does speak, her choice of vocabulary and topic are equally important. Garin lo Brun in his *Ensenhamens* sums up this ideal succinctly: "Que mais val uns taisars / Assaz c'uns fols parlars" (341–42), i.e., that silence is preferable to the foolish prattle of a female.[2] The Provençal writer is not unique in his counsel.[3] Similar opinions are held by Robert de Blois who, in his *Chastoiement des Dames,* comments that women should not swear (a level of language considered improper for them), that they should speak little at the table as well as in church, and that they should not lie. In some situations, however, silence is the wrong tack. When a declaration of love is made to a woman, she must be able to reply using the conventions of the language of love, a discourse undoubtedly considered within her realm.[4]

The pervasiveness of such attitudes is equally apparent in the advice Saint Louis gives to one of his daughters: she should speak little yet wisely, and should know how to reply properly. These precepts are especially important when speaking to a man, for it is in that situation that the girl will be judged: "Fille, se vous voulez parler a homme, mettez garde que ne dictes chose ou l'on puisse mal penser; mais dictes parolles qui touchent a bon ediffiement, par quoy on puist jugier que vous estes fille saige et bien advisee" ("Daughter, if you want to speak to a man, make sure that you do not say anything that might seem improper; but speak words that are edifying, by which one can judge that you are a wise young lady and well instructed").[5] Moderation and propriety, or even Pauline silence: these are the ideals for women's speech.

Women as Verbal Victims: Fabliaux and the Power of a Name

While courtesy and proper speech in general terms are requisite for young girls of a certain social standing, in no area does the subject of decorous language become more immediate than in the realm of intimate relations. According to didactic treatises, coarse language is considered generally unfit both for a girl's mouth and ears—the subject of sex, and particularly the mechanics of the act, being particularly taboo. Such delicacy of vocabulary and subject matter in the language of courtly ladies was, however, fair game for ridicule in the fabliaux, with their traditional deflation of courtly values and customs, and, indeed, many an author in this genre shows himself as keen at burlesquing noble speech as noble action.

Consider the mother-daughter of *L'Escuiruel,* a fabliau in which such doctrines of language come directly into play. In that tale, a rich woman has a fifteen-year-old daughter to whom she gives precise instructions as to the bounds of acceptable verbal conduct:

> . . . Ne soiez mie
> Ne trop parlant ni trop nonciere,
> Ne de parler trop coustumiere,

> Car a mal puet l'en atorner
> Fame quant l'en lot trop parler
> Autrement que ele ne doit.
> Por ce chascune se devoit
> Garder de parler folement.
>
> (18–25)

("Be neither too talkative nor too foolish, nor too ready to speak, for a woman will be ill-spoken of if she is heard speaking more often than she ought. For this reason, each woman should refrain from speaking foolishly.")[6]

She distills all that the rhetoricians have decreed into a single precept—for the emphasis of this admonishment is on quantity, not quality. What words a woman may pronounce would seem of little import; the message will be distorted by the aspect of "trop." Less is better if one is to avoid falling into the trap of "fols parlars," that foolish prattle against which Garin lo Brun warns. Here, moderation is the key, and a well-spoken woman appears to be one who speaks little. This type of behaviour is simply part of her duty. The world of the fabliaux, however, would not be without its unexpected turn, as the mother goes on to add one more cautionary note in regard to vocabulary:

> Et une chose vous desfant
> Sor toutes autres mout tres bien,
> Que ja ne nommez cele rien
> Que cil homme portent pendant.
>
> (26–29)

("And one thing above all I forbid you: never name that thing that men carry hanging.")

The name of "cele rien" is one lexeme that should not be an active part of a woman's vocabulary. Forbidden fruit, however, often appears more sweet than it is, and once her curiosity is piqued, the daughter badgers her mother into revealing the word which when pronounced becomes imbued with an incantory power, as the daughter recites a litany that could well be called "le nom du vit." The name, however, is separated from its referent, and although its meaning is perfectly clear, the daughter does not necessarily possess sufficient knowledge to make the correct association between word and object.

A mother's fears for the propriety of her daughter's vocabulary do not, then, guarantee that chastity will be preserved. Indeed, in this tale we find that knowledge of the correct sexual term becomes a barrier to comprehension when we move from the realm of veridiction to that of deceit. A common motif in the fabliaux is the renaming of sexual organs, a ploy generally used by a young man to seduce a girl less sexually and, in this case, linguistically experienced than himself. In this regard the valet of *L'Escuiruel* is no exception to the rule. On the contrary, he proves himself a master exploiter of semantic opacity. Since he has overheard the mother's revelation of the name "vit" (a circumstance which has quite excited him), he plays upon the girl's newly acquired knowledge to take advantage of her sexually. His metaphor for intercourse is that of a squirrel with eggs in its nest who wants the nuts which can be found in the girl's belly. Substitution of one term for another effectively undermines the premise of the mother's concerns, that improper words can lead to improper acts and that the banishing of words describing danger can banish the danger itself. Interestingly enough, no substitute term is supplied for "con," defined as the entrance to the belly. The girl seems to be totally ignorant of sexual practices, and though she is familiar with the term "con," she does not appear to associate it with a sexual function. The squirrel begins to forage for nuts, but as the search intensifies, he is overcome and throws up, or so says the narrator who, falling into his own trap, metaphorically equates vomiting with sexual climax. The girl believes one of the squirrel's nest eggs has broken and admonishes the valet for his lack of care.

Throughout, the narrator has let it be known that the girl has not found this experience distasteful and from that circumstance draws a moral:

> Que tels cuide bien chastier
> Sa fille de dire folie,
> Et quant plus onques le chastie
> Tant le met l'en plus en la vie
> De mal fere.
>
> (202–6)

("That it's well thought of to punish one's daughter for saying foolish things, and when one no longer punishes her, one puts her on the road to doing bad things.")

Better to reprimand a girl for her language; ignorance is the road to perdition. The moral can, nonetheless, be read as being at odds with the tale, for the girl has a privileged role. She knows what she should not, yet her knowledge in no way precipitated her fall. This knowledge is limited to the word, not the act that it represents, and signs become easily interchangeable when deceit is the goal. Thus one finds that for the purpose of deceit, a simple substitution of terms can bring about the desired result. Whether the girl is so naive as to not know that she has engaged in a sexual act is secondary. A system of signs has been created which is unique to that couple: "escuiruel" does not generally mean "vit." While she might recount a bizarre incident to others, no immediate understanding is available to those outside the very narrow linguistic community where such idiosyncratic terms are used in this fashion. The act would be couched in a double entendre that cannot be decoded by those not privy to the rules of their private linguistic game. Although her virtue is no longer intact, her honor (how she is spoken of) remains safe.

The central topos around which this tale revolves is the equation of the foraging animal and the sexual organs, a linguistic association which allows such confusions as are generally at the heart of fabliaux. This animal-nourishment topos is repeated in a number of fabliaux which are all variants on the same theme: *La Dame qui aveine demandoit por Morel Porcelet, La Pucelle qui abevra le polain,* and *La Damoiselle qui n'ot parler de fotre* I *and* II. *Porcelet* and *Morel* both present young, married couples with varying attitudes towards sexual language. In one, the wife suggests that they give names to his "rien" and to her "con." Perhaps she has been instructed by her mother not to say the name of "cele rien"! Her "porcelet" (piglet) will have a source of "fromant" (wheat) when it is hungry and thus will her (sexual) appetite be satisfied—although her "porcelet" is true to its name. Indeed, it is quite a little pig and demands no small quantity of wheat, nearly killing the husband in his effort to be a provider. In *Morel,* the husband suggests that when his wife wants intercourse, she requests: "Biaux freres doux, faites Moriax ait de l'avoine" ("Sweet, fair brother, let Morel have some oats"). Her first reaction, one of anger, reflects again the difference in upbringing:

> . . . tu ies tous sos
> Qui veus que die tel outrage
> N'afiert à fame qui soit sage.
> (102–4)

("You're quite dumb; you who want me to say such an outrageous
thing have no business with a wise woman.")

A woman such as she is wise and knows what she can and cannot say.
"Sage" appears once again, recalling both Saint Louis's urging to
speak wisely, and in opposition to "fols parlars." "Sage/folle" become
a contrastive pair, not only for language but also for conduct.[7] Her
resolve breaks down as her husband will withhold his sexual favors
unless she asks, thus enabling "folle" to win out over "sage." Once
given free rein, Morel, that dark horse, reveals an insatiable appetite
that the poor husband nearly dies in the effort to satisfy. In both of
these tales, the women assume the role of a gaping mouth which
must be fed; they embody the hungry animal, while the men are the
providers, the source of food. The image makes of them types of the
Hell Mouth and places them far from the domain of the virgins they
once were.

The situation undergoes a reversal in the remaining three tales
within the group. Each presents a young girl whose sensibilities are so
refined that the very mention of the word "foutre" or other such
"lecherie" causes a violent physical reaction: fainting (*Damoiselle II)*
and nausea *(Damoiselle I* and *Pucelle).* In each, a young man will
mimic her sensibilities in order to get into her bed: two do so before
marriage, one after. And from there, this version of medieval "pré-
ciosité" begins. Substitute terms continue to refine/redefine sexual
language. In these stories, the male is characterized as a thirsty
animal, again a horse, which will drink at the woman's fountain if he
can circumvent the guards. Not unlike the "Amant" who must brave
"Danger" and company and avoid the temptation of the fountain of
Narcissus, our stallion finds his reward in a fountain that is definitely
to his liking. Here, it is the woman who is the provider. However,
whether the female is portrayed as animal in need of food, or supplier
of water, the animal/nourishment pair is maintained, and the substitution of eating for intercourse leads to the same result. Intercourse
does take place and is enjoyed by both partners.

While this type of sexual game playing is, as we have seen, not
uncommon among young couples, it is used here to mock that
element of "women's language" which strives to eliminate coarseness
and use only refined terminology. The apparent irony of this situation
is that these female characters are objects of ridicule because they
follow too well the verbal proscriptions of society: they wish to
banish those words that they themselves are forbidden. As the narrator of *La Pucelle* tells us:

Que femes n'aient point d'orgeuil
De foutre paller hautement,
Quant il foutent tot igalement.
Mieldres raison est que se haucent:
Teus en parolent qui l'essaucent,
Quar molt a entre faire et dire.

(224–29)

(Let women not be too proud to speak aloud of fucking when they fuck in any case. Better they should raise themselves up; speaking of it glorifies it, for there's a lot between doing and saying.)

That they do not wish to banish sexual intercourse as well seems a contradiction to some narrators but perhaps not to the characters whose stories they relate. The moralistic conclusion to this fabliau points to the basic dichotomy between actions and words as the contrast between "faire" and "dire" underscores the facility with which one thing can be said, yet another meant.[8]

In a related but slightly different fabliau, *La Grue,* we see a young girl whose education also brings about her downfall. A chatelain keeps his daughter locked in a tower with only her nurse, a woman responsible for whatever knowledge the girl has of the outside world. The nurse, we are told, "mout l'avoit bien endotrinee" ("very much had indoctrinated her" [25]). The consequences of such schooling are seen when, left unguarded for a brief time, the girl happens to look out a window and see a young man with a crane. In what can be read as a rather muddled version of Leda and the swan, the girl finds the bird so fascinating that she asks to buy it. The valet will be a willing seller if he gets his price: ".i. foutre." The term is unknown to the girl; indeed, she claims to have none but will let the valet search her chamber. Need we add that the girl does pay the price asked, but the valet, in a most ungentlemanly way, walks off with the crane. The valet does not attempt to conceal what he wants from the girl; his language is straightforward, but the vocabulary is not part of that taught to the girl by her nurse. The girl is a victim of her own ignorance, an ignorance which has been imposed upon her by society, especially if we are to conclude by extension that, like the girl in *L'Escuiruel,* her sexual education has also been completely lacking.

Another girl gets into trouble because of a bird, albeit in a slightly different fashion. Renowned for her beauty and courted by all, this young woman is not interested in marriage. *La Pucelle qui voulait voler* would emulate Daedalus. A clerk, who pretends to be skilled at outfitting fliers, finds a way to cater to her ambition and, at the same time, upbraid her for it. She needs a beak, wings, a tail like a bird—how else could she expect to fly? Up in her bedroom she receives the first treatment. Since the process is not found to be unpleasant, she authorizes the clerk to repeat it until she can fly. The result of the clerk's labor is not what she wanted. Instead of being light as a bird, she becomes heavy with child and laments her fate as she berates the clerk's duplicity. He counters by saying:

> Vos m'alez a grant tort blamant . . .
> Se grosse estes, ce est nature
> Mais ce estoit contre nature
> Que par l'air voliez voler.
> (90, 93–95)

("You blame me unfairly . . . If you're pregnant, it's only natural, but what was unnatural was your wish to fly through the air.")

The girl's desire to fly was unnatural, whereas childbearing is not. She ends up like Icarus whose foolish ambition caused his downfall. But, unlike Icarus, she never even gets off the ground. Naive, prudish, or ambitious girls have much to learn when it comes to dealing with sexual linguistics, and it seems that this education is not generally forthcoming from those responsible, their mothers or nurses.

From Victim to Victimizer: Women as Verbal Manipulators

What we have seen so far are a series of initiatory sexual encounters in which young girls are, for the most part, at a distinct disadvantage. The advice that they receive from their mothers or others charged with their upbringing and education often serves to create many a foolish virgin, for the level of development of their skills in language is severely circumscribed. Language is imposed upon them; they are given an inadequate stock from which to draw. A fast-talking man of the world can easily dupe a young girl sequestered from both world and word. The pitfalls of sexual double entendres are many, and many are caught in them. When faced with unfamiliar language and/

or actions, they cannot distinguish deceit from truth. They try to follow as best as possible what they have been taught to accept as proper, in words as well as in conduct. Often, however, when their conduct is compared to this ideal, there is a significant gap between actions and words. If we attempt to read through the mockery of those young girls, we realize that much of what is reflected is the double standard of conduct which existed for women and men in society, applied to male and female characters. Those fabliaux that make light of what women will and will not say point to a distinction between men's language and women's language, and remind us that it is men who dictate what women's language ought to be.

Can the disadvantages with which these girls enter the world be overcome? Given this lamentable track record, one might well begin to wonder what it is that was so threatening in women's use of language that necessitated such control. The fact is that credulous husbands are as wont to fall victim to the verbal wiles of not-so-naive wives as were these young girls to their would-be lovers.

La Sorisete des estopes provides an excellent example of the more experienced woman using the game of renaming genitalia in a topsy-turvy yet highly succesful fashion. So that she might spend time with her lover, a newlywed takes advantage of her husband's inexperience and sends him to her mother's cottage to pick up the "con" she has stored there—having saved herself, as it were, for her husband. Her mother plays along, showing a certain complicity,[9] and hands the husband a pail of wadding material in which there is a mouse. The husband assumes the furry creature to be the "con," and on his way home, overcome by lust, he attacks. The mouse runs off, leaving the husband to return home disconsolate. His wife, upon hearing the story, takes pity on him and explains that the "con" has returned home on its own. In this instance, the tables are turned, and the wife can deceive her husband because of his ignorance. He knows the word "con" and even has some idea (albeit a confused one) of what it represents, but lacking sufficient experience, he cannot tell a *"con"* from a mouse in a basket, much as the girl we spoke of earlier could not distinguish a "vit" from a squirrel.

La Sorisete depicts the wife in terms more common for the fabliaux, that of a sly and deceitful character. Facilitating rendezvous with their lovers is an art at which the women of the fabliaux excel, and the author of this tale takes care to warn his readers:

> . . . fame set plus que deiable
> Et certeinement lo sachiez . . .

Qant el viaut ome decevoir,
Plus l'an decoit et plus l'afole
Tot solement par sa parole
Que om ne feroit par angin.
                (236–37, 240–43)

(Woman knows more than the devil, and that you're sure to know.
When she wants to deceive a man, the more she deceives him, the
crazier she makes him. She makes him crazier just by her words alone
than a man could by his own schemes.)

Women, he fears, know far too much. In fact, Eve has outdone her
tutor since, if we consider the *Jeu d'Adam,* she succeeds where the
devil has failed; it is Eve, not the Devil, who corrupts Adam. What is
worse is that if she takes it into her mind to deceive or confuse a man,
she can accomplish more by words that a man could do by all his
wiles. The "fols parlars" so undesirable in a woman's speech may
indeed be that very element which makes her so formidable an
enemy: her speech can "afole"—that is, make others act in a foolish or
senseless manner. While this identification of women's capabilities to
deceive through words would seem to run against those examples we
have just seen, that conclusion would be premature.

The young wife of *La Sorisete* shows us that she is just as capable of
verbal manoeuvers as any of the valets or clerks. The young girl,
however, must learn through experience, and this learning must also
entail an unlearning of what came before. She must also learn to
manipulate the language that has been imposed upon her, to turn it
against its creators if she is to hold her own and not be unfairly
exploited. The sensibilities are different, for though she may often
take advantage of a husband, she can show kindness as well: the valet
took back his crane even though he had been paid his "foutre"; the
wife of *La Soriesete* will share her husband's bed even though he
nearly lost her "con." Perhaps it is her own experience which has
taught her temperance and clemency. What is certain is that once
women have learned the mechanisms of deceit they are as adept as any
at employing them. Should they choose to make language serve their
own ends, triumph is at hand. The salesman may be able to fool the
farmer's daughter, but he'll be hard pressed to fool anyone's wife.

In the Court as well as the Cottage:
Noblewomen and the Deceptive Sign

Country wives, however, are not the only ones capable of turning a phrase to their own benefit. That a noblewoman's words can be equally adept in the deception of husbands and the commanding of lovers is again evident if we consider another of Chrétien's works, *Lancelot*. Twice during the course of battle, Lancelot hears Guinièvre say that he should temper his attack (3805–12, 5016–22),[10] and he proceeds to do so, greatly imperiling his own life. Seemingly banal sentences encode her messages to Lancelot, so that her commands remain unknown to those who remain outside the lovers' linguistic circle. As with her less noble sister of the fabliaux, her reputation, if not her honor, remains intact since she may deal in terms which the rest of the world may not decode. For his part, however, "Lancelot a bien entendu" (5019): he hears and understands her message and does her bidding. Communication, however, depends greatly on the speaker's intentions, and more often than not, we encounter women who use their skills not to deliver a message directly but rather to befuddle, to deceive, or to communicate only what they wish to be understood, as in the case of Guinièvre. Women make use of various sorts of linguistic ruses, and of these talents the reader (male) is warned by the narrator of *Les Perdrix*:

> Femme est fete por decevoir
> Mençonge fet devenir voir,
> Et voir fet devenir mençonge.
> (151–53)

(Woman is made to deceive. She'll make lies become true and truth become lies.)

Nor is he alone in his alarm; his observation recalls the cry of alarm cited above by the narrator of *La Sorisete des Estopes*. Both quotations are particularly revealing of the caution with which a woman speaking must be approached. The *Perdrix* emphasizes women's ability to turn falsehood into truth and truth to falsehood—a technique that can be used with amazing success to cover up indiscretion.[11] In *La Sorisete*, we see that women as well as men are capable of dealing in metaphor, which by its nature is language that "speaks other" and is, hence, a form of lie. What the authors of these fabliaux tell us is that women by their words can change the truth, confuse, or deceive—a formidable verbal armory is at their disposal. While it is true that warnings of this sort apply most frequently to characters in the fabliaux, the manifestations of women's linguistic abilities are not limited to that genre.

These examples of women's manipulation of language, what one might call linguistic ruses, are numerous. Perhaps the most common occurrence is the use of ambiguous or deceptive language to cover up a sin, generally of a sexual nature. In this category, *Lancelot* again can serve. When blood is discovered in Guinièvre's bed and Kay is accused of treachery, Guinièvre is quick to come to his defense and flatly deny any relations between Kay and herself:

> Se Damedex me gart,
> ce sanc que an mes draps regart,
> onques ne l'i aporta Ques.
> (4779–81)

("May God protect me, this blood that you see on my sheets was not brought there by Sir Kay.")

This is, in fact, the truth; for she knows that Lancelot, not Kay, was in her bed. How the blood got there, however, is a mystery to her since neither she nor Lancelot noticed his bleeding fingers, and so she explains it away by claiming a nosebleed. A lie? Or simply a plausible explanation? Whatever Guinièvre intends by the nosebleed story, her opening statement clearly avoids the intent of the question by couching her response in terms ambiguous enough to be interpreted both truthfully and falsely. The crux of the issue—whether or not she has slept alone—is masked by her words. Kay then denies his guilt, and rightly so. Yet, when Lancelot arrives, Guinièvre hastens to explain the nature of the accusation made against her. Lancelot once more understands her message, one which is veiled by her words, and knows to swear (truthfully) that Kay was never in her bed. The deception is successful enough for Lancelot to do battle with Guinièvre's accusers with "right on his side."

What Guinièvre accomplishes by omission and invention, Iseut does through a half-truth and complete honesty. When asked by Arthur to swear that,

Tristran n'ot vers vos amor . . .
Fors cele que devoit porter
Envers son oncle et vers sa per.
(4193, 4195–96)[12]

("Tristan has towards you no love other than that which he should bear towards his uncle and his wife.")

Guinièvre boldly states,

Qu'entre mes cuises n'entra home,
Fors le ladre qui fist soi some,
Qui me porta outre les guez,
Et li rois Marc mes esposez.
(4205–8)

("No man has gone between my legs except this leper, who served as a beast of burden to carry me across the ford, and King Marc, my husband.")

The propriety and appropriateness of Tristan's love is the subject of Arthur's question, a question that Iseut does not answer. Rather, she responds to the unasked but implied question—her sexual relations with Tristan—and her response goes directly to what men have "been between her legs." In that regard she answers truthfully. The truth of her reply derives from the double entendre. Marc and the leper who carried her on his back across the river are the only two men who have been between her legs. The court understands Marc as a sexual partner and the leper in his capacity as beast of burden. The ambiguity of Iseut's statement is clear to those who know the truth; thus, Iseut will be misunderstood in a way that, as Michelle Freeman suggests, she had probably anticipated.[13] That the leper in question was Tristan in disguise is, on the other hand, a fact she neglects to mention.

Lancelot and *Tristan et Iseut* offer typical instances of deceit through half-truths. Each work finds the women in an extremely dangerous situation in which death, if they are proven guilty, is fairly certain. Yet both Iseut and Guinièvre are exonerated thanks to their manipulations of the gap between word and deed, signifier and sign. The varieties of deceit are many, and one does not need to be thrust into a life or death situation to put them to use. Marital infidelity, as we have seen, affords ample situations for lies in less serious circumstances. Again we can look to a fabliau for quick-witted women. Indeed, it would be safe to say that the epitome of all women in the fabliaux is the *Bourgeoise d'Orleans*. The story is one of adultery: a husband sets out to prove his wife's infidelity, but she catches on and plays along. She announces to her servants that in her bedroom she has entrapped the young man who had tried to make a pass at her and bids them to give him a sound beating, knowing, of course, that it is her husband in disguise. Her husband is the classic "cocu battu et content"—convinced by her subterfuge of her loyalty and love. The wife's deliberately false statement to the servants is construed as truth. Since their actions, culminating in the beating, occur at the wife's behest, the husband construes them as a sign of his wife's fidelity. The theme is stock fabliau; nonetheless, it underlines the fact that women can successfully make people—be they husbands, servants, or even lovers—believe what they wish.

The double entendre can also be used to facilitate infidelity. *Guillaume au faucon,* a "courtly" fabliau, turns upon a single pun. The eponymous hero has pressed his lady for her love, which she stoutly refuses. He will begin a hunger strike which eventually catches the lord's attention. For what reason, inquires the lord. The lady replies that Guillaume has asked for the lord's "faucon"—a gift which he hesitates to bestow. Yet, taking pity on the poor Guillaume in his plight, she urges her husband on:

> "Sire," dit el, "or li donnez,
> Puisque faire si le volez;
> Il nel' perdra mie par moi.
> Guillaume, foi que ge vous doi,
> Quant messire le vos ostroie,
> Molt grant vilenie feroie,
> Se vos par moi le perdiez . . . ."
> (602–8)

("Sire," she said, "now give it to him if that's what you wish to do; he won't lose it because of me. Guillaume, by the faith I owe you, when my sire gives it to you, I would act quite basely, if because of me you were to lose it . . .")

Her words are clear to Guillaume; like Lancelot and Tristan, he can catch her message. The husband understands only the most literal

level. Thus do her statements lend themselves to two radically different interpretations, making Guillaume a double winner: not only
will he get his lord's favorite bird, the falcon, but also the wife's favor
as she becomes the homophonic "fau[x] con." In a way not dissimilar
to that in the *Bourgeoise d'Orleans,* she makes her husband the instrument of his own cuckoldry. As she says, how could she refuse that
which her husband has offered?

An even more outrageous use of the double entendre appears in the
fabliau *La Sainresse.* There, the wife's effeminate-looking lover is able
to pass himself off as a woman who will ease the wife's aches and
pains through a bleeding. The two leave the room and have their
pleasure while the husband waits on. After the "sainresse" leaves, the
wife proceeds to give a detailed account of her supposed bleeding and
proceeds to describe graphically, though in veiled terms, the intercourse that has taken place:

> Et m'a plus de .C. cops ferue
> Tant que je sui toute molue . . .
> Tant que je fui toute guerie.
> (71–72, 89)

("And he gave me more than 100 blows—so much that I was quite
softened, so much that I was quite cured.")

All the while, her husband "n'est pas aperceu / de la borde qu'ele
conta" (100–1: "never caught on to the joke she told"). The tale is
purely for her own (and, of course, the hearer/reader's) amusement,
for her husband does not understand what he is being told. Thus, the
wife's language is opaque and at the same time transparent, with the
humor of the story coming not so much from the telling itself but
from the complicity that ultimately exists between the wife and her
absent but implied audience.

Deceit need not serve only the sin of adultery. The wife of *Les
Perdrix* must hide the fact that during her husband's absence she has
eaten the two partridges that were to serve as dinner for him and the
local priest. At first she stalls, finally telling him to sharpen his
carving knife for the priest is coming. She greets the priest somewhat
wildly to warn him of her husband's rage and plan to castrate him.
The husband returns, knife in hand, to see the priest fleeing madly,
running off with the partridges, or so says his wife. As the husband

leaves to chase the priest, the wife can breathe a sign of relief for the gluttony is never known. She fabricates the entire story, and once her plot is in motion, it is she who is in control. Like an able playwright, she sets the scenes, directs the actions, and exploits the ambiguity of the husband with knife as well as the fleeing priest. In each case the victim believes the wife's lies because of stereotyped images: a jealous castrating husband chasing a gluttonous, lecherous priest. While what she actually says does not correspond to the truth, it does correspond to a possible interpretation of what is seen, and thus the deceit is successful.

Another way that women make language work for themselves is through the willful distortion of its meaning or deliberate misunderstanding. The former again appears in a situation of sexual infraction. The priest in *L'Evesque qui beneï lo con* is found to have a mistress. To punish this infraction of clerical standards of conduct, his bishop forbids him to drink ("boire") wine. The mistress will not suggest that he disobey the order:

> Qui vin à boivre vos deffant;
> Biau sire, son commandemant
> Covient tenir, ja n'en bevroiz,
> Mais, par foi, vos lo humeroiz.
> (47–50)

("You should obey the command, fair sire, of he who forbids you to drink wine; you won't drink it, but, upon my faith, you'll sip it.")

Sipping ("humer"), however, is not forbidden, so sip they shall. When the bishop then forbids goose ("oie"), the mistress counters with gander ("jars"). And if her lover is not to sleep upon a mattress, she will make him "un lit . . . de cousins" (100: "a bed of pillows"). Thus, in each case, she has changed the category into a sub-category; the success of her ruse depends upon the preciseness of the language the bishop uses. While understanding full well what the bishop meant, she prefers to misunderstand and thereby circumvent his intent. She obeys the letter of the law, but not its spirit.

As easily as a bishop can be thwarted, so too can a knight who tries to abduct a shepherdess. Marion in Adam de la Halle's play *Robin et Marion* prefers her shepherd lover, Robin, to a passing knight who tries to seduce her. She will have none of him and puts him off by playing dumb. When, for example, he inquires if she has seen a heron ("hairon"), she speaks of of herrings ("heren") and Lent, thereby taking advantage of the minimal pair involved. After three such fruitless exchanges, the chevalier admits: "N'anic mais je ne fui si gabes" (46: "Never was I so mocked") and soon gives up.[14] Her answers to questions he asks are deliberately wrong—that is, she misunderstands him on purpose. Later, at their second encounter, the knight once again admits: "Vraiment, sui bien caitis / Quant je met le mien sens au tien!" (316: "Really I'm quite the victim if I mix my meanings and yours"). He seems to recognize that his "sens" or meaning is not the same as Marion's. Just as the fabliaux told us earlier, a woman can easily befuddle a man if she wants to. Marion is able to twist language in such a way that she avoids communication and at the same time is able to get her message across. We should note that while Robin fails to free Marion from the knight whose force is greater, Marion talks her way out of her abductor's grasp.

Misogyny and Violence:
The Suppression of Women's Language

This small sampling of successful linguistic ruses initiated by women does not, admittedly, put these female characters in a very favorable light. The portrait of woman as deceiver, as a true daughter of Eve, appears a commonplace. Of those few "good" women mentioned, only Marion puts the technique of purposeful confusion of her listener to positive use—that is, to foil her abductor. Leaving judgments of good and bad aside, we can discern certain pervasive attitudes relating to women and language reflected in a variety of texts, texts which cross the barriers of comic and serious, of lay and ecclesiastic, and of genre. That language, specifically speech, is associated with women is evident. But it is also equally evident that language as a property to be owned and controlled is placed by these authors under the stewardship of men.

Didactic literature of the period concerns itself with what women should say and how they should say it. These theoretical works all point to a suppression of "free speech" in women, for if allowed to develop unfettered, women's language will be detrimental to the social fabric. In regard to women, the free use of language is clearly equated with sexual mores that are equally freewheeling. Wives, those women with sexual experience, are clearly more likely to be verbal manipulators than inexperienced maidens. So it follows that the keeping of women is the keeping of language. Women's fecundity and the similarly dangerous creativity of the word must equally be kept under wraps. It becomes apparent when the first level of control fails (i.e., when women are able to overcome the limitations of their education), secondary measures in the form of physical controls come into play. More than once do we find violence directed against women in order to silence them. Often as not, women are chastised for speaking out of turn, speaking their minds, or simply speaking the truth.

Perhaps the most flagrant example of this type of aggression can be found in *La Dame escoille*. An upstart woman, failing to control her speech, affirms that she is wiser than her husband. In response, she is told that the source of her willfulness is her "testicles," and she is "castrated;" that is, to cure her of her "folse parlor," she is held down and her right and left hips are cut open, and bull's testicles (no doubt the source of her unfemininely aggressive verbal behavior) are drawn from the wounds. The woman faints from loss of blood during surgery, and it is little surprise that she is afterwards cowed into submission to her husband. Language and sexuality are inextricably linked. To appropriate language is to appropriate a creativity—testicles—that is, from the point of view of the author, appropriately male.

And yet, so completely are women associated with language that this type of violence is generally unsuccessful. On the contrary, more often the victim will find a way to overcome. In the version of *Philomene* attributed to Chrétien de Troyes, Tereus will cut out Philomene's tongue after he has raped her so that she might not reveal what has happened. Yet, she is able to communicate despite her handicap through woven writing in a tapestry she fashions.[15] Her message reaches its destination, and she is saved from further violation. Moreover, unlike Ovid's version of the tale, Chrétien follows Hyginus so that at the moment of metamorphosis, Philomena, not Procne, is turned into a nightingale.[16] Thus does Chrétien restore her voice.

Finally, the fabliau *Le Pre tondu* presents a semantic battle between husband and wife over the state of a field. He maintains it was mown; she, that it was clipped. When she refuses to accept her husband's assessment, he beats her senseless: "A la terre est cheue pamee . . . / La elle ne peut mot soner." (122–25: "She fell senseless to the

264   LAUGHING AT THE VOID

ground . . . There she can't say a word"). He has effectively prevented her from further speech. Yet, she reiterates her opinion
through sign language, forming her fingers into a scissors. At this
point, her husband concedes: "ja ne la vaintra / A deibles la com-
manda." (131–32: "Never will he defeat her. To the devil he sent
her"). His defeat is complete for, even when she is unable to speak,
she can find a way to convey her message. Her husband recognizes his
inability to counter, and it is her opinion which prevails. These
examples seem to point to a fundamental recognition of the potential
of women's speech, one which construes their linguistic abilities as
hostile and threatening.

The fabliaux—in comic, albeit often violent, mode—point to
many of these concerns. Those fabliaux that joke of what women will
and will not say point to a distinction between women's language and
men's language, while those in which a girl is duped because of
her naivete reflect the effect of the linguistic limits imposed upon her.
Yet, it is clear that women's skills in manipulating words can serve to
confound those they want to confound and still be comprehensible to
others, all of which reflects a deliberate and sophisticated use of
language almost surprising in its effectiveness. Use of verbal strategies by women easily transcends the boundaries of genre and class:
fabliaux and courtly tales will allow the same attributes—Iseut's "between my legs" is worthy of any fabliau wife, and queens lie as easily
as bourgeoises. The universality of the trait cannot be ignored, reflecting a fundamental belief that women are able manipulators of
language and that their skill can only be construed as threatening to
established order. Indeed, when compared to those young girls confounded by their own ignorance, the counter-examples of the more
sophisticated women who triumph through speech point to a simple
truth: lacking other arms to defend themselves, female characters
must depend upon their tongues to help them get by in the world.
And, that even lacking that organ of speech, they will persevere
against all odds to get their message across.

Notes

1. Cited in Alice Hentsch, *De la Littérature didactique du Moyen Age s'adressant
spécialement aux femmes"* (Cahors: A. Coueslant, 1903), p. 28.
   2. Ibid., pp. 45–48.

3. Nor is he unique among Provençal writers whose reverence for "la dompna" is more frequently recalled than is their particular brand of "gauloiserie." Take for example Peire de Bossinhac's judgment: "E saubran vos pagar / Tan gen ab lur mentir, / De lurs enjans / Nulhs om no's pot gandir" ("And they know how to pay you back so sweetly with their lies that no man can protect himself against their trickery"). For a discussion of this type of marginal troubadour poetry, see Pierre Bec's *Burlesque et obscenité chez les troubadours* (Paris: Stock, 1984).

4. Hentsch, *Littérature didactique,* pp. 75–80.

5. Translated and cited in Diane Bornstein, *The Lady in the Tower: Medieval Curtesy Literature for Women* (Hamden, CT: Archon Books, 1983), p. 6.

6. All translations are my own. All quotations are from: Anatole de Montaiglon and Gaston Raynaud, *Receuil général et complet des fabliaux des xii*e* et xiv*e* siècles,* 6 vols. (reprint, New York: Burt Franklin, 1966).

7. The pair itself is not without liturgical resonances, since the wise and foolish virgins were an often exploited trope.

8. "Faire" and "dire" are also contrasted in the mother's admonition in *L'Escuiruel,* though in a proscriptive way.

9. This same type of complicity between female characters is exhibited elsewhere in French texts, as for example, between Brangien and Iseut in *Tristan et Iseut* or Thessala and Fenice in *Cligès.*

10. All references and quotations are from Chrétien de Troyes, *Lancelot, or the Knight of the Cart,* ed. W. W. Kibler (New York and London: Garland Pubs., 1981).

11. The only truly unsuccessful such lie that comes to mind immediately is in the "Snow Child" tales.

12. All quotations are from Thomas, *Les Fragments du roman de Tristan,* ed. B. Wind (Genève: Droz, 1960).

13. Michelle A. Freeman, "Marie de France's Poetics of Silence: The Implications for a Feminine *Translatio,*" *PMLA* 99 (Oct. 1984): 868.

14. All quotations are from Adam de la Halle, *Le Jeu de Robin et Marion,* ed. F. Gennrich (Frankfurt a. M.: Langen, 1962).

15. See also Michelle A. Freeman, "Poetics of Silence," pp. 860–83.

16. See my article, "Hyginus's Influence on Chrétien's *Philomene,*" *Romance Philology* 36 3(1983): 403–6. Chrétien also treats the theme of silence and speech regained in a considerably less violent way in *Erec et Enide.* In a typically male move, Erec forbids Enide to speak to him unless he initiates the conversation; she thrice ignores this interdiction, each time saving his life and probably her own as well, compelling him to think better of his act and once again restore her speech. This tale is one of the few instances where the results of women speaking are positive, indeed lifesaving, and perhaps indicates on Chrétien's part a more liberal view of what restrictions should be placed on women's access to language.

PART VII

WORDS INTO DISCOURSE
The (Re)creation of Meaning

EDITORS' INTRODUCTION

In the previous chapter, Edith Joyce Benkov discussed language as a social behavior, the central issue being which group or individual would gain and maintain dominance over the other, the struggle for power being the struggle to control discourse, largely by controlling the naming process (as in the fabliaux) or by squelching speech (as in *Erec et Enide*). Language, as it is portrayed in such works, is the interaction of signs signifying shared values which, like those values, are constantly redefining themselves.

The final two essays in this collection consider language on the social level. Kathleen Ashley returns to one of the more common themes in this collection, the attempt to shape reality by changing names. As Ashley notes, the idea of a name change "introduces the somewhat subtler perception from moral psychology: the perception that while men may indeed want to sin, they prefer to do it under the guise of something innocuous or virtuous." In fact, what is surprising, at least in regard to this trope, is how much the verbal strategy of the popular sermon has in common with the seemingly antithetical fabliau. For both the would-be seducer of the maiden and the Devil renaming his daughters utilize the same means: false-seeming signs are used to beguile the innocent. (It is well to remember that this is an age in which Eric the Red might name a rather inhospitable stretch of land "Greenland" in hopes of keeping the far fairer "Iceland" for himself.) In the sermon *topos,* Ashley, however, discusses mutability of sign as an indication of corruption, not of creativity. In such changing of names one sees the "potential for corruption and manipulation inherent in the use of language in a fallen world." For the Lollards, in a more extreme case, the deceptive change of name "becomes an example of the perversions wrought by the Antichrist and his followers, the clerks and friars, who use 'fals fablis' rather than the plain gospel." Yet, despite differences in emphasis and in embodying the theme, the exploitation of linguistic instability remains constant, as do the forces that keep this instability in check.

Such dialectics lead Ashley to consider the discursive theories of

269

Bakhtin, who sees language as the site of dynamic struggle and contradiction, rather than of stability and fixedness—especially the vying for domination between devil and victim where the battlefields are the "open spaces" inherent in words. Sign, far from being fixed, is an active component of speech, constantly modifying and transforming—not even a relatively fixed knot in the skein but more like an amorphous node in a moving net of fabric constantly changing shape as it is pulled this way and that. This means that culture, the accumulation of signs, is an open-ended, creative dialogue resulting in both domination and synthesis of the competing subgroups of the speech community. If such "dialogue" seems to result in babelic chaos, the solution is to integrate the various voices into a new Hegelian synthesis. In this light, the privatization of language, whether in Erec's romance retreat or in the cloistering of fabliau maidens, is doubly antisocial and is bound to fail with each reintegration of the privatized speech community into the larger linguistic whole. Dialect is permitted as a subset of the mother tongue, but linguistic idiosyncracy, like the uncontrolled fecundity of sign, poses a definite social threat. For the romance knight, linguistic separatism necessitates the quest and the subsequent reintegration into society. For the less fortunate denizens of the fabliau, reintegration usually means the collapse of linguistic illusion.

While Ashley provides something of a Bakhtinian 'coda' to the issue of renaming, Peggy Knapp begins where Ashley leaves off by applying Bakhtinian ideas of discourse to the linguistic jockeying that comprises the storytelling contest among Chaucer's pilgrims. In particular, Knapp focuses her attention on the struggle to "fix discourse" between the Knight as representative of the dominating Boethian mode of thought and the subculture represented by the Miller. As Knapp notes, the *Canterbury Tales,* with its speakers from so many different social classes, is ample refutation of the concept of the Middle Ages as a monolithic, linguistically homogenous speech community. Instead, in the competing, often antithetical tales of the Canterbury pilgrims, we see a linguistic conflict that mirrors the social conditions of the period. What we repeatedly find is the clash between authority and subgroup, between prestige dialect and non-standard; we witness the battle between those whose language is authorized and those whose language is not. Thus, we end where we began, with Chaucer's Knight acting the part of the Heideggerian positivist and Robin the Miller taking up the "nominalist" banner of Derrida. Knapp presents us with a Knight whose Boethian code contains a fundamentally meaningful unity and with a Miller who sees only the mocking silence in the cracks. Finding a lack of substance in the Knight's signs, Robin changes the names and recasts the characters in his own "churl's terms," revealing the essential emptiness in which he believes. That this recasting is taken as wit arises from what David Hiscoe points to as the disparity between the ideal recalled and that idea presented in the new context, the new skein. Just as Genius's tale of Bardus is comic by virtue of the disparity between its origin and the purposes to which the tale is now put, so Robin's reworking of the now-recalled Knight's tale is comic. In the end, in this discourse Robin's tale takes its meaning from its relation to the set of signs proffered by the Knight he is quitting. And the *Knight's Tale* takes its new meaning from the absent present, whose absence becomes the presence or essence of its successor, and together they form the interplay, the discourse, with which they create themselves anew.

13

RENAMING THE SINS
A Homiletic Topos of Linguistic Instability in the Canterbury Tales

KATHLEEN M. ASHLEY

Chaucer's fondness in the *Canterbury Tales* for dramatizing homiletic rhetoric and tone is undeniable. Even his characters attest to it: "Ye been a noble prechour in this cas," the Pardoner tells the Wife of Bath after her *auctoritee*-laden monologue. Nevertheless, Siegfried Wenzel makes the point that "creating a handful of characters who sound like preachers because they moralize and quote Scripture is not the same as actually borrowing verbal material from contemporary sermons."[1] Wenzel does believe that a case can be made for some specific borrowings, and he provides examples of images, story plots, and proverbial sayings probably familiar to Chaucer through the medium of sermon literature. Indeed, Wenzel's discussion of technical terms like the sermon phrase "knytte up," repeated by both the Host and the Parson (Parson's Prologue, 27–28, 46–47), has especially important thematic implications for the final tale, for, as he says, "when the Parson agrees 'to knytte up al this feeste,' Chaucer not merely signals the end of his collection of tales, but also hints that somehow we are approaching the gist of his poetic enterprise."[2] I would like to suggest another important and equally specific Chaucerian borrowing from preaching materials—the motif of renaming the sins.

Renaming the seven deadly sins to make them seem more attractive to sinners was a widespread and popular *topos* during the medieval period. It took two basic forms: one, a narrative *exemplum* about the Devil's unmarriageable daughters, the other a non-narrative exposition about whitewashing sin by euphemistically renaming it. The first section of this essay traces both forms of the *topos* through several centuries and several genres, including sermons, satirical poems, treatises, and moral drama. Then the second section takes up Chaucer's use of the same topos in the *Canterbury Tales*.

A search for "sources" is usually assumed to lead to firmer conclusions about how to interpret a work of art. Here, however, the
suggestion that Chaucer is adapting the *topos* of renaming the sins will
only highlight further the ambiguities of his literary enterprise. Unlike Wenzel, who finds Chaucer's adoption of sermon materials
straightforward and unambiguous, I will argue for problematic differences between the *topos* in its homilectic uses and its uses in the
Canterbury Tales. These differences stem from Chaucer's narrative
techniques, many of which seem designed to destabilize our firm
identification of moral stance and literary mode. The process of
renaming the sins, with its exploitation of language's instability, is
central to the world of the *Canterbury Tales.*

Renaming the Sins: Tracing the Topos

The *topos* of renaming the sins is based on moral psychology. Such
theologians as Gregory the Great, Augustine, and Bernard of Clairvaux were acutely aware of the human tendency to self-delusion, for
which they adopted the metaphor of the Devil with his disguises.
Gregory in his *Moralia in Job* says:

> And there are some vices which present an appearance of rectitude, but
> which proceed from the weakness of sin. For the malice of our enemy
> cloaks itself with such art, as frequently to make faults appear as virtues
> before the eyes of the deluded mind. . . . For cruelty is frequently
> exercised with punishing sins, and it is counted justice; and immode-
> rate anger is believed to be the meritoriousness of righteous zeal. . . .
> Frequently, negligent remissness is regarded as gentleness and for-
> bearance. . . . Lavishness is sometimes believed to be compassion. . . .
> When a fault then appears like a virtue we must needs consider that the
> mind abandons its fault the more slowly, in proportion as it does not
> blush at what it is doing.[3]

By pretending that what it does is both reasonable and good, frail
human nature accepts evil.

The *Book of Vices and Virtues,* a fourteenth-century English translation of the thirteenth-century *Somme le Roi,* says that one of the gifts
of the Holy Ghost is to recognize the languages of the Devil and
know all his falseness. This work cites the spiritual psychology of

Bernard of Clairvaux, who says great skill is required to distinguish between the thoughts that the heart brings forth and those that the enemy sets when they both come as friends or as merchants who show him sins that are "so likynge and delitable."[4] This idea of vices masking as virtues is a type of temptation associated with the weakness of the flesh and the abuses of the reason, and it is a worldly sin which may account for its recurrent connection with satire.

The medieval roots of the *topos* of renaming the sins are clearly homiletic. We find its earliest versions in sermons or *materia predicabilis*. G. R. Owst tells us that the *topos* was popular in the twelfth and thirteenth centuries in the form of the marriages of the Devil's daughters. Those daughters (according to different versions they are 7, 8, or 9 in number) are named Pride, Simony, Hypocrisy, Rapine, Usury, Fraud, Bad Service, Sacrilege, and Luxury. Their father the Devil wishes to marry them off, and this is eventually accomplished.[5] Pride is married to the high clergy or to women, Simony to the clerics, Hypocrisy to monks and false religious, Rapine to the knights, Usury to the bourgeoisie, Fraud to the merchants, Sacrilege to the peasants, Bad Service to workers and servants, and Luxury to all classes of men. Thus, from the earliest evidence, the narrative of the Devil's daughters served estates satire.[6] Owst makes no distinction between this story, in which names are unchanged, and what I have called "the *topos* of renaming the sins." We should note, however, that in this story the World is only too happy to marry the Devil's daughters. No linguistic transmutations are necessary to persuade the estates to accept them; they welcome the sins with open arms. To Owst, the important element is the idea of a marriage; I will show, however, that we can still trace the *topos* even when the marriage is not present, because its basis is the action of renaming.

The story of the Devil's daughters changes when it is used for individual moral rather than estates satire, for the sins are now the seven deadly sins. John Bromyard, an English theologian who compiled a compendium of sermon materials as a preacher's tool about 1348, describes the daughters of the Devil who were married to many under pleasant names and with beautiful false new clothes.[7] Bromyard cites in full the passage from Gregory as an authority beyond the *exemplum* or popular saying *(dictum)*. Some of his examples of name-changing include social types like the tyrant, simoniac, or usurer, but others center on the sins: "Ita diabolus & eius ministri peccata sub pulchris abscondunt verbis: superbiam vocantes honestatem: vindictam correctionem: gulam satietatem, avariciam providentiam &

pietatem . . . Luxuriam naturalem complexionem. Malum lucrum prudentiam . . ."8 ("Thus the devil and his minions conceal sins beneath attractive words: calling pride nobility: revenge correction: gluttony satisfaction: avarice thrift and conscientiousness . . . luxury natural employment. Usury prudence . . ."). Bromyard's *Summa Predicantium* contains the fullest and most definitive account of the *topos* as it was understood in the fourteenth century.

In fifteenth-century sermon collections, the allegorical narrative is popular, especially addressed to individual rather than group morality. A sermon from Gloucester Cathedral library tells the story of the name changes of the seven daughters—the seven deadly sins—concluding: "Be well ware that ȝe marry not with the dowȝtter of the devyll!"9 One sermon in MS. e. Museo 180 in the Bodleian library is structured totally around the narrative of the seven daughters, whose "ivell names and fowle" were changed to "þe gayest names that he myȝte fynde" by their father:

> Be this man þat had vii dowȝters is understonde þe devill, and his vii
> dowȝters is understonde the vii dedly synnes, the whiche everi cristen
> creature scholde voyde, and exchewe the felischipe of hem. Consid
> eryng þe fende of þe fowlnes of his fowle dowȝters namys he hathe
> chaungid þe names of his dowȝters that were so odious, and now he
> hathe set on hem the goodliest namys þat he cowde fynde.10

The eldest daughter's name is Pride; the Devil "sett on hyr a gay name, and sche is called Honestye, so þat a prowde man or a prowde woman is called an honest man or honest woman." The second daughter is called Envy, "but now sche is called Iusticia, þat is Ryȝtwysnes." The sermon continues: "And therde dowȝter was calde Ira, Wrathe, but now sche is callyd Virilitas, þat is to sey manhode for he that is a fracer or a bracer, a grete bragger, a grete swerer or a gret fyȝtter, soche men ben calde manly men." The fourth daughter is Sloth, whose new name is "Impotencia," or "Unmyȝty." The fifth daughter is Luxuria or Lechery, but "for þe devyl wold have hyr maried well, he called hyr Luffe." The sixth daughter is Gluttony, "but þis name is turned nowdays into a feyre name and is cald Good Felischipe. For he þat is a riatowre and a revelowre and a grete hawnter of the taverne or the alehowse, and a grete waster of his gooddys, then is he callyd a good felow." The seventh daughter is Covetise, whose name is changed to "Alms Dede."11 This *exemplum* is directed both at the individual sinner and at the state of the world "nowadays" which, the preacher tells us, cares more about the pleasure of the body than about the salvation of the soul.

What then is the identity of this *topos?* Owst conflates the marriage of the devil's daughters with the idea of renaming the sins, as if they were identical. Yet, if the daughters are simply married openly, as named sins, to the estates, then the point of the *exemplum* is that the various estates of society embrace sin. Changing their names, however, introduces the somewhat subtler perception from moral psychology, the perception that while men may indeed want to sin, they prefer to do it under the guise of something innocuous or virtuous. The change of names, therefore, shifts the point of the satire to man's perennial tendency to delude himself, and to his characteristic mode of self-delusion: linguistic manipulation. It is significant that the rewriting of this allegory to include a linguistic shift takes place during the fourteenth century, the century in which language becomes the focus of intense philosophical discussion. Heightened philosophical awareness of the conventionality of language can become moral awareness of linguistic shiftiness, of the potential for corruption and manipulation inherent in the use of language in a fallen world. These fourteenth-century themes are also Chaucerian themes, as part II of this essay will suggest.

We have been examining the *topos* of renaming the sins in the narrative form which it took in many sermons. However, in Lollard sermons it is unattached to the *exemplum* of the Devil's daughters, for the use of "fables" was regarded by Lollards as one of the most reprehensible aspects of fraternal activity.[12] The Lollard preachers were unanimous in rejecting *exempla*—the humorous, racy, or otherwise vivid stories through which generations of preachers had conveyed their *moralitees.* When we encounter the motif of renaming the sins in Lollard sermons, therefore, it has been shorn of its narrative structure and reduced to its linguistic essentials.

A sermon in Ms. Bodl. 95 at the Bodleian Library briefly summarizes the alternate names for the sins:

> If he be a lechere they say hit is but ȝouþe hode and kyndely thynge.
> . . . If he be a proude man they sey hit is but honeste . . . If he synne
> yn glotony they clepe hit good felowschipp . . . If that he be
> wrathefull to ber hit longe in his hert and soon to take venyaunce they
> clepen hit lordelynes and seyen he were full semely to have lordshipp. If
> that they synne in slouthe they sey they ȝett begynne all in good

tyme to serve god . . . Envye is clepede but ryȝtwesness for to hate
thyne enmye . . . Covetise they clepen wysdome a man to helpe hym
selve.[13]

The preacher obviously knows that the theme can take a narrative
mode, since he concludes: "And thus mareth the devyll here his vii
douȝters by councell of antecrist, þat is the devel bawde." Unlike the
preacher in the earlier sermon (e. Mus. 180), this preacher only
alludes to the traditional narrative framework and makes the telling
comment that the Antichrist had counselled the Devil to this action—
a comment which substantiates the Lollard affiliations of this sermon,
for the Antichrist was a familiar character in Lollard invective, the
ultimate Lollard symbol for evil. The *Rosarium Theologiae,* a Lollard
sermon compendium, tells us that the Antichrist is a reasonable
creature pretending himself most holy, using deceiving, persuasive,
feigned miracles, gifts, or—if he is a preacher—telling errors, using
fables, dreams, and poesies to mislead his auditors.[14]

In another Lollard sermon, the preacher specifically condemns
those who tell stories rather than use Holy Scripture ("Summe pre-
chen fablis and summe veyne stories; summe docken hooli writt and
summe feynen lesyngis; and so loore of Goddis lawe is al putt abac.")
In this context of attack on ecclesiastical authority and the fraternal
orders, the *topos* of the renaming of sins becomes a weapon. According to the Lollards, the "glosing" of God's law by "contrarie wordis"
has transformed the Church into the body of the fiend and transformed the virtues into vices:

> As mekenesse to cowardise, and felnesse of pride is clepid riȝtwisnesse
> for to maintene Goddis riȝt, and wraþ is clepid manhed, and my-
> ldenesse is schepischeness, and envye is condicioun of Goddis child to
> venge him, and sleuþe is lordlynesse (as God restiþ everemore); covet-
> ise is prudence to be riche and myȝti, glotenye is largesse, and lecherie
> is myrie pley; Goddis servant is an ypocrite and an heretik is sad in
> feiþ; and þus alle vertues ben transposid to vicis, and so hooli chirche
> to synagoge of Sathanas.[15]

For the Lollard preachers, then, the *topos* of changing the names of the
sins becomes an example of the perversions wrought by Antichrist
and his followers, the clerks and friars who use "fals fablis" rather
than plain Gospel.[16] The satire is thus ecclesiastic, not personal, when

our *topos* is used by Wycliff in the fourteenth century and by his Lollard followers in the fifteenth.

Both in Lollard propaganda and in non-Lollard satires, the renaming *topos* is used to define a "world upside-down," the popular idea that all norms—linguistic, social, or moral—have been reversed.[17] Normally in these "complaints on the times" or poems on the "abuses of the age," evil reigns unchecked, and the virtues have been turned to vices.[18] In John Ball's letter, for example, we are told,

> now raygneth pride in price,
> covetise is holden wise
> lechery without shame,
> gluttony without blame,
> envye raygneth with reason
> and sloath is taken in great season,
> God doe boote for nowe is time.[19]

Satire on the degenerate state of England thus may or may not employ all the sins in their new guises; only one line in John Ball's letter really echoes the *topos* ("covetise is holden wise"), and even then the linguistic element of renaming has been deemphasized. Another satirical poem, however, cited in Robbins's *Historical Poems of the xivth and xvth Centuries,* does retain the theme of linguistic perversion, first for the virtues and then for the vices:

> vertues & good lyvinge is cleped ypocrisie;
> trowþe & godis law is clepud heresie;
> povert & lownes is clepud loselrie;
> trewe prechinge & penaunce is clepud folie."

In the envelope of virtues, which are now considered vices, is our familiar list of the seven deadly sins renamed by a corrupt world:

> pride is clepud honeste,
> and coveityse wisdom.
> richesse is clepud worþynes,
> and lecherie kyndely þing,
> robberie good wunnynge,
> & glotenye but murþe.
> envye and wraþþe men clepen riʒtfulnes;

slouþe men clepen nedfulnes
to norshe mennes kynde.[20]

The end of the poem returns to the abuses of the virtues.

The *topos* in truncated form may even be found in fifteenth-century Spain. The *Libro de la Consolacion de Espana,* which laments the decadence of the nation "nowadays," gives a picture of vice and decay which reminds the anonymous clerical author of the fate of Sodom and Gomorrah: "Agora en este tienpo tenemos e reputamos por vertudes a los vicios e pecados e los tales nonbres les ponemos, ca llamamos a la luxuria de la carne e al adulterio amores e bien querencias. . ."[21] In connection, then, with general satire on the corrupt state of a world "upsodoun," the *topos* of renaming the sins was drawn on either as a whole list or in part.

We have now traced the *topos* of renaming the sins through sermon *exempla* in the narrative form and through the non-narrative Lollard sermons, as well as through satirical poems on the abuses of the age and through prose complaints. In the fifteenth century, this theme also becomes popular in the morality play. We are most familiar with it, perhaps, not from a morality but from the N-Town cycle (which has such other characteristics of the morality as personifications of vices and of virtues). In N-Town's Passion Play I, the Devil reveals to the audience how he will seduce mankind by inverting all standards and norms: "Loke þou sett not be precept. nor be comawndement / Both sevyle and Canone. sett þou at nowth" (93–94). At first Satan describes the actions of a world socially upside-down:

A beggerys dowtere to make gret purvyauns
To cownterfete a jentyl woman. dysgeysyd as she can
And yf mony lakke, þis is þe newe chevysauns.

He then articulates the *topos* in its traditional form of linguistic and moral inversion:

I have browth ʒow newe namys, and wyl ʒe se why
Ffor synne is so plesaunt, to ech Mannys intent
ʒe xal kalle pride. oneste. and naterall kend lechory
And covetyse wysdam. there tresure is present.
Wreth manhod, and envye callyd chastement.

(109–13)[22]

The N-Town Satan's offer of "newe namys" balances John the Baptist's speech which immediately follows it at the beginning of Passion Play I. Where Satan sows confusion by renaming the sins, John counsels man to "reforme all wronge / in our concyens of þe mortall dedys sevyn" (5–6). In an interesting echo of Bromyard, the N-Town Satan's offer to "false þe wordys" (52) is accompanied by offers of new clothing to his followers (pointing to his own disguise as a gallant): "By-holde þe dyvercyte of my dysgysyd varyauns" (65). On stage, linguistic disguising is symbolized by costume changes and disguise, both in N-Town and throughout the morality drama.

The morality play *Wisdom,* written about the same time as N-Town (c. 1465), also features Lucifer. Disguised as a courtier, he seduces Mind, Will, and Understanding, transforming them into Pride, Avarice and Lechery (381–550).[23] As the three perverted faculties cavort in their "new aray," symbolic of their moral perversion, they invoke the *topos* of renaming the sins. Mynde reassures himself with the code phrase: "It ys but honest, no pryde, no nay" (555); Will echoes the code language: "I am so lykynge, me seme I fle. I have atastyde lust: farwell chastyte" (567–68); and Understanding is the most explicit in the use of the *topos:*

> The riche covetouse wo [who] dare blame,
> Off govell and symony thow he bere þe name?
> To be fals, man report yt game;
> Yt ys clepyde wysdom.
>
> (601–4)

When the three faculties of the soul are the spiritual protagonists, only three sins appear renamed; in *Wisdom* the other four do not have functions.

The *topos* is found in its straightforward and complete form as late as Henry Medwall's *Nature* (c. 1490). Pride admits that he is commonly called Worship in places where he dwells, and later Sensuality and Worldly Affection have a conversation which recalls the name changes among the seven deadly sins:

> Sirra! there is first Pride, as ye wot well,
> The sweet darling of the devil of hell:
> How his name is changed ye can tell.
> Wor. Aff: Yea, marry! on the best wise—
> Worship I ween is now his name.

Sensual: Yea, by the rood! even the same.
           And Covetise, to eschew all blame,
           Doth his name disguise,
           And calleth himself Worldly Policy.
           Wrath, because he is somewhat hasty,
           Is called Manhood. Then there is Envy,
           And he is called Disdain.
           Gluttony for Good fellowship is taken;
           And Sloth his old name hath forsaken,
           And as fair a name hath he shapen
           As ever man could ordain—
           He is called Ease; right comfortable to the blood.
           Specially for them that lust to do no good.
           And, among all other I would ye understood
           That Lechery is called Lust.[24]

These names so appeal to the Mankind figure in *Nature* that for a time he gives up his reason, the only thing that distinguishes man from the beasts, and follows the sensual appetites which lead him to sinful dissipation.

We have now defined the *topos* as a verbal code which, with fair consistency, replaces the seven sins with alternate appellations, usually with a satiric motive. Even in the fifteenth-century drama we can find the verbal code intact, although new dimensions have been added by the theatrical context. In the shift from sermon or poetry to morality drama we gain a generic context of considerable import. Visually, the name changes are accompanied by costume changes, sartorial disguise paralleling verbal disguise. Even more fundamental, though, the idea of renaming the sins becomes the impetus for the whole plot. Bernard Spivack has commented that "the dramatic energy that moves the plot is, in fact, the allegorical energy latent in their names, defining and prescribing their monolithic natures. No literary feature is more constant for the whole body of moralities than just such an exposition of his name by the Vice as the logical preliminary to his aggression."[25] Persuasion of the mankind figure to take the vices for virtues, and then his discovery of their true natures, *is* the structure of the morality play. Thus the function of the renaming *topos* in the drama is more than exemplary: it provides the basis for all the characterization and all the dramatic action.

What happens in the sixteenth-century drama is a permutation of the changed-names *topos,* transmuting the seven deadly sins into the various sins found at court. In Skelton's *Magnyfycence* (1516), for example, the seven deadly sins have been replaced by decadent advisors who lead the weak and witless king into tyranny and his kingdom into ruins. These courtiers adopt false names which mask their true natures: Fancy becomes Largesse, Crafty Conveyance becomes Surveyance, Counterfeit Countenance becomes Good Demeanance, Courtly Abusyon becomes Lusty Pleasure, Folly becomes Merry Conceit, and so on. Fair names have here become masks for courtly abuses in a satire of political life.[26]

At mid-century (1553), Nicholas Udall in *Respublica* also adopts the technique of disguised "gallants" at court: Avarice goes under the name of Policie (a version of Wisdom), Insolence assumes the name of Authority (Wrath = Manhood?), Oppression becomes Reformation (Envy = Righteousness?), and Adulation becomes Honesty, surely a version of Pride which changes its name to Honesty in our *topos*. Respublica, true to this form of satire, fails to recognize her enemies in their new guises, and only when Mercy and Veritee arrive are the evil counselors unmasked and shown to be "ravynyng wolves in the clothing of sheepe" (1366).[27] Euphemistic renaming is carried on in other mid-sixteenth-century plays, such as John Redford's *Wit and Science* or *Health and Wealth,* in which the vices Ill-Will and Shrewd Wit change not only their names but also their nationalities in an effort to escape detection. In *Impatient Poverty* (1560), Envy passes for Charity; Impatient Poverty pretends to be Prosperity; and when Misrule joins the gang, Envy counsels him to change his name so he chooses Mirth.[28]

In these Renaissance moralities, the republic rather than the individual soul has become the focus of dramatic attention, while the transmutation of the vices' names is the chief characteristic of a mutable world dominated by Fortune. Virtually every one of these plays contains a speech which links the disguising of the vices through name-change with the rule of Fortune. In the medieval tradition, the name changes were metaphorically a plot of the Devil, that is, an objectification of the individual's propensity to whitewash evil in order to accept it more readily. In the Renaissance satires, however, linguistic change becomes the characteristic of the worldliness at court, which corrupts all men who come there. Examination of these sixteenth-century plays reveals that their authors, even though they drop the sins and substitute other vices, are drawing on a morality tradition in which the *topos* of changing the names is one of a repertoire of dramatic devices.[29]

This survey of generic and ideological contexts for what I have called the "renaming the sins" *topos* concludes with an affirmation.

Despite wide variations in the way the *topos* is used and despite its ambiguous identity at the beginning and at the end of its career (the marriage of the Devil's daughters in the twelfth and thirteenth centuries, and the euphemistically-named political vices in the sixteenth century), we can posit the existence of the *topos* as a verbal code in the homiletic and moral literature of the late Middle Ages and early Renaissance.

Chaucer, Bakhtin, and the Discourse of Renaming

To argue that throughout the *Canterbury Tales* Chaucer is using the sermon *topos* of renaming the sins poses a more difficult challenge. However, there is a striking correlation between the *topos* of renaming the sins and the language Geoffrey the narrator and the other pilgrims use. The narrative technique Chaucer employs makes it often unclear whose point of view we are getting: Chaucer's, Geoffrey's, or the pilgrims'. Actually, as John Fyler has noted, Geoffrey's impartiality is "in fact a too ready willingness to accept other people's valuation of themselves."[30] What we seem to have in the *General Prologue* and in various prologues to tales are the pilgrims' self-evaluations. As a result, with the authoritative voice of preacher, moralist, or satirist absent from the code language of the *topos*, we are less sure of how to judge the euphemistic terms.

The Friar's portrait, for example, culminates in an ironic depiction of a man on the make, socially and financially:

> For unto swich a worthy man as he
> Accorded nat, as by his facultee,
> To have with sike lazars aqueyntaunce.
> It is nat *honest*, it may nat avaunce.
>   (243–46)[31]

This "honesty," which forbids the Friar to consort with beggars and sick men, looks like Pride, as our *topos* would have it. Similarly, in *The Merchant's Tale,* January is described as attempting

> In *honest* wyse, as longeth to a knyght,
> Shoop hym to lyve ful deliciously,

> His housynge, his array, as *honestly*
> To his degree was maked as a kynges.
> Amonges othere of his *honeste* thynges,
> He made a gardyn . . .
>
> (2024–29)

The repetition of the word "honest" is suspicious in Chaucer, as are all repetitions, especially when what is being described is a life-style that is as luxurious as a king's—a form of pride in a knight. But without the clear ironic structure of the *topos*, how can we be sure that Chaucer means the word "honest" as a code for pride? The ironies in any Chaucerian description or declaration are always subtle and difficult to pin down, depending as they do upon a reading of the whole complex work.

Within the homiletic tradition, probably the most unvarying element in the *topos* is the code name of "Wisdom" for Avarice. An excessive concern with "getting" characterizes many of Chaucer's pilgrims and appears to be a recurrent theme in his satire as well. If we accept Terry Jones's argument that the Knight is presented as a mercenary,[32] then the "sovereyn prys" he gets and the statement that he was "wys" could well be signals of his sin of avarice. We are on firmer ground, however, with the Merchant of the *Shipman's Tale*, "That riche was, for which men helde hym wys" (1192), and in the *General Prologue* portraits of the Merchant (274–84), the Man of Law (309–20), the Guildsmen (369–73), the Manciple (569–85), and Harry Bailly (754–55)—all of whom are described as avaricious and to all of whom the epithet "wys" is applied.

The portrait of the Guildsmen is most explicit:

> Wel semed ech of hem a fair burgeys
> To sitten in a yeldehalle on a deys.
> Everich, for the *wisdom* that he kan,
> Was shaply for to been an alderman,
> For catel hadde they ynogh and rente.
>
> (369–73)

The "wisdom" at first sounds innocuous enough; an alderman would, one assumes, be among the more perspicacious of the guildsmen. In the next line, however, "wisdom" is redefined as the possession of property and money ("For catel hadde they ynogh and rente"), undercutting our first assumption. The ironies here depend upon the deadpan tone of the narrator, who elicits from his readers one implied definition of "wisdom" and then with perfect timing gives us information which forces us to construct a much less flattering view of the materialism upon which the political power of the bourgeoisie is built. The satire depends upon ironic narrative techniques which by their very nature work through implication rather than explicit statement. Chaucer gives us only the euphemistic terms, never the names of the sins, leaving it up to the reader to perceive the lack and make the moral judgments.

It is also up to the reader to supply the missing information in the Man of Law's *Prologue,* where the narrator apostrophizes poverty as a situation causing many sins, whereas his source (Innocent III's *De miseria humanae conditionis*) condemns both poverty and riches. Everything the narrator says connects him with those who are avaricious, a state he repeatedly calls "wise": "Herkne what is the sentence of the wise: / 'Bet is to dyen than have indigence'" (113–14). All the days of the poor are wicked, he continues; if you are poor, your brother hates you, and all your friends flee from you. His idols are the wealthy merchants who, it turns out, have provided him with the story of Custance that he will recount for the pilgrims.

> O riche marchauntz, ful of wele been yee,
> O noble, o prudent folk, as in this cas! . . .
> Ye seken lond and see for yowre wynnynges;
> As wise folk ye knowen al th'estaat
> Of regnes. . . .
>
> (122–23, 127–29)

This attitude that the pursuit of wealth is wisdom, which the renaming *topos* satirizes, is here simply dramatized through the narrative voice of the Man of Law. Again, moral judgment is left to the reader.

When we look back at the code and see that lechery is renamed "natural kind" or "natural inclination," it is difficult not to think of the Wife of Bath's *Prologue,* where she argues from experience that the sexual organs were made for man's pleasure as well as for procreation: "In wyfhod I wol use myn instrument / As frely as my Makere hath it sent" (149–50). The Wife's naturalistic argument has long been recognized, although most critics find it more rewarding to attack her misinterpretation of the Bible than her argument from kind. But, of course, this is not the whole of the Wife of Bath. Her interest in sexual pleasure and her lifelong experience with the "olde daunce" are less central to her tale than her psychological warfare with husbands over "maistrye." Hers is not a character dominated by one moral tradition, but a combination of truly Chaucerian brilliance. One contributing strand, however, may be our *topos* of renaming the sins to make them palatable.

Turning from Lechery to Gluttony, in the *topos* of renaming the sins gluttony is usually called "Good Fellowship," and the gluttonous man a "Good Fellow." When Geoffrey calls the Shipman a "good felawe" (395) and notes his stealing of the wine in his cargo, the term certainly has the satirical significance of "rascal," but does it also suggest the glutton? Geoffrey also calls the Summoner—who loves garlic, leeks, onions, and strong red wine—"a bettre felawe" than men can find. Perhaps some resonances of the *topos* of euphemistic renaming cling to the term "good fellow" here. Harry Bailly is in many ways the most fully dramatized "Good Fellow" on the pilgrimage. Repeatedly called a "myrie man" by Geoffrey, he compliments the pilgrims for being a "myrie" company, and he cultivates their mirth through the game of tale-telling along the route. But it is also Harry Bailly who wines and dines the pilgrims at the beginning of the trip and sets up the meal which will supposedly celebrate the end of their pilgrimage and return to London. Harry is the tavern owner who reminds us of Gluttony, a reveler and rioter and frequenter of taverns and alehouses, as our sermons point out.

Throughout most of the *Canterbury Tales,* we are in the unrepentent world, one of whose chief characteristics is linguistic instability. The Parson says that "in mannes synne is every manere of ordre or ordinaunce turned up-so-doun" (259). In the world "up-so-doun," language is unreliable: words and deeds rarely coincide, and evil masquerades under the name of good. In his lyric *Lak of Stedfastnesse,* Chaucer adopted a melancholy tone to describe the world turned "up-so-doun," with its correlatives that truth is put down and reason is held a "fable" (1–7, 15–16, 19–21).[33] In the *Canterbury Tales,* however, the tone is far more ambiguous. In place of the censorious preacher of sermon narrative or the vaunting Devil of morality play, both of whom openly explain their motivations and methods, as narrator we have Geoffrey. Geoffrey is a humanly obtuse narrator, one who consistently subverts his own self-assigned goal that "the word moot accorde with the dede." Only the reader, however, is in a position to perceive or make such a judgment.

The tight story structures and explicit lists of linguistic inversions which characterize the renaming *topos* are absent from the *Canterbury Tales*. Instead, the narrative is recounted by Geoffrey, who describes his fellow pilgrims in their own euphemistic terms. He is the genial if superficial Everyman, who accepts the world at its nominal definition. It is possible, however, to see the other set of terms as supplied by the Parson, in his treatise on the seven deadly sins. In his tale, the Parson reveals the true identity of the sins. He strips away the linguistic veils which had provided the central ironies and delights of Chaucer's narrative. The presence of such a full analysis of the seven deadly sins at the end of the *Canterbury Tales* is neither incidental nor accidental. As the Parson points out, the process of repentance begins with correctly naming one's sins and acknowledging one's culpability.

But we must also attend to Chaucer's proportion. The *Canterbury Tales* overwhelmingly presents a linguistically unreliable world, a world dominated by euphemistic language and self-justifying rhetoric, rather than by the Parson's stark terms. Thus, there is no rush to self-judgment in Chaucer; rather, we have the continual deferring of moral conclusion. Even if Chaucer adopted the *topos* of renaming the sins from the sermon materials or satires of his day, he has in fact transformed those materials so radically, subsumed them so completely within his larger narrative strategies, that we can question in what sense the *topos* is "there" at all. Dramatizing a world of verbal manipulation and verbal self-creation—both of which depend upon ambiguities of language—seems closer to Chaucer's goal in writing the *Canterbury Tales* than satirizing linguistic perversion and inversion.

For this reason, we might profitably apply Bakhtin's idea of "polyphony" to Chaucer. Bakhtin's chosen subject was the nineteenth-century novel, which he valued as a genre that represented speaking subjects in a field of multiple discourses (Heteroglossia). In the novels of Dostoevsky and Dickens, for example, he discovered a resistance to monologue—a resistance to the totalizing power that reduces nonhomogeneous wholes to one voice.[34] Bakhtin's theory of the novel has been summarized by James Clifford in terms which could also apply to Chaucer's medieval narrative, the *Canterbury Tales:*

A "culture" [for Bakhtin] is, concretely, an open-ended, creative dialogue of subcultures, of insiders and outsiders, of diverse factions; a "language" is the interplay and struggle of regional dialects, professional jargons, generic commonplaces, the speech of different age groups, individuals, and so forth. For Bakhtin, the polyphonic novel is not a tour de force of cultural or historical totalization (as realist critics like Lukacs and Auerbach have argued), but rather a carnivalesque arena of diversity. Bakhtin discovers a utopian textual space where discursive complexity, the dialogical interplay of voices, can be accommodated.[35]

While one hesitates to see Chaucer the ironist as "utopian," certainly Bakhtin's concept of a "textual space" in which discursive complexity, the "dialogical interplay of voices," can be accommodated is a remarkably accurate characterization of the narrative structure of the *Canterbury Tales.* Jill Mann, in her study of the influence of estates satire upon the portraits in the *General Prologue,* comes close to this conclusion when she says that "the method of the work is not additive, but dialectic; the tales modify and even contradict each other, exploring subjects in a way that emphasizes their different and opposed implications."[36] Furthermore, with regard to individual characters, "Chaucer calls forth contradictory responses—a positive emotional or sensuous response conflicting with an expectation that moral disapproval is called for—in order to make us feel the complexity of his characters." This is accomplished in part by incorporating "an awareness of their point of view—their reactions to the traditional attitudes to their existence, their terminology and standards of judgment."[37]

Bakhtin's theory of the novel and Chaucer's *Canterbury Tales* both favor the mimetic form, with its "dispersion of authority among multiple voices, as against philosophically unified forms that reveal a singular, sovereign voice."[38] Within the didactic or exemplary tradition, the *topos* of renaming the sins is unified by the totalizing voice of the preacher or satirist, which subordinates morally the euphemistic "new names" to the older and more truthful names of the seven deadly sins. When, however, the advocates of Good Fellowship or Natural Inclination or Manliness or Wisdom are given voices which not only articulate those positions engagingly but also enter into a dialogue with the proponents of other points of view—as the Wife of Bath takes on the critics of her "lecherous" life-style—the result is a medley of voices, a polyphony, which resists easy categorization into "authentic" versus "deceptive" language.

As Terry Eagleton notes, for Bakhtin the sign itself was not a fixed unit (like a signal), but

an active component of speech, modified and transformed in meaning by the variable social tones, valuations and connotations it condensed within itself in specific social conditions. Since such valuations and connotations were constantly shifting, since the "linguistic community" was in fact a heterogeneous society composed of many conflicting interests, the sign for Bakhtin was less a neutral element in a given structure than a focus of struggle and contradiction. It was not simply a matter of asking "what the sign meant," but of investigating its varied history as conflicting social groups, classes, individuals and discourses sought to appropriate it and imbue it with their own meanings. Language, in short, was a field of ideological contention, not a monolithic system.[39]

Bakhtin's insight into language as a field of ideological contention may well be his most valuable contribution to our study of the *Canterbury Tales,* for within Chaucer's most complex narrative the power to 'name' oneself and others is shown to be political power. Furthermore, contrary to the assumption which seems to underlie much Chaucer criticism of the past thirty years, Chaucer is bent on destabilizing meaning precisely by revealing the process of ideological contention at work. In the *Canterbury Tales,* Harry Bailly's rivalry with the Parson over the definition of "myrie," the Wife's challenge to male interpretations of female behavior, the contests of power between the aristocrats, the bourgeois, and the lower classes as to what defines "honest," "wise," and "manly" behavior—that is, ideologies of religion, gender, and class—voice a polyphony of conflicting discourses which are never resolved into a monologue. The power to fix the discourse, to name without ambiguity, is simply not available in this fiction. Rather than celebrating the fluidity with Bakhtin or condemning the instability with the preachers, Chaucer mirrors a world which is recognizably Early Modern in its dispersal of power. The world he represents is one in which no social or political group can establish hegemony and silence its rivals. It is thus a world in which the power of renaming represents all that was in disruptive and comic dispute.

Notes

I would like to thank Derek Pearsall and David Raybin for perceptive critiques of this essay.

1. Siegfried Wenzel, "Chaucer and the Language of Contemporary Preaching," *Studies in Philology* 73 (1976): 139.

2. Ibid., p. 157.

3. Quoted from Bernard Spivack, *Shakespeare and the Allegory of Evil* (New York: Columbia University Press, 1958), p. 156; see Gregory's *Moralia* III, 544–46; also I, 174–75 and III, 18, 455.

4. *The Book of Vices and Virtues,* ed. W. Nelson Francis, EETS o.s. 217 (1942), p. 157.

5. G. R. Owst, *Literature and Pulpit in Medieval England,* 2nd. rev. ed. (Oxford: Blackwell, 1961), pp. 93–96. There is some variation among sermon writers, who include Jacques de Vitry, Odo of Cheriton, Guy d'Evreux, and Adam de la Vacherie; see B. Haureau, "Les Filles du Diable," *Journal des Savants* (1884): 225–28; P. Meyer, "Notice du Ms. Rawlinson Poetry 241," *Romania* 29 (1900): 54–72.

6. The story of the devil's nine daughters is common in the thirteenth century in Anglo-Norman and Provençal as well as Latin, according to Meyer, who gives not only the Latin sermon *exempla* but also a Provençal prose version (Ms. 17920 Add. of the British Library) and an Anglo-Norman verse version (Ms. 24 Fairfax at the Bodleian; also in Ms. Rawlinson Poetry 241). A distant version of the story may be used by John Gower in "Mirour de l'Omme," where Sin and her seven daughters are sent to win the World to the Devil. World eventually marries the seven daughters, and their offspring tempt man; see *The Complete Works of John Gower, Vol.* I, ed. G. C. Macaulay (Oxford: Clarendon Press, 1899), pp. 1–334.

7. John Bromyard, *Summa Predicantium, Vol.* I (Venice, 1586), "Falsitas" Cap. I, 270.

8. Bromyard, *Summa Predicantium, Vol.* II, "Peccatum" Cap. V, 200.

9. Cited by Owst, *Literature and the Pulpit,* p. 96. He notes that the eldest daughter was called Pride, "And for by cawse that the fende wolde marry hyr to the pepull of the worlde, he hathe sett on hyr a gay name and now sche is callyd 'Honestye'. . . ."

10. Bodleian Library Ms. e. Museo 180, fols. 69v–75r. Sermons from this manuscript have been the subject of Alan J. Fletcher's Oxford B. Litt. thesis (1978), "A Critical Edition of Selected Sermons from an Unpublished Fifteenth-Century de Tempore Sermon Cycle."

11. Typically in the *exemplum,* Avarice or Covetise are renamed Wisdom.

12. The tradition of questioning storytelling, even in the service of truth, is an ancient one. St. Jerome raises the theme of *adulterium linguae,* the preference for pagan classical literature over the Word of God, in a letter to Eustochium: "What communion hath light with darkness? What concord hath Christ with Belial? What has Horace to do with the Psalter, Virgil with the Gospels, and Cicero with Paul?" *Jerome: Selected Letters,* ed. F. A. Wright (London: Loeb Classical Library, 1954), p. 125. Alcuin's letter to the monks at Lindisfarne, who were telling heroic legends instead of Christian ones at their refectory, asks, "What has Ingeld to do with Christ?" In the later Middle Ages, friars adopted classical stories and fables of all kinds to teach Christian lessons in their sermons. See J. T. Welter, *L'exemplum dans la littérature religieuse et didactique du moyen âge* (Paris: Occitania, 1927).

13. Ms. Bodl. 95, f. 100–100v. Another sermon, one of two in Bodleian Library's Douce 53 identified by Anne Hudson as Lollard, mentions the Devil's linguistic malfeasance but omits reference to the marriages of his daughters: "lo how þe devel baptiseþ synnes undir þe names of honestee þat þei be þe lasse orrible to men. þus is

now pride callid honestee, veniaunce manhood, glotenye good felowschip, lecherie kyndely solace, covetise wysdom, symonye oon good turn for anoþer and usurie, chevyshaunce" (f. 17). Anne Hudson, ed., *Selections from English Wycliffite Writings* (Cambridge: Cambridge University Press, 1978), pp. 178–79, 233.

14. Christina von Nolcken, "An Edition of Selected Parts of the Middle English Translation of the *Rosarium Theologie, Vol. I.*" (D. Phil. thesis, Oxford, 1976), p. 49.

15. BL MS Royal 18. B. ix (G), fols. 191v–194v, reprinted in Hudson, *Selections from English Wycliffite Writings* (Cambridge: Cambridge University Press, 1981) pp. 75–83.

16. Other Lollard works which incorporate the list of changed names for the sins within an anti-fraternal context include *Jack Upland*, an anonymous polemic c. 1419; see P. L. Heyworth, ed., *Jack Upland, Friar Daw's Reply and Upland's Rejoinder* (Oxford: Oxford University Press, 1968), p. 56. Wycliff's own sermons inveigh against preaching with *exempla*; see Thomas Arnold, ed., *Select English Works of John Wycliff, Vol.* II (Oxford: Clarendon Press, 1871), pp. 11, 166. In a sermon on Ephesians 5:1, Wycliff appears to draw on the *topos*: "Poul biddiþ here to trewe men, 'þat no man bigile hem in bileve bi veyn wordis' which þei speken, þat þes ben no synnes or liȝt; as *lecherie is kyndeli*, as þei seien, and mankynde kyndely haþ love of his owne excellence, siþ þat God haþ ȝovun it him. . . . Siche veyn wordis þat excusen synne done myche harme amonge men, as Adam and Eve weren bigilid bi veyn speche of þe serpent, and so weren many oþer after, unbilevynge treuþe of Goddis lawe." (p. 276).

17. Lollard propaganda was especially fond of the image of an inverted world. "The Perversion of the Works of Mercy" describes how "Sathanas and his children turnen werkis of mercy upsodoun and disceyven men therinne and in here fyve wittis": N. F. Blake, ed., *Middle English Religious Prose* (London: Edward Arnold, 1972), p. 139. In this text, the Devil's teachings exactly invert Christ's commandments to do the works of mercy: "And thus in stede of werkis of bodely mercy and charite is comen in ypocrisie of worldly name and coveitise and norischynge of synne and sotil excusynge therof; and evyl is clepid good and good evyl" (p. 142).

18. As Ernst Curtius suggests, the "World Upsidedown" is a *topos* of the complaint on the times, which are seen as out of joint. The classical ancestor of this medieval form is the *impossibilia,* where the order of things is changed to its opposite. It was adopted in Carolingian poetry for contemporary criticism of the Church and monastic degradation. See also the *Carmina Burana,* Nigel Wireker's *Mirror of Fools* (c. 1180), and Alanus's *Anticlaudianus* (c. 1183), as well as Chrétien's *Cligès* (3849 ff.), where the dog flees from the hare, the fish hunts the beaver, the lamb the wolf: "Si vont les choses a envers," *European Literature and the Latin Middle Ages,* trans. Willard R. Trask (New York: Harper & Row, 1963), pp. 96–98.

19. Rossell Hope Robbins, ed. *Historical Poems of the XIVth and XVth Centuries* (New York: Columbia University Press, 1959), p. 54.

20. Ibid. pp. 144–45.

21. Agapito Rey, "Libro de la Consolación de España," *Symposium* 9 (1955): 249.

22. K. S. Block, ed. *Ludus Coventriae*, EETS, e.s. 120 (1922). The fifteenth-century code word for this type of disguise is "gay"—in the morality *Mankind* (c. 1468), Mercy asks to know the names of the Worldlings when they introduce themselves as New Gyse, Nowadays, and Nought, Mercy responds that they "betray many men" (117), but New Gyse tells him, "Betray! nay, nay, ser, nay, nay! We make them both fresch and gay" (118–19). After the Worldlings have departed, Mercy tells

Mankind that he does not forbid the "goode new gyse" but only the "vycyouse gyse" and that his reason will help him distinguish the two; Mark Eccles, ed., *The Macro Plays*, EETS, e.s. 262 (1969), pp. 154–84.

23. Eccles, *The Macro Plays*, pp. 114–52.

24. John S. Farmer, ed., *Recently Recovered "Lost" Tudor Plays* (London: EETS, 1907; reprint, N.Y.: Barnes & Noble, 1966), pp. 43–133.

25. Spivack, *Shakespeare and the Allegory of Evil*, p. 180.

26. Philip Henderson, ed., *The Complete Poems of John Skelton* (London: J. M. Dent & Sons, 1959), pp. 165–244. On the political and literary contexts of Skelton's satire, see A. C. Spearing, *Medieval to Renaissance in English Poetry* (Cambridge: Cambridge University Press, 1985), pp. 224–34.

27. *Respublica*, ed. W. W. Greg, London: EETS, o.s. 226 (1952; reprint, 1969).

28. These three plays are also edited by John S. Farmer in *Recently Recovered "Lost" Tudor Plays*, pp. 137–75, 275–348.

29. Spivak in his analysis makes no differentiation between the speech of Satan in the N-Town cycle, which is much closer to the homiletic tradition, and the later Tudor uses of euphemistic disguise. For Spivak, they are "the same thing."

30. John Fyler, *Chaucer and Ovid* (New Haven: Yale University Press, 1979), p. 148. See also Judith Ferster, *Chaucer on Interpretation* (Cambridge: Cambridge University Press, 1985), especially Chapter I. Indeed, the reader of the *Tales* is invited to examine his own assumptions as well because he has been cast fictionally as a member of the pilgrimage, along with Geoffrey the narrator and the other pilgrims, as Walter J. Ong points out in "The Writer's Audience Is Always a Fiction," *Interfaces of the Word* (Ithaca: Cornell University Press, 1977), p. 70. Barbara Nolan also takes up the issue of point of view and voice in the *Canterbury Tales,* terming it "a series of impersonations" in "'A Poet Ther Was': Chaucer's Voices in the General Prologue to the *Canterbury Tales,*" *PMLA* 101 (1986): 154–69, especially 161–63.

31. *The Works of Geoffrey Chaucer*, ed. F. N. Robinson, 2nd ed. (Boston: Houghton Mifflin, 1957). All quotations are from this edition. Emphases added.

32. Terry Jones, *Chaucer's Knight: The Portrait of a Medieval Mercenary* (Baton Rouge: LSU Press, 1980), pp. 31–32, 100–108.

33. Chaucer's lyric fits the satirical "World Upsidedown" tradition discussed above; see Robinson, ed., *Works*, p. 537.

34. As Michael Holquist points out in the "Introduction" to *The Dialogic Imagination by M. M. Bakhtin: Four Essays*, trans. Caryl Emerson and Michael Holquist (Austin; University of Texas Press, 1981), Bakhtin offers a theory of the novel which does not fit neatly into established literary histories of the "rise of the novel" as a genre after the seventeenth century: "Rather, 'novel' is the name Bakhtin gives to whatever force is at work within a given literary system to reveal its limits, the artificial constraints of that system. Literary systems are comprised of canons, and 'novelization' is fundamentally anticanonical. It will not permit generic monologue" (p. xxxi).

35. James Clifford, "On Ethnographic Authority," *Representations* 1 (1983): 136–37.

36. Jill Mann, *Chaucer and Medieval Estates Satire* (Cambridge: Cambridge University Press, 1973), p. 190.

37. Ibid. p. 189. She argues that the *General Prologue* is "based on an ethic of this world"; the *Prologue* "presents the world in terms of worldly values, which are largely concerned with an assessment of facades, made in the light of half-knowledge, and on the basis of subjective criteria. Subjectivity characterizes both the pilgrim's attitude,

and the world's (or the reader's) attitude to the pilgrims" (p. 201). Mann concludes therefore that Chaucer's inquiry is epistemological as much as moral.

38. Michael D. Bristol, *Carnival and Theater: Plebian Culture and the Structure of Authority in Renaissance England* (New York: Methuen, 1985), p. 21.

39. Terry Eagleton, *Literary Theory: An Introduction* (Minneapolis: University of Minnesota Press, 1983), p. 117.

14

ROBYN THE MILLER'S THRIFTY WORK

PEGGY A. KNAPP

"Lat us werken thriftily"—Harry Bailly

*G*od's plenty" the *Canterbury Tales* certainly is. Dryden's memorable phrase captures the breadth, the specificity, and the coherence of Chaucer's fictional world, the ways we are tempted to regard it as "real" instead of humanly constructed, God's rather than Chaucer's creation. Without wishing to quarrel with the power of the text to hide its art, I would like to call Chaucer's great poem "culture's plenty," to enable discussion not of an image of the fourteenth-century world, but of an image of fourteenth-century discourses, each associated with a certain social and philosophical view of that world. Chaucer's narrative moves forward entirely on the basis of impersonated language, including the impersonated language of the created pilgrim called "Chaucer," and that fact has led to a number of interesting, and not altogether reconcilable, interpretive observations. Even so straightforward a tale as the Miller's may be profitably revisited as the site of intersecting strands of linguistic coding.

Marshall Leicester has recently argued that Chaucer's pilgrims' personalities are constituted as they speak, by their speaking; they are not predetermined by supposed counterparts in the "real" world outside the fiction.[1] The conclusion he draws from the immediacy of the unfolding fiction is that the social and moral tensions involved in the narrator's voice are "embodied precisely *as tensions,* not as a resolution or a synthesis" (220). In Leicester's view, the Miller's ability to tell such a clever tale cannot be prejudged according to the social typing the presence of the other pilgrims provides. Indeed, his tale "quites," among other things, that very typing (218).

Such a view contrasts sharply with the notion of the doctrinal, theological Chaucer called up for us by the school of patristic exegesis—the notion of a workmanlike Christian poet bringing order out of the potential complexity of the world by creating pilgrims and characters as types and anti-types in the Scriptural tradition, and producing precisely a "resolution" and a "synthesis." Thus, to D. W. Robertson in *A Preface to Chaucer,* the Miller was recognizable as a type by reason of his bagpipe playing, his wrestling, his drunkenness, and his impropriety.[2] The brilliance of his characterization of Alison is neither realistic nor suggestive of a specific character (any more than is the Wife of Bath). The Miller's Alisoun is merely "a manifestation of *woman*" as object of lust (249). Jealous husbands like John are icons of avarice (369), and Absolon is "vainglory" (385). These characters are not expressions of the teller's "personality and outlook as embodied in the unfolding 'now' of the telling" (Leicester, 215) but, rather, are fixed in and by a tradition which predates and frames them. Neither the pilgrims nor their "creations" fall or could fall outside this massive signifying system, which is, Robertson argues, the language of the *Canterbury Tales* and of the medieval world.

M. M. Bakhtin, however, proposes in *The Dialogic Imagination* that a single system of meaning-assignment as monolithic as Robertson assumes is really more appropriate to the age of epic than to later literary languages, which contain, as history moves along, greater and greater "indeterminacy" and "semantic openendedness, a living contact with unfinished, still-evolving contemporary reality."[3] In Bakhtin's analysis, the voice of an author who speaks through characters, as Chaucer does, is "refracted as it passes through these planes [the speech diversity of the characters]" and "does not give itself up to any one of them" (311). That voice is the orchestrating gesture of the whole, capable of subjecting the speaking voices it represents to irony, but producing no direct discourse of its own. Although Bakhtin does not specifically mention Chaucer, my contention in this essay is that his are appropriate terms for discussion of the *Canterbury Tales,* and particularly the *Miller's Tale.* Bakhtin's view allows for the immediacy and idiosyncracy which makes Leicester's position attractive, but it insists on the co-presence of an authoritative discourse which is called up within the fiction to contend with its idiosyncratic voices. The *Canterbury Tales* does, I think, create new voices and meanings, but it does not create them out of nothing; there are already languages—social, philosophical, rhetorical—through which its dialogues are carried on.

The Word of the Fathers

Bakhtin levers his analysis of the "heteroglossia," the internal mixedness of the language of the novel, against the univocal and distanced language of epic. Epic language he describes as taking an authoritative, internally unchallenged view of the dominant ideology of the era that produced it; it becomes the official word, underwritten by political power, either personal or institutional, and "it stands or falls together with that authority" (343). When that authority disappears from the social world, the discourse associated with it becomes "simply an object, a *relic*" (344). This way of reaching the *Canterbury Tales* and other medieval works, as if they were products of an epic era, is what the school of patristic exegesis is asking us to produce, a reading based on the authority of the institution of the Church Universal. Readers who do not now accept that authority must call upon it as a relic of the past.

The "novel," on the other hand, does not rest on authoritative discourse alone, but combines with it discourse which is "internally persuasive." Such discourse is not prior to the present moment, is interwoven with everyday life, and is seen as being in "*struggle* with other internally persuasive discourses" (345–46). This internally persuasive discourse is "denied all privilege, backed up by no authority at all" (342). Its persuasiveness rests on what Alisoun of Bathe is defending: *experience*.

Bakhtin's position here is much like Michel Foucault's analysis of discourses at odds with the authoritative institutions of the era in which they appear. In *Power/Knowledge* he calls them "subjugated knowledges," "those blocs of historical knowledge which were present but disguised within the body of functionalist and systematizing theory."[4] An attempt to resuscitate the "subjugated knowledges" of the *Miller's Tale* or to account for the persuasiveness of its internally persuasive discourse might enable us to do justice to both the tale's witty intelligence and its social force.

In order to consider the Miller's discourse as normally subjugated during the Middle Ages, we must posit an overarching "functionalist and systemizing theory" which informs the dominant discourse of the period. This is an important and, I believe, an unavoidable step in the inquiry, but it must be taken with care lest it suggest that the culture of any given moment is a more closed and "metaphysical" system than it ever can be. To posit a dominant discourse, then, is not to ignore social difference and flux, but to avoid regarding history, in

Fredric Jameson's words, "as sheer heterogeneity, random difference, a coexistence of a host of distinct forces whose effectivity is undecidable."[5] Thus, the notion of a dominant discourse allows us to gather the impulses of dissent and change around certain foci, thereby recognizing conflict without positing cultural chaos.

The reference to a dominant discourse with which the storytelling in the *Canterbury Tales* begins is Boethian, and it occurs in the *Knight's Tale*. I agree with Judith Scherer Herz that the "real center of the tale is a vision of the noble life where all that happens belongs to a providential order and has its role, even if that role be tragic."[6] Whether Chaucer's Knight perfectly renders that vision may justifiably be questioned; but the Knight is not presented, I think, as judging and subverting it. The irony sometimes apparent in the tale may signal the Knight's lack of control of the philosophical system he represents. Whether or not the vision is fully realised, however, is irrelevant to identification of the Boethian trust in an orderly providential scheme, along with the moral and social obligations which follow from it, as an authoritative discourse of late fourteenth-century England.

The *Knight's Tale* drew praise from young and old in "al the route," especially from the nobles. This is what an "official" Middle Ages wanted to think of as its kind of ideal, expressing through its calm equanimity in the face of suffering the dominant discourse of the time. Theseus's "Firste Moevere" speech, which allows the philosophical resolution of the Knight's story, directly reproduces the "word of the father" Boethius. This elegant passage has all the earmarks of Bakhtin's authoritative discourse: its authority is "already fused to it" by its familiarity; it is strongly demarcated, magisterial; and it assumes unconditioned allegiance (342–43). As I see it, the authority of this discourse is recognized and embraced by the storyteller's voice—the Knight reveres this world view and therefore does not find it necessary to actually "prove," through his plotting, that its lessons are "preeved by experience," as Theseus claims they are (I, 3001).[7]

Robyn's Anti-Aristocratic Language

Robyn the Miller, however, finds all this celestial and earthly harmony highly suspect. He refuses to defer to a "bettre man," as the

Host asks, and thereby prevents the pilgrims from working "thriftily" (I, 3131). "Thrift" in the Middle English denotes success, prosperity, or welfare; "thriftily" could mean properly or providently. The
unthrifty Miller is disrupting propriety and order by attempting to
interfere with the authority fused to the Knight's lovely story.

The dominant discourse is at work in the Miller's tale, but to
altogether different ends than in the Knight's. Robyn apparently
understands the ideological point of his predecessor's story well
enough. He sees in it the way fathers (Theseus and Egeus) and The
Father control discourse in order to bring sons (the unruly, passionate
Palamon and Arcite) into conformity. The Knight has been candid
about this lesson, since he presents Theseus as controlling both the
discursive scene (through his eloquence) and the social scene (through
his rule, his direct power over life and death). It is a critical commonplace that the Miller's tale requites the Knight's by replicating its
formula (a woman under the guardianship of an older man sought by
two young lovers) but debasing its tone and direction. I am arguing
more than that. I think that Robyn is replacing a story ultimately
referable to an authoritative discourse, Boethius and the Patristic
tradition generally, with a story in the same form which rests on a
subjugated but internally persuasive discourse, and which makes an
entirely different point about the social world.

Where the Knight asserts Emelye's beauty abstractly, through her
likeness to a goddess (a female in the realm of the Father):

> I noot wher she be womman or goddesse,
> But Venus is it soothly, as I gesse.
> (I, 1101–2)

Robyn renders Alisoun's beauty concretely through her likeness to
desirable items in the everyday world:

> As any wezele hir body gent and smal
> . . . .
> She was ful moore blisful on to see
> Than is the newe pere-jonette tree,
> And softer than the wolle is of a wether.
> . . . .
> Wynsynge she was as is a joly colt,
> . . . .

> She was a prymerole, a piggesnye,
> For any lord to leggen in his bedde,
> Or yet for any good yeman to wedde.
>   (I, 3233, 3247–49, 3263, 3269–71)

What is being invoked here is, in Bakhtin's phrase, the "everyday rounds of our consciousness" (345), especially those usually called "lower." Chaucer seems to have deliberately emphasized the lower, scatological force of his nearest analogue (the Flemish version) of the "misdirected kiss" story, especially in enlarging Alisoun's active role in the joke.[8] In appreciating the force of Emelye's beauty, the reader must align himself or herself with the abstractly-expressed system of worth already approved in medieval culture and linked to theological sources of worth through terms like *shene, bright, faire, fresh, as an aungel hevenysshly.* To appreciate Alisoun's appeal, however, is to refer directly to one's senses: to sights in the ordinary world, to the odors of pears and apples, to pleasantly soft tactile sensations, and to sex itself—"for any lord to leggen in his bedde."

Where Palamon's and Arcite's unruliness is linked with the aristocratic conventions of courtly love (a secondary target for the Miller's irony), Nicholas and Absolon, in different ways, act out the basic appetites of lust and desire for power. The point is not that the Knight's story is unrealistic and the Miller's is not—indeed, both stories are fabulous (examples of Cicero's rhetorical figure *fabula,* which neither is nor seems to be true).[9] The point is the different systems of conventions. The Knight's characters answer to the exaggerated demands of the romance epic, the Miller's to the equally exaggerated intricacies of fabliau plot, especially timing.

In social terms, what is portrayed in both the Knight's and Miller's tales is competition and disorder among young men, those not yet married or incorporated into the guilds and professions. Such groups were a source of anxiety to the populace, especially when they formed a large proportion of the men in a village (as must have been the case in Oxenford). The threat offered by Arcite and Palamon is recognized by Theseus's open-air trial and sentencing but then, through his pity, is transformed into a public spectacle, a lawful, and perhaps socially instructive, tournament.

In medieval France, such young men celebrated a ritual of misrule which, Natalie Zemon Davis argues, allowed them to learn the social conscience of the community by becoming its "raucous voice" in charivaris.[10] In the ancient Athens of the *Knight's Tale* we may be seeing an analogous case of the competition of the young used for public edification. England had similar rites of misrule and charivaris which might be explained in similar ways. Nicholas and Robyn (and perhaps Absolon too) are aware of the "gross disparity in age between the bride and groom" in John's household, such disparity often being the occasion for charivaris. But in the Miller's story, of course, the young men are not engaging in a traditional form of social ridicule which could clear the air by expressing loud disapproval (Davis, 107). Rather, they are expressing self-interested reaction to the inappropriate marriage of delightful Alisoun to a man not likely to keep her sexual interest.

The *Knight's Tale* treats the taming of the young by positing their cooptation, their adoption of the self-restrained behaviors, the patience, the meekness in the face of "necessity," which is the counsel of the dominant ideology. The *Miller's Tale* posits just the opposite: the triumph of the uninitiate, their successful embarrassment of the "rich gnof" who technically possesses what they both want, Alisoun. An eighteenth-century eruption of this kind—younger, poorer men acting out a ritualized violation of their landlord's household—is discussed by Robert Darnton in *The Great Cat Massacre*. Darnton writes that the young men, in this case apprentices to a printer, made their "sedition" meaningful "by playing with the themes of their culture,"[11] just as Nicholas achieves his victory (shortlived though it may be) by using in a distorted way the dominant discourse of obedience to Biblical injunction which his life is an attempt to discount or circumvent. The aggressiveness of the *Miller's Tale* is aimed at unmasking the serene universal assurance that informs the *Knight's Tale*. Perhaps it is not going too far to see a deliberately debased, not-easily-recognized image of the Knight himself in the good-hearted, conservative, gullible John the Carpenter. The Reeve thinks himself Robyn's satiric target, and in a surface reading he is; but the *Tale* at its deepest reaches is stalking bigger game.

The Ideology of Robyn's Discourse

The Miller's reply to the Knight uses genre to make a philosophical (or, perhaps more broadly, an ideological) point. This fabliau is, according to Charles Muscatine, "so completely realized that the genre is virtually made philosophical."[12] I agree with Muscatine's argument that the philosophical point of the genre is "the sovereignty of animal nature" (I would rather say, though, the compellingness of material conditions). I will therefore not replicate his excellent marshalling of the evidence that the details of the story are arranged to create "an extraordinary solidity" for the physical "real" world. (Robertson seriously mis-characterizes the setting when he calls it "vague" except for the lowness of the window and therefore "only sufficient to make the action understandable," thereby allowing only iconic settings to be detailed [258].) But the tale is philosophically telling in a more extended sense as well, since it insists, in both plot and language, on what I will call a nominalist mode.

The protagonists of the *Knight's Tale* enact a thinly plotted, thickly decorated, fiction. They act, but their actions do not count for very much. The mere fact that critics have waged such a convoluted debate about whether Arcite and Palamon differ at all should make the point that the center of the tale is not the individual men, but the ordered, and order-replicating, world in which their story moves.

In the *Miller's Tale,* however, the opposite is true. The plot is intricate, careful, and yet surprising. The characters individually plan for what they want and, at least temporarily, they get it. The story moves forward because of the cooperation and interference of one person's planning with another's. First, Nicholas successfully tricks John into separating himself from his wife for the night, but this plot eventually results in John's noisy response to the cry "Water." Second, John, misled about the flood, plans to save himself and his wife. Note that Robyn does not suppress the likeable traits John shows here: his concern for Nicholas, his desire to save Alisoun, his willingness to endure discomfort to abide by what he thinks is the law ("This ordinance is seyde" [I, 3592]). Third, Absolon, who plans to be kissed for his serenade, is at first frustrated and humiliated but later successfully revenged, although not on his intended victim. His strategem has no connection with Noah's flood—it is pure happenstance that *his* victim's need to quench fire with water intersects with *Nicholas's* victim's obsession with water. The tale is built neither on a predictable "faire cheyne of love" which binds "the fyr, the eyr, the water, and the lond / In certeyne boundes" (I, 2191–93) nor on the orderly moral assignment of rewards and punishments predicated on it.

The very basis of the Miller's story is thus entrepreneurial and nominalist, in contrast with the authority-ridden, philosophically realist Knight's. This story is not referrable to a universal system but, rather, to the ungoverned desires and talents of Nicholas and Absolon. Yet this nominalist point is made by refashioning some conventional languages, primarily Nicholas's management (or mismanagement) of Christian doctrine and astrological lore and the courtly idiom with which the Miller surrounds Absolon. A several-sided dialogue is thus heard throughout the tale.

As it concerns Absolon, the humor cuts two ways. Absolon is trying to fulfill the dictates of a code of love, no matter how silly his attempts actually sound, so he sweetens his breath and sends gifts to speed his suit along. The humor in his presentation is the result of his "success," his incorporation of the courtesies which elevate Absolon himself and Alisoun to lover and beloved lady and which ought to ensure his acceptance. He is reaching for a definition of courtship which, although still seeking sexual consummation, is finicky about noticing the body—he himself is "somdeel squaymous of fartyng." The trouble is that Alisoun is not. The other half of this joke is that she responds to the direct, unrule-bound approach of Nicholas. The prize in this competition does not go to the patient, self-restrained suitor (whose self-restraint is, of course, on a far lower and less serious plane than Arcite's and Palamon's) but to the one who seizes the main chance.

The *Tale* should also be called nominalist because words—signifiers—are irreverently pried loose from what they signify. No guaranteeing order prevails to keep everything in place. The story proceeds because Nicholas, in his con of the carpenter, plays fast and loose with the faith the dominant discourse had placed in the revelatory meaning of words. In his vivid description of the world after the flood, Nicholas almost goes too far imitating the dominant discourse in its idyllic mode:

> Whan that the grete shour is goon away,
> Thanne shaltou swymme as myrie, I undertake,
> As doth the white doke after hire drake.
>
> (I, 3574–76)

He powerfully calls up both the apocalyptically destructive powers of water and the calm of the cleansed state which will follow the destruction. It makes sense, then, that the climax of the tale comes when the word "water," linked with the nonlinguistic sound of Nicholas's thunderous fart, is made to function in two competing schemes simultaneously. In Nicholas's trick, the predictive power of science (in this case astrology) and the sacred power of Scripture (the Noah story) are used cynically to authorize a scam completely of Nicholas's own manufacture.

The concern of the story with astrology makes several points. By suggesting for Nicholas a student's keen interest in the subject, the Miller is referring to a discourse which did, as Keith Thomas points out, prove a likely locus for intellectual curiosity, the "desire to reduce things to order."[13] Nicholas, like Aurelius's brother's friend in the *Franklin's Tale,* is one of those learners who has both an intellectual fascination and a practical application for this science. At the same time, since in England "astrology was primarily the concern of Court, nobility, and Church" (Thomas, 301), John is characterized as being favored to be let into the circle of those who could see into these recessed corners of learning. His quick, secondhand glimpse into this facet of "Goddes privetee" makes yet another point about the social hierarchies of the *Miller's Tale.* John is richer than Nicholas, but his access to this privileged discourse can come only through his poorer boarder. This advantage is, of course, just what Nicholas is both counting on and hoping to prove by his trick:

> "A clerk hadde litherly biset his whyle,
> But if he koude a carpenter bigyle."
> (I, 3299–300)

A further irony for us, which may also have been a commonplace in Chaucer's day, concerns William Lily's assertion (1675) that Noah's flood could not have been foretold astrologically, since only events with natural causes could be predicted, whereas the flood was the result of God's direct intervention (Thomas, 336). If fourteenth-century astrologers shared this viewpoint, Chaucer would be stressing again Nicholas's affront to the authorized discourses of his day.

Nicholas is not afraid of the consequences of diverting authorized discourses—biblical and astrological—to his own ends, nor does the outcome of the tale reveal that he should have been. In Max Horkheimer and Theodor Adorno's discussion of enlightenment, the link is made between the abandonment of an animistic world through rationality and a movement toward nominalism.[14] The power of the word to direct nature through magic or myth is replaced by power over the word, like that exercised by Odysseus in the Polyphemus episode when he abandons his "real" name and adopts the name "Nobody," in Greek ("Udeis") a name sounding like his own, to effect his escape (60). Nicholas seized the power of the word through cunning (and "cunning is defiance in a rational form" [Bakhtin, 591]), and Robyn the Miller allowed him to get away with it. Like pretty Alisoun, authoritative language allowed itself to be appropriated by a resourceful ("hende") young man who will not recognize the "authority already fused to" the system he distorts for his own ends (Bakhtin, 342).

Nicholas takes a chance when he manipulates language this way (one might say he links himself with Odysseus and other trickster figures), but he does not suffer the "scalded towte" which is his punishment because an orderly universe stands behind the authorized language in which it is expressed. He suffers because another willful young man had another scheme going and was not so stupid as to be trickable the same way twice. Nicholas should have trusted the stability of language less, not more. The very real world of the hot colter and his singed ass produced the automatic call for "Water," and made him forget both the elaborate fiction he had invented concerning water and his own habitual control of language.

The fabric of Robyn's telling is also nominalist. It continually distorts and mocks the solemnity of the Knight's sober formulations. The line in which the Knight phrases his melancholy description of Arcite's grave, "Allone, withouten any compaignye" (I, 2779), appears unchanged to describe Nicholas's strategically private bachelor pad. The featured term "queynte" in Emelye's temple scene (in which she prays to Diana to protect her maidenhood) (I, 2333) is employed obscenely in the description of Alisoun's "wooing" (I, 3275–76), first to mean "quaint" and then "cunt," and later, in the phrase "queynte cast" to mean both at once (I, 3605). The narrator's voice is as unafraid as Nicholas's to reappropriate language for its own cunning and irreverent uses. It is equally important to note that these signifiers that Robyn exploits *already had* the double edge that allowed his outrageous linguistic alchemy, suggesting the possibility for dialogic discourse in this society.

The Languages of Wit

The reception of the *Miller's Tale* is that of a joke. Bakhtin argues that "comic familiarity" is itself corrosive of the high, straightforward genres, both because of its implied reference to everyday life and its "contradictory and heteroglot" language (55). How the comic familiarity works may be explored through Freud's thinking on jokes as psychic and social phenomena.

Robyn's joke looks both obscene and tendentious in Freud's system of classification.[15] The Miller forces the company, perhaps especially the Knight and Harry Bailly, who had offended him by their deference to the hierarchical world, to see disorder and sex graphically. He embarrasses the women and affronts the men (as the narrator acknowledges in his advice to "chese another tale" and his defence of himself for including this one, lest he should "falsen som of my mateere" [I, 3177, 3175]). The Knight had carefully banished Emelye's sexual nature from his telling, although the sexual possession of her is the motive force for the contest between the two young men. He also hides it in the description of the temple of Venus, although there, some hints of physical sexuality and its chaotic sufferings do appear. The Miller forces the physical into the center of his picture and into the consciousness of his hearers:

> And prively he caughte hire by the queynte . . .
> . . . .
> And heeld hire harde by the haunche-bones.
> (I, 3276, 3279)

These lines are an affront to the Knight and Host in that they force the company to laugh (all but Osewold the Reeve), to make a common bond on the Miller's own turf, since "laughing over the same jokes is evidence of far-reaching psychical conformity" (Freud, 151). But the company in fact does not normally share that ground—that is why Robyn's joke is such a tour de force. The Miller *creates* the common ground which allows the company to laugh together, and he does so in the awed hush which followed the *Knight's Tale,* a mood inhospitable to the "state of feeling" he wishes his joke to induce (Freud, 145). How is Robyn able to produce "psychical conformity" among such sondry folk? And why is his tale taken as funny rather than insulting by everyone but Osewold?

The *Miller's Tale* is on one level merely an example of the "cheerful humor" which "those who work" find in obscene jokes—it is on this level that Osewold sees himself as its victim. Told to a public which shared his suppositions about sex and society, Robyn's joke would be an everyday matter of shared humor among men and possibly seductiveness toward women. In the aftermath of the universally-admired *Knight's Tale,* however, the Miller's story becomes instead a campaign in a philosopical and social struggle to establish a common understanding about life within the company. When the pilgrims laugh, Robyn has won at least tolerence, and perhaps a measure of acceptance, for his point of view. Since his discourse has no institutional authority fused to it, he must have accomplished this feat by creating internal persuasiveness.

As an attack on the Knight's philosophical pretension and social coyness about sex, the *Miller's Tale* uses the two techniques Freud mentions specifically: *degradation,* exposing "dependence on bodily needs," and *unmasking,* uncovering "the physical demands lying behind the claim of mental love" (Freud, 222). Robyn strips the authoritative discourse of its exalted status by pointing out what he takes to be the common needs of all people—John's ungovernable curiosity about Nicholas, both suitors' sexual longings, Alisoun's desire for a young lover, Nicholas's getting up "for to pisse," and the like.

These are, of course, exactly the features the Knight leaves out of his telling, especially by devising the attenuated time scheme which keeps the young men in his story waiting until middle age to "attain the love" of Emelye. In arranging his telling this way, of course, the Knight is not speaking merely idiosyncratically "for himself," but on behalf of a philosophical tradition which asserts the lower and peripheral nature of the physical realm, superintended by Fortune, to the concerns of life. The other aristocratic tradition he invokes— courtly love—also allows the suppression of the everyday realities of loving in favor of the extravagant gestures of courtship—the return from exile and the tournament—offered by Arcite and Palamon. Such mental and social games are associated with the upper social echelons, Robyn's technique implies, but those exalted and authoritative types nonetheless laugh at his story because something in them finds his discourse internally persuasive.

Jokes "evade restrictions and open sources of pleasure that have become inaccessible" because of our "high" level of civilization (Freud, 103). They allow the teller's obscene, hostile, or cynical thoughts, normally kept repressed, to be expressed and shared so as to enlist support among listeners. The listeners, who might take offense at argument or invective because of *their* proprieties, are bribed by the pleasure in wit afforded by the joke. The joke liberates pleasure by getting rid of inhibitions, protecting the pleasure from the criticism of reason by being "nonsense" without losing the pointedness of "sense" (134, 131). If the Miller is indeed registering a protest against the Knight's philosophical and social conservatism, his tale is a perfect vehicle both for masking the hostility in his rejoinder and for affording pleasure to the company—pleasure which could not be gained by direct argument, and could not, presumably, have won him the prize for storytelling. That is one sense in which the Miller has been thrifty (economical) in serving his own cause, though unthrifty (improper) in terms of the dominant ideology.

Another sense of Robyn's thrift is the brevity of his tale. Brevity, as everyone since Polonius knows, is the soul of wit. According to Freud, wit entails a psychic shortcut. Something is used where it is unexpected but not unfamiliar; something repeated or rediscovered saves the psychic energy of introducing new subject matter (124). The economy of the *Miller's Tale* is the strongest feature of its wit, for the single word "water" brings to a climax the two plots being worked out simultaneously.[16] Water has figured centrally in Nicholas's plot against John. The water Nicholas needs later to cool his burning behind is a comic economy in that it suddenly links the two plots, just when the audience had nearly forgotten the first, and in that it degrades Nicholas's flight of imagination about water, thereby associating him with the comic type of Icarus, a high flier who gets wet.

When Harry Bailly admonishes Robyn to "werken thriftily," the Miller's reply is:

> "By Goddes soule," quod he, "that wol not I,
> For I wol speke or elles go my wey."
>
> (i, 3132–33).

As things unfold, Robyn both speaks and goes his way, and in the end even "werkes thriftily." And all this happens so "naturally" that the fiction looks like the "real world," God's creation, rather than a weaving together of the languages of our own.

Notes

1. Marshall Leicester, "The Art of Impersonation: A General Prologue to the *Canterbury Tales*," *PMLA* 95 (1980): 215. Subsequent references to this article appear in the text.

2. D. W. Robertson, Jr., *A Preface to Chaucer* (Princeton: Princeton University Press, 1962), pp. 133, 243. Subsequent references to this book appear in the text.

3. M. M. Bakhtin, *The Dialogic Imagination,* ed. Michael Holquist, trans. Caryl Emerson and Michael Holquist (Austin: University of Texas Press, 1981.), p. 7. Subsequent references to this book appear in the text.

4. Michel Foucault, *Power/Knowledge: Selected Interviews and Other Writings, 1972–1977,* ed. Colin Gordon (New York: Pantheon Books, 1980), p. 82.

5. Fredric Jameson, "Postmodernism or The Cultural Logic of Late Capitalism," *New Left Review* 146 (July/August, 1984): 17.

6. Judith Scherer Herz, "Chaucer's Elegiac Knight," *Criticism* 6 (1964): 223.

7. The edition used throughout is *The Complete Poetry and Prose of Geoffrey Chaucer,* ed. John H. Fisher (New York: Holt, Rinehart and Winston, 1977).

8. Peter G. Beidler, "Art and Scatology in *The Miller's Tale,*" *Chaucer Review* 12 (1977): 90–102.

9. Morton W. Bloomfield, "*The Miller's Tale*—An UnBoethian Interpretation," in *Medieval Literature and Folklore Studies,* ed. Jerome Mandel and Bruce A. Rosenberg (New Brunswick, N.J.: Rutgers University Press, 1970), p. 207.

10. Natalie Zemon Davis, *Society and Culture in Early Modern France* (Stanford: Stanford University Press, 1975), p. 108. Subsequent references to this book appear in the text.

11. Robert Darnton, *The Great Cat Massacre* (Princeton: Princeton University Press, 1983), p. 99.

12. Charles Muscatine, *Chaucer and the French Tradition* (Berkeley: University of California Press, 1957), p. 224.

13. Keith Thomas, *Religion and the Decline of Magic* (New York: Charles Scribner's Sons, 1971), p. 327. Subsequent references to this book appear in the text.

14. Max Horkheimer and Theodore Adorno, *Dialectic of Enlightenment,* trans. John Cumming (New York: Continuum Books, 1982), pp. 5, 23. Subsequent references to this book appear in the text.

15. Sigmund Freud, *Jokes and Their Relation to the Unconscious,* trans. and ed. James Strachey (New York: W. W. Norton and Company, 1960). Subsequent references to this book appear in the text.

16. My approach here is in some ways similar to that of Eugene W. Holland, "Boccaccio and Freud: A Figural Narrative Model for the *Decameron,*" *Assays* 3 (1985): 85–98.

AFTERWORD

Four thousand years after Shvetaketu learned from his father that from nothing can come infinity, far on the other side of the world, on a warm night in a New Orleans backyard, a small child stood with her father looking up at a giant fig.

"Daddy, where did the fig tree come from?"

"I don't know."

"Daddy, what's that bad noise?"

"Crickets, I think."

"Daddy, I want to go inside."

"There's nothing to be afraid of. You know Jiminy Cricket, don't you? He's nice, isn't he? He's not scary."

"But I'm afraid of the ones that don't have names."

—Casey Wasserman

INDEX

Abelard, Peter: *Sic et Non,* 119
Abuse of language, 146–48
Adam, 6–7, 31–32, 255
Adorno, Theodor, 303, 308
Aenigmata (conundrums), 114, 115
Aesop, 117, 131, 135, 233
Alain de Lille, 111, 216, 229; *Anticlaudianus,* 291; *De Planctu Naturae,* 21–22, 28
Albert of Saxony, 136
Alford, John, 242
Allegory, 232, 237–38, 241, 292; and dreams, 118–19; and exegesis/interpretation, 13–14, 77; as narrative, 275–76; and secular literature, 230
Allen, Judson, 13, 25–27
Allen, Peter, xx, 6, 7, 48–49, 95–97, 141, 266
Alphonsi, Petrus, 233–34
Ambiguity, 95–97, 100, 108–10; and fate, 195–214; and oaths, 203–5, 258; of signs, 108–10, 115–34; of visual evidence, 57–60, 261
Andreas Capellanus, xix, 227
Aquinas, Thomas, 36, 44, 125, 136
Arabic, 200
Arbery, Glenn C., 6–7, 47, 142, 226
Arbitrariness, 5, 38, 77, 199–200, 202–3, 213, 218, 227
Aristotle, 11, 25, 132, 136, 229
Arnold, Thomas, 291
Arthur, Ross G., 47, 48, 141, 178, 226
Ashley, Kathleen, 48, 141, 226, 269–70
Astrology, 12, 303
Augustine, 152–54, 167, 178, 190, 239, 246, 273; on allegory and exegesis, 124, 161, 233; *Confessiones,* xix, 22–23, 29–30, 157–60, 172–73, 181, 188, 189, 197–98, 217–18, 230; on creation; *Contra mendacium,* 172; *De civi-*

tate Dei, 91, 137, 158–59, 161, 162, 172–74, 198, 218, 242; *De doctrina Christiana,* 80–81, 83, 88–89, 90, 128, 159, 163, 206, 229; *De Genese contra Manichaeos,* 229; *De magistro,* 159–60, 161, 172, 221, 242–43; *De ordine,* 221; *De Trinitate,* 163, 173, 218, 242; *De vera religione,* 198; *Enarrationes in Psalmos,* 23, 29; on signs, 47–48, 114–18, 200, 225, 229, 230; on thought and language, 36, 142
Austin, J. L., 215

Babel, 199, 270
Bailly, Harry, xviii, 149, 284, 286, 289
Bakhtin, M. M., 270–71, 287–89, 292, 295–97, 304, 308
Ball, John, 278
Ballard, Edward G., 243
Barthes, Roland, 25, 98, 109–12
Bec, Pierre, 265
Bede, xix, 82, 92
Benkov, Edith Joyce, 48, 141, 226, 227, 269
Bennett, H. S., 218
Bennett, J. A. W., 243
Benoît de Sainte-Maure: *Roman de Troie,* 100–101
Beowulf, xix
Bersuire, Pierre: *Ovide Moralisé,* 232
Bezzola, Reto R., 77
Birney, Earle, 152
Blake, Norman, 218
Blanch, Robert J., 218
Bloch, R. Howard, 26, 29, 111
Bloomfield, Leonard, 219
Bloomfield, Morton W., 171, 215, 308
Boasts, 70
Boccaccio, Giovanni, 29, 123, 126–29,

311

SIGN, SENTENCE, DISCOURSE

was composed in 10½ on 12 Bembo on a Merganthaler Linotron 202
by Coghill Book Typesetting Co.;
with initial caps in Caxton;
printed by sheet-fed offset on 50-pound, acid-free Glatfelter Natural Hi Bulk,
Smyth sewn and bound over binder's boards in Holliston Roxite C,
and adhesive bound with paper covers,
with dust jackets and paper covers printed in 2 colors
by Braun-Brumfield, Inc.;
and published by

SYRACUSE UNIVERSITY PRESS

Syracuse, New York 13244-5160